In Our Own Voices

Rosemary Skinner Keller and

Rosemary Radford Ruether, editors

In Our Own Voices

FOUR CENTURIES OF
AMERICAN WOMEN'S
RELIGIOUS WRITING

HarperSanFrancisco

An Imprint of HarperCollins*Publishers*

The authors and editors wish to acknowledge particularly the
Louisville Institute for the Study of Protestantism and Culture,
whose grant was the major support for the research and writing of
this volume. Rosemary Keller and Rosemary Ruether thank Garrett-
Evangelical Theological Seminary, whose support from the Institute
for the Study of Women in Church History also helped fund research
and writing of this volume.

Ann Braude thanks Riv-Ellen Prell and Tamar Frankiel for
generous contributions to this project and Michael McNally for
excellent research assistance.

Emilie Townes wishes to thank the members of the Womanist
Approaches to Religion and Society Group of the American
Academy of Religion for their support in her work on her chapter.

Permissions acknowledgments are on p. 537 and constitute a
continuation of this copyright page.

HarperCollins Web Site: http://www.harpercollins.com
HarperCollins®, ▟®, and HarperSanFrancisco™ are trademarks
of HarperCollins Publishers, Inc.

FIRST HARPERCOLLINS PAPERBACK EDITION PUBLISHED IN 1996

Library of Congress Cataloging-in-Publication Data:

In our own voices : four centuries of American women's religious
    writing / Rosemary Skinner Keller and Rosemary Radford Ruether,
    editors. — 1st ed.
    Includes bibliographical references and index.
    ISBN 0-06-066843-1 (cloth)
    ISBN 0-06-063292-5 (pbk.)
    1. Women in Christianity—United States—History—Sources.
2. Women in Judaism—United States—History—Sources.   I. Keller,
Rosemary Skinner.   II. Ruether, Rosemary Radford.
BR515.I45   1995
200'.82—dc20   94-37808

96 97 98 99   RRD(H)   10 9 8 7 6 5 4 3 2 1

We dedicate this book to our mothers and grandmothers,
Rose Zeckman Braude,
Vicci Sperry,
Clarita Martinez Talamantez,
Ruth Lucille Parr Hardesty,
Helen Monroe Longworthy,
Mary Morley,
Rebecca Cresap Ord Radford,
Mary Doris McLean Townes,
and Ruthe Carlson.

CONTENTS

viii

Gender and the Multicultural Worlds of Women and Religion in America

Rosemary Skinner Keller

I N 1637 Anne Hutchinson spoke in her own voice declaring that she had received a revelation directly from God. This action led to her excommunication from the Massachusetts Bay Colony because the ordained clergy saw themselves as designated mediators of God's word to laypeople. But Anne became her own person and a model of woman-hood for us over four and one-half centuries later.

Sister Blandina Segale found her own voice when she stopped a lynch mob and kept the Billy the Kid gang from scalping doctors in Colorado in the 1870s.

At the turn of the century, Ida B. Wells-Barnett claimed her own voice to expose the evil of lynching propagated against her African American brothers by white persons. Her forthrightness led to the burning of her office and to threats against her life, but she never allowed her voice to be silenced.

Sally Priesand gained her voice to preach and officiate at Jewish religious services when she became the first woman rabbi ordained in the Reform Movement of Judaism in 1972.

Pilulaw Khus, Native American elder of the Chumash tribe, found her own voice when she fought oil companies to prevent them from desecrating Chumash ceremonial areas in California in the 1980s.

These are only a few of the stories told by women in their own voices in this book. Gender and multiculturalism intersect in every chapter as we share accounts of women trying to gain their full and equal stature as persons before God and their sisters and brothers. *In Our Own Voices* becomes a metaphor of women's efforts to speak and act as persons with authority in their own right.

Many of us who have come of age in the late twentieth century believe that the struggle to speak "in our own voices" has taken place only in our day. We think that the issues of rights gained for women and rights still denied first surfaced in our generations. When we look at secular or religious history books of the past several decades we find few if any stories of women who have had a voice and place in the decision making of our past. The traditional way of writing history has been through the voices and actions of white male leaders in church and society.

History is revised in this book, and a new vision of the past is conceived. Until history is revised, neither the writer nor the readers can imagine how a different story of the tradition will change their lives or the shape of history itself.

When history is revised, the writer and the reader are led to new beginning points for interpreting their heritages. Neither person can accept the old story as it was told before!

Rosemary Radford Ruether and I embarked upon personal exploratory journeys when we edited the three-volume documentary history of *Women and Religion in America* for Harper & Row in the 1980s (1981, 1983, 1986). Along with other contributors, we began to chart a new field of history. The history of women itself had just been birthed, and little work had been done to substantiate a hypothesis that many scholars agreed with and believed was important: one could not interpret where women have been throughout four centuries on American soil without understanding the impact of religious faith on their lives and their participation in religious institutions.

We were further convinced that religious history itself in the United States had been impoverished because the place and contribution of women had not been a part of the story.

No one person had the expertise to write the history of women and religion in America. But, with our contributors, we opened the treasure chests of countless previously unknown documents and sifted, compiled, edited, and analyzed them. In bringing together the three volumes of *Women and Religion in America,* we realized that we barely had uncovered one layer of the treasure chests' holdings.

The field of women and religion in America has come a long way in the decade and a half since Marie Cantlon, our original editor at Harper & Row, helped us conceive this project. A host of monographs have been written on diverse subjects involving women, gender, and religion, representing many faith perspectives, locales, time periods, and analytical viewpoints. The subject of women and religion has gained its foothold in the larger fields of women's, social, and religious histories. Hardly anyone would dare write a survey of American Christianity or religious history without making some semblance of including women's experience and contributions in it.

However, all who write and read in this field realize that we are still in the early stages of discovering, analyzing, and integrating women and religion into American religious history. The luxury does not exist to complete the work stage by stage, compiling all the primary source documents, writing all the monographs, integrating all the studies into a new religious and social history, and then writing a new comprehensive history of the United States. Research and writing must continue at all these points simultaneously, just as in all areas of history, where new truth is unfolding daily.

Almost fifteen years after the first of the original three volumes of *Women and Religion* was published, we embark on this new one-volume edition. Some of the material is taken from the earlier volumes, and other parts are brought together for the first time. While the former volumes did not go beyond 1960 in their research, this book continues into the feminist period of the mid-1990s. This one-volume study is intended to be more accessible, both for reading by the general public and for classroom use. We again edit a documentary history out of our conviction that history comes alive most vividly for laypeople and scholars as they read the original documents for themselves and have some guidance in interpreting them.

CONCEIVING A NEW VISION OF THE PAST: THE CYCLE OF REVISING HISTORY

The shift from the twentieth into the twenty-first century marks a crucial turning point in writing the story of the past. However, this new cycle in the writing of history was set in motion a quarter of a century ago, and the history of women and religion needs to be understood in this larger context. In the 1970s historians charted a new direction in the recovery of tradition, and particularly in interpreting American religious history. That process led to the discovery of new fields of history, among them the stories of women and of women in religion.

In 1972 Sydney Ahlstrom caught the spiritual significance of the 1960s in his monumental *A Religious History of the American People*, which became my first real textbook in American religious studies. He stated in his first chapter, "Social and intellectual developments of the last decade have profoundly altered our interpretation of the entire course of American history. The terrible moral dilemmas that began to intensify during the sixties have had an especially rude impact on long-accepted views of the country's religious development."[1] Ahlstrom points to the first step in revising history: conflict arises among scholars and the basic consensus regarding the essential content of historical inquiry breaks down. Contemporary social events create the need for a new approach to the past.

Ahlstrom's very title, *A Religious History of the American People*, testified that denominational and institutional church histories, the prominent focus of the day, marginalized and even isolated the significance of religion in the nation's and individuals' lives. Religious history needed to be interpreted as a part of the larger world of American culture, as well as an aspect of the story of institutional developments.

The second step in revising history is closely tied to the first. Historians begin to explore sources from the past that had been "hidden histories"—concerns and materials previously considered nonexistent or unimportant for historical purposes. These sources are called "new," but in fact they always had been there. Historical work at this stage is disparate and fragmented. Personal letters, journals and autobiographies of women and laypeople, sources tucked away in attics of homes and churches or rescued from the trash bins are recovered as invaluable treasures.

A third step is taken in revising the tradition: new fields of history emerge as historians recognize the significance of their disparate sources against the backdrop of the social events around them. Ahlstrom speaks of the "terrible moral dilemmas that began to intensify during the sixties" and that have accelerated since then. The social revolution of the sixties brought to light a host of subcultures, and the "new social history" led established and newly minted historians in the 1970s and '80s to spotlight them. Attention was directed to previously ignored themes in the study of American history, among them women, gender, African Americans, race and ethnicity, class, urban and local communities, youth, and aging.

If the term *American culture* seemed to imply one predominant, defining middle-class mainstream, we suddenly acknowledged that many cultures always had been living right before our eyes, though historians had seen little of them. We finally recognized that in the United States we lived in a multicultural and a cross-cultural world, a world where many cultures interact with one another. American history no longer could be defined primarily in terms of the public leadership of white men in government and the military.

We took the fourth step in the cycle of revisionism, the incorporating of new and disparate fields of history into a revised social and cultural history. It came naturally and almost imperceptibly, but it also created jarring dislocations among diverse constituencies. For social activists and historians, the looming question became: if historians of African American experiences, racial and ethnic studies, and women's and gender concerns all became lumped together as "new social historians," would not their distinctive emphases and the advocacy of each be diluted and dissipated? The fear was not well founded. For, while the "new social history" has become a recognized field today, research within it continues to deepen gender, racial, and ethnic topics.

Applying the new social history to American religious history meant that the field could no longer be interpreted as the study of white male bishops, preachers, and steepled churches. Other contributions had to be included. No longer could we focus almost exclusively on Protestantism in interpreting Christianity. And "the history of Christianity" was insufficient for interpreting American religious history. In addition to Christianity, particularly Roman Catholicism and Protestantism, and Judaism, the interreligious worlds of Native American spirituality, Hinduism, Buddhism, Islam, lesbian options, New Age spirituality, and Goddess religion had to be recognized. The pluralism of faiths also was seen as intrinsically related to race and ethnicity, as cultural diversity became one of the new directions explored in American religious history in the 1990s.

A new consensus is emerging in religious historiography, the fifth and final step in the cycle. Religion and American culture is the broad category to be studied, with American religious studies, not simply American Christianity, at its heart. The pluralism of religious movements and institutions means we must address cultural diversity, including race, ethnicity, women, gender, class, and congregational studies. Perhaps no single volume can bring all of this diversity into one unified study. But this vision of wholeness should be held before us as we read and write the stories of religion and American culture and the history of women and religion in America at the end of the twentieth century.

SOUNDING OUR OWN VOICES

In this book, *In Our Own Voices,* we hear and interpret the words of women through the theme of gender in the multicultural worlds of women and religion in America. In ten chapters, the volume brings together primary source documents from diaries, letters, speeches, sermons, essays, and books by women from the earliest colonial settlements in North America until the present. Each chapter begins with an essay integrating the distinctive voices of women in their multicultural worlds into a broader interpretative framework.

The three opening chapters present and interpret the words of women in the major historic faith traditions of North America: the multicultural worlds of Catholicism, Protestantism, and Judaism. We then turn to five chapters representing five distinctive voices through which the life and work of women in American religion may be heard: the stories of African American women, evangelical women, women in social reform movements, in traditions of preaching and ordination, and in utopian and communitarian traditions. Most of these women, both Black and white, have their roots in mainline or marginalized Protestant churches, though some come from Catholicism and Judaism. In the two concluding chapters we begin to hear the voices and write the histories of women in American religious traditions whose stories are only now emerging, including Native American, Muslim, and Buddhist women. The ten chapters draw upon written and oral words, some never published before, from the early seventeenth century until the mid-1990s.

In the first chapter, "Catholic Women in North America," Rosemary Ruether presents voices that describe the clash of cultures of Roman Catholic nuns and laywomen with the hierarchy of priests, bishops, and the pope throughout American history. In the colonial period, Hispanic nuns developed scholarly lives within the convent, and activist French sisters from Canada to New Orleans established progressive-thinking religious orders, hospitals, and educational institutions for girls of all races. Women religious also were the most independent women professionals in the nineteenth century, founding and administering a myriad of service institutions.

From 1900 to 1950, nuns were subjected to more restrictive control by the church hierarchy and often described as "the serf labor of the church." The inheritance of independence from the nineteenth century and of repression in the first half of the twentieth century activated sisters in the Catholic feminist movement, including Black and Hispanic nuns, in its stirrings dating from 1950 until today.

Chapter 1 further traces the cultural dissonance characterizing the attitudes of institutional officials toward laywomen. Ruether concludes, "American and global Catholicism entered the 1990s more deeply polarized than at any time since the Reformation, divided between movements of searching self-criticism calling for change and a hierarchy unable to accept the possibility of significant error. . . . The conflict between a creative Catholic feminism and deep hostility to women's independence is a central expression of this polarization."

Rosemary Keller focuses on the culture of women's organizations in chapter 2, "The Organization of Protestant Laywomen in Institutional Churches." Women first gained voices in the churches through women's societies, the initial doors opened to provide them with larger social space outside the home. However, these societies arose most often because women were not permitted to serve on governing boards of churches at both local and national levels.

Further, volunteer laywomen's separatist societies were perpetuated because rules of exclusion continued, in most cases, until the late-twentieth-century wave of feminism. When such organizations were merged with general church boards, women often lost their governing authority and power, and they were co-opted into auxiliary roles. Wisely, women often sought to maintain their separation. They knew that their societies provided training in organization and administration from grass-roots to national organizational levels for countless thousands, even millions, of women who would have received it nowhere else.

Finally, male leaders often sanctioned women's separatist societies as a means of marginalizing and even isolating women's place in church structures. However, women found "safe space" in organizations "for women only," where they experienced mutual support, affirmation, encouragement, and momentum to accept themselves and to become new and empowered beings in Jesus Christ.

Both Black and white women claimed "God-given sanction" to step out boldly. The mutual support of their sisterhoods in missionary service provided a subculture of empowerment within the larger structures of Black and white churches.

The clash between gender and culture within Judaism related to the cross-cultural worlds of deeply ingrained religious practice and the process of Americanization, writes Ann Braude in chapter 3, "Women and Religious Practice in American Judaism." This reality was more prominent for Jewish women than for either Roman Catholic or Protestant women.

The development of women's organizations within Judaism, similar to those in both Catholic and Protestant American Christian churches, led to major cultural clashes between rabbis and women in Jewish orthodoxy. "Failure to adapt to the American norm in which women supply the bulk of time, energy, and money for maintenance of religious institutions would have meant 'organizational suicide' for American Judaism," writes Braude. Yet, on the other hand, "once exposed to American freedom, many Jewish women could not accept the restrictions placed on them by Jewish traditions."

Women within the Conservative, Reform, and Reconstructionist wings of Judaism have been active in social reform since the late nineteenth century and have gained ordination within the last two decades. The dissonance of cultural worlds may be most striking today within Orthodox Judaism, where women's voices have been raised in separatist prayer meetings. Braude states that within Orthodoxy "women's prayer groups represent a more radical departure from Jewish gender expectations than the egalitarian models pursued first within the Reform movement and now, more cautiously, in Conservative Judaism as well. Rather than incorporating women into the male-dominated sphere of the synagogue, these groups create a space within Jewish ritual that is completely controlled by women."

Emilie Townes articulates the emerging strong voices of Black women in chapter 4, "Black Women: From Slavery to Womanist Liberation." In the 1740s, when conversions of slaves began, more Black women than men became Christian. African folk beliefs blended with evangelical enthusiasm to form a distinctive African American celebration by the early nineteenth century. Simultaneously, Black Christianity helped instill a strong sense of identity in the women.

As the Black Church emerged into an identity of its own in the nineteenth century, Black women remained within the orthodoxy of African American Christian institutions, just as most Catholic, Protestant, and Jewish women had done. But, also like their white sisters, Black women created their own social space. Townes states that in their own voices, African American women "restated that orthodoxy" in language more freeing to women. "Black women in religious circles did not depict themselves as the larger society portrayed white women—fragile and impressionable with little capacity for rational thought," Townes writes. "Black women viewed themselves as having a capacity to influence men and consistently described their power of persuasion over men as historically positive."

African American women adopted the dual image of Christ as feminine and masculine, passive and aggressive, meek and conquering to describe their self-understanding. They defined themselves as both homemakers and soldiers. Such self-declared identity provided a strong foundation in later generations for women to critique the church from within and to move into social reform through the Black women's club movement.

Women who have entered the public world through preaching and social reform have gained stronger presence and voice within streams of evangelicalism and revivalism than in other religious traditions. Nancy Hardesty traces the multicultural worlds of evangelicalism and the place of gender within them in chapter 5, "Evangelical Women."

The culture of evangelicalism has shifted radically within Protestantism in the American past and present. During the seventeenth and eighteenth and much of the nineteenth centuries it was at the center of mainline Protestantism and social reform.

By the late nineteenth century, evangelicalism became identified with the Holiness movement, creating a subculture of a whole family of denominations outside mainstream Protestantism. Many Holiness women were increasingly marginalized, becoming identified with faith healing and speaking in tongues. Some founded denominations and churches of their own.

The broad culture of evangelicalism holds contradictions with regard to gender, as do denominations and racial groups. Some Holiness and Pentecostal churches granted full ordination to women while mainline denominations vigorously resisted it. In contrast, women have gained little stature in Fundamentalism, and their voices have been largely quelled.

The clash of gender expectations within evangelicalism continues today, with women as well as men representing the continuum of social views from radical to conservative, through such organizations as the Evangelical and Ecumenical Women's Caucus, Christians for Biblical Equality, the Council on Biblical Manhood and Womanhood, and Concerned Women for America.

In chapter 6, "Protestant Women and Social Reform," Joanne Brown recovers voices that women of religious conviction brought to secular reform movements. By the age of reform in the nineteenth century, however, women of sacred and secular conviction banded together to found organizations outside specifically defined religious institutions.

Many, though not all, of these societies were devoted to particular causes, including temperance, women's rights, education, abolition of slavery, freedmen's aid, moral reform, fair wages, and care of the insane. Women generally founded separate-sex reform societies because they were banned from participating in general reform agencies begun by men. Here, as in laywomen's societies within the churches, women discovered strength and mutual support in bonding and demonstrated their innate gifts of organizing, administering, and fund-raising.

Religious women brought a distinctive voice to social reform: they claimed divine sanction, a greater mandate than could be mustered for any secular motivation. God willed the good society. And, while God intended that women work for the improved life of all persons, a particular sanction was placed upon women to address the basic human needs of their own sex.

For many of the women, reform became their religion, a faith as much as a cause. Social reform held a sacred quality for the women involved; it equaled practical Christianity, the living out of the ethics of Jesus. Most female reformers saw Christianity as the foundation of, not an impediment to, their work. Some also felt led to critique the church so that its message and its practice would be brought more closely together.

Many historical issues, such as race, women's rights, and economic justice, remain on the agenda of religious women social reformers today. But, in this age of pluralism and secularism, issues also have changed. Having gained a foothold in secular society, women grapple as never before with issues of success and professionalism. Religious language also has changed. But the motivation to live and act out of the call of God still causes religious women to seek new, along with well-tested, ways to work for social change.

Prior to the nineteenth century, women in the preaching tradition primarily sought the right to speak publicly in their own voices. But by the late nineteenth century and especially in the twentieth century, their foremost goal became ordination: the institutional accreditation of their ministries to sacrament and order as well as to preaching the word. In chapter 7, Barbara Brown Zikmund traces the relationship between "Women and Ordination" in many branches of Christianity and Judaism.

The fight for ordination of women in mainline Protestant denominations and Judaism has been won in the twentieth century, notably in the second half of the century. Zikmund documents those steps within the Presbyterian, Methodist, Lutheran, and Episcopal denominations of Protestantism, in Wesleyan and Holiness churches, in Black churches, and in Judaism. She further outlines the struggles that continue to be waged in Roman Catholicism and Orthodoxy.

Ordination has been rightly evaluated as the major achievement in gaining equal status of women with men in the churches. In ordination, women are seeking not increased power and participation in separatist organizations, but full admission to all the rights of the mainstream power structure of the churches. The weight of ordination is dramatically witnessed by the fact that until 1977, only 17 percent of female clergy served in the ten major Protestant denominations, while the majority of ordained women have consistently found their home within Pentecostal, evangelical, and paramilitary denominations, such as the Salvation Army.

"The idea of America as a new land with an open future early attracted people holding utopian and millenarian visions," writes Rosemary Ruether in opening chapter 8, "Gender in Utopian and Communal

Societies." Visions of the good society have been a continuing theme uniting religious reformers active in church and society since the early Puritan experiments. The chapter focuses on women's participation in alternative social and religious movements and specific issues, both positive and negative, that defined their place in these societies in terms of gender.

Ruether traces the many utopian and communal societies to which women were related that have arisen in this country, from the colonial communities of the late seventeenth century through the explosion of communal experiments in the 1960s. "Despite great diversity in ideological inspiration, all these utopian groups share some kind of vision about the perfectibility of humanity through reorganized social relations," she states. She documents four areas of the transformed self and society found in these utopian movements, including androgynous visions for both God and the new humanity, alternatives to the family, female founders and leaders, and gender-based division of labor and social equality.

Through their own voices, primarily of women but also of men, we hear what utopian visions have meant in the lives of women within the movements. Communities often have betrayed their promises to women, while male domination typical of mainstream organizations has been perpetuated. "Pioneering men and women deeply alienated from the dominant society and seeking a visionary alternative" will continue to be attracted to alternative communities "in a time of growing economic and ecological crisis of the late twentieth century." The recurring question remains: how egalitarian and empowering for women will their utopian vision and practice be?

In the final two chapters, we begin to recover the history of women in the North American religious tradition whose stories are only now being written. The challenge in earlier chapters has been to retrieve the written documents of women who, in their own voices, speak representatively for larger segments of women in their traditions. But, regarding women in the American Indian heritage and in a myriad of other emerging religions in the United States today, the challenge lies elsewhere: in these traditions women speak "in our own voices" to begin to conceive of a living past, a historical tradition, that addresses their condition at the end of the twentieth century.

In chapter 9, "Seeing Red: American Indian Women Speaking of Their Religious and Political Perspectives," Inés Talamantez explores the sense of self and place that Indian women ancestors have transmitted to Native American women and girls today. The ancestors' perseverance for social justice and religious freedom provides the model for indigenous women in their contemporary struggle for education, health care, and possession of the land for themselves and their sisters and brothers, as well as for ecological vision and practice in caring for the created order.

Talamantez begins to recover the world of native women's spirituality through female initiation rites and tribal myths disclosed in limited recent printed materials and, more important, in her interviews with clan mothers, medicine women, and female elders on reservations today. Initiation rituals become the instruments of empowerment used by Native American mothers, stripped away from their foremothers by white patriarchal domination, to raise their daughters to the full stature of womanhood.

Understanding the present as a pivotal moment in history, Talamentez hopes that future generations will look back to our time and see that as human rights activists, mothers, artists, scholars, women demanded accountability from the religious and political institutions of our time.

People within the broad mainstream of American culture have been blind to the extent that religious diversity always has been present in the United States. Increasing recognition of the multicultural religious worlds is markedly changing the contours of what it means to be individuals and societies of faith in the late twentieth century. One paragraph from the tenth chapter, "Women in American Religions: Growing Pluralism, New Dialogue," by Rosemary Ruether, brings together a striking demographic picture:

> From being the historically dominant form of religion in the United States, Protestant churches in 1993 account for about 35 percent of Americans, and other forms of Christianity another 25.5 percent. Jews are about 2.4 percent. While many of the other 37 percent of Americans (some 93 million people) are nominally Christian, perhaps as many as 20 million of these belong to other religions. They are Muslims, Hindus, Buddhists, Sikhs, Zoroastrians, Bahais, or members of New Age spiritualities, such as

the Covenant of the Goddess. The 1993 World's Parliament of Religions reported that, in the greater Chicago area, there are more Muslims than Jews, more Thai Buddhists than Episcopalians. In this area alone there are seventeen Hindu temples.

In the concluding chapter, Ruether points out that a host of women's voices have emerged in the last quarter century, including those of Christian feminist, womanist, and *mujerista* theology, along with voices of Jewish, Muslim, and Buddhist feminist theology and those of Wiccan thealogy. The reality of women's experiences in one of these traditions, Islam, suggests affinity with the conditions that have confronted women in the dominant Protestant, Catholic, and Jewish faiths. Riffat Hassan, a feminist scholar of the Qur'an, points out that "unless and until the theological foundations of misogynistic and androcentric tendencies in the Islamic tradition are demolished, Muslim women will continue to be brutalized and discriminated against, despite statistical improvements relating to female education, employment, or social and political rights." Her point well applies to the experiences of women in other emerging cultures, as presented in this chapter.

Black and white, as well as Hispanic and Native American, women have lived in multicultural worlds of faith since the founding of their religious movements and institutions on American colonial soil almost four centuries ago. Today the stories of women of Roman Catholicism, Protestantism, and Judaism are being joined with those of almost countless emerging religions representing wide racial and ethnic diversity.

The barriers that women in Christianity and Judaism have faced in relating to the hierarchical structures of their faith institutions bear affinity with the barriers facing women in emerging religious movements in the United States today. In their own voices, women here speak of both the distinctiveness of their experiences and the affinities of their experiences with those of other women.

A deeper understanding of our close connection with people of similar and differing beliefs and needs will help all of us, both women and men, better analyze oppressive conditions and envision a transformed

future of personal and social wholeness and well-being for all God's people. We trust that this purpose underlies all religious faiths. As our understanding of this goal deepens, may we commit ourselves to particular
expressions of this vision in our personal experience.

Through listening to our own voices, we seek to share our histories.
This effort is meant to be a step in creating cultural bridges, opening dialogue, and furthering support among women and men for a liberating
persuasion in traditional and emerging faiths today.

CHAPTER ONE

Catholic Women in North America

Rosemary Radford Ruether

Documents

THE COLONIAL ERA

1. Marie Madeleine Hachard: The Ursulines Arrive in New Orleans
2. Margaret Brent: A Demand for a Seat in the Maryland Assembly

WOMEN RELIGIOUS, 1790–1950

3. Sister Blandina Segale: Pioneer Nuns on the Frontier
4. Sisters of Providence: Nuns Struggle with Bishops over Their Rights
5. Sisters of Mercy: Nurses in Epidemics

CATHOLIC LAYWOMEN AND SOCIAL REFORM, 1890–1950

6. Mother Jones: Organizing the Women and the Miners
7. Katherine Conway: A Leading Woman Editor Rejects Women's Suffrage
8. Mrs. Francis E. Slattery: Catholic Women Use the Vote to Defend the Family
9. Dorothy Day: The Catholic Worker, Still Pacifist in World War II

THE BIRTH OF CATHOLIC FEMINISM, 1950–1993

10. The Grail: From Rural Utopianism to Feminism
11. Patty Crowley: The Christian Family Movement and Birth Control
12. Sister Madeleva Wolff: The Education of Sister Lucy
13. Leadership Conference of Women Religious: Educating Nuns for Feminist Consciousness
14. Las Hermanas: Hispanic Nuns Confront Racism and Sexism
15. Rosalie Muschal-Reinhardt: Feminist Theology Claiming Ordained Ministry
16. Catholics Speak Out: The Failure of the Bishops' Pastoral on Women
17. Women-Church: Creating Feminist Communities

T HE Catholic community in the United States is ethnically diverse. The first Catholics to invade the Americas were the Spanish in the sixteenth century, followed by the French in the seventeenth century. English Catholics colonized Maryland in 1634. Irish and Germans were the major Catholic immigrants of the nineteenth century. In the 1880s waves of Polish and Italians began, followed by other southern and eastern Europeans. The occupation of Puerto Rico and the Philippines in 1900 brought immigrants from these lands. Black Catholics would grow in numbers in the twentieth century through urbanization and migration from the Caribbean. The number of Asian Catholics would expand after the Vietnam War with the arrival of Vietnamese.[1] In 1990 Catholicism was the largest U.S. Christian denomination (58.5 million), with a growing sector of Hispanics (21 million).[2]

WOMEN IN COLONIAL CATHOLICISM

The Spanish, who built a vast Latin America colonial empire, brought a church with religious orders for women as well as for men. Hispanic nuns shaped an intellectual life within the convent walls, writing mystical treatises, poetry, and plays. The most notable of these women was Sor Juana Ines de la Cruz (1648–1695), a brilliant Renaissance humanist who struggled to nurture her scholarship against the restrictive environment of the convent.[3]

Women of seventeenth-century New France came from a more open society where the equality of women and men was much discussed.[4] French Canadian women founded schools for girls of all races, hospitals, and activist religious orders.[5] Moving down the Mississippi, the French planted New Orleans in 1718 as the jewel port city for their trade. The Ursuline nuns arrived in New Orleans in 1727 from France and for many years provided the main education available in the city, teaching only women (document 1).[6]

Catholics in the British thirteen colonies were constricted by religious hostilities that reflected the rivalries among the British, French, and Spanish colonial empires in the new world. English Catholics were accustomed to separating political from religious loyalties to avoid being suspected of partisanship for one of the two European Catholic powers. In England, Catholicism survived in the Reformation era as a private religion observed quietly in the home. Women were the mainstay of the faith, gathering the family for prayer, educating children, observing the rounds of feasts and fasts, hosting and hiding the clandestine itinerant priests. The prestige thus acquired by Catholic women of property is reflected in Lord Baltimore's provisions for land grants in the colony of Maryland, in which women heads of family are treated the same as men in claiming tracts of land.[7]

Among the women who came as settlers to Maryland were the Mistress Margaret Brent and her sister Mary. As owner of a considerable manorial estate, Margaret Brent had the right to hold courts-baron, where she heard disputes and received fealty for land granted to dependents. Margaret Brent's name appears 134 times in the records of the provincial court of Maryland between 1642 and 1650, as she managed her affairs of property. She often acted as attorney for relatives and friends. When the governor, Leonard Calvert, left the colony and later died, Brent was named executrix of his estates. In 1647 she was virtually the governor, quelling uprisings and paying soldiers.[8]

Brent then appeared before the Maryland Assembly, asking for a seat and two votes, one in her own right and one as representative of the governor. The assembly refused her this request, although it expressed its appreciation for her services (document 2). Brent's relation to the church is indicated by the fact that when the Jesuit missionaries converted the leaders of the Piscataway Indians, she was named the guardian of the orphaned Indian princess, Mary Killamaquund.[9]

Maryland Catholics defended equal treatment of all Christians, but their lands and political predominance aroused the hostility of their Protestant neighbors. In 1689 Catholics were disenfranchised, and the Church of England became the official church. A series of penal laws passed against Catholics removed them from any public role. One such law testifies to the power of women to transmit religious faith. It decrees that a Catholic widow of a Protestant man could lose custody of her children, so they would not be raised Catholics.[10]

The American Revolution, enthusiastically supported by Maryland Catholics, lifted these bans against Catholics. Catholics could again act as delegates to political assemblies. But women did not share in the new "rights of man." In seventeenth-century Maryland a woman property holder could exercise power of attorney in her own name but not in the new republic. In 1689 Maryland women were denied legal standing as Catholics, in 1776 as women.

WOMEN RELIGIOUS, 1790–1950

Women religious were the most independent women professionals in nineteenth-century America. They were self-supporting and educated, and they owned and administered large properties: convents, schools, orphanages, homes for the aged, delinquents, and other needy groups, hospitals, and farms. But they were also viewed as embodying the epitome of the feminine ideal of sexual repression, docility to male authority, and self-effacing service to others.

Twelve religious congregations of women were founded between 1790 and 1830, six by American women, and another one hundred and six between 1830 and 1900, twenty-three by Americans. By 1900 there were over 40,000 nuns in the United States, outnumbering priests four to one. By 1950 their numbers had grown to 177,000 in 450 distinct congregations.[11] They ran thousands of schools on the elementary, secondary, and college levels, hundreds of hospitals, and many other special institutions of social service.[12]

The first religious congregation for women to be founded by an American was the Sisters of Charity of Emmitsburg, Maryland. Elizabeth Bayley Seton (1774–1821) was a wealthy widow with five children who converted to Catholicism and opened a school for girls in Baltimore in 1806. In 1809 she founded a community for herself and a circle of friends and relatives modeled after the French third-order Daughters of Charity (an order without rules of cloister or solemn vows).[13]

Another congregation founded by American women was the Sisters of Loretto in Bardstown, Kentucky. Mary Rhodes (1783–1853) belonged to Maryland Catholic families who migrated to Kentucky in 1785, seeking land and escape from religious intolerance. Rhodes and two friends began a log cabin school for these families in 1811. In 1812 they formed an order with the assistance of Charles Nerinckx, a Belgian priest.[14] Between 1816 and 1820 the Lorettos founded several other schools in Kentucky. They expanded their work to Missouri (1823), Pine Bluffs, Arkansas (1838), Osage, Kansas (1847), Santa Fe and Taos, New Mexico (1850s), Denver (1864), Salinas, California (1886), and El Paso, Texas

(1891). In the 1920s they were operating one hundred schools, including two senior colleges and one junior college.[15]

The pioneer era of American sisterhoods contains many stories of risk taking with few resources other than an indomitable faith. Nuns who arrived from Europe with little knowledge of the language or culture were sent alone or in small bands of women into the frontiers. They entered unsettled territories, braving lynch mobs and bandits, as did Sister Blandina Segale (document 3). Mary of Jesus of the Sisters of Charity of the Incarnate Word traveled alone on mission through Texas in the 1860s, driving a team of horses and holding a brace of pistols at her side.[16]

Catholic nuns in nineteenth-century America struggled with severe contradictions rooted in the Catholic view of women as mentally and morally weak. Canon law imposed strict enclosure on all nuns under solemn vows. Even third-order nuns with simple vows, supposedly able to do charitable work in the community, were subject to strict limitations on their movements and work. Such rules were unsuitable to the American situation. Almost all orders were founded or came to the United States to teach, nurse, or do other social service. They lacked the endowments, dowries, and wealthy benefactors that allowed European nuns to pursue a monastic regime of continual prayer. Their work was viewed as free charitable service, but they also had to support themselves. They often ran both free and tuition-supported schools, did their own farming, taught extra classes in music and art, did laundry and sewing, printed books, and engaged in many other occupations to support themselves and their projects.[17]

Their constitutions, inherited from Europe, reflected a monastic regime of prayer and fasting, but in America this was combined with full-time teaching, domestic work, farming, and other self-support projects. They wore heavy clothing unsuited to the weather and endured inadequate sleep, food, and medical care. The result was a high mortality rate among nuns.

Some priest-counselors and superiors from European mother houses insisted that nuns remain faithful to European monastic regimens, despite their unsuitability to the American context.[18] Other advisers urged sisters to relax their rules of enclosure, monastic hours of prayer, and restrictions on the type of work they could do (such as not teaching boys) in order to be more available for the many needs of the American pioneer church. Many bishops preferred diocesan orders that were directly under their jurisdiction.

American sisterhoods were often in conflict with church authorities as they resisted pressures to adapt their rules to be more available for the work that a bishop wanted them to do and more directly under his power (document 4). Some congregations gained independence from their European orders to be able to adapt their constitution to the American context; others appealed to European superiors or to Rome to counteract a bishop who wanted to interfere in their way of life or the work that they were doing.

Catholic sisters in the United States were the butt of anti-Catholic hostility, particularly in the pre–Civil War period. Protestant literature depicted the nun either as an indolent and morally corrupt aristocrat or else as the victim of a repressive regime that captured and imprisoned her. Nuns wore secular garb outside the convent to avoid insults and physical assaults. At times they suffered raids and even destruction of their convents by mobs incited by anti-Catholic preachers or literature.[19]

This hostility to nuns was tempered by laws protecting religious freedom and also by the respect many Protestants felt toward nuns as selfless servants of social welfare. Many upper-class Protestants also saw convent schools as good places to educate their daughters in French language, culture, and social graces. The Visitation convent school in Washington, D.C., founded in 1799, educated the daughters of many high-ranking Protestant government leaders, and its graduations were presided over by presidents such as James Madison and John Quincy Adams.[20]

A significant change in American attitudes toward nuns came as a result of their dedicated nursing during the Civil War in both Northern and Southern hospitals. Nuns in nineteenth-century America nursed soldiers in every war from 1812 to the Spanish American War; they also nursed the victims of diseases, such as the cholera and yellow fever epidemics that ravaged the country in 1832–34, 1849–50, and 1855 (document 5). Six hundred forty nuns responded to the call for nurses during the Civil War. This service earned high tribute from American leaders and the general public and was a major factor in changing the negative image of nuns that had existed earlier.[21]

From 1900 to 1950 the roles played by Catholics nuns narrowed while their numbers were greatly increasing. In 1900 U.S. Catholics gained permission from Rome to organize as a church with a recognized hierarchy. The Vatican also recognized the third-order apostolate as a true form of religious life but imposed partial cloister and monastic rules on it. Strict control, limiting activity outside the convent or contact with the lay world, became normative for nuns.[22] The U.S. Catholic bishops sought uniformity and control over their diverse flock. One means was the promotion of parochial schools, which the 1882 Plenary Conference of the Catholic bishops endorsed as the norm for all Catholic children.

Teaching in parochial schools became the primary role for nuns. The need for teachers in the parochial schools mandated for every parish meant that women in their late teens, after a one-year novitiate, were pressed into on-the-job training in large classes of working-class children. Bishops were unreceptive to efforts of nuns to further their own educations and typically felt that two or three hundred dollars a year, paid to the superior and not directly to the individual, was sufficient remuneration for these services. Nuns were the serf labor force of the church.[23]

From 1900 to the 1940s the gap widened between the educational and professional opportunities available to laywomen and those of nuns. Nuns, who earlier had been pioneers for women in nursing, were forbidden to study anatomy and physiology or to nurse in maternity wards, sights seen as threatening to their purity.[24] Concerned about their inferior training compared to that of lay professionals in nursing and teaching, nuns struggled to complete their education through summer and Saturday courses. Many of their academies grew into full colleges to provide adequate education for themselves and their women students.

CATHOLIC LAYWOMEN AND SOCIAL REFORM, 1850–1950

Few Catholics participated in the abolitionist movement of the 1840s.[25] However, some religious orders educated and served the poor of all races. On several occasions Catholic schools with Black students found themselves in conflict with local mores that forbade education of Blacks.[26] In the antebellum period free Black women founded two religious orders to educate their own people: the Oblate Sisters of Providence in Baltimore, Maryland, in 1829, and the Sisters of the Holy Family in New Orleans in 1842. A third order, the Franciscan Handmaids of Mary, was founded in Savannah, Georgia, in 1916 and moved to Harlem in 1922.[27] A white order, the Sisters of the Blessed Sacrament for Indians and Colored People, was founded in 1891 by Katherine Drexel.[28]

By the 1880s American Catholics felt enough at home in U.S. society to begin to participate in the questions of social reform. As a largely working-class population, many Catholic women and men had strong ties to the labor movement.[29] The gap between rich and poor was widening, worsened by waves of economic depression. Workers responded by militant labor organizing and strikes. The official Catholic response to poverty was charity. Charitable organizations run by religious orders redoubled their efforts. Urban parishes took on some of the functions of settlement-house work, providing gyms, kindergartens, adult education, libraries, and food pantries. Temperance was a popular solution to poverty among Catholics, inspiring groups such as the Catholic Total Abstinence Union.[30]

By 1900 the official Catholic hostility to labor organizing changed to support for unions but in a framework of antisocialism and defense of the rights of private property.[31] Yet even priests and bishops supportive of labor ignored the problems of working women. Like most Americans, including many men of the labor movement, they assumed working women were "unnatural," the normative role for women being homemaking and motherhood. But most immigrant women had no choice but to work. The majority of the women employed by the Knights of Labor and the American Federation of Labor to organize working women were Irish, such as Elizabeth Flynn Rogers, Mary Kenny O'Sullivan, and Leonora Barry. Mother Jones, famous for her work with miners, was only one of many Irish women labor organizers in this period (document 6).[32]

Mutual benefit societies were a popular strategy immigrants chose for combating economic insecurity. These societies provided insurance and home loans and tided workers over during times of adversity. Such societies were usually formed along ethnic lines and fostered ethnic cultures and languages threatened by the Anglo-American "melting pot." Immigrant women formed women's auxiliaries of ethnic societies, such as the Fenian Sisterhood, which supported the independence of Ireland from England and fostered Irish identity in the United States. Some immigrant women's mutual benefit societies, such as the Polish Women's Alliance, arose independently of male groups to provide support not available elsewhere for working women. Unlike women labor organizers, women's mutual benefit societies, linked to ethnic cultures and parishes, enjoyed good support from priests and bishops of their national communities.[33]

Women's suffrage was another major movement of the time. The official Catholic view of it was overwhelmingly negative. Bishops, priests, even prominent Catholic women writers, such as Katherine Conway, a novelist, journalist, and editor, strongly opposed it as a threat to woman's "true nature" as mother and homemaker (document 7). Feminism was linked to socialism and seen as an assault on the family, divine law, and social stability. This opposition was not total. Priests and bishops associated with the rights of labor were more favorable to feminism, and there were some Catholic women suffrage leaders.[34]

Once women won the vote, however, the Catholic bishops quickly dropped their opposition and turned instead toward organizing Catholic women to use the vote for socially conservative causes. In 1920 the bishops set up the National Council of Catholic Women under the bishops' social agency, the National Catholic Welfare Conference, to coordinate Catholic women's groups.[35]

Officially recognized Catholic women's groups championed a view of women as having a totally different nature from males. The older view of women as morally inferior was played down in favor of an exalted idea of women as "naturally" more moral and altruistic, but this was harnessed to a conservative social agenda. Women had a special role to oppose liberalism, secularism, socialism, and feminism, with their "insidious" social reforms, such as birth control, divorce, child labor laws, and the Equal Rights Amendment, which were intended to undermine the family and society. This ideology was linked with an aggressive Americanism among Catholics who saw themselves as saviors, not only of true Christianity, but of the true American society as well (document 8).

Despite the regnant conservativism in official Catholicism in the 1930s to 1950s, the period also saw the rise of a number of important lay movements, most of them led by women or having predominantly women members. These grassroots groups represented a new type of

Catholic movement. Organized and run by laypeople, they nevertheless saw themselves as fully and distinctively Catholic. They sought good relations with the hierarchical church but avoided any direct control by it.

One such movement was the Catholic Worker, founded by Dorothy Day in 1933 with French peasant philosopher Peter Maurin. The Worker was a unique blend of social radicalism and asceticism that drew thousands of idealistic young Catholics to embrace a life of poverty and insecurity in solidarity with the most downtrodden of the American urban poor. The Worker also broke with Catholic teaching on "just war" and enunciated a Catholic ethic of total pacifism (document 9).[36]

Catholics, like most white Americans, were slow to respond to racism as an issue distinct from the rights of labor. In the twenties the Irish and Italians were becoming middle class and moving into better neighborhoods, and their places in the urban slums were being taken by Blacks migrating from the South. Many Catholic parishes in former white ethnic neighborhoods were deeply threatened by these new migrants, seen as both racially and religiously alien. However, some priests saw these new neighbors as potential church members who could benefit from the schools and other organizations of the now half-empty parishes. They began evangelizing urban Blacks and brought tens of thousands into the Catholic fold. Such priests became sensitive to racism and founded groups to combat it, such as the Catholic Interracial Council.[37]

The major lay movement that focused on racial injustice was Friendship House, which started in Harlem in 1937 in the style of the Catholic Worker, and then spread to other cities. Founded by Russian émigré Catherine de Hueck, its leadership was almost entirely female. Its typical staff of volunteers were young Catholic women in their twenties, graduates of Catholic women's colleges, who broke with the values of their suburbanized parents and expressed their social idealism by moving to the urban ghettos and identifying with the problems of the Black urban poor.[38]

THE BIRTH OF CATHOLIC FEMINISM, 1950–1993

Catholic feminism, which would blossom in the 1970s, did not arise just from the liberalizing movements unleashed by the Second Vatican Council of 1961 to 1965. Its incubation lay in the fifties, in lay movements, and in initiatives among nuns to improve the education of Catholic sisters. Two lay movements that would be important seedbeds for Catholic feminism were the Grail and the Christian Family Movement. These movements are examples of how traditional Catholic values that promoted women as saviors of the family against masculine vices could develop into progressive rather than conservative movements.

The Grail was brought to the United States in 1940 by two Dutch women, Lydwine van Kersbergen and Joan Overboss. While its core group followed the evangelical counsels of poverty, chastity, and obedience, it avoided becoming defined as a religious order under hierarchical control. From its beginnings, the empowerment of women as social transformers was central to its vision, but it initially saw this in terms of women's distinctively feminine nature. The early Grail promoted a renewal of rural life and helped popularize liturgical renewal (document 10).

In the sixties the Grail became involved in the civil rights and peace movements, and in the seventies it became a major promoter of feminist theology. From 1974 to 1978 the Women's Seminary Quarter in Loveland, Ohio, would bring women seminarians to the Grail center there to explore feminist theology and spirituality. These programs helped generate a new era of feminist theological reflection, not only among Catholics but also among Protestant and Jewish women as well.[39]

The Christian Family Movement began in 1949 as couples' groups using the methodology of Catholic Action to reflect on their social responsibilities. This method taught couples to "see, judge, and act" in examining social issues of the day, although sexuality and women's roles were ignored. Although Catholic Action was officially defined as "the participation of the laity in the apostolate of the Hierarchy" and was intended to be strictly controlled by priest-chaplains, CFM was lay organized from the beginning, with positive relations to, but not under the control of, its clerical friends.[40]

In 1964 CFM's leaders, Pat and Patty Crowley, were asked to participate in the Papal Birth Control Commission. The Crowleys polled CFM membership on birth control and brought to the commission their findings that the rhythm method was deeply resented by these "good" married Catholics because it inhibited sexual relations at ovulation, the very time when women desired it the most. The arguments in favor of the rhythm method were seen as reflecting a male celibate view of sexuality (document 11).

As a result of the testimony of the Crowleys and other couples and lay experts, the clerical members of the commission changed their minds and voted overwhelmingly to reject the traditional Catholic teaching that there was a significant moral difference between rhythm and other forms of contraception. When Pope Paul VI rejected the majority view of his own commission and opted to reaffirm the traditional teaching, the Crowleys and many other CFM couples were stunned and forced to re-examine their naive views of papal teaching authority. Such new critical consciousness would lead Patty Crowley and many other CFMers increasingly to recognize that the problem of Catholicism was not so much sexuality as sexism.

In the late forties and fifties Catholic nuns were also restive. They began to challenge the pattern that had forced young nuns to teach in Catholic schools with inadequate education and social maturity. The result was the Sister Formation Movement, which demanded that nuns complete college and earn a teaching credential before being put into schools as teachers (document 12). The stress on holistic formation fostered critical consciousness about the meaning of the Christian vision and women's role in it.[41]

In response to the Vatican's call to renew their orders, many U.S. women's orders democratized their structures and diversified their work. In the 1970s the Leadership Conference of Women Religious, the official organization of Catholic nuns, saw education in feminist consciousness as an important means toward the spiritual and social formation of its members and sponsored a series of study packets on feminism (document 13). Hispanic and Black nuns also created their own organizations in order to combat both racism and sexism in the church (document 14).[42]

These changes of consciousness and social organization among nuns resulted in bruising confrontations with some bishops, who saw the nuns as "out of control." Because of these conflicts many nuns who had been most involved in the reforms left their orders, often to pursue social ministries in autonomous lay movements. In one notable confrontation between the Sisters of the Immaculate Heart in Los Angeles and Cardinal McIntyre, 90 percent of the order left as a body to refound themselves as an independent lay community.[43]

In the early 1970s the question of women's ordination became a pressing issue for U.S. Catholic women, as Episcopal women moved through a deep conflict and won a majority vote for ordaining women. In November 1975, 1200 Catholic women gathered in Detroit to examine the question of women's ordination and to found the Women's Ordination Movement. The newly emerging leaders of Catholic feminist biblical exegesis and theology provided the critical arguments for the change. The goal, however, was never simply women's ordination but a more participatory understanding of the church as a community of mutual ministry (document 15).

Conflicts between U.S. Catholic feminists, both lay and religious, and the Vatican heightened in the 1980s as the Vatican, under the new Pope John Paul II, became increasingly conservative and sought not only to block liberalizing trends but even to retreat to pre–Vatican II understandings of the church. A major display of this conflict took place when ninety-seven prominent Catholics, including twenty-six nuns, signed a New York Times ad that appeared October 7, 1984, stating that a diversity of opinions existed among Catholics on the morality of abortion.[44]

The Vatican saw such a statement as a direct challenge to its teaching authority. It insisted that all the nun-signers either recant or leave their orders.[45] Since these women were leading feminists and social activists, the conflict became a major struggle over the right of nuns to act as independent agents in society. Many feminist nuns, such as Maureen Fiedler and Marjorie Tuite, had departed from traditional apostolates under the hierarchy and were engaged in political organizing that challenged American foreign policy in places such as Nicaragua. A series of confrontations took place between the Vatican and social activist nuns, together with their orders, over the right of nuns to engage in political life.[46]

Some bishops already in the late 1970s realized that the church could only lose by such conflicts with its best-educated women. As the number of priests was dwindling, it was evident that the church would have to depend more and more on nuns and laywomen for ministry. A dialogue was authorized between the Women's Ordination Conference and the Catholic Bishops' Committee on Women in 1978. For three years they met in a dialogue on women's issues in the church.[47]

The bishops of the committee emerged feeling they had learned much and should create a similar process of education for their fellow bishops. The result was the decision to write a pastoral letter on women.

As each draft of this letter became more contradictory than the last, the profound inability of Catholicism to accommodate feminist critique without admitting that it had erred in the past became painfully evident. By 1992 even liberal bishops were urging that the project be dropped and that the bishops simply try to spend more time listening to women (document 17).[48]

Not all Catholic women were happy about the new feminist thought among their sisters and even some of their brothers in the faith. For some Catholic women such ideas were evidence that a deep spirit of infidelity and even "paganism" had erupted in the heart of the church itself. They believed such dissidents must be purged in order to save both the church and society. Echoing the conservative ideology that had been standard in the pre–Vatican II era, but now with a sharper edge of polarization within the Catholic Church itself, these women formed groups such as Women for Faith and Family to organize against contraception, abortion, and feminist theological goals such as inclusive language.[49]

For other Catholic women the polarization only confirmed their belief that the institutional church could not accommodate feminism. It was necessary to bring to birth a new feminist religious community within the dying body of the old church. The women-church movement grew within the Women's Ordination Conference as the emphasis shifted from the pursuit of ordination to the development of feminist base communities to organize alternative worship services. The first women-church conference was held in 1983, with successive conferences in 1987 and 1993. In an expanding network, Catholic feminist organizations grouped themselves under the umbrella of women-church (document 18).[50]

American and global Catholicism entered the 1990s more deeply polarized than at any time since the Reformation, divided between movements of searching self-criticism calling for change and a hierarchy unable to accept the possibility of significant error, particularly on matters related to women, sexuality, and centralized power. The conflict between a creative Catholic feminism and deep hostility to women's independence is a central expression of this polarization.[51]

Sister Blandina Segale's pioneering work in the American Southwest is recorded in her letters to her sister, Justina, during the last decades of the nineteenth century.

Sister Marjorie Tuite, O.P., a leading feminist and social activist nun of the late twentieth century, struggled for the rights of sisters to engage in political life and act as independent social agents.

Board of Directors of the Polish Women's Alliance, 1918. The alliance arose independently of male groups to provide support not available elsewhere for working women.

Representatives of the Sisters of the Holy Family, centered in the picture among Black church leaders. Their order was founded in New Orleans in 1842 to educate Black children.

Members of the Catholic Family Movement at the Papal Birth Control Commission meeting in 1964: Pat and Patty Crowley (U.S.A.), Dr. and Mrs. Laurent Potvin (Canada), and Dr. and Mrs. Charles Rendu (France). They were the only three married couples present. No pictures were allowed of the commission's deliberations. This photo was snapped with a Polaroid after the final session.

Mother Jones, an Irish immigrant, became a major labor organizer, particularly with the railroad and mine workers.

Documents

THE COLONIAL ERA

Document 1. Marie Madeleine Hachard:
The Ursulines Arrive in New Orleans

The Ursuline Sisters from Rouen, France, were the first order of religious women to arrive in territory that would become the United States. Twelve nuns left France on February 22, 1727. After a harrowing voyage of five and a half months, in which they encountered several pirate ships and ran aground off the American coast and had to dump much of the cargo, they finally arrived in New Orleans on August 6, 1727. Marie Madeleine Hachard wrote five letters to her father in Rouen describing their voyage. The following excerpts recount the last stage of the journey and their establishment of their convent and school.[52]

We had left Balize on the feast day of St. Ignatius and the launch did not arrive here in New Orleans until the day of the Octave. . . . There are no lands cultivated the whole length of the river, only great wild forests inhabited solely by beasts of all colors. . . . We slept twice in the midst of mud and water which fell from the sky in great abundance and penetrated both us and our matresses which almost swam in the water when a rainstorm with thunder and lightning broke in the middle of the night. . . . On this occasion several of our Mothers were greatly inconvenienced, getting colds and inflammations, some with faces and legs swelling, and one of them even contracted a more severe malady. All these little annoyances began to bother us with time, but we were well rewarded afterwards with the pleasure that one gets from telling of life's little adventures. It is true that the ardent desire we had to see this promised land made us endure everything with joy. . . . Our present lodging is all the way at one end of the town and the house they are building for us all the way at the other. We do not plan to take possession of our Monastery and the Hospital beyond a year or longer, because workmen are not as plentiful here as they are in France. . . . Meanwhile they are at this moment building a small lodging at our residence to be used for instructing the day students and lodging the boarders. . . . There are already thirty boarders from here and as far away as Balize. . . . Fathers and mothers are carried away with joy when they see us because they no longer fear they must return to France since they now have the means of assuring an education for their daughters.

In a later letter written April 24, 1728, Hachard wrote:

Our little community increases each day. We have twenty boarders, eight of whom made their First Communion today, three ladies who are also boarders and three orphan girls whom we took in out of charity. We also have seven slave boarders to instruct for Baptism and first Communion, a large number of day students and Negresses and Indian girls who come two hours each day for instruction. . . . I am still very happy to be in this country and following my vocation. My joy redoubles with the approach of my final vows, to be made in a foreign land where Christianity is nearly unheard of. It is true that there are many honest people in this country, but there is not the slightest indication of devotion, or even of Christianity. How happy we would be if we could establish it here.

Document 2. Margaret Brent:
A Demand for a Seat in the Maryland Assembly

When Governor Leonard Calvert died, Margaret Brent was named his executrix. To better handle his affairs, she appeared before the Maryland Assembly on January 21, 1647, and asked for a seat and a vote in that body. Her power of attorney for Calvert was upheld, but her request for a seat was denied. Brent protested against all proceedings of the assembly unless she was present and with vote.53

Came Mrs Margarett Brent and requested to have vote in the howse for her selfe and voyce allso for that att the last court 3rd: Jan: it was ordered that the said Mrs Brent was to be looked upon and received as his Lordships attorney. The Governor denyed that the said Mrs Brent should have any vote in the howse. And the said Mrs Brent protested against all proceedings in the present Assembly unlesse shee may be present and have vote as aforesaid.

Brent's handling of Calvert's estate forced her to sell some of his property to pay the expenses of the colony's affairs, including the payment of soldiers. When Leonard Calvert's brother, Lord Baltimore, ignorant of the disorders in the colony, complained against her handling of the estate, the Maryland Assembly defended her in a letter dated April 21, 1649.

As for Mrs Brents undertaking and medling with your Lordships estate (whether she procured it with her own or others importunity or no) we do Verily Believe and in Conscience report that it was better for the Collonys safety at that time in her hands than in any mans else in the whole province after your Brothers death for the Soldiers would never have treated any other with that Civility and respect and though they were even ready at times to run into mutiny yet she still pacified them till at the last things were brought to that strait that she must be admitted and declared your Lordships Attorney by an order of Court (the Copy whereof is herewith inclosed) or else all must go to ruin. Again and then the second mischief had been doubtless greater than the former so that if there hath not been any sinister use made of your Lordships Estate by her from what it was intended and ingaged for by Mr Calvert before his death, as we verily Believe she hath not, then we conceive from that time she rather deserved favour and thanks from your Honour for her so much Concurring to the publick safety then to be liable to all those bitter invectives you have been pleased to Express against her.

WOMEN RELIGIOUS, 1790–1950

Document 3. Sister Blandina Segale: Pioneer Nuns on the Frontier

An example of the intrepid style of many nuns who ministered on the American frontier with few resources except their faith is Sister Blandina Segale (1850–1941). Italian born, Segale was sent by her order at the age of twenty-two to Colorado and New Mexico, where she worked for eighteen years building schools and at times confronting outlaw justice. The following excerpts are from the journal that she kept during those years as a series of letters to her sister Justina, also a Sister of Charity.[54]

Stopping a lynch mob in Trinidad, Colorado: November 14, 1874

One of my oldest pupils came to me. . . . He looked so deathly pale that I inquired, "What has happened?" He answered . . . "Sister, dad shot a man. He's in jail. A mob has gathered at Mr. McCaferty's room. The instant he breathes his last, the signal of his death will be given, and the mob will go to the jail and drag dad out and hang him." "Have you thought of anything that might save him?," I asked. "Nothing, Sister; nothing can be done." "Is there no hope the man may recover?" "No hope whatever; the gun was loaded with tin shot."

"John, go to the jail and ask your father if he will take a chance at not being hanged by a mob." "What do you propose doing, Sister?" "First to visit the wounded man and ask if he will receive your father and forgive him, with the understanding that the full force of the law will be carried out." "Sister, the mob would tear him to pieces before he was ten feet from the jail." "I believe he will not be touched if I accompany him," I said. "I'm afraid he will not have the courage to do as you propose." . . . Immediately after school, with a companion, I went to see the wounded man. . . . I looked at the young man, a fine specimen of honesty and manliness. My heart ached for the mother who expected frequent word from her son, then to receive such news! To be shot by a stranger, to die in a strange land, among strangers, so young! . . . The subject of the present visit was broached. The young man was consistent. He said, "I forgive him, as I hope to be forgiven, but I want the law to take its course." . . . Will you tell Mr. —— this if he comes to beg your pardon?" "Yes, Sister," he answered.

Friday evening the prisoner's son came to say that his father was very much afraid to walk to Mr. McCaferty's room, but if Sister would walk with him, he would take the chance. . . . Early Saturday morning we presented ourselves to the Sheriff in his office. . . . "Good morning Sheriff. Needless to ask if you know what is taking place on our two principal streets." "You mean the men ready to lynch the prisoner who so unjustly shot the young Irishman?" "Yes, what are you going to do to prevent the lynching?" "Do! What has any sheriff here ever been able to do to prevent a mob from carrying out its intent?" "Be the first sheriff to make the attempt!" . . .

The prisoner was asked if he would be willing to walk between the sheriff and Sister to the victim's bed and ask his pardon. The sheriff interrupted: "Sister, have you ever seen the working of a mob?" "A few, Mr. Sheriff." "And would you take the chance of having the prisoner snatched from between us and hanged to the nearest cottonwood?" "In my opinion, there is nothing to fear." He straightened himself and looked at me, shrugged his shoulders and said, "if you are not afraid, neither am I." We—the sheriff, my companion and myself—started to walk to the jail. All along the main street and leading to the jail were men at about a distance of a rod apart. These were the men who were to signal Mr. McCaferty's death by three taps of our school bell in order that the mob might proceed to the jail, take the prisoner and hang him. Our group arrived at the jail, where we encountered the greatest discouragement. The prisoner . . . was trembling like an aspen. We saw his courage had failed him. . . . We assured him he was safe in going with us. . . . We hastened to the sick man's door. The crowd made way. Intense fear took possession of me. . . . I said quietly to the prisoner, "Go in." . . . The culprit stood before his victim with bowed head. Fearing the prolonged silence, I addressed the prisoner: "Have you nothing to say?" He looked at the man in the bed and said: "My boy, I did not know what I was doing. Forgive me."

The sick man removed the blanket . . . revealing a sight to unnerve the stoutest heart. The whole leg was mortified and swollen out of proportion, showing where the poisonous tin had lodged and the mortification was creeping toward the heart. "See what you have done!" said the wounded man. "I'm sorry, my boy, forgive me." "I forgive you, as I hope to be forgiven, but the law must take its course." I added, "Yes, the law must take its course—not mob law." Those outside with craned necks distinctly heard the conversation. We returned to the jail where the prisoner was to remain until the Circuit Court convened.

Encounter with Billy the Kid, November 1876: Sister Blandina had previously visited and won the trust of a member of Billy the Kid's gang who had been shot. On a second visit she discovered that Billy the Kid was coming to town to scalp the physicians who had refused to remove the bullet from the wounded man.

Saturday 2 PM came and I went to meet Billy and his gang. When I got to the patient's room, the men were around his bed. . . . The leader, Billy, has steel-blue eyes, peach complexion, is young, one would take him to be seventeen—innocent looking, save for the corners of his eyes, which tell a set purpose, good or bad. . . . "We are glad to see you, Sister, and I want to say, it would give me pleasure to be able to do you any favor." I answered, "Yes, there is a favor you can grant me." He reached his hand toward me with the words: "The favor is granted." I took the hand, saying, "I understand you have come to scalp our Trinidad physicians, which act I ask you to cancel." Billy looked down at the sick man who remarked: "She is game." . . . Billy then said: "I granted the favor before I knew what it was, and it stands. Not only that, Sister, but any time my pals and I can serve you, you will find us ready."

Document 4. Sisters of Providence: Nuns Struggle with Bishops over Their Rights

The constitutions of religious orders set forth the accepted relationships between religious orders and bishops, but many bishops assumed that they could treat women's orders as directly under their jurisdiction in all matters. One such case was the Sisters of Providence at Saint-Mary-of-the-Wood, Indiana, who suffered repeated interference in their internal affairs by Bishop de la Hailandiere of Vincennes. On March 8, 1846, Mother Theodore Guerin and her sisters requested the bishop to respect their rights.[55]

My Lord, It has not been possible to reply sooner to your letter of January 25: even today we can speak of only one item of that letter. We are confronting circumstances too grave to be deterred by personal considerations. You say that we are mistaken in thinking that your refusal to reply to our letter of the month of August is equivalent to a refusal of those things we asked of you. If such is the case, we take the liberty to renew, once more, the same requests.

The first is, as you know, that you give in writing, with your signature and under your episcopal seal, permission to dwell in your diocese according the the Rules and Constitutions which we brought from France, in order that we may have the assurance of being allowed to follow them as perfectly as possible for a body not yet organized. The second is that you give us the deed to the property of Saint Mary's so that we may begin to build. Your Lordship knows that we have never asked aught but these things in order to establish ourselves in Indiana as a Congregation subject to you. Many times you have said, and even written, that you intended to grant us these things, but that we have put obstacles. These obstacles are now all removed—all the Sisters of Providence can now hold property legally; therefore we dare hope that you will not delay to give us this last proof of your good will, which, in putting an end to a state so painful for all, will open to our view a brighter future and afford us the occasion to prove to you by our gratitude and submission how it has pained us to be, in any way, compelled to afflict your heart.

However, faithful to the spirit of candor which we have always followed, we must say that, after all that has occurred since our first request, your silence, or any reply which would not be the Acts we ask for, could not but be regarded by us, this time, as a formal refusal: in which case we would consider ourselves obliged to take a definitive resolution and that with very little delay.

The fate of our Congregation is yet in your hands. We shall pray with even greater fervor than in the past that God may inspire you to act in the manner that will procure Him more glory and unite us more closely with Him. In these sentiments we remain, with the most profound respect, my Lord.

Of Your Lordship, the very Humble and obedient servants,

Sister St. Vincent	*Sister Mary Joseph*
Sister St. Francis Xavier	*Sister Mary Cecilia*
Sister Mary Liguori	*Sister St. Theodore*

Document 5. Sisters of Mercy: Nurses in Epidemics

In the following account a Sister of Mercy describes their work during the yellow fever epidemics that ravaged Charleston, South Carolina, in the 1850s.[56]

The first yellow fever I remember was the terrible epidemic of 1852. . . . In 1854, 1856 and, I think, 1858, the city received visits from the same dread disease. During these years the Sisters had no hospital, but went about from street to street, through lanes and alleys, wherever the sick might be found, carrying baskets filled with the necessities of life and medicine, as these were needed. They worked heroically, all through the periods of disease, and all classes of citizens recognized the debt of gratitude due to these noble women. Some, such as Sister Mary Joseph and Sister Mary Peter, fresh from Ireland and full of vigor in body and soul, were as little alive to human respect as they were to danger, and I remember on one occasion during the wet season, it was quite laughable to see them wade through the mire, with large boots, their habits and cloaks tied up, and lugging along their baskets, which seemed twice as large as themselves, that they might bring relief to the sick in the poor quarter of town. When the troubles were over, our Sisters quickly returned to their schoolrooms and seemed to have forgotten what no one who had seen them could ever forget, that they had but a short time before been active amid the dark scenes of death from yellow fever haunting the entire community. . . . In later years when the epidemic broke out, the Sisters were supplied with vehicles in order that they might carry out their mission to the sick with greater facility and dispatch. At times no one was seen in the streets but the doctors, the priests and the Sisters on their rounds, and no sound heard but the rumble of the carts carrying off the dead.

CATHOLIC LAYWOMEN
AND SOCIAL REFORM, 1850–1950

Document 6. Mother Jones:
Organizing the Women and the Miners

Mary Harris Jones was the best-known Irish woman labor organizer. Her family migrated from Ireland when she was a child. Jones taught in a convent school in Michigan and then ran a sewing shop in Chicago. She married a union organizer, but her husband and four children died in the yellow fever epidemic in 1867. Jones became involved with the Knights of Labor and later the American Federation of Labor and was employed as an organizer by the United Mine Workers. She identified herself as a socialist and was hostile to priests because of their antilabor attitudes. She described her work as an organizer in her autobiography.[57]

In Hazelton, Pennsylvania, a convention was called to discuss the anthracite strike. I was there when they issued the strike call. One hundred and fifty thousand men responded. . . . Not far from Shamokin, in a little mountain town, the priest was holding a meeting when I went in. He was speaking in the church. I spoke in an open field. The priest told the men to go back and obey the masters and their reward would be in Heaven. He denounced the strikers as children of darkness. The miners left the church in a body and marched to my meeting.

"Boys," I said, "this strike is called in order that you and your wives and your little ones may get a little bit of Heaven before you die." We organized the entire camp. The fight went on. In Coaldale, in the Hazelton district, the miners were not permitted to assemble in any hall. It was necessary to win the strike in that district that the Coaldale miners be organized.

I went to a nearby mining town that was thoroughly organized and asked the women if they would help me get the Coaldale men out. This was in McAdoo. I told them to leave their men at home to take care of the family. I asked them to put on their kitchen clothes and bring mops and brooms with them and a couple of tin pans. We marched over the mountains fifteen miles, beating on the tin pans as if they were cymbals.

At three o'clock in the morning we met the Crack Thirteen of the militia, patroling the roads to Coaldale. The colonel of the regiment said "Halt! Move back!"

I said, "Colonel, the working men of America will not halt nor will they ever go back. The working man is going forward!" "I'll charge bayonets," he said. "On whom!" "On your people." "We are not enemies," said I. "We are just a band of working women whose brothers and husbands are in a battle for bread. We want our brothers in Coaldale to join us in our fight. We are here on the mountain road for our children's sake, for the nation's sake. We are not going to hurt anyone and surely you would not want to hurt us."

They kept us there until daybreak and when they saw the army of women in kitchen aprons, with dishpans and mops, they laughed and let us pass. An army of strong mining women makes a wonderfully spectacular sight. Well, when the miners in the Coaldale camp started to go to work they were met by the McAdoo women who were beating their pans and shouting, "Join the union! Join the union!"

They joined, every last man of them, and we got so enthusiastic that we organized the street car men who promised to haul no scabs for the coal companies. As there were no other groups to organize we marched over the mountains home, beating on our pans and singing patriotic songs. . . . When I got back to Hazelton, Mitchell[58] looked at me with surprise. I was worn out. Coaldale had been a strenuous night and morning and its thirty mile tramp. I assured Mitchell that no one had been hurt and no property injured. The military had acted like human beings. . . . I told him how scared the sheriff had been. He had been talking to me without knowing who I was. "Oh Lord," he said, "that Mother Jones is sure a dangerous woman."

Document 7. Katherine Conway:
A Leading Woman Editor Rejects Women's Suffrage

Katherine Conway was a successful novelist and journalist. She was assistant editor for the Buffalo *Catholic Union and Times* and then editor for three Catholic newspapers, the *Catholic Union,* the *Republic,* and the Boston *Pilot.* She also taught at St. Mary's College in Indiana. A single professional woman all her life, Conway rejected feminism and women's suffrage and made herself the spokesperson for the traditional ideal of the retiring wife and mother, defending these views in a panel on "The Woman Question Among Catholics" in the August 1893 issue of the *Catholic World*.[59]

To the writer it seems settled beyond question that woman, as woman, can have no vocation to public life. . . . Woman, being after man and from man, does not represent humanity in the full and complete sense that a man does. It cannot be necessary, nor even useful, that she should try to do what she cannot do. . . . Woman, as woman, has been created for a peculiar and definite purpose; and the equipment for it, not to speak of the accomplishment of it, debars her, broadly speaking, from public life. . . . The vocation of the overwhelming majority of women is to wifehood and motherhood; and their bodily and mental sensitiveness and timidity, and the fixed adversion, or at least indifference, of most of them to public work are safeguards raised by God's own hand about the sanctuary of life. We Catholics recognize for women another and higher vocation, to which but a small number are called. But the instinct against publicity, so strong in the woman of the home, is intensified in the woman of the convent. Natural love moves the normal woman to self-sacrifice, almost of self-effacement. She is proud to surrender her name, to merge her identity in that of her husband. Supernatural love acts on the lines of nature, and the nun gladly sinks her individuality in her order, her membership in which is the sign of her special and exclusive union with the divine. The territory between the home and the convent is small, and the Catholic women within it are ordinarily there in fulfillment of some very evident filial or sisterly duty—another manifestation indeed of the sacrificial spirit of normal Christian womanhood. . . .

While believing that woman, as woman, has no public sphere, she believes also that woman as an intelligence, a rational creature, responsible for her own deeds and free to choose her own state of life, may be or do what she can; and that some women by virtue, not of their womanhood, but of their strong individualities, marked ability and the demands of unusual environment, may have a special call to some public duty. . . . But these things having been at all times granted by the Catholic Church. . . . The state, not the church, has ruled on the question of women in government and politics. . . .

The indifference of Catholic women of every grade of intelligence and education to woman suffrage, and the disinclination of most of them to identify themselves with the public work of organized women in its recent manifestations of "Women's Congresses," "Woman's Days," etc, furnish a strong argument against women in public life. For the Catholic woman is the normal woman. . . . In all this "woman question" the partisans of alleged progress seem to forget one foundational fact: that, as between men and women, it is not so much a question of better or worse, as a question of different.

Document 8. Mrs. Francis E. Slattery: Catholic Women Use the Vote to Defend the Family

Mrs. Francis E. Slattery, president of the Boston League of Catholic Women from 1919 to 1932, represented the new sense of public responsibility to use the women's vote to counteract what were seen as the threats to the traditional family and society. In her talk, delivered as a radio address during the Christmas season, 1929, Catholic ideals, womanhood, and Americanism merge.[60]

Today, after the Church, the greatest single influence for the good of the people, for the protection of their morals and the preservation of their spiritual idea is woman. . . . Under the authority of her husband, she rules the Christian home, she influences the standards of the community, she leaves her impress upon the works of the State. In the arts, in sciences, in politics, in religion, in industry and trade and community movements, her influence cannot be discounted today. Yes, her influence is great, but is it properly effective? Is it fully used? Are we women alive to our responsibility and opportunities? In other words are we doing our full duty to our God and our country? . . .

To be specific, are we content with conditions on the stage and screen? Are we indifferent to the violent attacks on the family and the home: divorce, trial and companionate marriage, birth control and the aims of the Feminist movement? Are we satisfied with our public educational system that forgets God in its scheme? Have we no concern with a Federal movement that menaces the inherent rights of parents and the welfare of their children? . . . Here, then, is our duty and our opportunity. Men, God bless them, are our natural guides and protectors in most things, but in matters of morals women should be leaders, not merely followers. It is our particular province to stress the moral virtues, to uphold the moral standards, to develop the underlying principles, to spread a knowledge of them in the public mind, and to insist upon their application to the great political and ethical issues of the present day. . . . The heart of the nation is the home, where it beats happily in peace and contentment. . . . Our home is our castle, made legally impregnable to intruders, . . . [yet] in danger from insidious and powerful enemies. . . . Their aim is to destroy the family and family life. Under their attack the castle weakens and Bolshevism enters.

Are you familiar with the purpose of the so-called Equal Rights Bill which, under the guise of emancipating women, attempts to make her the competitor rather than the companion of man? This proposal, if enacted into law, would wipe off the statute books all those humanitarian safeguards that are now thrown around woman for her physical, mental and social welfare. It would even separate the identity of husband and wife and, by retention of her unmarried name, encourage the use of separate domiciles: measures calculated to deprive children of a protecting home influence and sending the family to the four winds. But an even greater problem confronts the home. If these so-called leaders of thought have their way, the problem of children and their upbringing will eventually cease to be a problem at all, because there will be no children. Those who preach birth control can hardly appreciate what they are doing.

We Catholic women know that the practice they advocate is contrary to the laws of God and nature, and we stand firm and determined against its practice and its sanction in the law. We know also that it is un-American, because no less distinguished an authority than the late President Roosevelt called it race suicide. . . . Finally, the attack is on marriage itself, the very basis of the Christian family and the American home. Divorce is rampant. Its numbers are appalling. . . . Let us safeguard marriage and save civilization itself.

For examples of this maneuvering I ask you to re-call the so-called Child Labor Amendment, the Maternity Act and the Federal Education Bill. Women of all classes and creeds in the Commonwealth of Massachusetts, scenting the perils of the Child Labor Amendment, organized in opposition . . . and succeeded in defeating this Amendment by the overwhelming vote of three to one. . . . The same Patriotic forces in this State and throughout the land have fought the Maternity Act and the Federal Education Bill with conspicuous success. . . . There must be no North, no South, no East, no West, no sectionalism, no divisions, but a united America working together for one purpose, the preservation of American ideal and the common good of all. . . .

These, my dear friends, are some of the things that have engaged the attention of the League of Catholic Women of Boston. Under the impulse of our great Churchman and distinguished citizen, Cardinal O'Connell, we have cooperated with all who have sought to maintain our national ideals. . . . Let us fashion ourselves to the model of the Holy Family. Let us bow our head in deepest reverence to the Cross of Christ and rise our arm in salute to the flag of flags—the Stars and Stripes of America.

Document 9. Dorothy Day:
The Catholic Worker, Still Pacifist in World War II

The Catholic Worker, founded by Dorothy Day and Peter Maurin in 1933, deeply influenced Catholic social activists. Its houses of hospitality, where the transient poor of American urban slums were welcomed, fed, housed, and clothed, spread rapidly. Day also laid the foundations for a Catholic pacifism. In editorials in The Catholic Worker in January and February of 1942 Day defended this unpopular pacifist stance during the Second World War.[61]

Dear Fellow Workers in Christ,

Lord God, merciful God, our Father, shall we keep silent, or shall we speak? . . . We are at war, a declared war, with Japan, Germany and Italy. But still we can repeat Christ's words, each day, holding them close to our hearts, each month printing them in our paper. . . . We are still pacifists. Our manifesto is the Sermon on the Mount, which means that we will try to be peacemakers. Speaking for many of our conscientious objectors, we will not participate in armed warfare or in making munitions, or in buying government bonds to prosecute the war, or in urging others to these efforts. . . . Our Works of Mercy may take us into the midst of war. As editor of The Catholic Worker, I would urge our friends and associates to care for the sick and the wounded, to the growing of food for the hungry, to the continuance of all our Works of Mercy in our houses and on our farms. . . . Because of our refusal to assist in the prosecution of war and our insistence that our collaboration be one for peace, we may find ourselves in difficulties. But we trust in the generosity and understanding of our government and our friends, to permit us to continue to use our paper to "preach Christ crucified."

In reply to critics, Day's tone became more militant in her February editorial.

"But we are at war," people say. "This is no time to talk of peace. It is demoralizing to the armed forces to protest, not to cheer them on in their fight for Christianity, for democracy, for civilization. . . ." One reader writes to protest our "frail" voices "blatantly" crying out against war. . . . Another Catholic newspaper says it sympathizes with our sentimentality. This is a charge always leveled against pacifists. We are supposed to be afraid of the sufferings, of the hardships of war.

But let them who talk of softness, of sentimentality, come to live with us in cold, unheated houses in the slums. Let them live with the criminal, the unbalanced, the drunken, the degraded, the perverted. . . . Let them live with rats, with vermin, bedbugs, roaches, lice. . . . Let their flesh be mortified by cold, by dirt, by vermin; let their eyes be mortified by the sight of bodily excretions, diseased limbs, eyes, noses and mouths. Let their noses be mortified by the smells of sewage, decay and rotten flesh. Yes, and the smell of the sweat, blood and tears spoken of so blithely by Mr. Churchill. . . . Then when they have lived with these comrades, with these sights and sounds, let our critics talk of sentimentality. . . . Our Catholic Worker groups are perhaps too hardened to the sufferings of the class war, living as they do in refugee camps, the refugees being, as they are, the victims of the class war we live in always. We have lived in the midst of this war now these many years. It is not a war recognized by the majority of our comfortable people. . . . They even pretend it is not there. Many friends have counseled us to treat this world war in the same way. "Don't write about it. . . . Don't jeopardize the great work you are doing among the poor, among the workers. Just write about the constructive things like Houses of Hospitality and Farming Communes." . . . But we cannot keep silence. We have not kept silence in the face of the monstrous injustice of the class war, or the race war that goes on side by side with this world war (which the Communists used to call the imperialist war). . . .

Perhaps we are called sentimental because we speak of love. We say we love our President, our country. We say that we love our enemies too. . . . Love is not starving whole populations. Love is not the bombardment of open cities. Love is not killing, it is the laying down of one's life for one's friends. . . . We must all admit our guilt, our participation in the social order which had resulted in this monstrous crime of war. . . . That should be our cry. . . . O God, take away my heart of stone and give me a heart of flesh.

THE BIRTH OF CATHOLIC FEMINISM, 1950–1993

Document 10. The Grail: From Rural Utopianism to Feminism

The Grail, founded in the Netherlands in 1921, came to the United States in 1940. The Grail promoted women as transformers of church and society but initially saw women as representing the "feminine" qualities needed to redeem harsh "masculinity." In the 1940s to 1960s it promoted Catholic back-to-the-land movements and liturgical renewal. It became involved in issues of urban justice and feminism in the 1960s and '70s. In the 1980s it renewed its concern for the land through study programs and demonstration projects on ecological awareness and sustainable agriculture. Janet Kalven's 1944 address to the National Catholic Rural Life Convention represents the early Grail mystique of womanhood and rural living.[62]

. . . No healthy, balanced, sane pattern of rural living is possible without the wholehearted interest and cooperation of the woman. Agriculture needs the influence and the unique contribution of woman to achieve a human and satisfying way of life on the land. . . . Every woman is made to be a mother, to find her center outside herself in other human beings who are dependent on her loving care. Her motherhood need not be realized physically, but it must be realized spiritually if she is to achieve her fulfillment and her true happiness. Woman is most truly herself when she is utterly forgetful of self, absorbed in the service of those around her, alert to their needs and spending herself without stint for them. She is made to be the heart of the home, the center of light and warmth, and physical and spiritual wellbeing in the family. . . . Woman's nature demands close contact with the beauties of creation and with growing plants and animals for her fullest physical and spiritual development. She needs the simple, rhythmic life on the land, with its fresh foods and outdoor work, to build abundant health and vitality. . . . Women have always been great agriculturalists, mothers of the earth. The mystery of the seed is very close to her, for she bears the seed of new life in her womb and nurtures it with her blood. A rich experience of the cycle of birth and death in plants and animals is in harmony with the deepest tendencies of her nature and develops her womanly talents. . . . The new pattern of life on the land must meet the fundamental requirements of woman's nature if it is to win her enthusiastic interest and active support. . . . First of all, the woman needs the small, diversified family farm. . . . Because it is family centered, organized first of all to supply what the family requires for a full life, the homestead is deeply satisfying to the mother of the family. . . . She enjoys the homestead with its few cows to furnish butter, milk and cheese for her family; its few pigs for meat, its few sheep for lambs and wool; its small flock of chickens for really fresh eggs; a few bee hives for honey. . . . She wants to plant an orchard, a vineyard, a berry patch, an herb and flower garden, as well as a plot of vegetables.

Another fundamental requirement of woman's nature, and one which the rural pattern in the country has not met, is the need for strong community life. . . . The fact that women connect farming with loneliness constitutes one of the formidable barriers to the rural movement, a barrier which can only be broken down by the development of flourishing, closely knit, rural communities. It is the task for the rural apostolate to demonstrate the fulness of Catholic community life on the land by establishing homestead communities which will exemplify concretely the doctrine of the Mystical Body of Christ. Under the influence of a stable and well-integrated community, inspired by the Catholic vision of life, women will blossom forth and be stimulated to contribute the best of their qualities and talents to the creation of a new social order.

Document 11. Patty Crowley:
The Christian Family Movement and Birth Control

The Christian Family Movement arose in 1949 among Chicago couples seeking meaningful Christian family life in society. Led for twenty years by Pat and Patty Crowley, it grew into a major international movement. In 1964 the Crowleys were invited to be members of the Papal Birth Control Commission to reconsider the Catholic teachings on contraception. The Crowleys surveyed CFM members and brought to the commission a testimony of these couples' dissatisfaction with the rhythm method. In her address to the commission from "A Woman's Viewpoint," Patty Crowley documents their findings.[63]

Since our appointment to this Commission we have asked people how they feel about these momentous questions. We have asked them informally, in casual conversation, where so much can be said in so few words, and we have asked them in three formal scientific surveys. So we think that we can speak with some authority on how the married people we know and work with feel. Let me summarize a few of our conclusions.

Is there a bad psychological effect in the use of rhythm? Almost without exception, the responses were that, yes, there is. *Does rhythm serve any useful purpose at all?* A few say it may be useful for developing discipline. Nobody says that it fosters married love. *Does it contribute to married unity?* No. That is the inescapable conclusion of the reports we have received. In marriage a husband and wife pledge themselves to become one in mind, heart and affection. . . . Some wonder whether God would have us cultivate unity by using what seems to them an unnatural system. . . . These reports seem to indicate that instead of unity and love, rhythm tends to substitute tension, dissatisfaction, frustration and disunity. *Is rhythm unnatural?* Yes—that's the conclusion of these reports. Over and over, directly and indirectly, men and women—and perhaps especially women, voice the conviction that the physical and psychological implications of rhythm are not adequately understood by the male church. Over and over again, respondents point out that nature prepares a woman at the time of ovulation to have the greatest urge to mate with her husband. Similarly at that time her husband wants to respond to his wife. She craves his love. Yet month after month she must say no to her husband because it is the wrong date on the calendar or the thermometer isn't reading right. No amount of theory by men can convince women that this way of making and expressing love is natural.

Notice how the reactions in our report contradict what in the past has been the stereotyped, conventional way of looking at the Catholic husband and wife and their large family. These mothers and fathers, surveying their children, do not sit back with pride and satisfaction. Instead they reflect a hardly muted bitterness at a condition in their lives that has forced them to stay apart from each other when their natures cry out for each other.

We think it is time for a change. We think it is time that this Commission recommend that the sacredness of conjugal love not be isolated by thermometers and calendars. . . . Couples want children and will have them generously and love and cherish them. We do not need the impetus of legislation to procreate—it is the very instinct of life, love and sexuality. It is in fact largely our very love for children as parents and our desire for their full development as committed Christians that leads us to realize that numbers alone and the large size of a family is by no means a Christian ideal unless parents can truly be concerned about and capable of nurturing a high *quality* of Christian life.

Document 12. Sister Madeleva Wolff: The Education of Sister Lucy

The Sister Formation Movement arose in 1954 out of discussions in the National Catholic Educational Association of the inadequate educational preparation of American nuns teaching in parochial schools. In her 1949 address before the NCEA, Sister Madeleva Wolff, president of St. Mary's College in South Bend, Indiana, and foremost educator of Catholic women, dramatized the educational plight of Catholic teaching sisters.[64]

For overlong, many of us had struggled with our academic consciences and put the seal of discretion on our lips over the flagrant *status quo* in Catholic education. Even recent indictments of the mediocrity of the Catholic mind scarcely advert to the untrained or inadequately trained sisters who have been teaching generations of parish school-children. . . . With inadequate plants and only partially trained teachers for three hundred years, we have been taking care of our young people. The valor of the achievement is not always patent to us. . . . Needs imperative for schools and staff have precipitated young sisters scarcely out of the novitiate into parish schools.

For years a stubborn group of the college section of the National Catholic Educational Association had dreamed of, had asked for a section in the Association for teachers' preparation. Reasons for refusal now seem absurd. Then they were effective, final and fatal. At the meeting of the Association in the spring of 1948, I asked for the last time that such a section be authorized and put to work. . . . We projected a program in which the training procedures then in operation in six teaching orders were submitted. In addition a possible schedule was formulated by which a young sister beginning her education in a postulancy of one year, continuing through two or three years after her canonical novitiate, could earn her teacher's credential and degree. The plan was set up for a hypothetical Sister Lucy. . . .

Our new section on Teachers' Education was assigned the smallest committee room, the last hour of the last day of the [1949 NCEA] convention. The room assigned proved absolutely too small. We moved in and out of the cafeteria for the same reason. We settled in the gymnasium with people sitting on the steps and in the aisles. The Education of Sister Lucy proved the big event of the week. The tremendous spontaneous response to the cause established its importance and its need. . . . Those present will never forget the hour. . . . Within two months a neat brochure, "The Education of Sister Lucy," was off the press at South Bend.

. . . Presently the superior general of the Sisters of the Immaculate Heart at Monroe, Michigan, asked me to come to the mother house to talk over with her council some of the needs, the feasibilities and the professional "musts" of this tentative program. Later Sister Patrick and her companion came to Saint Mary's to continue planning. Surveying the problems of organization, ways and means, Sister Patrick said, "Sister Emil is just the person to do this." Sister Patrick was right. When the

Institute for Religious held its first great historic meeting at the University of Notre Dame in 1952 I was asked to present the case of completed professional training for religious teachers before they were assigned to their life apostolate of teaching. During that same session Sister Patrick made her memorable plea, "Share the sisters." The facts of sister-shortage, sisters' education, sisters' salaries were emerging. We were coming at this late hour to the use of reason. Sister Lucy has been admitted to college. I leave her education to those qualified and authorized to educate her, the mothers general, the mothers provincial in the organized Sister-Formation Program.

•

Document 13. Leadership Conference
of Women Religious:
Educating Nuns for Feminist Consciousness

The LCWR, the body representing American nuns, committed itself in the 1970s to educating women religious on their relation to feminism. A study packet, *Focus on Women,* was prepared for the 1975 LCWR assembly. The final booklet summarized the problem.[65]

Human history has been one constant and cumulative oppression of women on the basis of sex. The existence of such oppression has been gradually construed as the fact of female inferiority and has emerged as one of the major tenets of social mythology throughout the world, ironically related as it is to the possible previous myth of female power. Religion (as an effect rather than as an original cause of such oppression) has been a major force in its continuance, perpetuation and "canon"ization. The mainstream of tradition within the Catholic Church—in significant opposition to the central revelation of human personhood, sexuality and redemptive fulfillment embodied in Christ's life and teaching—is one of the most oppressive of all religious superstructures. There is a growing awareness and bonding among women today who refuse to subject themselves and their sisters to such institutionalized injustice.

Document 14. Las Hermanas:
Hispanic Nuns Confront Racism and Sexism

Las Hermanas, the major organization of Hispanic sisters in the United States, arose in 1970 to challenge ethnic prejudice in the Irish-dominated U.S. Catholic Church. It also became increasingly critical of sexism in the church and in Hispanic culture.[66]

[An] element in the historical context for the birth of LAS HER-MANAS was the situation of Hispanic women religious in the U.S. Church. Hispanic nuns in the United States were roughly divided into two distinct ways of life: those employed as domestic servants who were mostly from Mexico, and the small number of Hispanic women who entered religious life in U.S.-based communities. Almost all of the latter entered religious community at the price of leaving their people and their cultural identity behind them at the convent door. Sister Teresita Basso described the "strife" of the Mexican American or Chicana religious at that time as threefold, i.e., society's discrimination toward women, paternalism toward women in the Church and the Mexican American culture's restrictive view of women. The Chicana sister who sought to find her identity amidst this strife often found her religious community to be more harmful than helpful, pushing her to accept a middle class orientation which had no reference to the religious and cultural values of her ethnic background. Basso called for a move to regain these cultural roots so that Chicana religious could better serve their own people. The loss of identity which so often accompanied entrance into U.S. communities, the assignment of sisters from Mexico to mere housekeeping tasks and the call for efforts to reverse these trends were further impetus for the creation of LAS HERMANAS.

Another instance of HERMANAS challenging Church officials occurred in March of 1985 when Beatriz Diaz-Taveras, Maria Teresa Garza, Ada Maria Isasi-Diaz and Carmen Villegas testified before a consultation committee for the U.S. bishops' pastoral letter on women. After presenting their reflections on the oppression of Hispanic women in the Church, in society and in family life, the HERMANAS' representatives read Matthew 7:9–12, a text which includes the line, "Would one of you hand your child a stone when they ask for a loaf?"

They then handed a stone to each of the six bishops at the meeting and said, "we have asked for bread and you have given us stone. Put these stones on your altars when you celebrate Eucharist and remember us Hispanic women, struggling for our liberation and the liberation of our people." . . .

Present organizational leaders see LAS HERMANAS as a forum for the articulation of Hispanic women's experience, spirituality and liberationist methodology. In these efforts HERMANAS are rooting themselves in the experience of their foremothers. . . . In both its early concern for Hispanics in general and its later more focused concern for Hispanic women, the purpose of LAS HERMANAS has remained multifaceted. The organization has functioned as an educational group, a support group, a cultural awareness group, a leadership training institute, a grassroots organizing group and the lobbying or advocacy groups. . . . For LAS HERMANAS to remain a vital force it must be immersed in the cause of liberating Hispanic women as Catholics and as members of U.S. society.

Document 15. Rosalie Muschal-Reinhardt: Feminist Theology Claiming Ordained Ministry

In the 1960s and '70s more Protestant churches were allowing the ordination of women. In 1975 Catholic women organized a major conference in Detroit to examine the theological bases for changing the church teaching on women's ordination. Twelve hundred women, both religious and lay, attended this conference, and the Women's Ordination Conference was created to promote the issue in the church. One of the organizers of the conference, Rosalie Muschal-Reinhardt, read a statement written by a workgroup, defining women's call to priesthood.[67]

We have been called to the priesthood, and we want to be ordained, not because we want to exercise power, but because we are motivated by love and concern for our Church. Indeed, we are already functioning as ministers, but under limitations and handicaps, owing to the lack of official recognition and authorization for our ministry, especially in the sacramental area.

A major focus of the love and concern that move us is our firm conviction that we as women are indispensable to the full humanness and wholeness of the priesthood. Unquestionably, new models of priesthood are needed. We believe that women in the priesthood will inevitably produce these sorely needed new models. We call on the people of God to engage in dialogue on the nature of ministry and priesthood. . . . We who feel called to ordination see the Eucharist as the very center of our life and our ministry. We desire to unite who we are and what we do as priests with the life-giving dynamic of the Eucharist. Leaven; in every age people are called to be leaven, which gives rise to new dimensions in humanness, love and service to the Church and the world. We are leaven when in our deep consciousness we recognize a call to ordained ministry and work toward that day when that call will be tested. We are leaven when we encourage one another to explore every avenue, to knock on the door of every human heart. We are leaven when we proclaim, in faith, that the Lord has done wonderful things in our lives and when we walk with confidence toward a sacramental ministry in the Church that is home for us.

Document 16. Catholics Speak Out: The Failure of the Bishops' Pastoral on Women

From 1982 to 1992, the American Catholic bishops worked on a pastoral letter on women's issues in the church and society. Some bishops wanted to affirm women's new roles in society and in (lay) ministry but also had to uphold the bans on birth control and the ordination of women. The Vatican feared that the pastoral left too much room for change on these issues and insisted on more explicit reassertions of traditional teachings. As the pastoral became more unacceptable to more liberal Catholics, the Catholic action group Catholics Speak Out circulated an open letter to the bishops to reject the pastoral. On November 17, 1992, the pastoral failed to get the required two-thirds vote and was tabled by the bishops.[68]

Dear Brothers who serve as bishops,
Your hour of decision has come. You will soon vote on *One in Christ Jesus,* the fourth draft of your Pastoral on Women's Concerns.

Your vote will witness to the world whether you have the courage to stand with women who have been oppressed for centuries by the structures of our church or whether you stand with those who want to reenforce the very patriarchy and sexism which have caused so much pain, division and even loss of faith.

We speak to you strongly, plainly and publicly because the 4th draft of this Pastoral is so seriously flawed and such a departure from the message and example of Jesus that its approval and publication would be a real source of scandal for us as believing Catholics. Its internal contradictions will open you to ridicule and undermine your credibility to speak on other issues of justice. It will increase the pain of Catholic women and caring Catholic men who believe sincerely that our church is called to embrace a New Spirit which gives prophetic witness to equality and the rights of women, practicing and advocating them in the life of our faith community and civil society. *For the sake of women, for the sake of the gospel, for the future of our church—we urge you in the strongest possible terms to vote "NO.".* . . . When you bishops began to form a broad consultative process to prepare for the Pastoral, we hoped that the document might reflect the voices of women. But successive drafts of this Pastoral have muffled and muted the voices of women and moved to embrace the very sexism and patriarchy which they purported to condemn.

The 4th draft is a stark embodiment of the sin of sexism itself. It hides behind the rhetorical mask of equality as it denies women equal access to the deaconate, priesthood and implicitly the episcopacy. Its theology of priesthood attempts to sanctify male domination and shut women out from church decisions which intimately affect their lives. It offers not even the possibility of dialogue on complex and sensitive issues of reproduction such as birth control and abortion which cause so many women and men great pain. It is deeply insensitive to the special suffering and discrimination lesbian women face. . . . The Pastoral is blind to the ways the church has supported sexism in civil society. . . .

We challenge you bishops to do more than merely reject this Pastoral. It is no secret that many of you disagree with key Vatican positions in the Pastoral and want our church to embrace equality and dialogue. It is time for you to speak your consciences publicly. . . . It is time for you to move from talk to action. Implement equality. Liberate a "New Spirit" in our Church.

Document 17. Women–Church:
Creating Feminist Communities

As the Vatican reiterated its teachings against women's ordination, many U.S. Catholic feminists felt that the demand for institutional ministry should be secondary to a deep renewal of church life as community. They began to develop feminist groups to explore spirituality and social change. Mary Hunt, leading Catholic feminist theologian, defines the vision of women–church in a handbook designed to develop such groups.[69]

My definition of women–church is a global, ecumenical movement made up of local feminist base communities of justice-seeking friends who engage in sacrament and solidarity. . . . While the expression of women–church differs according to cultures, there are certain common elements. There are local groups in which one participates; one cannot be women–church simply in one's imagination. . . . These groups are composed of individuals who form a movement. Women–church is a relational reality; the term describes my being as a person of faith who as a woman in a patriarchal culture must create the context of my spirituality. It is not that I am women–church, but that we together are trying to be women–church. Women–church groups are feminist. . . . Women–church groups seek to change social structures and personal attitudes to stop oppression. . . . Women–church is made up of local base communities. . . . These are groups in which the deep unity of reflection and action, prayer and politics, or what I call sacrament and solidarity, is taken seriously. . . . From a feminist perspective, a sacrament is an act of lifting to public expression the every-day life of people because such life is holy. Prayer is sustained attention which does not make the divine present, but simply recognizes it as so. . . .

We do not demand unilateral allegiance to women–church. Nor do we make it a practice of criticizing other churches. We are church. Our primary attention is on being church. . . . Women–church is not schismatic. It is the spiral expression of the deepest aspects of the Christian tradition taken to new depths by women's faithfulness. Further it is a springboard for investigating, practicing and evaluating other traditions so that what results is a new synthesis of religious experience. . . .

What is the theology of women-church? We do not seek a creed or a set of dogmas. . . . Rather with our feminist brothers and children we seek to live out a theology of "mutual relation," . . . a praxis of radical love and commitment to justice-seeking. Of course we need to articulate beliefs and a framework for action, but that will take place in local groups according to local needs as part of a larger national and international conversation. The theology per se comes later, after we have lived a little more in this new reality called women-church. It comes only when many can speak, when more can sing, when all can dance. It must be done by theologians and non-theologians alike; it is a different process of theologizing, as well as the difference in theological content, which heralds a new religious moment.

Moving toward that day as women-church is the task ahead. As Women-church we are well accompanied by one another and by the Spirit of Sophia in our local groups and around the world. This accompaniment is the source of our power.

CHAPTER TWO

The Organization
of Protestant Laywomen
in Institutional Churches

Rosemary Skinner Keller

Documents

THE SEVENTEENTH AND EIGHTEENTH CENTURIES

THE NINETEENTH CENTURY

THE TWENTIETH CENTURY

WOMEN and men "have still a long stretch of unexplored country to be traversed before the perfect democracy of Jesus is reached," wrote Helen Barrett Montgomery in 1910 in her book, *Western Women in Eastern Lands*.[1] As president of the interdenominational National Federation of Women's Boards of Foreign Missions and the Woman's American Baptist Foreign Missionary Society, she celebrated the accomplishments of women's missionary work in the preceding fifty years and sharply raised challenges that remain in the late twentieth century (document 14).

Montgomery provides a notable theme in the evolution of women's organizations in Protestant churches from the colonial period through the late twentieth century. She hoped that the day would come "in the growth of the kingdom" when women and men could work together in organizations side by side. But she questioned whether, in her day, men had been "emancipated from the caste of sex so that they can work easily with women, unless they be head and women clearly subordinate."[2]

In this chapter I trace the rise of women's organizations within Protestant churches from their origins in colonial times until the late twentieth century. I note the challenges related to sexism that persist in the churches as well as the gains that have been made over almost four centuries.

THE SEVENTEENTH AND EIGHTEENTH CENTURIES: COLONIAL AND REVOLUTIONARY AMERICAN SOCIETY

Women began to organize within mainstream Protestant churches along the entire Atlantic seaboard from the settlement of the first colonies in North America. These groups took several forms, including prayer, Bible study, and charitable giving to persons of need within the church and community.

The trial and excommunication of Anne Hutchinson from the Massachusetts Bay Colony in 1637 shows that women's groups were an accepted form of gathering under auspices of Puritan churches from the founding of the colony in 1630. The official complaint against her was that she shared her direct revelation from God not only with the group of women, who had been meeting regularly, but also with a "promiscuous assembly" of both men and women (document 1 and its source).

Most women probably accepted without question their subordination in the highly structured hierarchical society. Yet some of the first organizations of women became avowed threats to the Puritan order. Anne Hutchinson insisted that salvation was not earned by good works but was given through the covenant of grace. Redemption was a spiritual gift given individually and personally to whomever God chose to give it, regardless of that person's status in the social order. She further testified at her trial for heresy that she had received a direct revelation from God that the clergy of Massachusetts Bay were not able ministers.[3]

In New Haven, Connecticut, a network of female supporters also developed around Anne Eaton, the daughter of an English bishop and the unhappy wife of Governor Theophilus Eaton (document 2). Mrs. Eaton had denounced infant baptism and left church services before the Lord's Supper and baptism were administered, since she had not been baptized. She also had failed to seek help from her husband, her pastor (John Davenport), or the members of the church. She was tried and excommunicated in 1644.[4]

The "party" that formed around Mrs. Eaton included a Mrs. Brewster, a Mrs. Moore, and a Mrs. Leach. These three women were brought before the court at New Haven in June 1646. Mrs. Brewster was charged with claiming that Pastor Davenport identified church membership with salvation in Christ. It was further alleged that Mrs. Brewster declared herself "sermon sick" of his preaching and that she had her son "make waste paper" of the notes from Davenport's sermon after Sunday church service.[5]

Mrs. Moore, too, was charged with high heresy for declaring that "pastors and teachers are but inventions of men" and that no one in the congregation could be turned to the Lord "until the veil before the eyes of the minister and the people of this place be taken away." Mrs. Moore denied the allegation. However, her daughter, Mrs. Leach, readily accepted the charge against her; Mrs. Moore, her daughter said, had formerly "had a mind to join the church, but now declined it, because she found so many untruths among them."[6]

The more isolated existence of many Southern women on plantations, unlike the communal lives of women in New England townships, made it difficult for Southern women to congregate or to envision mutual support. Anglican women of the Church of England in Virginia and Maryland viewed their role in society as one of helping to maintain their precarious civilization. Advice literature, which combined secular rationalism and sacred piety, admonished women not to stray from the domestic scene. Southern women gathered in small clusters of female relatives and slaves and encouraged the development in younger women of private devotions, religious exercises, and prayer.[7]

Within these various denominations, only Quaker women had a voice in the affairs of the meeting house or could preach the word of God. The institution of the Women's Meetings by Margaret Fell, known as the "mother" of the Society of Friends, was a controversial innovation in early Quakerism. Women's Meetings gave Quaker women an official role in the administration and government of the society. The groups both supervised internal morality and managed extensive works of charity. They gathered and administered funds for the relief of the imprisoned and the poor as well as for the sick, widows, orphans, and the aged. The societies organized projects such as spinning groups for unemployed women, and they placed orphans in apprenticeships. They supervised marriages and the payment of tithes within the society. Correspondence among Women's Meetings encouraged the development of such meetings throughout the Friends' societies in the American colonies (document 3).[8]

In both the Puritan and the Wesleyan movements, evangelicalism became women's primary means of expanding their religious sphere. The evangelical spirit loosed by the First Great Awakening of the mideighteenth century began with a series of local revivals in the 1730s and 1740s. It became the most significant experience in the spiritual life of colonial America, reviving and dividing churches from New England to the southern colonies. The most important expression of the First Great Awakening was the rise of lay power. Laywomen, as well as men, attacked unregenerate ministers and at times took over their clerical functions. Women stopped short of preaching, however.

A few women, such as Sarah Osborn of Newport, publicly displayed doctrinal knowledge in evangelical tracts; her *Nature, Certainty and Evidence of True Christianity* (1755) evinced an erudition equal to that of many ministers (document 4). She was also among the women who founded prayer societies, which gave their activities an organizational basis. Osborn's group, begun about 1741, met weekly under her guidance until her death in 1796. Her esteem as a religious leader drew men as well as women to her. In 1766 and 1767, when hundreds pressed into her home for weekly religious meetings, she felt compelled to defend her behavior in an eight-page letter to a male critic.[9]

Barbara Heck went even further. Though she never preached, she is credited with being the "Mother of American Methodism" and possibly the founder of the Methodist movement. The distinction grew from her colorful evangelical witness in which she broke up a game of cards, threw the cards in the fire, and summoned her cousin, Philip Embury, to "preach to us, or we shall all go to hell" (document 5). This act led to creation of the earliest extant Methodist society in North America, the John Street United Methodist Church in New York City. Heck provides an early instance of a woman effecting the organization of the entire church, not simply working with her own sex.[10]

During the War for Independence, the revolutionary commitment of the American patriots became defined by an intimate connection between national reverence and Christian piety, a linkage that in our time is known as civil religion. Many women took part in activist social causes, organized by and in the name of the churches, whose meetings were held on church property. The Daughters of Liberty undertook door-to-door campaigns to raise money for cloth to make shirts and other clothing for soldiers. The first campaign, for the benefit of Washington's army, was launched in 1780 in Philadelphia by the Ladies Association.[11]

These organizations marked a departure from the women's previous noninvolvement in public affairs. They are a symbol of women's religious protests for social and political justice—protests that would be a major emphasis of churchwomen's work in the future.

As early as 1767, churchwomen organized economic boycotts of tea and other items taxed by the Townshend Act of that year. Increasingly activist expressions of female protest found women forcibly opening stores owned by Tory sympathizers, removing hoarded goods, and distributing them to patriot supporters and needy citizens of the town.[12]

A popular form of propaganda was the broadside, which was posted on trees and buildings in town squares. Such broadsides, written by Daughters of Liberty of Massachusetts, indicate an ideology of religious patriotism held by large numbers of patriot women (document 6).

THE NINETEENTH CENTURY

Women's groups that arose informally during the colonial and revolutionary eras provide instances of the same types of women's organizations that have existed in mainstream Protestant churches down to the present day. However, women's societies spread widely in the early years of the nineteenth century, with a variety of organizations springing up in cities along the Atlantic coast from north to south and subsequently in towns and villages throughout the country.

"The 'feminization' of Protestantism in the early nineteenth century was conspicuous," wrote historian Nancy Cott. Much larger numbers of women than men had joined the churches throughout the seventeenth and eighteenth centuries, and women disproportionately filled the churches of the early nineteenth century. "Women's associations before 1835 were *all* allied with the church, whereas men's also expressed a variety of secular, civic, political, and vocational concerns." After 1835 women also founded and joined social reform organizations related to abolition, temperance, women's rights, prisons, and education, though the church continued to be their primary base of organization.[13]

The proliferation of women's organizations within the church was, foremost, a response to the Second Great Awakening of the early nineteenth century, but groups also arose in areas not associated with outbreaks of revivalism. These groups drew women ecumenically from all Protestant churches in a given community. Even women's groups related to a specific church, however, were generally organized by women themselves rather than being initiated by male officials of the churches.[14]

The variety of names women gave their groups—including the Colored Female Religious and Moral Society of Salem, the Maternal Association, the Female Mite Society, the Female Charitable and Benevolent Society, and the Female Religious Biography and Reading Society—indicates the diversity of their emphases. Women moved with ease from one to another group and often belonged to several at the same time. The freedom with which they circulated among the groups shows that group support and intimacy and the theological grounding of evangelical Protestantism were more basic to these women than were the specific goals and causes of the groups. Societies were prominent among Black churchwomen as well as white. In giving charity, white women often distinguished between the "worthy and the unworthy" poor, whereas Black women reached out to their sisters and brothers without distinction. White women, more than Black women, focused their work on aid to other women. Founding of orphanages and schools and help for destitute children demonstrate the women's early championing of the needs and rights of children.[15]

By the nineteenth century, it was generally accepted that women were more naturally fitted for religion than were men. Prominent male clergy, however, debated the historic question: just what was proper and improper for women to do organizationally? Selected documents present two widely held positions: the conservative view that women's organizations should be limited to prayer groups, and the more liberal belief that women's contributions to revival meetings should be encouraged (documents 7, 8, 9).

Organizational work of women in individual Protestant denominations began after the Civil War in the 1870s. Now women's groups were sanctioned by the churches, and women worked under the auspices of denominations. During the late nineteenth century, women were denied ordination, voting privileges, and equal administrative authority with men on national, conference, and local church boards in many of the same denominations. Laywomen were not yet allowed to lead or participate in established structures of the denominations.

During these years, expanded roles and power for females came through creating organizations "for women only," particularly missionary societies ministering at home and abroad and deaconess orders. Women raised large sums of money to support mission programs and to send deaconesses into foreign and national fields. For the first time, women were appointed by their denominations to be missionaries. It was no longer assumed that they would serve in that capacity simply because their husbands were missionaries. Through self-created separatist organizations, women also enlarged their churches' programs. However, they did not directly challenge the established clergy and lay power structures of their denominations.[16]

More women became involved in women's missionary society work after the Civil War than in all areas of the social reform and woman's rights movements combined. Between 1861 and 1894, foreign missionary societies were organized by and for women in thirty-three denominations and home missionary societies in seventeen. Women organized missionary societies in both white and Black churches and in most immigrant denominations established in the United States by the late nineteenth century. Women's ability to build grassroots organizations and to consolidate those groups into regional and national societies created a new basis of community among women in the churches. The surprising power of women to raise thousands of dollars from the gleanings of "mite boxes" was a major factor in making missions an identifying mark of late-nineteenth-century Protestantism.[17]

Women defined the purpose of their societies and deaconess orders in the late nineteenth century as contributing to the church's mission of evangelizing the world. Until the late 1800s women had left that responsibility to men, who had not offered to share it with them. These women believed, too, that their special evangelical duty was to bring the good news to other women, to the five hundred million women held in forced subjection by false religions and oppressive social customs in non-Christian countries. Education and moral uplift of women were intrinsic to their organized evangelistic effort (document 10 and its sources). The distinctive feature of the movement became "woman's work for woman." This phrase was the title of the Woman's Presbyterian Board of Missions's monthly publication, referring to the service of society members and deaconesses to women of non-Christian lands and urban ghettos.[18]

The key to the success of national mission programs was the commitment and contributions of women in every congregation. Pages of society journals were filled with detailed instructions for organizing local units and for fund-raising. The aim was to enlist every churchwoman in the society and to hold unit meetings often and regularly—every week, month, quarter—to instill the mission in their members, build commitment, and accomplish their tasks (document 11).

By advancing causes that required widespread cooperation, women created ties of sisterhood and built networks of support across the country. Three types of organizations were developed, varying from regional to national structures in different denominations: first, societies that were incorporated independently to cooperate as supplemental arms of denominational agencies, such as the African Methodist Episcopal and the Congregational women's boards; second, those that were independent and understood themselves as equal to the general agency, like the

Methodist Episcopal society; and, third, women's groups that were dependent upon and subsidiary to denominational boards, as in the Episcopal Church (document 12).[19]

Women saw the dedication of deaconesses, who ministered to the neediest and lowliest at home and abroad, to be a reflection of the ministry of Christ. By 1894 the thirty-three women's foreign mission societies had sent one thousand women missionaries abroad, most of whom were trained in over 140 deaconess homes. The deaconess homes were another organizational enterprise strongly supported and endowed by women's societies of mainstream Protestant denominations. A major focus of deaconesses' ministry in this country was to Christianize and Americanize the immigrants who crowded the inner cities. The deaconess movement provided the first organization of professional laywomen in the church, offering liberating choices for women who were employed outside the home by the church (document 13). However, the services rendered by the deaconesses did not necessarily provide expanded options for the newly arrived immigrant women outside their homes. Primarily, deaconesses trained them to provide better care for their children and their homes.

THE TWENTIETH CENTURY

At least six types of women's organizations, most of which originated in the colonial era and continue into the twentieth century, could be distinctly identified by the early 1900s: prayer, Bible, and support groups; missionary societies; ladies aid societies; altar guilds; separatist orders; and social protest organizations.[20] These types existed denominationally and interdenominationally, though all were not found in each denomination. Their causes often overlapped so that each kind of group did not always constitute a distinct body. In surveying these forms, their historic and contemporary interconnections become clear.

The oldest type in American history, dating from the first decade of the Puritan settlement, was prayer, Bible, and women's support groups. As the Anne Hutchinson and Anne Eaton circles demonstrated, these groups were potentially the most radical theologically because from their prayer and Bible study they gained sanction to advocate for the rights of their sex. Among the heirs of these informal gatherings in the late twentieth century are special women's task forces and commissions organized denominationally and interdenominationally. One such organization, the General Commission on the Status and Role of Women of the United Methodist Church, advocates for the rights of women both within the church and in society, particularly seeking to open official structures in the church on the basis of equity (document 20). Begun in 1972 by a vote of the General Conference, GCOSROW is an official commission of the denomination. Its national leadership has been seated in a two- or three-member General Secretariat, representing women of ethnic and racial diversity, to signify a team approach of shared leadership.

A very different legacy of the seventeenth-century prayer groups is the World Day of Prayer, which is distinguished in the late twentieth century as "the most universal expression of Christian unity in the world." The annual event was begun in 1890 through the vision of two Baptist women and ecumenical pioneers, Helen Barrett Montgomery and Lucy Waterbury Peabody. World Day of Prayer services are committed to the international inclusiveness of women beyond denominational and racial identity and to the liberation of women from the social, political, economic, and ecclesiastical bondage that confronts them even in the 1990s. Its centennial was commemorated in 1987 with an affirmation that the World Day of Prayer is a gift "passed from heart to heart by mothers and sisters in Christ who dared to live beyond the limits of creed and race, daily circumstance and tradition."[21]

Separatist societies "for women only" have proven to be the base of women's power in the church. Ironically, they were begun throughout the colonies and have been sustained over four centuries because male leadership in established denominational structures did not allow or enable women to work equally with men on denominational boards. The ecumenical strength of separatist women's missionary society work in the twentieth century is demonstrated in Lucy Waterbury Peabody's description of a campaign for higher education of Asian women in 1922 (document 15). The organizational genius of the campaign was an example of "prayer, publicity, and power-wielding," which enabled women to tap rich philanthropic sources beyond the church.[22]

Organizations "for women only" generally have taken highly acceptable form within denominations, yet in the process they have carried out radical protests and reforms. The description of the Quaker

Women's Meeting, likely deriving from the 1675 Newport, Rhode Island, meeting, demonstrates the many facets of such groups in their Bible study, mutual support, advocacy of the equality of women with men, and their outreach to provide support for persons in all conditions of need. The conservative evangelical missionary goal—to individually convert natives on all continents of the world until all the world accepts Christ— underlay Protestant women's missionary society work at least through the first quarter of the twentieth century. However, the work of Anna Kugler, first Lutheran female medical missionary to India, demonstrates a deeper underlying religious unity (document 16). In her daily medical service in the early twentieth century, sponsored by the women of the United Lutheran Church, interreligious unity took precedence over Christian triumphalism in the mission field.[23]

Women's separatist orders, such as orders of deaconess sisters, con- tinue to provide a professional option for Protestant women well into the last quarter of the twentieth century, though fewer women have entered these orders in recent years. Today diaconal ministry has replaced dea- coness orders in most denominations. Open to both women and men, the contemporary diaconate is defined today either as an office of eccle- siastical assistantship to pastors or as consecrated work of service to church and society, distinct from ordination to ministries of word and sacrament. Seen in this way, diaconal ministry in the 1980s and '90s keeps a strict demarcation between the ministry of laypeople and that of clergy. The diaconate thus addresses the threat that deaconess orders were earlier thought to present to clergy—the possibility of serving as a "stepping stone" to ordination. Arguments formulated in the first decade of the twentieth century regarding the distinction of clergy and dea- conesses have been transposed in recent decades to preserve the separa- tion between the diaconate, as laity, and the clergy, as the primary and "higher" form of ministry.[24]

The major organizational work of women in churches, both in the twentieth century and earlier, has been ladies aid and missionary soci- eties. Historically, ladies aid societies helped their own churches raise money to meet budgetary expenses, while missionary societies raised funds to support programs and personnel in national and foreign mission work. By the 1930s, these functions were generally brought together in most individual congregations into one women's society of Christian service. Altar guilds, the work of women in arranging flowers and preparing the church altar weekly for communion, have sometimes remained separate or also have been merged.[25]

"Women's work for women" in national structures of denominations during the twentieth century characteristically has been subsumed under general boards of denominations. In 1910, when Helen Barrett Montgomery questioned whether men were emancipated sufficiently from the caste of sex to be able to work on a basis of equality with women, she directly confronted the question of whether it would "not be better to have one great organization of the entire church to which both men and women contributed" (document 14).

Montgomery knew that in the early twentieth century the time was not yet right. Her warnings were borne out in consolidations made within many denominations in the 1920s and '30s. Some women of the denominations saw that in being subsumed under their denominations' general boards, women's boards had lost autonomy in decision making and the raising and distribution of their own money for women's work for women, and that these developments had been counterproductive. Priscilla Stuckey-Kauffman evaluated the consolidation of women's missionary boards into the male-led American Board of Commissioners for Foreign Missions in the Congregational Church. She wrote that "especially the younger generation of women were eager to join the ecclesiastical mainstream." But men and women had different ideas of what their organizational life together should be. "National leaders (mostly men) pursued consolidation, whereas women preferred *cooperation* among separate organizations." Consolidation was the outcome, but

> consolidation did not accomplish the positive goals that congregational leaders had promised. Rather, it reinforced trust in bureaucratic solutions, and it furthered a system of male-dominated leadership in the church. Women gave up autonomy, and their unique contributions to foreign missions strategy were lost. It was a high price to pay.[26]

Two twentieth-century critiques published in *The Christian Century,* one in the 1930s and the other in 1965, point to the issues that repeatedly surface as women continue to expand their rightful place and work toward inclusivity and equality. A voice of the early 1930s, identifying itself simply as "The Churchwoman," spoke in these words, seeking space for women in the churches beyond missionary societies and ladies aid work: "The place for an adequate organization of churchwomen is not in the kitchen, not yet in the obsolete parlor, but in the spacious living room of our social household" (document 17). As the "Daughters" of the Revolutionary Era had publicly protested for the patriots' causes, "The Churchwoman" of 1930 was claiming the right of churchwomen's organizations to advocate for world peace, law enforcement, rights of labor for women and children, and racial equality and inclusiveness.

Thirty-five years later, in 1965, Hannah Bonsey Suthers wrote a "sister" article in *The Century,* and this article earns the distinction of being the churchwoman's initial response to the modern feminist movement (document 18). Suthers wrote that churches must put to rest "the Christian Mystique," which means that women's "work, money and prayers are most acceptable." Still "limiting women's church work to housekeeping . . . and omitting capable women in the policy-making executive or liturgical areas" results in "a failure to see women as persons, to accept them as persons."

Women in the United Methodist Church and its antecedent denominations were the only ones who maintained and gained authority throughout the denominational consolidations of the twentieth century. In 1993 the Women's Division, which works in cooperation with other arms of the United Methodist Board of Global Ministries, contended that work with women and children must still be its focus. "We continue to face the historic dilemma which assigns only to women the concern for ministries with women, children and youth. We must continue to make these 'women's concerns' our priority because the larger church and the society are reluctant to take the lead" (document 19).

The final document of this section, the report of the General Commission on the Status and Role of Women to the 1992 General Conference of the United Methodist Church, noted the major gains of the last two decades toward including clergy- and laywomen in the structures of the church. However, as an advocacy agency for women within the denomination and in society, the commission itemized the very specific areas in which it must continue to challenge the church to assume its responsibility to gain equity for women, both within its own organization and in the world. The document concludes with the challenge that today men and women must "be in partnership as the issues are addressed."

Anne Hutchinson preaching to a religious gathering in her home in the 1630s, a practice that led to her excommunication from the Massachusetts Bay Colony.

Barbara Heck (1734–1804), the "mother of American Methodism," helped to organize America's first Methodist society in New York City in 1766.

The Senders supported women's pioneer mission work throughout the world in the nineteenth century. They were middle- and upper-class women and their young children, trained from an early age to regularly contribute their own "mite for missions."

TOMORROW

To-morrow, we have faith and hope to believe, these same children, older grown, will put into practice the methods they have learned to-day.

To-morrow, we hope to have no *ignorant* poor.

The idealism characteristic of the early deaconess movement is reflected in this cover of the bulletin of the Chicago Training School for Home and Foreign Missions. Through their efforts to raise a new generation of children in the inner cities, deaconesses hoped to eradicate ignorance and poverty.

Black deaconesses performed essential functions as "extensions" of local pastors, just as did their sisters in white churches. These seven deaconesses graduated in 1902 from the first training school for Black deaconesses in the United States, located in Cincinnati.

Helen Barrett Montgomery (1861–1934) was a pioneer in Baptist and ecumenical women's missionary society leadership in the late nineteenth and early twentieth centuries. The first woman to head a national Protestant denomination, she was elected president of the Northern Baptist Convention for 1921–1922.

President Barbara Thompson and the three-member General Secretariat of the General Commission on the Status and Role of Women of the United Methodist Church, Nan Self, Kyoko Fugiu, and Trudi K. Reed (formerly Preciphs), in the early 1980s. The first women's advocacy commission of a national denomination, it was founded in 1972.

Throughout the American past, as well as the much longer Christian history, women as members of the laity have fulfilled most of the—largely overlooked—roles in Christian service. This involvement in the ministry of the laity has sometimes domesticated women, but just as often it has led them into larger fields of involvement in transforming the world.

This dual potential of laywomen's organizations—to constrict women within the home or to liberate them in the world—runs throughout women's experience in Protestantism. Notably, that potential for the liberation of women and, in turn, of the church, is vested in Anne Hutchinson and the New Haven Circle of women in the early seventeenth century, just as in the Women's Division of the Board of Global Ministries and the Commission on the Status and Role of Women in the United Methodist Church at the end of the twentieth century. The difference is that today women's organizations draw large numbers of women and are at the heart of the institutional structures of the churches.

Documents

THE SEVENTEENTH AND EIGHTEENTH CENTURIES: THE AMERICAN COLONIAL AND REVOLUTIONARY PERIODS

Document 1. "Here Hath Been Much Spoken Concerning Mrs. Hutchinson's Meetings": From Her Trial in the Massachusetts Bay Colony

Anne Hutchinson's meetings in the Massachusetts Bay Colony may have been the first informal but regular organization of women in the American colonies. Excerpts from her trial and excommunication in 1637 demonstrate the explosive potential of the gatherings, in that men as well as women were attracted to her radical message.[27]

Mr. Winthrop, governor. Mrs. Hutchinson, you are called here as one of those that have troubled the peace of the commonwealth and the churches here; you are known to be a woman that hath had a great share in the promoting and divulging of those opinions that are causes of this trouble . . . and you have maintained a meeting and an assembly in your house that hath been condemned by the general assembly as a thing not tolerable nor comely in the sight of God nor fitting for your sex.

Gov. Why do you keep such a meeting at your house as you do every week upon a set day?

Mrs. H. It is lawful for me so to do, as it is all your practices and can you find a warrant for yourself and condemn me for the same thing? . . .

Gov. For this, that you appeal to our practice you need no confutation. If your meeting had answered to the former it had not been offensive, but I will say that there was no meeting of women alone, but your meeting is of another sort for there are sometimes men among you.

Mrs. H. There was never any man with us. . . . I conceive there lyes a clear rule in Titus, that the elder women should instruct the younger [Titus 2:3–5] and then I must have a time wherein I must do it.

Gov. All this I grant you, I grant you a time for it, but what is this to the purpose that you Mrs. Hutchinson must call a company together from their callings to come to be taught by you?

Mrs. H. Will it please you to answer me this and to give me a rule for then I will willingly submit to any truth. If any come to my house to be instructed in the ways of God what rule have I to put them away?

Gov. But suppose that a hundred men come unto you to be instructed will you forbear to instruct them?

Mrs. H. As far as I conceive I cross a rule in it.

Gov. Very well and do you not so here?

Mrs. H. No Sir for my ground is they are men.

Gov. Men and women all is one for that, but suppose that a man should come and say Mrs. Hutchinson I hear that you are a woman that God hath given his grace unto and you have knowledge in the word of God I pray instruct me a little, ought you not to instruct this man?

Mrs. H. I think I may.—Do you think it not lawful for me to teach women and why do you call me to teach the court?

Gov. We do not call you to teach the court but to lay open yourself. . . .

Mr. Dudley, dep. gov. Here hath been much spoken concerning Mrs. Hutchinson's meetings and among other answers she saith that men come not there, I would ask you this one question, then, whether never any man was at your meeting?

Gov. There are two meetings kept at their house.

Dep. gov. How; is there two meetings?

Mrs. H. Ey Sir, I shall not equivocate, there is a meeting of men and women and there is a meeting only for women.

Document 2. "Pastors and Teachers
Are But the Inventions of Men":
The New Haven Circle of Women

The spirit of independent judgment spread throughout the circle of women who gathered around Anne Eaton in New Haven. Their own study of biblical texts led these women to believe that God gave all followers—clergy and laity, men and women—the authority to discern God's message and to share it in organized settings.[28]

At the Court held at New Haven this 2nd June, 1646:

Mrs. Brewster, Mrs. Moore & Mrs. Leach being warned about several miscarriages of a public nature, appeared and were charged severally as followeth.

Job [Hall] and Elizabeth [Smith] both affirm that Mrs. Brewster speaking of his sermon said, "Mr. Davenport makes the people believe that to come into the church is as much as the receiving of Christ." Job said she added, "Mr. Davenport carrieth it as if they could not have salvation without coming into the church." What concerneth Job in this part of his testimony he gave in writing, and affirmed before the magistrates, yet now in court was somewhat doubtful whether he heard the words from Mrs. Brewster herself, or only heard Elizabeth repeat them from Mrs. Brewster. . . .

Elizabeth said, that twice or thrice she [Mrs. Brewster] spake to that purpose, that she was sermon sick, and that proceeding in conference she presently said that when she came home she bad her son make waste paper of it, which she then said Elizabeth's conceiveth was spoken in reference to the notes of Dr. Davenport's sermon.

Mrs. Brewster denied these words, sermon sick, or that it was in reference to the sermon, & those words of making waste paper &c, but confessed she said her stomach wrought, smelling an ill savor in the seat, wherein she gave no satisfaction to the court.

3rdly, Job & Elizabeth affirm that Mrs. Brewster (in conference speaking of scandalous persons), asked Mrs. Moore whether she had not heard for what Mrs. Eaton was cast out of the church. Mrs. Moore asked Mrs. Eaton why she did not confess her sin. Mrs. Eaton answered she had done it, but not to the church's satisfaction. Mrs. Brewster said "if Mrs. Eaton had seen her light before she came into the church, she would not have come in."

Job Hall, servant to Mr. Leach saith, that Mrs. Moore in prayer with Mr. Leach's family saith . . . "when Christ ascended, he gave gifts to men, some to be apostles, some pastors, some teachers, but they are gone through the word & are now ascended into heaven." That in opposition, as he conceiveth to Mr. Davenport's sermon upon Ephesians 4.11 verse, she added that night in prayer, that "now pastors & teachers are but the inventions of men." That in conference with Mrs. Brewster, she said "a veil is before the eyes of ministers and people in this place, & til that be taken away, they cannot be turned to the Lord." He saith further, that Mrs. Moore "used to express content & satisfaction when Mr. Davenport holdeth forth the excellency of Christ in his ministry, but she saith she loveth not to hear him preach for practice." . . .

Mrs. Moore again denied the charge, & particularly that ever she said, pastors & teachers were the inventions of men. She affirmed herself to be a member of a church. She was asked of what church, but made no reply. She was told that by three witnesses it is affirmed she had upon several times & upon several occasions said, that pastors & teachers are the inventions of men. . . .

Mrs. Moore's daughter, Mrs. Leach, being charged that, upon a question or conference about joining with this church, she had said to Mrs. Brewster, (as formerly to Mrs. Wackman or some others of the church,) that she sometime had a mind to join, but now declined it, because she found so many untruths among them.

Document 3. God "Can Make Us Good and Bold and Valliant Souldiers of Jesus Christ": Quaker Women's Meetings

This document was probably sent from the Swarthmore Monthly Meeting, led by Sarah Fell, the daughter of Margaret Fell, to all the Quaker women's meetings in England and America. A copy preserved in the depository of the Arch Street Friends' Meeting House in Philadelphia likely derives from an original sent to the Newport, Rhode Island, Meeting about 1675. The letter, which details the duties of women's meetings, also contains the militant theology of women's equality in Christ that appears in the writings of Quaker founder George Fox but particularly in those of Margaret Fell.[29]

From our Country Women's meeting in Lancashire to the Dispersed abroad, among the Women's meetings every where.

Dear Sisters,

In the blessed unity in the Spirit of grace our Souls Salute you who are sanctified in Christ Jesus, and called to be Saints. . . . Where there is neither male nor female &c. but we are all one in Christ Jesus. . . .

So here is the blessed Image of the living God, restored againe, in which he made them male and female in the beginning. . . . And he makes no difference in the seed, between the male and the female, as Christ saith, they were both the work of God in the beginning, and so in the restoration. . . .

Soe all Dear friends and sisters, make full proofe of the gift of God that is in you, and neglect it not. . . .

And first, for the women of every . . . monthly meeting, where the mens monthly meetings is established let the women likewise of every monthly meeting, meet together to wait upon the lord, and to hearken what the lord will say unto them, and to know his mind, and will, and be ready to obey, and answer him in every motion of his eternal spirit and power. . . .

If there be any that walks disorderly, as doth not become the Gospell, or lightly, or wantonly, or that is not of a good reporte: Then send to them, as you are ordered by the power of God in the meeting, (which is the authority of it) to Admonish, and exhort them, and to bring them to Judge, and Condemn, what hath been by them done or acted contrary to the truth. . . .

And if there be any that goes out to Marry, with priests or joineth in Marriage with the world, and does not obey the order of the Gospell as it is established amongst friends, then for the womens monthly meeting to send to them, to reprove them. . . .

And dear sisters it is duely Incumbent upon us to look into our families, and to prevent our Children of running into the world for husbands, or for wives, and so to the priests: for you know before the womens meetings were set up, Many have done so, which brought dishonour, both to God, and upon his truth and people. . . .

And also all friends, in their womens monthly, and particular Meetings, that they take special care for the poore, and for those that stands in need: that there be no want, nor suffering, for outward things, amongst the people of God, . . .

And so let Care be taken for the poore, and widdows, that hath young Children, that they be relieved, and helped, till they be able and fitt, to be put out to apprentices or servants.

And that all the sick, and weak, and Infirme, or Aged, and widdows, and fatherless, that they be looked after, and helped, and relieved in every particular meeting, either with clothes, or maintainance, or what they stand in need off. So that in all things the Lord may be glorified, and honoured, so that there be no want, nor suffering in the house of God, who loves a Chearfull giver.

So here was the womens meeting, and womens teachings of one another, so that this is no new thing, as some raw unseasoned spirits would seem to make it:

And though wee be looked upon as the weaker vessels, yet strong and powerfull is God, whose strength is made perfect in weakness, he can make us good and bold, and valliant Souldiers of Jesus Christ, if he arm us with his Armour of Light, he who respect no persons, but chuseth the weak things of this world, and foolish things to confound the wise: our sufficiency is of him, and our Armour, and strength is in him.

Document 4. To Give "Account of My Conduct as to Religious Affairs": Sarah Osborn's Religious Bands

A widow of twenty-six when the Great Awakening began, Sarah Haggan Wheaton Osborn (1714–1796) of Newport, Rhode Island, found in evangelicalism a means to religious influence and a relief from a life of drudgery. As her activities expanded from guiding a female prayer society to leading a revival, she met clerical opposition. She explains her role in Newport's 1766–1767 revival to her spiritual adviser, Reverend Joseph Fish of Stonington, Connecticut.[30]

Revd and Worthy Sir

. . . And now believing Zions cause is as dear as ever to my venerable friend, permit me to set my self as a child in the Presence of her Father to Give you the Most satisfactory account of my conduct as to religious affairs I am capable. I will begin with the Great one respecting the poor Blacks on Lords day Evenings, which above all the rest Has been exercising to my Mind. . . . To avoid Moving beyond my Line, while I was anxiously desirous the poor creatures should be savrd with some sutable one to pray with them, I was Greatly distresst; but as I could not obtain [help] I Have Given it up and Thay Have not Had above one [prayer] Made with them I believe Sir Since you was here. I only read to them talk to them and sing a Psalm or Hymn with them, and then at Eight o clock dismiss them all by Name as upon List. They call it School and I Had rather it should be calld almost any thing that is good than Meeting. I reluct so much at being that Head of any thing that bear that Name. . . . You Might almost Hear as we say the shaking of a Leaf when there is More than an Hundred under the roof at onece (I mean with the young Mens Society in the chamber) for all there was so Many. . . .

As to the young Men that did in sumer visit us on tusday Evenings and spend the Evening in religious Exercises, praying in turn etc. but as soon as time come to work on Evenings in Sept that ceasd. The Boys fills that vacancy now and the young Men Haven only the priviledge of Meeting in our chamber on Sabath Evenings. I Have no thing to do with them, only Have the pleasure of Seting my candlestick and Stool. . . . So I dare not desire the young Men to remove from Hence as

I know not that any one of them has conveniency and our female Society was broke up Many years on that very account. . . .

There is usually 30 odd young garls every Monday Evening except and weather is excessive bad and indeed it is surprising to see their constancy thro almost all weathers—yet I know of no Extraordinary Effects but *Here* they behave quite serious and the Pashions are sometimes toucht I think. . . .

As to My ability I can only say I trust christs Strength is Made perfect in my weakness, and at sometimes am Made open to Glory Even in my infirmities that the Power of christ May rest upon me and rejoice that I am nothing and can do nothing without Him. . . .

> *sincier tho unworthy friend*
> S Osborn
> *March 7 1767*

Document 5. Barbara Heck Empowers the First Extant Religious Society—and Becomes the "Mother of American Methodism"

Debate continues today as to whether Robert Strawbridge, an early Methodist preacher in the Baltimore area, or Barbara Ruckle Heck (1734–1804) should be credited as the true founder of American Methodism. Heck's organizational work went beyond women's meetings. One year after she migrated to New York City in 1765, Barbara Heck made a colorful evangelical witness that distinguished her as the "Mother of American Methodism."[31]

Many of the Palatines who accompanied Embury and Barbara Heck from Ireland, had by this time lost even the form of godliness, and had become adept at card playing and other sinful amusements. . . . One evening in the autumn of 1766, a large company were assembled playing cards as usual, when Barbara Heck came in, and burning with indignation, she hastily seized the cards, and throwing them into the fire, administered a scathing rebuke to all the parties concerned. She then went to Embury's house, and told him what she saw, and what she had done, adding, with great earnestness, "Philip, you must preach to us, or we shall all go to hell, and God will require our blood at your hands!"

Philip attempted a defence by saying, "How can I preach, as I have neither house nor congregation?" "Preach," said this noble woman, "in your own house, and to your own company." Before she left, she prevailed on Philip to resolve to make the attempt, and within a few days, Embury preached the first Methodist sermon in New York, in his own hired house, to a congregation of five persons. Such was the origin of the Methodist Episcopal Church in the United States—now the largest and most influential church in the American Continent. "Who hath despised the day of small things."

Document 6. "New England, Now to Meet Thy God Prepare": The Daughters of Liberty During the American Revolution

The stern and sobering words of "An Address to New-England: Written by a Daughter of Liberty" in Boston in 1774 could have been preached from a pulpit in Boston by any Puritan preacher of the revolutionary generation. These words, posted in a public place, demonstrate women's early organizational work of social critique and social activism, taking women beyond the bounds of the church in the name of their faith.[32]

> . . . Unhappy Boston! wherefore doth thy God
> Thus scourge thee with a Tyrant's Iron Rod?
> How art thou spoil'd, O City of Renown? . . .
> Before the final Storm upon thee fall.
> What Sins, what crying Sins did God provoke,
> To cause his Wrath against this land to smoke?
> . . . Crushing the Poor and Needy to the Ground,
> In every Place is common to be found:
> These Sins have call'd for Vengeance from Above,
> Thy Glory stands just ready to remove. . . .
> New England, now to meet thy God prepare,
> Awake Repentance, Faith and earnest Prayer. . . .
> The Wound is deep but God doth thee assure,
> Attend the Lord's endearing gracious Call,
> Accept this Call and turn unto thy God,
> Fear not the Tyrant's Yoke nor threatning Rod:
> The Lord our Lawgiver our Judge our King,
> Shall in the Mount appear and Succor bring.

Happy O People! Saved of the Lord,
He is the Shield and Safety will afford:
Safely the People here alone shall dwell,
In vain shall rage the Sons of Earth and Hell:
We shall not fear although the Earth remove.

THE NINETEENTH CENTURY

Document 7. "The Little Band of Pious Females": Evangelical Presbyterian Women

Women's promotion of revivals in the early nineteenth century naturally followed from their conversions. Prayer meetings became their most common revival effort. By the 1820s women's evangelical efforts were so accepted that a clergyman writing in a Presbyterian magazine suggested that God showers down divine grace in direct proportion to women's prayers.[33]

. . . At a lecture in a part of the parish remote from the centre, there were found three persons evidently under the special operations of the Holy Spirit. One of this number, to the great joy of these sisters in Christ, soon gave evidence of a change of heart. A second lecture, without much delay, was preached in the same neighborhood, at which meeting eleven persons were found, who were deeply affected in view of their spiritual state. . . . Their pastor was then necessarily absent from town a few days.—On his return, his first business was to visit these anxious sinners; but alas, he found them not in a state of anxiety like that in which he left them. All, without exception, were far less solicitous respecting the salvation of their souls; and the serious impressions of no small proportion of them were erased, and they were unwilling to make religion a subject of conversation. It was so ordered, that on the same day in which this mournful fact was ascertained, the little band of pious females, of whom mention has been made, were assembled together. Their minister, without communicating to them a knowledge of this fact, asked them individually, what had been their religious feelings and conduct for a few days previous. There was, substantially, but one answer given to the interrogation. Each person was constrained to confess, that she had not, during that period, had so lively an interest at the throne of grace—she had been involved more deeply in the cares of the world—and had thought less of the condition of impenitent sinners. It was then stated to them, that the persons, who were a short time before viewed as being convicted of sin, were now in an unpromising state, having lost, in a great degree, their serious impressions.—This statement called forth, as we trust, tears of repentance. A resolution was unanimously adopted, to devote a certain portion of time to special fasting and prayer. The convictions of the eleven persons, to whom allusion has been made, were renewed—their hopeful conversions succeeded, one after another; and all of them, together with *fifty-six* other persons, were in a few months added to the church.

Document 8. "Cultivating These Fields of Pious Usefulness": The Conservative View of Women's Evangelical Activity

The conservative view of women's evangelical activities limited their religious activity outside the home to prayer meetings made up only of females. Ashbel Green (1772–1848), influential Presbyterian minister, president of the College of New Jersey (1812–1848), and president of Princeton Seminary's Board of Directors (1812–1848), affirmed this position while guardedly approving of a public role for women in carefully delineated church-related organizations.[34]

The supposition is, that in female prayer meetings, women *only* meet with women. In the devotional exercises carried on in such circumstances, there is surely no ground for the charge of arrogant assumption, or of any trespass on female decorum. Why then should any object to this sacred communion of sisterhood, in which devout women mingle their prayers and their praises—their prayer for each other, for their husbands, for their children, and for the church of God? Verily, we believe that these female offerings come up as sweet incense, before the throne of a prayer-hearing God; and that often, in the most signal manner, he returns to the offerers answers of peace. . . .

Bible Societies, Tract Societies, Education Societies, Jews Societies, Charity Schools, Orphan Asylums, Widow Asylums, and all institutions of a similar character to these, present to Christian women objects and opportunities for manifesting their love to their Saviour and his cause, which they may seize and improve, with the greatest freedom and advantage. And truly they have, in our day, seized and improved them, with an activity, and to an extent, which are worthy of the highest praise. In several instances, within the knowledge of the speaker, the energy, perseverance, and success of Christian women, in cultivating these fields of pious usefulness, have reproved the more sluggish efforts of men. It was reserved for the age in which we live, and it is among the indications, as we hope, of a better age approaching, that female agency should be called on, to take part in almost every plan and effort for extending the Gospel, or for abating the sufferings, or meliorating the condition of mankind. . . .

Document 9. "If You Don't Appoint an Anxious Meeting, I Shall Die": Charles Grandison Finney Defends Women's Evangelical Work for the Entire Church

During the 1830s, Charles Grandison Finney delivered a series of sermons in New York City on how to create a revival. They inadvertently suggest his dependence on women, beyond praying, in furthering what he saw as the chief work of religious institutions: promoting revivals. Most of his examples of successful lay revival efforts featured women rather than men, and many of those women were more strongly evangelical than their ministers. The evangelizing woman in the following account sought an "anxious meeting" to enable people to acknowledge their sins and demonstrate the need for a revival.[35]

A revival may be expected when Christians have a spirit of prayer for a revival. That is, when they pray as if their hearts were set upon a revival. . . . A clergyman in W——n told me of a revival among his people, which commenced with a zealous and devoted woman in the church. She became anxious about sinners, and went to praying for them; she prayed and her distress increased; and she finally came to her minister, and talked with him, and asked him to appoint an anxious meeting, for she felt that one was needed. The minister put her off, for he felt nothing of it. The next meeting she came again, and besought him to appoint an anxious meeting; she knew there should be somebody to come, for she felt as if God was going to pour out his Spirit. He put her off again. And finally she said to him, "If you don't appoint an anxious meeting I shall die, for there is certainly going to be a revival." The next Sabbath he appointed a meeting, and said that if there were any who wished to converse with him about the salvation of their souls, he would meet them on such an evening. He did not know of one, but when he went to the place, to his astonishment, he found a large number of anxious inquirers. Now don't you think that woman knew there was going to be a revival? Call it what you please, a new revelation or an old revelation, or any thing else. I say it was the Spirit of God that taught that praying woman there was going to be a revival. "The secret of the Lord" was with her, and she knew it. She knew God had been in her heart, and filled it so full that she could contain [it] no longer.

Document 10. "Woman's Work for Woman": United Brethren Define the Purposes of Women's Missionary Societies

Two articles graphically illustrate the beginnings of women's missionary society organizations in established denominations of mainstream Protestantism after the Civil War. They were published in 1882 in early issues of the *Woman's Evangel,* journal of the Women's Missionary Society of the United Brethren Church, a comparatively small denomination. They demonstrate ways in which women sought to expand their sphere of usefulness alongside men in evangelizing the world for Christ.[36]

To every intelligent creature God has given capacity for doing some kind of work in the world. As individual Christians we have our distinct duties, our several spheres of usefulness, to be filled by ourselves alone. . . . For long years we as women seemed to have had but limited views of our duty. We were content to save our own souls and let men attend to all the rest. But the door has opened, and at last our timid feet have crossed the threshold. The women of other denominations have begun the work before us; but we are now arousing to our duty. . . . God has given us this work, the work of sending the gospel to those who are without its light and influence, to teach and elevate them mentally and morally, and thus to lead them into the fair light of the gospel and civilization.

In beginning women's missionary society and deaconess work, the early leaders were especially concerned to convert, educate, and raise the status of other women. Leaders understood that women were not being adequately reached under present national and foreign mission programs, and they believed this emphasis was possible only through "woman's work for woman."[37]

. . . "Fear not: behold, I bring you good tidings of great joy, which shall be to all people." . . . This glad announcement was "to all people." To us as women it has come, making the name of wife and mother sacred, which is only true of Christian nations. It has been to women a glad evangel; and because we *love much* do we wish to make our work— as the name of our paper signifies,—an announcement of glad tidings to some of the five hundred millions of women in the degradation and ruin of false religions and oppressive social customs of heathen nations. . . . Many centuries have passed since the command was given to women, "Go and tell that Jesus has risen," but not till this century (the latter part of it) have Christian women come together with one mind and heart to roll away the stone from the living sepulcher, where her heathen sister sits in total darkness. She has heard that "the Master is here and calleth for thee."

Document 11. "Let Them Form an Auxiliary to the Woman's Missionary Society": Baptist Women Develop Organizational Techniques

"Suggestions for the Formation of Auxiliaries" from the *Missionary Helper* (July 1878) outline the detailed, meticulous instructions that central offices provided local churchwomen as they organized for the first time.[38]

One of the objects which the Woman's Society aims to accomplish is to secure, from each woman in the denomination, a pledge of two cents per week or a dollar a year to carry on our work. To accomplish this, we do not wish you to withdraw the contributions you are accustomed to give to other branches of Christian work, but we do ask you to do the following specific things in addition to what you are now doing:

1. Write on an envelope, "Woman's work for woman," lay it in some safe place, and deposit in it two cents each week, or more if you can.

2. To persuade each woman in your church to do the same, using the means that in your judgment will best secure the object, whether it be by private solicitation or by calling a meeting.

3. As soon as a few—if not more than three or four—will make the weekly pledge, let them form an auxiliary to the Woman's Missionary Society, and meet once a month for prayer, reading missionary intelligence, and devising means to interest others. Once a quarter, at a specified meeting, let all your members bring in the contents of their envelopes and pay to your Treasurer, who shall keep an exact account of all the money she receives and from whom, and forward the same quarterly to Miss DeMeritte.

4. When your society is formed, report it to the district secretary of your Quarterly Meeting or, if you do not know her address, report to the Home Secretary of the Society, and ask for some definite work for which you may become responsible. See that one of the officers is an agent for the *Helper.*

    Some of you may not understand that a person in each Quarterly Meeting is appointed a district secretary, or agent, whose duty it is to aid each church to organize an auxiliary. But don't wait for her action. She may be so situated that she can't attend to the work, and if she can, she will be cheered and encouraged to learn that you have moved in the matter.

5. Ask yourself if it is not your privilege to become a life member. The payment of $20, even if made in installments within one or two years, constitutes a life membership.

Document 12. "The Steady Activity and Increasing Interest in the Work Among Our Women": African Methodist Episcopal Women Model a National Society

The Women's Parent Mite Missionary Society drew together local church units of women from the African Methodist Episcopal Church into one national organization. This essay describes graphically the origins of the earliest missionary society of women in a Black denomination. Further, it lifts up essential features of national organization by women in all denominations: their pride of accomplishment, their relationship to established male governing authorities, and the careful planning, organization, and content typical of female societies. This document was written by Sarah E. Tanner, who was married to a prominent bishop of the denomination.[39]

It was in the year 1874, that the first meeting was held in Washington, D.C., to consider a plan whereby the women of the church could be brought in line to assist the Home and Foreign Missionary Society in its efforts to carry the gospel, not only to those of our own land who are in ignorance of the atoning blood, but to those in foreign lands also. In furtherance of this purpose, a convention was called to meet in Philadelphia May 8, 1874, and from this assembly sprang the Parent Mite Missionary Society of to-day. The sisters of the church rallied to the work, and with the assistance of both bishops and elders, the society was put on a firm basis; auxiliary societies in the meantime springing up in all sections—societies that have greatly assisted in the work, and helped to keep the missionary fire burning. At times it would really seem that only a flicker could be discovered; yet the warmth ever remained, until in all our twenty-one years the treasury, like the widow's oil, has not failed us. . . . Seeing the need of more concerted action, the Parent Society thought it wise to call a conference of missionary workers to meet in Philadelphia, Nov. 7, and continue to the 11th inclusive. The purpose was to take a retrospective view of the past, and, if possible, map out plans for more effective work in the future. . . .

As to the business of the conference, we held three sessions every day, each beginning with devotional exercises. . . . The second day proved to be a busy one. . . . The evening session was devoted to work on the "Dark Continent." A letter was read from our missionary, Rev. J. R. Frederick, by Mrs. M. E. Wilmer. It was full of information in regard to our work in Sierre Leone. Mrs. Sarah J. Early was here introduced and made an address so full of pathos, that the vast audience was stirred to its depth. Mrs. Amanda Smith concluded by one of her happy talks on the many incidents connected with her world-wide missionary work. . . .

The closing exercises at 7 p.m., began by Mrs. Amanda Smith. It was simply a Pentecostal shower. Sisters Radcliffe, Aldridge and others led off in singing, after which the Lord's Supper was administered by the Bishops present. . . .

In conclusion, we say: One of the most cheering indications in the Mite Missionary department, and in the conference just adjourned, is the steady activity and increasing interest in the work among our women, both old and young. Especially do we note the enthusiasm of our young women. And what more hopeful sign need we ask than to have our young mothers throwing themselves into the missionary work? Of a necessity the children will be inspired by the example of the mothers; and so we may hope to perpetuate the zeal and devotion to the great cause. Our prayer is that some of these dear little ones now being nestled to sleep by the sweet voice of a mother, singing "Over the Ocean Wave," or some other missionary song of Zion, will be consecrated to missionary work; and when the years of maturity are theirs, and we mothers who have laid the foundation, be resting in the "Sweet bye and bye," they will be endowed with the holy fire to go forth, proclaiming the Word.

Sarah E. Tanner

Document 13. The "New Woman" of Protestantism: Deaconess Institutions, the First Professional Laywomen's Organizations

Begun in 1884, the Chicago Training School was the first deaconess home in the Methodist Episcopal Church. It was a model for deaconess institutions of other denominations, which followed shortly thereafter. Deaconess institutions constituted the first professional organizations of females, all of them laywomen, in Protestantism.

In the excerpts included here, Lucy Rider Meyer, superintendent of the Chicago Training School and editor of the *Message and Deaconess Advocate,* acknowledges the stereotype of the deaconess. Then she proceeds to shatter it.[40]

A deaconess is often pictured as a goody-goody kind of woman who goes softly up dirty back stairs, reading the Bible to poor sick women and patting the heads of dirty-faced children. But there is nothing a woman *can* do in the line of Christian work that a deaconess may not do. Her field is as large as the work of woman, and the need of that work. In deaconess ranks to-day may be found physicians, editors, stenographers, teachers, nurses, book-keepers, superintendents of hospitals and orphanages, kitchen-gardners and kindergartners. In Omaha not only the superintending nurse, but the superintendent of the Methodist Episcopal hospital, an institution that within two years has cared for 1040 patients, are deaconesses. . . .

. . . A bit of history [shows] that the "new woman" is not an invention of the last decade but that, in the character of Hilda, Abbess of Whitby, (b. 614) she played an important part in the history of the English church. . . . The foundress of a double monastery—that is, both for monks and nuns—she became the abbess of each. . . .

And more even than this, we find Hilda in the councils and conferences of the church taking part in that Synod of Whitby which determined the form and fate of the church in England. "Her counsel," says J. R. Green, "was sought even by nobles and kings." . . .

I closed the life of this noble Abbess of Whitby, wondering if God sent a St. Hilda to Methodism *what would we do with her.*

THE TWENTIETH CENTURY

Document 14. "Are Men Ready for It?"
Helen Barrett Montgomery
Challenges Women Ecumenically

Nineteen ten marked the fiftieth anniversary of the first woman's board of missions in the United States, the Woman's Union Missionary Society. From this original interdenominational board came the inspiration for work in home and foreign missions by women in all Protestant denominations. Helen Barrett Montgomery's book, *Western Women in Eastern Lands: Fifty Years of Woman's Work in Foreign Missions,* is perhaps the most important single piece produced from this era of "woman's work for woman." She calls women to confront the hard organizational questions that present enormous challenges for continued progress in their work.[41]

With the very great expansion of women's work for women has come questioning of the organized relations which these organizations sustain to the general Boards. . . .

Would it not be better to have one great organization of the entire church to which both men and women contributed? This is the quest that is most agitated to-day. Some of the brethren say: "Let the women collect, they are such splendid collectors. We will spend it far more wisely than they can." Others say, "Let us all work together, have men and women on the Board, men and women in the work."

The first plan will commend itself to few women. The opportunity for self-expression and the development that comes through responsibility are as necessary to women as to men. The modern educated woman has ideas not only on the way to collect money but on the way to spend it, and the purposes for which it should be spent.

The second plan is very attractive. It looks ideal to have one tremendous organization with men and women working side by side. Perhaps the day will come in the growth of the kingdom when this can be, but let us look at all sides of the argument before hastening out of organizations which have been so blessed of God.

In the first place, are men ready for it? Are they emancipated from the caste of sex so that they can work easily with women, unless they be head and women clearly subordinate? Certain facts seem to indicate that in spite of the rapid strides undoubtedly made in this direction we have still a long stretch of unexplored country to be traversed before the perfect democracy of Jesus is reached. . . .

The Laymen's Movement is the real answer to the question. Organize, inspire, inform, the men of the church. Bring to bear their splendid, solid, thorough, businesslike study of the whole situation, and such methods will be devised, such systems installed, such enthusiasm roused, that in the thunderous answer of the men to the appeal our little feminine treble will rejoice to find itself submerged. . . .

Let us get down to some principles in the matter. It is good for women to give; their husbands cannot do it for them. It is good for men to give, their wives cannot do it for them. Each has certain interests separate from the other. Both have certain interests together. It is a woman's task to see that the poor, downtrodden, backward women of the non-Christian world have a chance. Let us take care of the kindergartens, orphanages, asylums, and schools that appeal most to us; let us touch the home side of life, believing that in so doing we are aiding the whole great enterprise to which as men and women we are committed.

Document 15. "College Days": The Campaign for Higher Education of Asian Women

Lucy Peabody's leadership of "College Days," the yearlong campaign to fund Asian women's colleges, demonstrates the ability of women to conceive new movements, to administer broadly based programs, and to mobilize support. A description of "Dollar Day," the last major project, which brought the campaign to successful completion, is a dramatic legacy to "professional volunteers" for generations to follow.[42]

The last lap of the race, as Mrs. Montgomery expressed it in a recent number of *Missions*, for the Seven Union Christian Colleges of the Orient is on, and Washington's part in the event is to be of a decidedly signal character. It will be remembered that the race started in Washington last year at the time the College Day luncheons were inaugurated, which are still being given in the leading cities of the country. At that time the churches of the Capital City, of nearly all denominations, united in a campaign for the seven Union Christian colleges and succeeded in raising $25,000. Now Washington is having its full share in the closing triumphs that are being staged in all parts of the country.

Mr. Rockefeller's gift of $1,000,000 from the Laura Spelman Rockefeller Fund to the Union colleges, provided the women of the United States would raise $3,000,0000, is too well-known to be repeated here. More than $2,000,000 of the $3,000,000 has been secured, and to attain the remainder of the amount before the time limit on the Rockefeller gift expires, January 1, 1923, Mrs. Peabody, chairman of the building committee for the colleges, devised plans for inaugurating a day of dollar gifts, which by a Nation-wide popular movement would bring in all money that is still lacking. She selected Saturday, December 9, as the date of the Dollar Day, and the project is in full swing all over the country to make the day a success.

As the matter eventually developed there will be two evenings devoted to a Nationwide broadcasting of the Dollar Day plan for the Union Christian colleges. On Monday evening, December 4, the broadcasting station at Arlington will be used. Mrs. Coolidge, the wife of the Vice-President of the United States, will introduce the speaker, who will represent Dr. Ida Scudder to the people of the Nation in the interest of the colleges. Then over the Arlington radio the story of the seven colleges will be told, as well as some of Dr. Scudder's experiences as president of one of the seven colleges—the Women's Medical School at Vellore, India.

In addition to this Mrs. Peabody has secured the Associated Press, and announcement of the plan and a story of the Dollar Day will be sent out by that far-reaching medium. In very many of the States the daily papers will keep that plan before their readers during the week beginning December 3, and leading weekly papers will publish the story of the colleges in full at that time.

Do you ask, How is the plan for the Dollar Day to be worked out? In the same way that has been used by the Red Cross and the Near East Relief—dollar gifts for the millions! Every one who reads these lines is going to give on Saturday, December 9, at least $1 toward these seven wonderful union Christian colleges. Moreover, will not every one try to get someone else to give also in order that the

DOLLAR DAY

will become

THE MILLION DOLLAR DAY?

Document 16. "We Are Not Converts in the Strict Sense": The Relationship of Christianity to Interreligious Unity in Lutheran Medical Missions

Anna Kugler was the first female medical missionary of the United Lutheran Church to India. This document, taken from a letter to Anna Kugler from a Hindu rajah, testifies to his family's acceptance of the evangelistic goals and medical service offered by women's missionary societies. It is clear that conversion to Christianity and interreligious unity were not necessarily antithetical for the American women missionaries.[43]

Mission hospitals for women and children are doing wonderful work in this land, to alleviate the temporal and spiritual condition of the unfortunate women whose customs preclude them from any contact with the outside world. The Rainy Hospital at Madras, the A.E.L.M. Hospitals at Rajahmundry and Guntur, and the Bethsaida Hospital at Pittapuram are a few amongst such institutions personally known to me. My family is frequently visiting the A.E.L.M. Hospital for women and children at Guntur for medical relief for the last twenty years. Before our first visit to this hospital my wife and children never heard the name of the Good Shepherd—no, not even once. After their acquaintance with this hospital, though we are not converts in the strict sense of the term, my family regularly pray every morning and evening in the name of the Lord, read their Telugu Bible and meditate on some passage or other. We do not now feel ashamed if people call us Christians to mock at. It is needless to say that this change in my family is mainly due to the saintly character of the most able physicians in charge of the hospital.

Document 17. "The Spacious Living Room of Our Social Household": Challenging Women's Organizations to Confront Social Issues

This prefeminist essay, published in The Christian Century in 1930 under the simple title of "The Churchwoman," sounds contemporary to the 1990s in its call to develop women's organizations within the church to directly confront the crucial social issues of the day.[44]

. . . Women have been taken for granted. Their relation to the church has never defined itself as a problem which required looking into. The traditional loyalty and labor of churchwomen have been left to those forms determined by tradition and habit, without any critical examination as to the adequacy of these forms to express the full possibilities of woman's church membership. . . .

. . . The Ladies' Aid as a money-making organization has ceased to appeal to the mind of the modern churchwoman. About a generation ago there began to be a decided recoil against it. . . . The question was seriously discussed as to whether a church could make ends meet without the support of the Ladies' Aid.

In the Woman's Missionary society we have a type of local church organization which stands in apparent contrast to the Ladies' Aid. Here we find a group of women, generally a much smaller group than that of the Ladies' Aid, gathering once a month to study the work of Christian missions, chiefly foreign missions. . . . It marks a definite advance from the Ladies' Aid society type of expression. It is an advance, one might say (we recognize the danger of such a metaphor), from the kitchen to the parlor. . . .

Clearly, the place for an adequate organization of churchwomen is not in the kitchen, nor yet in the obsolete parlor, but in the spacious living room of our social household. Churchwomen are now called upon consciously to set themselves to the task of investing their church membership with all the significance which the modern church is beginning to take to itself. By this, of course, is meant the whole round of social responsibilities in the discharge of which religion meets its most decisive test. The responsibility of the church for bringing the influence of Christ's gospel to bear successfully upon the social order will never be discharged so long as churchwomen—we are not discussing men's part of the responsibility now—so long as churchwomen are either ignorant of the social gospel, or unorganized on its behalf, or confine the expression of their social impulses and intelligence to women's clubs outside the church. Powerful and helpful as women's clubs are, the salvation of the social order is not in them. Unless the church of Christ saves the world, it cannot be saved. And unless the womanhood of the church can be given a mode of self-expression within the church, by which its peculiar gifts may function under religious sanctions on behalf of a social order worthy to be called Christian, the church itself cannot save the world.

. . . For example, the issue of world peace, it is inevitable that the question of world peace will soon or late become a subject of study and action by every local group for which the central body speaks. Likewise the law enforcement. Likewise with hours of labor by women. Likewise with child labor. Likewise with race relations. Likewise with every issue which arises upon which the mind of Christ throws a clear light.

Document 18. "Religion and the Feminine Mystique": Early Feminist Critique Within Protestant Women's Work

In "Religion and the Feminine Mystique," published in 1965, Hannah Bonsey Suthers applies Betty Friedan's *Feminine Mystique* to religious institutions. Churches must put away the "Christian Mystique" and lead the way toward liberating women within its structures and in society.[45]

In order to take up Mrs. Friedan's challenge to be what we were created to be, we must see our way out of the "Christian mystique"—a mystique more difficult to escape than the feminine mystique because it holds its victims with the power of the religious "ought." . . . The church in its official stand seems at best only to be taking the traditional cultural viewpoint and giving it a religious rationale and sanction. While Christ gives woman a new stature, the church in practice sells woman short in the following ways: (1) By producing theology that claims that women are "mysteriously different," the implication being that women are inherently incapable of life in its fullest sense. (2) By quoting and interpreting Scripture either to limit women to a feminine role or to enable women to stomach their servitude and lack of full personhood. The same Scripture interpreted in view of the personhood of all believers is dynamic. (3) By endorsing marriage manuals that present marriage as an exclusive profession to be chosen over other vocations, paid or voluntary, when the truth is that marriage is but one part of life. (4) By offering pastoral counseling that tries to "adjust" women to their "feminine role" instead of giving them courage to hear that inner voice which says, "This is not the whole of life: take the courage to be." (5) By limiting women's church work to housekeeping-teaching-calling functions and omitting capable women in the policy-making, executive or liturgical areas.

All of which adds up to a failure to see women as persons, to accept them as persons, though their work, money and prayers are most acceptable.

Yet the attainment of the "measure of the stature of the fullness of Christ" is a goal inseparable from the attainment of personhood, including stewardship of given capacities and responsible personal relationships. The realization of this can be tremendously liberating to anyone enslaved by limitations on physiological, biological, functional living. To achieve the "glorious freedom of the children of God—the freedom to be—we must labor painfully to heal and restore capacities that have been diseased or atrophied by traditional neglect: the capacities for autonomy, independence, individuality, self-fulfilment, self-realization, the grace to grow from strength to strength.

We must hold suspect that Christianity which calls itself the minus sign across the "I," forming a cross of self-sacrifice, which tends to masochism and falls short of the outgoing concern of a mature self which Jesus exemplifies.

Document 19. "Transformation Is Where We Believe the Gospel Compels Us to Move": Women's Work for Women and Children at the End of the Twentieth Century

In its 1993 statement of identity and vision, the Women's Division of the United Methodist Church's Board of Global Ministries responded to the historic challenge to rid the church and society of the "Christian Mystique."[46]

The combined barriers of racism, sexism and class divisions become inseparable in the lives of an individual woman suffering oppression, a youth seeing no future, or a child struggling to survive. These same barriers work within our United Methodist Churches and agencies. They limit each of us from fully carrying out God's mission in the world. Confronting these barriers in ourselves, our institutions and our world underlies all of our mission.

We continue to face the historic dilemma which assigns only to women the concern for ministries with women, children and youth. We must continue to make these "women's concerns" our priority because the larger church and the society are reluctant to take the lead. Until women and youth have a stronger voice in the decisions affecting their lives, this will be our number one concern. Until children have strong advocates in the general population, we will champion their cause. Our call is for the whole of church and society to share the urgency of this mission. . . .

Now in the final decade of the 20th century and with more than 100 years behind us, the Women's Division is engaged in invigorating our programs with women, children and youth. We have initiated new structures with the other units of the General Board of Global Ministries to ensure that these concerns are given higher priority. Both the National and World Divisions of the Board have established offices that deal primarily with ministries with women and, in the World Division with children and youth as well. These offices keep before the divisions and the church special issues and programs. They are catalysts and energizers working with other staff and Board members to sensitize them to the continuing situations of women, children and youth and to provide arenas for networking.

While these things were occurring in the internal structure, other things were occurring in the church and in the society. For example, the 1973 General Conference created an independent General Commission on the Status and Role of Women dedicated to eliminating sexism. Although this move was initiated and strongly supported by the Women's Division, it was seen as a necessity for the whole church.

The Women's Division is a lay movement directed by volunteers and with an executive staff of laywomen. It heartily supports the role of women clergy and the role of women as bishops, but the emphasis of United Methodist Women is toward laywomen's empowerment for mission. . . .

We can go on being "reactive" through programs that take care of people after they are broken, or we can be "transformers" by changing the systems, eliminating barriers and being pro-active. Transformation is riskier, but it is where we believe the Gospel compels us to move.

In humility, we state our belief that the simple and powerful message of liberation is being spoken to and through women, children and youth in a new way today. We believe this is a valuable gift for the whole Church, and we ask for support as we continue to recall, tell and celebrate our story.

Document 20. "Equity and Opportunity, a Continuing Challenge": GCOSROW Challenges the United Methodist and the Ecumenical Church

The General Commission on the Status and Role of Women of the United Methodist Church raises the question of why a major Protestant denomination includes an organization devoted to advocacy of rights and justice for women today. The commission's statement of purpose points both to the historical legacy of almost four centuries and to the continuing challenge of gaining full recognition for the dignity and stature of women in religious institutions and the world.[47]

In its report to General Conference 1992, the Commission celebrates its accomplishments and looks ahead to the challenges that remain.

Consider these statistics:

- 60 percent of the 8,908,741 members of the United Methodist Church are women.
- 10.6 percent of the 42,423 clergy are women, an increase from 1.0 percent in 1970, including 4 women bishops.
- 34.4 percent of delegates to General Conference are women compared with 13.4 percent in 1972.

Concerns that continue

The church has made progress in recognizing, respecting and appreciating the gifts of women, but current trends and data indicate that we have more to do to realize the disciplinary mandate of the Commission. GCOSROW is charged "to challenge The United Methodist church, including its general agencies, institutions, and connectional structures, to a continuing commitment to the full and equal participation of women in the total life and mission of the Church, sharing fully in the power and policy-making and mission of the Church's life." (Para. 2202, *Book of Discipline, 1988.*)

As the church struggles to strengthen the participation of women at all levels, the Commission continues its key role in voicing the needs of women and responding to concerns identified during the quadrennium:

- Pay inequity for persons with the same job descriptions
- Sexual harassment in local churches, general agencies, theological schools
- Uneven pension benefits for lay church employees
- Unfair performance reviews of female general staff members.
- Reorganization of annual conferences and general agencies, which may result in job losses for women
- Discriminatory procedures in clergy appointments
- Underutilization of women's gifts and leadership in the Church. . . .

To determine direction for the work beyond this quadrennium, . . . priority issues reported include:

1. Need for the church to be present in difficult life situations surrounding *controversial issues* faced by women, such as abortion, racism, sexism, and homosexuality.

2. Opportunities for a *more fulfilling spiritual life* for women that include women's unique experiences.

3. *Violence against women,* including tragedies of rape, spouse and child abuse.

4. Special needs of women and men in *challenging living situations* such as single parenting, blended family parenting, child care needs, older adult care, divorce, homelessness and unemployment.

5. The need for increased acceptance of *women in leadership* positions and increased collegiality among women leaders.

6. Visible and positive *role models* for young women and men.

7. Continued threat of *sexual harassment* in the work place, both in the church and in the secular arenas.

8. Need for *equal opportunity* for women in the ministry including salary, benefits, and career advancement.

9. Ways for the church community to be in *solidarity with women* throughout the global community.

10. More examples of *collegial working styles* and change in structures to accommodate the different styles of operation.

Responding to the issues reported by the constituents of the General Commission will take constant attention, sensitivity, commitment, and vigilance by the Church as a whole community of God's people. In the spirit of the 1988 resolution to participate in an "Ecumenical Decade: Churches in Solidarity with Women," men of the Church and in society are joining women in acts of reformation and even recreation. It will be important for men and women to be in partnership as the issues are addressed.

CHAPTER THREE

Women
and Religious Practice
in American Judaism

Ann Braude

Documents

THE first Jews arrived on the North American continent in 1654 when twenty-three Dutch Jews landed at the port of New Amsterdam. By the end of the seventeenth century, they had gained the right of public worship and established the Portuguese-speaking Congregation Shearith Israel (the remnant of Israel). As late as 1820 there were only about three thousand Jews in the United States, about half of them Sephardic (Spanish, Portuguese, or Mediterranean) and half Ashkenazic (western and eastern European). Between 1820 and 1880, two or three hundred thousand Jews arrived as part of a mass migration from Germany. These German Jews and their children were the dominant force in the emergence of American Judaism during the nineteenth century.[1]

The vast majority of American Jews trace their ancestry to the flood of immigration from Russia and eastern Europe that accompanied increasing anti-Semitism and anti-Jewish violence beginning in the 1880s. This group would total about three million before the United States closed its doors to immigrants in 1923. During and after World War II about a quarter million Jews gained entrance to the country, many of them survivors of concentration camps, all of them dislocated by Nazi atrocities. During the 1970s and '80s over 150,000 Jews emigrated to the United States from the Soviet Union, with additional immigrants coming from Israel, Iran, and other countries in the Middle East. Since the destruction of European Jewry by the Nazis, American Jews have comprised the largest Jewish community in the world. As of 1992 approximately six million Jews live in North America, comprising 2.4 percent of the population of the United States and 1.2 percent of the Canadian population.[2]

WOMEN IN JEWISH TRADITION

Judaism is based on a covenant between God and the Jewish people, in which the people agree to do the will of God as given to them in his law, the Torah. Halachah, the body of Jewish law derived from the Torah and the Talmud, governs not only synagogue ritual but every aspect of life, from the preparation and serving of food to economic activities and sexual relations. For Jews who live in accordance with the law, every action performed in fulfillment of the law is sanctified as a religious obligation (mitzvah). This means that centuries-old beliefs and practices about the

different roles and natures appropriate for men and women are not simply a matter of tradition but are codified in religious law.

The law specifies very different roles for men and women, both in
religious practice and in areas considered to be matters of civil law in
contemporary America (marriage and divorce, for example). Of the 613
commandments incumbent on adult males, women were exempted from
those that had to be performed at a specific time, because time-bound
obligations were considered to conflict with their roles as bearers and
nurturers of children and homemakers. While Orthodox Jews hold that
this reflects a sanctification of the different roles of men and women
(document 9), others question whether women are actually included in
the covenant if they are not bound by all its commandments (document
6). Many debates in contemporary Judaism hinge on whether "exemption" of women from important mitzvot means that they are incapable of
performing those religious duties and must be excluded from them or
whether it means that although women are not required to observe those
mitzvot they may voluntarily assume those obligations and fulfill them
equally with male Jewish adults (documents 4, 7).

In normative rabbinic Judaism, the exemption of women from certain religious obligations was interpreted as disqualifying them for those
mitzvot. Thus women could not be counted in the minyan of ten adults
required for public prayer. Because a minyan was required, they could
not say kaddish, the memorial prayer for the dead, for their own parents.
They could not serve as witnesses. Because daily public prayer was not a
commandment for women, and women's voices and appearance might
arouse men and distract them from their prayers, women were secluded
behind a barrier (mechitza) in the synagogue, far from the bimah, where
men read from the holy Torah. In addition, married women were required to wear wigs to hide the attractiveness of their own hair.

In early American history, similar restrictions on women were shared
by many religious groups. Separate seating for men and women was
common, as were requirements for modesty in dress and the belief that it
was improper for women to speak in public. When the Protestant evangelist Charles Grandison Finney encouraged women to pray aloud in
"promiscuous assemblies" comprised of both men and women in the
1830s, he was roundly condemned. But as the nineteenth century wore

on, American Protestants drifted away from the practice of separate seating and from squeamishness about women's voices in public worship.

But for Jews separate seating, like virtually every limitation on women's role, was not simply a practice that could drift out of style; it was a law incumbent upon the Jewish people as a whole in fulfillment of their covenant with God. Every question about lifting restrictions on women's religious practice involved a basic challenge to long-accepted interpretations of Jewish faith. Change required confrontation with the basic understanding of Jewish law as a comprehensive system that could be elaborated but never reduced. Even traditions that could not be traced directly to the Torah were considered to be religious obligations if they helped build "a hedge around the Torah" to encourage observance of other commandments. Attempts to expand women's religious role aroused fears about the loss of the religious distinctiveness that generation upon generation of Jews had struggled so hard to preserve.

While normative or rabbinic Judaism excluded women from many religious practices, Jewish women over the centuries developed their own traditions for the sanctification of everyday life. As in most cultures where there is a high degree of sex segregation, rituals performed exclusively by women in some ways constituted an unofficial parallel religion from which men were excluded. The rabbis recognized four "women's mitzvot": lighting Sabbath candles in the home; setting aside a sacred portion while baking challah (egg bread) for the Sabbath; following the laws governing the separation of husbands and wives during and after menstruation (niddah); and purifying oneself in the mikvah (ritual bath) following menstrual separation. Women had their own prayer books, printed in the vernacular. These contained techinot (supplicatory or devotional prayers) for the specific events of a woman's life, including prayers for the safe delivery of a child, prayers for the safe return of a husband from a journey, prayers for a woman married to an irreligious husband, and so forth.[3] In addition, many of men's ritual obligations, such as following dietary restrictions and observing the Sabbath, could not be fulfilled without the active cooperation of wives and mothers.

Since Jews came to America, questions about women's role in Judaism have sparked constant debate and inspired broad religious innovation. The great internal debate of American Judaism in the nineteenth century was what amount of American practice could be adopted before religious practice ceased to be Jewish. Americanization and the participation of women in public worship reform were converging trends that encouraged a new religious role for women.

JEWISH WOMEN IN THE NINETEENTH CENTURY

Although considering themselves orthodox, early American Jews showed great flexibility about adapting to American standards for women's participation in public worship. The letters of Rebecca Gratz (document 1) are among the most vivid and intimate accounts of American Jewish life before the beginning of the German immigration. She and her gentile sisters-in-law read the Bible and other religious books together and discussed them in their letters. The ease and frankness of their religious discussions shows a remarkable lack of friction between their faiths. Gratz's description of the 1826 dedication of the new synagogue of Philadelphia's Mikveh Israel Congregation suggests that Jews accepted certain American practices without question until later arrivals from Europe reasserted more traditional practices. The mixed choir that sang at the dedication ceremony attracted attention only for the sweetness of its song, while the propriety of mixed choirs was much debated over the next decades because of the traditional view that women's voices caused sexual arousal in men.

The German Jews who came to the United States in the nineteenth century brought with them a new movement that hoped to preserve the essence of Judaism while modernizing its rituals and practices to bring them in accord with the dictates of reason and of modern life—the Reform movement. Reform Jews wanted to participate fully in the opportunities offered by life in America, and they were anxious to shed traditional practices that stood as barriers between themselves and other Americans. To them menstrual taboos, dietary restrictions, and other traditions practiced by women seemed embarrassingly archaic. The Reform movement made women the religious equals of the male laity. Isaac Meyer Wise, the leader of the American Reform movement, advocated sweeping changes in women's religious status. Besides counting women as full congregational members, seating them in the main body of the synagogue, and extending equal access to religious education, Wise deleted the word *obey* from the marriage ceremony, instituting reciprocal vows to replace the traditional marriage ceremony in which the woman was silent and passive. He also advocated women's suffrage and ordination, but neither of these was instituted during his lifetime.[4]

The Reform movement and the lack of facilities, such as mikvahs (ritual baths) and kosher food, discouraged the traditional religious activities of Jewish women: going to the mikvah, keeping kashrut (dietary laws), and keeping the Sabbath in the home. With some significant exceptions, the architects of Reform Judaism found that male religious practices were rational and essential and should be preserved, while women's practices were irrational and outmoded and should be abandoned. This peculiar bargain, of being offered equality in exchange for the abandonment of women's practices, often placed women in the position of the defenders of orthodoxy. Women controlled whether their families observed dietary restrictions as well as whether they and their husbands observed the laws of ritual purity. In the United States the "kitchen religion" of Jewish mothers sometimes outlasted religious observance by husbands and sons. The first synagogue in Chicago, Kehilath Anshe Mayriv, is said to have been founded because a pious woman, Dilah Cohn, refused to eat meat that was not kosher. Her sons, unwilling to see their mother subsist on vegetables, organized a congregation able to support a kosher butcher.[5]

Women who accepted the Reform movement rechanneled their religious lives into the formerly male realm of the synagogue. They were included in confirmation classes and Sunday schools, often making a majority of both students and teachers. The expanding role of women in the synagogue was not limited to the Reform movement. Women committed to tradition saw themselves as guardians of orthodoxy in the synagogue as well as the kitchen, just as their Christian contemporaries saw themselves as the guardians of Christian piety. In response to the radical reforms adopted by Congregation Beth Elohim in Charleston, a group of women started a coeducational religious school. The Jewish press noted that "this sacred and laudable undertaking emanates from the mothers and daughters of Israel who are opposed to the innovations lately established in this congregation, and whose zeal and energies will be actively employed in impressing upon the tender minds of their pupils the *orthodox* tenets of our religion."[6]

EMIGRATION FROM RUSSIA AND EASTERN EUROPE

Starting in 1881, tens of thousands of Jews each year fled the poverty and persecution of Russia and Eastern Europe to make new lives in the "Goldene Medina" (golden land) of America, which was said to offer a life of freedom and riches. Among the three million Jews who arrived from eastern Europe was a larger proportion of women than in any other immigrant group arriving during this period. While some immigrant groups consisted mainly of men who hoped to save money and then return to their homelands, Jewish immigrants had no homeland to which to return. They staked all their hopes on the prospect of a new life in America. They came as families, and they came to stay.

The majority of Jews who arrived in the United States disembarked at Ellis Island and made their way to Manhattan's Lower East Side as soon as they had cleared customs. Crowded into an area of a few square blocks, hundreds of thousands of Jews from all over Europe lived, worked, and worshiped in the same tenement buildings. Suddenly freed both from hundreds of years of censorship *and* from traditional European sex roles, Jewish women approached the challenge of forging a new life in America with immeasurable vitality.

Jewish women poured energy and determination into the maintenance of family life in the ghetto. A typical tenement floor contained four apartments of two or three rooms, each housing a family with several children, with a front room reserved for boarders.[7] Unmarried women and girls went into the sweatshops, while married women labored under equally oppressive conditions. In the crowded kitchens of tenement apartments, married women cooked and did laundry for boarders and fed their families in shifts, whenever this one or that one returned from the shop. Whether women wanted to adopt American ways or maintain traditions, poverty stood in the way (document 2). Homemakers struggled to keep Jewish observance alive in the ghetto. Settlement worker Lillian Wald wrote of one woman she visited on a Friday afternoon who had put two kettles of water on the stove to boil so that her neighbors would not know that she was unable to fulfill her sacred obligation to prepare a special meal for her family on the Sabbath.[8]

Crossing the Atlantic was not simply a geographic transition. Jews packed their bags in the semifeudalism of czarist Russia and disembarked in the most modern city in the world, New York. The Judaism they brought with them was embedded in cultural forms of another time and place. The customs of early marriage and large families facilitated men's halachic duty to procreate but also reflected the different economic and social conditions in the Old World and the New. To some Jews, America meant freedom to practice their religion unharassed. To others, it meant freedom from Judaism—freedom from religious authority and from the pressure to conform to the standards of the Jewish community. For all, life in America presented a conflict between a deeply ingrained heritage and the appeal of Americanization (document 3). For women, subject to men within Judaism, American ways had a special appeal. Novelist Mary Antin, in her paean to America, *The Promised Land,* lamented her sister's early marriage, which she attributed to the fact that at the time the family emigrated her sister was too old to attend school and "imbibe American ideas." Antin felt it was "a pitiful accident that my sister should have come so near and missed by so little the fulfillment of my country's promise to women."[9]

The sheitel, the wig worn by married women to hide the attractiveness of their own hair, visibly distinguished recently arrived "greenhorns," still immersed in traditional Jewish culture, from women who had adopted some measure of American values and dared to show their own hair. For mothers, the conflict between the new world and the old was experienced every day when their children returned from school, the primary vehicle of Americanization.

Jewish families were quick to take advantage of the public schools. In the old country, the chief function of education was to provide religious training for boys, so girls received little or no education. In the United States, the public schools brought boys and girls into the same classroom. So anxious were parents and teachers to have their children enjoy the benefits of life in America that Americanization was often encouraged at the expense of respect for Jewish traditions. Julia Richmond, the German Jewish district superintendent of the Lower East Side schools, forbade the use of Yiddish, the "mama loshen" (mother tongue) spoken in the Jewish home. Children caught speaking Yiddish to one another at recess had their mouths washed out with soap. In the attempt to Americanize immigrant children, the public schools taught them that their heritage was un-American and lower class.[10] Parents who spoke

Yiddish to their children were answered in English. It was often repeated: "In America, children become the teachers of their parents." Mothers who did not work outside the home had the least contact with American institutions and might become embarrassments to their acculturated children. Stories with titles like "Embarrassed by Mother" pervaded the Jewish press.[11] Children learned contempt for their families and their heritage in the public schools and from the examples of German Jews and other Americans. Educators used the "oriental conception of woman's status" held by Jews to condemn Jewish tradition.[12] America offered women opportunities for self-fulfillment clothed in anti-Semitism.

WOMEN AND RELIGIOUS OBSERVANCE BEFORE THE 1970s

"Perhaps the single most disruptive force . . . to American Jewish Orthodoxy," wrote the sociologist Marshall Sklare, "has been the position of woman." He found that failure to adapt to the American norm in which women supply the bulk of time, energy, and money for the maintenance of religious institutions would have meant "organizational suicide" for American Judaism.[13] Indeed, once exposed to American freedom, many Jewish women could not accept the restrictions placed on them by Jewish traditions. Emily Solis-Cohen, Jr., was shocked by the attitudes she encountered during fieldwork for the Jewish Welfare Board in 1932.

> It was disturbing to encounter, the country over, the notion that in respect to proscribed religious observances, to the conduct of public worship, to education, even to some phases of domestic life, Jewish law discriminates in favor of the sons of Israel, and that such favor springs from its fundamental attitude toward Israel's daughters. Personal experiences of many a girl are cited by her, as warrant for the assertion that apparently "woman does not count in Jewish life."[14]

Solis-Cohen, like Hadassah founder Henrietta Szold, accepted the view that exemptions from positive commandments "arise from a consideration rather than a disregard for women."[15] Szold extended the logic of this view to argue that the rabbis never intended to disqualify women from the mitzvot but only to excuse them. Having no maternal or household responsibilities with which religious duties would interfere, she did not believe that she was exempt from the ritual obligation of saying kaddish when her mother died in 1916, a responsibility usually limited to sons (document 4). This line of reasoning has been adopted by Jewish women across the religious spectrum who have taken on obligations formerly limited to men (document 7).

Sklare attributed the great success of Conservative Judaism to the increased role allotted to women. The Conservative Movement, which tried to adapt Judaism to American life without departing from the process of historical development, followed exactly the Protestant model of "formal equality coupled with limited participation." Women were seated with men in services and joined them in liturgical responses. However, the principle of equality was not extended to the most important part of the ritual, the handling and reading of the Torah scrolls, much less to ordination of women as rabbis. Conservatism enjoyed enormous success among the postimmigrant generation, becoming the largest sector of American Judaism during the 1950s and '60s.[16]

The incorporation of women into the synagogue service had also been a significant factor in the success of the Reform movement in the nineteenth century, which represented almost all American congregations until the influx of Jews from eastern Europe, beginning in the 1880s, introduced more traditional forms of worship. Across the religious spectrum there has been a persistent (though still incomplete) trend toward greater inclusion of women in religious practice. The bat mitzvah, in which girls, paralleling the bar mitzvah ceremony for boys, are called to the bimah and own the covenant, began in the Reconstructionist movement and was slowly adopted by other groups. The first bat mitzvah ceremony took place in 1922, celebrated by Judith Kaplan (later Eisenstein), daughter of Mordecai Kaplan, founder of Reconstructionism.[17] Until the late sixties bat mitzvahs in Conservative congregations were generally held on Friday nights, when the Torah is not read.

No less than Reform and Conservative Jews, Orthodox Jews were faced with American sex roles, in which women had freedom and opportunities unheard of in the old country. During the twenties, one Orthodox rabbi observed that the debate over seating women behind a curtain in the synagogue was so heated that "congregations are formed or dissolved" over it.[18] Another found that "the modern Jewess, more than the modern Jew, is responsible for the disintegration of our faith," because women were not spending enough time at home creating a "Jewish atmo-sphere."[19] Although the Orthodox have emphasized the benefits of traditional sex roles over the need for change, some Orthodox leaders responded to the American scene with a resolve to offer women increased opportunities within traditional Judaism. Yeshiva University, itself an adaptation to the desire of Orthodox youth for secular education, opened a high school for girls in 1948. In 1954 Yeshiva opened Stern College for Women, where students could pursue a collegiate program combined with an extensive Jewish curriculum under Orthodox auspices.[20]

FEMINISM AND RELIGIOUS INNOVATION

The emergence of the second wave of American feminism in the 1970s owed a substantial debt to the traditions of social activism and social crit-icism in the Jewish community. American Jewish women have always been activists, pouring enormous energy and commitment into building communal institutions like schools and hospitals, as well as supporting and leading a variety of political and social movements like labor, con-sumer advocacy, and socialism. The National Council of Jewish Women, founded by Hannah Solomon in 1893, addressed the needs of women among Russian immigrants during the early twentieth century and con-tinues to focus on issues like domestic violence (document 3).[21] Femi-nism continued the commitment to equality for women expressed by the women of the Zionist movement, who outnumbered men during the early twentieth century. The early women Zionists were visionary ideal-ists who worked to gain equal rights both for homeless Jews and for men and women. They envisioned a binational state of Arabs and Jews, which would be a model to the world of justice and cooperation (document 5). Hadassah, the Women's Zionist Organization of America, was founded in 1911 by Henrietta Szold to provide health care for the residents of Palestine. It was America's first national Zionist organization and has remained the largest. "The Zionist organization," according to Szold, "since it believes in the equality of men and women, must educate Jew-ish women not only to Judaism but to a realization of their civic and national responsibilities."

Betty Freidan, author of *The Feminine Mystique* and founder of the National Organization of Women, attributed her concern for women's rights to her "passion against injustice, which originated from my feelings of the injustice of anti-semitism."[22] Other Jewish founders of feminism include Gloria Steinem and Letty Cottin Pogrebin, cofounders of *Ms.* magazine; former Congresswoman Bella Abzug; and authors Grace Paley, Phyllis Chessler, and Andrea Dworkin—all of whom joined together for women's Passover seders during the formative years of the women's movement.[23] As Pogrebin recalled in her essay "Anti-Semitism in the Women's Movement," Jewish values might inspire feminist activism, but the movement they helped create was not always willing to accept their religious identities.[24]

But while the impact of Judaism on feminism may be somewhat covert, no observer could miss the impact of feminism on Judaism during the last twenty years. The desire of women to participate fully in their religion has been one of the most creative forces in recent developments in liturgy, theology, and piety (documents 8, 10, 11).

The Reform movement finally lived up to its promise of equality for women with the ordination of Sally Priesand in 1972. The Reconstructionists followed suit in 1974 with the ordination of Sandy Eisenberg Sasso.[25] Women quickly came to comprise half of the entering class at the Hebrew Union College (Reform) and a majority of students at the Reconstructionist Seminary. But because neither of these groups recognize observance of Jewish law as the basis for religious practice, these events did not send the shock waves that would emanate from the demands of women in more conservative sectors of Judaism. The same year that Sally Priesand was ordained, a group of young, well-educated Conservative women calling themselves Ezrat Nashim (the name used for the women's section of an Orthodox synagogue) began lobbying for lay rights for Conservative women. They went before the Rabbinical Assembly, whose Committee on Jewish Law and Standards establishes the legal precepts of Conservative Judaism. In an extremely controversial decision, the Assembly extended to women the right to be counted in a minyan and to be called to the Torah but stopped short of declaring women to be fully obligated Jews with responsibilities for religious observance equal to those of Jewish men.[26]

The following year Rachel Adler davened (prayed) with tallith (prayer shawl) and tefillin (phylacteries) at the first National Jewish Women's Conference. This startling action became a model for other women, who started experimenting with sacred practices that had never been performed by women before (document 7). In the midseventies a group of college students at Brown University started a women's minyan and published a women's prayer book that adhered to traditional religious forms but used specifically female language and imagery to refer to God.[27]

In 1983 the Faculty Assembly of the Conservative Jewish Theological Seminary (JTS) voted to admit women as rabbinical students. The swiftness of change following this decision indicates the readiness of many segments of the Jewish community to accept women's leadership and the ambivalence of American Jews toward religious law. Eighteen female students comprised half of the entering class of JTS the following year. The first woman rabbi ordained by the Conservative movement was Amy Eilberg in May 1985. In 1987 JTS began awarding women the diploma of *hazzan* (cantor), previously awarded only to men.[28]

While some Jewish women felt alienated from the tradition because they felt excluded, others felt motivated to challenge that exclusion because of their desire to observe Judaism more fully. In the late 1970s, Orthodox women began organizing their own prayer groups in order to be able to fulfill mitzvot that Jewish law prohibits women from performing in the presence of men or that allows them to perform only if a man is unavailable. Such groups meet on Shabbat mornings to conduct a full service, with the exception of prayers requiring a minyan of ten men. Because men are not present, they cannot be distracted by women's voices, and women are halachically permitted to lead prayers and to read from the Torah scroll. In a way, these women's prayer groups represent a more radical departure from Jewish gender expectations than the egalitarian models pursued first within the Reform movement and now, more cautiously, in Conservative Judaism as well. Rather than incorporating women into the male-dominated sphere of the synagogue, these groups create a space within Jewish ritual that is completely controlled by women.

Orthodox male religious authorities have universally condemned women's prayer groups. In 1984 a group of rabbis from Yeshiva University issued a responsum declaring such groups prohibited by Jewish law on the grounds that they falsify the Torah, that they are against Jewish tradition, and that they result from the influence of non-Jews in the feminist movement. Ironically, the rabbis accused women whose goal was to increase their observance of Jewish law with being influenced by non-Jewish practices. As Rivka Haut, a leader of the movement for Orthodox women's prayer groups, observed, "The rabbis who signed the responsum are apparently not aware that many Jewish women were among the founders of the feminist movement." In response to rabbinic condemnation, she and Judy Bernstein founded the Women's Tefillah Network in 1985 to provide resources and support for Orthodox women who want to form their own prayer groups.[29]

At the same time that increased inclusion is demanded by women in all segments of Judaism, the traditional path of the Jewish wife and mother whose spirituality focuses on maintenance of the home and family exerts a renewed appeal to women who feel alienated by the materialism, sexual exploitation, and instability of secular culture. The ba'alat teshuvah, the woman who rejects modern expectations for fulfillment in favor of a strictly observant lifestyle, has become a familiar figure in discussions of contemporary Judaism. The family-centered culture of Orthodoxy and Hasidism has attracted secular Jews, converts, and even an occasional feminist.[30] Like Judaism itself, these women defy the predictions of social scientists who saw secularization as a one-way street and assimilation into a predominantly Christian culture as inevitable for American Jews. By choosing to struggle with their tradition's challenges in a variety of ways, American Jewish women are bringing the same vitality to their religious lives that made their grandmothers legendary as bulwarks of the immigrant communities.

Havdalah (which means division, or separation), the ritual that observes the departure of the Sabbath, is performed over a cup of wine and is celebrated with a special candle made of two or more braided wicks, as in this summer camp for girls.

Woman on the Brooklyn Bridge reading Tasklikh (c. 1910), a ceremony performed on the first day of Rosh Hashanah, the days of repentance, traditionally at a body of water, in accordance with Micah 7:19: "I will cast their sins into the depths of the sea."

Henrietta Szold, founder of Hadassah, the Woman's Zionist Organization of America. Here she speaks to another group she founded, the Youth Alizah, which rescued thousands of Jewish children from the Nazis and relocated them in Palestine.

A women's minyan reading the Torah together at Brown University in the 1990s. Formerly, such religious assemblies were made up only of men.

Documents

Document 1. Rebecca Gratz, "Letters to Maria": Women in Early American Judaism

Rebecca Gratz (1781–1869) was born into a well-established Jewish family in Philadelphia, where she helped sustain a variety of voluntary organizations serving both Jews and non-Jews. In 1838 she founded the Hebrew Sunday School, the first Jewish Sunday school, which she served as superintendent for thirty-two years. The letter below was written to her brother's Christian wife, Maria.[31]

That which you call the misfortune of single ladies, My dear Sister, is in my case converted into a blessing—for by sharing the troubles I gain admittance into the affections of my friends—and what should I do with the heart nature had given me if all its warm pulsations were to beat against closed bosoms? . . .

I had my philosophy a little tried the other day by some good Christians, and as I dare not complain about it to anybody else (for I hate to set the subject in its true light at home)—I must make you my confidante—You know I promised our friend Mrs. Furness to apply for a little girl out of the Asylum for her—well there is a good little girl I have kept my eye on and she is ready for a place—and my application is rejected because it is for a Unitarian—but "Ladies," said I, "there are many children under my special direction—you all know my creed—suppose I should want one to bring up in my family?" "You may have one," said a church woman—"because the Jews do not think it a duty to convert"—but said a Presbyterian "I should not consent to her being put under the influence of a Unitarian"—and so my dear after putting the question to vote—I could get nothing—and when the meeting broke up, had a mischievous pleasure in telling one of the most blue of the board that I construed their silence into consent—for only one lady voted in the affirmative—and they were all ashamed to vote no—but I do not mean to let Mrs. F. know how she is proscribed, because notwithstanding my own position, I am ashamed of such an illiberal spirit—I got into a long discussion on the subject of religion, with a lady after the meeting and though we have been more than twenty years acquainted—I expect she will look shy on me for the rest of our lives— what a pity that the best and holiest gift of God to his most favored creatures, should be perverted into a subject of strife—and that to seek to know and love the most High should not be the end and aim of all— without a jealous or persecuting feeling towards each other. . . .

Document 2. Anzia Yezierska, Selection from *Bread Givers*: A Struggle Between a Father of the Old World and a Daughter of the New

Anzia Yezierska's (1885–1970) realistic stories of Jewish immigrant life on New York's Lower East Side emphasize the conflict between traditional Jewish ways and the new freedoms available to women in America. This excerpt from her novel *Bread Givers* suggests the elaboration of Jewish women's religious disabilities in popular culture.[32]

When we came to America, instead of taking along feather beds, and the samovar, and the brass pots and pans, like other people, Father made us carry his books. When Mother begged only to take along her pot for gefulte fish, and the two feather beds that were handed down to her from her grandmother for her wedding presents, Father wouldn't let her.

"Woman!" Father said, laughing into her eyes. "What for will you need old feather beds? Don't you know it's always summer in America? And in the new golden country, where milk and honey flows free in the streets, you'll have new golden dishes to cook in, and not weigh yourself down with your old pots and pans. But my books, my holy books always were, and always will be, the light of the world. You'll see yet how all America will come to my feet to learn."

No one was allowed to put their things in Father's room. . . . Of course, we all knew that if God had given Mother a son, Father would have permitted a man child to share with him his best room in the house. A boy could say prayers after his father's death—that kept the father's soul alive for ever. Always Father was throwing up to Mother that she had borne him no son to be an honor to his days and to say prayers for him when he died.

The prayers of his daughters didn't count because God didn't listen to women. Heaven and the next world were only for men. Women could get into Heaven because they were wives and daughters of men. Women had no brains for the study of God's Torah, but they could be the servants of men who studied the Torah. Only if they cooked for the men, and washed for the men, and didn't nag or curse the men out of their homes; only if they let the men study the Torah in peace, then, maybe, they could push themselves into Heaven with the men, to wait on them there.

And so, since men were the only people who counted with God, Father not only had the best room for himself, for his study and prayers, but also the best eating of the house. The fat from the soup and the top from the milk went always to him.

Mother had just put the soup pot and plates for dinner on the table, when Father came in.

At the first look on Mother's face he saw how she was boiling, ready to burst, so instead of waiting for her to begin her hollering, he started:

"Woman! when will you stop darkening the house with your worries?"

"When I'll have a man who does the worrying. Does it ever enter your head that the rent was not paid the second month? That to-day we're eating the last loaf of bread that the grocer trusted me?" Mother tried to squeeze the hard, stale loaf that nobody would buy for cash. "You're so busy working for Heaven that I have to suffer here such bitter hell."

We sat down to the table. With watering mouths and glistening eyes we watched Mother skimming off every bit of fat from the top soup into Father's big plate, leaving for us only the thin, watery part. We watched Father bite into the sour pickle which was special for him only; and waited, trembling with hunger, for our portion.

Father made his prayer, thanking God for the food. Then he said to Mother:

"What is there to worry about, as long as we have enough to keep the breath in our bodies? But the real food is God's Holy Torah." He shook her gently by the shoulder, and smiled down at her.

At Father's touch Mother's sad face turned into smiles. His kind look was like the sun shining on her.

"Shenah!" he called her by her first name to show her he was feeling good. "I'll tell you a story that will cure you of all your worldly cares."

All faces turned to Father. Eyes widened, necks stretched, ears strained not to miss a word. The meal was forgotten as he began.

Document 3. Hannah Solomon, Selections from *A Sheaf of Leaves:* The National Council of Jewish Women

In 1890 Hannah Greenebaum Solomon (1858–1942) was asked to organize a nationwide Congress of Jewish Women for the World's Parliament of Religions at the World's Columbian Exposition in Chicago. Through her efforts she brought together leading women from Jewish communities across the nation. At her urging, the congress resolved itself into a permanent organization, the National Council of Jewish Women. The council, composed primarily of Reform German Jews, became the first national Jewish women's organization in the United States, with Solomon as its president. The following excerpt is from an address at Sinai Temple in Chicago, February 14, 1897.[33]

. . . The position of woman today might have been foretold at the beginning, when, instead of creating her out of dust, the Lord waited until he could build her out of a strong, healthy, germ-proof bone. I would not say that the woman who places herself before the public in any way escapes criticism; yet it is not the persecution our pioneers received, and while it may sting, it is only for a moment. We are prepared to have those dear, good homemakers—the bachelors—mourn over our neglected children, and wonder how our husbands manage without us. But she who now enters any field finds many outstretched hands to lighten the way which once was thorny, friendless, cheerless. One word of encouragement to a strong heart is so powerful an elixir that it counteracts thousands of unkind ones. . . .

We cannot ignore the fact that the generation preceding ours observed so many forms and ceremonies that Judaism was ever present. We are removed but one generation from those who in love, reverence, and fear obeyed every injunction. We can all remember when no Jews would have opened the doors of their business houses from sunset to sunset upon holy days. To many of our own generation the ceremonial and the holiday have lost their appeal, and their hearts must be touched through the intellectual. We are in our day confronted by a question that has over and over troubled Israel: is Judaism worth saving? To some this question seems heresy. The daughters of Moses Mendelssohn and their friends solved it for themselves, deserting in the time when Israel was emerging from its gloom into the glorious day of religious liberty. From many the religious spirit is departing altogether. The world is asking: Is any religion worth saving? . . .

Women cling to old customs, and love their traditions, and often compel conservatism where radical thought would prevail. That this movement was undertaken by women was therefore natural. That we would have many critics was to be expected. Nothing is more deplorable than the attitude of the rabbis and the Jewish journals toward each other. How should we expect to escape where none, however excellent, are spared? We are criticized for the subjects we attempt to study, or to write upon. In order to stimulate thought and encourage individual effort, we write papers—some of us very bad ones, others very good. But there are worse ways of passing one's leisure moments. It cannot be proven that the sick children are always the unfortunate ones of mothers who write papers. As long as they are not compelled to listen to them, the children are comparatively safe.

. . . During the past year the council in its cities had seventy-five study circles varying in membership from five to two hundred, besides many lectures. The classes are led in many cases by rabbis; the interest is growing and we look forward enthusiastically to the coming winter's work. We have established nine mission schools, reaching several thousand children who are being instructed in our religion and ethics, and it is needless to say that their ranks are entirely made up of Jewish children. Many women have been placed upon the school boards of Sabbath-schools through our efforts, and many Sabbath-schools have been established by our members in cities where no synagogues exist. In our philanthropic department but few difficulties have presented themselves. One and all of our sections eagerly discuss philanthropic subjects and without exception they have adopted the newest methods of work.

Not a single almsgiving society exists. Our philanthropies take the form of industrial schools—sewing, manual training, kindergarten, creche, summer outing and personal service. In addition several thousand dollars were raised for the army and navy. If the deed is the supreme test of religion, then does our faith, as exemplified in this branch of our work, reach the highest ideal.

Document 4. Henrietta Szold to Haym Peretz: "On Saying Kaddish"

For many Jewish women, being excluded from saying kaddish (the memorial prayer for the dead) for one's own parent marks an acute revelation of the exclusion of women from Jewish tradition. When Henrietta Szold's (1860–1945) mother died, she wrote this classic explanation of her decision to recite kaddish herself. Fully committed to traditional Jewish observance, Szold was equally committed to an expanded role for women both in public life and within Judaism. Her belief that Jewish girls should receive the same religious education as boys and be encouraged to perform the same mitzvot presaged similar arguments offered fifty years later. Szold had a literary career as an editor and translator before founding Hadassah, the Women's Zionist Organization of America, and Youth Aliyah, which saved thirty thousand Jewish children from the Nazis and provided homes for them in Palestine.[34]

New York, September 16, 1916

It is impossible for me to find words in which to tell you how deeply I was touched by your offer to act as "*Kaddish*" for my dear mother. I cannot even thank you—it is something that goes beyond thanks. It is beautiful, what you have offered to do—I shall never forget it.

You will wonder, then, that I cannot accept your offer. Perhaps it would be best for me not to try to explain to you in writing, but to wait until I see you to tell you why it is so. I know well, and appreciate what you say about, the Jewish custom; and Jewish custom is very dear and sacred to me. And yet I cannot ask you to say *Kaddish* after my mother.

The *Kaddish* means to me that the survivor publicly and markedly manifests his wish and intention to assume the relation to the Jewish community which his parent had, and that so the chain of tradition remains unbroken from generation to generation, each adding its own link. You can do that for the generations of your family, I must do that for the generations of my family.

I believe that the elimination of women from such duties was never intended by our law and custom—women were freed from positive duties when they could not perform them, but not when they could. It was never intended that, if they could perform them, their performance of them should not be considered as valuable and valid as when one of the male sex performed them. And of the *Kaddish* I feel sure this is particularly true.

My mother had eight daughters and no son; and yet never did I hear a word of regret pass the lips of either my mother or my father that one of us was not a son. When my father died, my mother would not permit others to take her daughters' place in saying the *Kaddish,* and so I am sure I am acting in her spirit when I am moved to decline your offer. But beautiful your offer remains nevertheless, and, I repeat, I know full well that it is much more in consonance with the generally accepted Jewish tradition than in my or my family's conception. You understand me, don't you?

Henrietta Szold

Document 5. Alice Seligsberg, Address to the 1936 Hadassah Convention, and "The Woman's Way: A Brief Analysis of Methods": Hadassah, the Women's Zionist Organization of America

Alice Seligsberg was one of the tight-knit group of early Hadassah leaders who corresponded incessantly as they devoted their lives to Palestine and Zionism. She sailed to Palestine with Hadassah's American Zionist Medical Unit in 1918 and remained for two years as its director.[35]

An Address to the 1936 Hadassah Convention

No statement can be that attributes to the Jews all the virtue, all the strength of argument. Please do not think that I weaken in my conviction in the justice of our cause or that I would apologize to the Arabs. Not for an instant. But I admit that the means we have used, our ways of doing things, have not always been conciliatory. And the means we have failed to use to bring about not only Arab friendship, but understanding of our aims by the other peoples of the East—these omissions we must study, and, if it is still possible, rectify. Let us as Zionists accept responsibility for becoming a dynamic force in the solution of the Arab Jewish problem.

In conclusion, let me say that as all men and women who work for a collective purpose that lifts them out of merely personal concerns are fortunate in acquiring an expanded Self, so each of us has the inward joy and the gain of strength that comes from dynamic Zionism. But our Zionist collective endeavor and the concomitant enlargement of our individual lives through our identification of our own Self with our People, must, if it is to succeed, be seen by us as only a part, only our share, in a still greater endeavor, namely, the creation of a new society in which the interest of every individual, every People, will be in accord with the interests of us all. We must try to see life as a whole. Our collective endeavor, *if it is to succeed*, must be [geared?] to the still greater collective endeavor that is evolving out of the history of mankind.

The Woman's Way: A Brief Analysis of Methods

Instead of recording the achievements of women in the Zionist Movement, let me today rather call attention to the distinctive methods used by women in furthering the Jewish national cause. Hardly anyone will deny that there is a difference of method in the Zionist work of organized women and the organized mass. . . .

Where men interested in Palestine have engaged at one and the same time in many different kinds of undertaking, philanthropic, economic, social, educational—women have concentrated upon the preservation of life (by means of the medical aid already referred to and help given to orphans) though this intensive activity has gradually led them to develop on sidelines. For example, in the Training School for Nurses, and in some of the workshops for orphans established through the initiative of women, one can see how "life-saving" has led them into vocational undertakings that will fit the youth of Palestine to live as self-supporting citizens, who will ultimately contribute to the establishment of normal economic conditions in the country.

If women wish to contribute to the Zionist Movement those talents that are peculiar to women, they must unite as women. One of the explanations of Hadassah's persistence may lie in the desire of all human beings to count for the utmost; and the realization by the Zionist women of America that unless well organized, they will not count at all in the formation of opinion and the control of policies in those matters in which, as women, they have the deepest concern; namely, the protection of the weak, the healing of the afflicted, the safeguarding of the present and future generations.

Document 6. Cynthia Ozick, Excerpts from "Notes Toward Finding the Right Question": A Vindication of the Rights of Jewish Women

Cynthia Ozick (b. 1928), one of the most notable contemporary Jewish writers, explores the often-troubling aspects of modern Jewish life in her many novels, essays, and short stories. This text, originally published in *Lilith* magazine in 1979, sees the obliteration of so much of Jewish culture in the Holocaust as adding a special urgency to the call for equal participation of women in Judaism.[36]

In the world at large I call myself, and am called, a Jew. But when, on the Sabbath, I sit among women in my traditional shul and the rabbi speaks the word "Jew," I can be sure that he is not referring to me. For him, "Jew" means "male Jew."

When the rabbi speaks of women, he uses the expression (a translation from a tender Yiddish phrase) "Jewish daughter." He means it tenderly.

"Jew" speaks for itself. "Jewish daughter" does not. A "Jewish daughter" is someone whose identity is linked to, and defined by, another's role. "Jew" defines a person seen in the light of a culture.

"Daughter" defines a relationship that is above all biological. "Jew" signifies adult responsibility. "Daughter" evokes immaturity and a dependent and subordinate connection.

When my rabbi says, "A Jew is called to the Torah," he never
means me or any other living Jewish woman.

My own synagogue is the only place in the world where I, a
middle-aged adult, am defined exclusively by my being the female child
of my parents.

My own synagogue is the only place in the world where I am not
named Jew. . . .

Though we read in Scripture that Deborah was a judge in Israel,
under post-Biblical halachic rules a woman may not be a witness. In this
debarment she is in a category with children and imbeciles.

In the halachic view, a woman is not a juridical adult.

She is exempted from liturgical and other responsibilities that are
connected with observing a particular practice at a specific time. This, it
is explained, is a compassionate and sensible ruling. What? Shall she be
obliged to abandon the baby at her breast to run to join a prayer quorum at a fixed hour?. . .

Young girls, older women, and unmarried women do not have
babies at their breasts. Where is the extenuating ideal for them? They
are "exempted"—i.e., excluded, debarred—from public worship all
the same.

The halachic rationale for universal female exemption, however, is
not based on compassion for harried mothers, nor is it, as some erro-
neously believe, related to any menstrual taboo. It rests on a single
phrase—*kavod ha-tsibur*—which can be rendered in English as "the
honor (or self-respect) of the community." One infers that a woman's
participation would degrade the community (of men).

I am not shocked by the use of this rationale. (I *am* perhaps
shocked at a halachic scholar of my acquaintance who refers to the
phrase "the honor of the community" as a "concept that seems to defy
comprehension.") Indeed, I welcome this phrase as wonderfully illumi-
nating: it supports and lends total clarity to the idea that, *for Judaism, the
status of women is a social, not a sacred, question.*

Social status is not sacral; it cannot be interpreted as divinely fixed;
it can be repented of, and repaired. . . .

That these protests and claims are occurring in this generation and not in any earlier generation is *not* due to the parallel advent of a movement. The timing is significant: now and not forty years ago: but it is not the upsurge of secular feminism that has caused the upsurge of Jewish feminism.

The timing is significant because the present generation stands in a shockingly new relation to Jewish history. It is we who have come after the cataclysm. We, and all the generations to follow, are, and will continue to be into eternity, witness-generations to Jewish loss. What was lost in the European cataclysm was not only the Jewish past—the whole life of a civilization—but also a major share of the Jewish future. We will never be in possession of the novels Anne Frank did not live to write. It was not only the intellect of a people in its prime that was excised, but the treasure of a people in its potential.

We are the generation that knows more than any generation before us what mass loss means. It means, for one thing, the loss of a culture, and the deprivation of transmittal of that culture. It means lost scholars of Torah—a lost Rashi; a lost Rambam; a lost Baal Shem Tov; a lost Vilna Gaon. The loss of thousands upon thousands of achieved thinkers and physicians, nourishing scientists and artists. The loss of those who would have grown into healers, discoverers, poets. . . .

To think in terms of *having lost so much and so many* is not to "use" the Holocaust, but to receive a share in its famously inescapable message: that after the Holocaust every Jew will be more a Jew than ever before—and not just superficially and generally, but in every path, taken or untaken, deliberate or haphazard, looked-for or come upon.

The consciousness that we are the first generation to stand after the time of mass loss is knowledge that spills inexorably—how could it not?—into every cell of the structure of our lives. What part of us is free of it, or can be free of it? Which regions of discourse or idea or system can we properly declare to be free of it? Who would risk supposing that the so-called "women's issue" can be free of it?

Put beside this view, how trivializing it is to speak of the "influence" of the women's movement—as if Jewish steadfastness could be so easily buffeted by secular winds of power and pressure and new opinion and new perception. The truth is that it would be a blinding mistake to think that the issue of Jewish women's access to every branch and parcel of Jewish expression is mainly a question of "discrimination" (which, if that were all, *would* justify it as a feminist issue). No. The point is not that Jewish women want equality as women with men, but as *Jews with Jews*. The point is the necessity—*having lost so much and so many*—to share Jewish history to the hilt.

Document 7. Amy Eilberg, Excerpts from an Interview by Raye T. Katz: Taking On the Yoke of the Law

Some Jewish women take on ritual obligations previously limited to men in an attempt to participate more fully in their tradition. For Amy Eilberg, the desire for fuller acceptance of Jewish obligations led ultimately to the rabbinate. The first woman Conservative rabbi, Eilberg was ordained in 1985.[37]

I come from a Conservative family, one very strongly identified as Jews on an ethnic and cultural level; *halacha* and ritual observance were not a primary concern in our home. We went to *shul* every now and then—always on the High Holy Days. I went to Hebrew school, lit candles Friday night, had a Bat Mitzvah as a matter of course.

When I was 14, I went on a United Synagogue Youth—USY-on-wheels summer program—a 6 1/2-week cross-country tour. It was my first experience with the traditional Jewish lifestyle: we *davened* (prayed) three times a day, and observed Shabbat very strictly, kept kosher very strictly, in all sorts of very odd places. That was a watershed point in my life. From then on, I got progressively more observant of various *mitzvot* (commanded actions). I started to take my Jewish education much more seriously. By the time I entered college, I knew I wanted to be a Jewish educator. . . .

Two things make [that experience] compelling for me now. One is the sense of connectedness with the faith community, both vertically and horizontal. Vertically, a sense of connection with an ancestral community—with millennia of ancestors—and a connection to the future. And a horizontal community, the community of Jews around the country and around the world with whom I had the sense that I had something special in common, as people who are working toward certain common goals and who share a past and a future.

The other element had to do with my sense of a system that addresses ultimate existential questions about one's place in the world and about God and the meaning of life. I had the sense—I still do—that ritual and liturgical activity represent a structured attempt to respond to some of those basic questions about life.

In 1972, I went to Brandeis. The community was tremendously supportive of women's equality and women's aspirations. It was the dawn of Jewish feminism. A very important feature of the community was Hillel Rabbi Al Axelrad—who took particular interest in helping women come into their own Jewishly.

When I got to Brandeis, the official service at the university had separate seating, no *mechitza* (partition between the sexes during prayer) but an aisle separating women and men, and from women's participation. The freshman class included a bunch of kids who had been in USY and Camp Ramah and some liberal Conservative congregations which were already calling women to the Torah. By the end of that year, we as a group had overturned the policy so that the official service of the university was an egalitarian one—traditional service with mixed seating and full participation by women.

In the spring of my freshman year (1973), the first National Jewish Women's Conference was held. My life was changed by that conference, which I did not even attend. When a friend told me that Rachel Adler had *davened* there with *tallit* (prayer shawl) and *tefillin* (phylacteries), this represented an answer to a question I had been asking.

I had come to Brandeis with a fairly strong traditionalist inclination, but also some feminist or at least egalitarian consciousness. But I did have the sense that the call for equality in the traditionalist Jewish community—by which I included the Conservative movement—would have to take into account the issue of obligation. For me, the blanket call for equality wasn't the whole story. Obligation, however you conceptualize it—from a personally commanding God or a sense of commandedness by God or in a Kaplanian sense of one's obligation to the community—was a concept that had to be factored into the discourse.

. . . I was very much struck by the connection between the *halachic* exemption of women from a whole set of *mitzvot* and women's exclusion from certain roles in the community.

After learning about Adler's action, I decided that I would take on the obligations of *tallit* and *tefillin;* these being only an example of that series of *mitzvot* from which women are exempt. I said to myself—and the community—that I rejected the notion that I was exempt and therefore excluded from a certain set of central activities simply by being a woman, and that by my repudiation of the exemption status I had made myself into the type of woman that the *halacha* would *have* to see as an equal. It was at that point that I began to feel comfortable leading services, reading the Torah. I had a male friend teach me to put on *tefillin*, read, lead services. I began to teach other women to be *shlichot tzibur* (prayer leaders). Two years later I began to think of the rabbinate.

Document 8. Judith Plaskow, "Beyond Egalitarianism": Listening to the Silences

Judith Plaskow is widely recognized for her contributions to contemporary Jewish theology, notably in *Standing Again at Sinai: Judaism from a Feminist Perspective.* She argues that allowing women equal participation in Jewish rituals does not adequately address the limitations of the patriarchal tradition in which they are embedded. Plaskow is professor of religious studies at Manhattan College.[38]

An interesting paradox is emerging in non-Orthodox Jewish communities. The very success of egalitarianism—the gains in equal access for women to educational opportunities and fuller participation in Jewish religious life—has generated new questions and uncertainties about whether egalitarianism is enough. Over the last twenty years, barrier after barrier has fallen before women. We have found ourselves being counted in *minyanim,* going up to the Torah, leading services, becoming ordained as rabbis, and studying Talmud alongside boys and men. These new opportunities, however, have brought women up against the *content* of tradition, and in doing so, have pointed to the need for changes far deeper and more frightening than the process of simply making available to women what all in the community acknowledge to be of value. . . .

Beyond egalitarianism, the way is uncharted. The next step is not nearly so obvious as fighting for *aliyot* or ordination. Beyond egalitarianism, Judaism must be transformed so that it is truly the Judaism of women and men. It must become a feminist Judaism: not a women's Judaism or a Judaism focused on women's issues, but a Judaism that all

Jews have participated in shaping. But how do we move from here to there? How does egalitarianism become the starting point for a fuller process of transformation?

I would suggest that there are at least five stages that any community has to move through on the path from egalitarianism to feminism or genuine equality. My treatment of these stages will be schematic, both because of limitations of space and because the content of any stage will be determined by the needs and problems of particular communities.

The first stage is *hearing silence*. Indeed, the impetus to move beyond egalitarianism stems from hearing the silence of the Jewish tradition and of particular Jewish institutions and events concerning the history and experience of women. Silence is difficult to hear. When a silence is sufficiently vast, it fades into the order of things. We take it for granted as the nature of reality. When I went through three years of graduate school without reading a single word written by a woman, it took me a long time to notice. After all, men are theologians; whom else should we study? Women have a long history of reading ourselves into silence. From childhood bedtime stories to the biblical narratives, from male teachers to male books on male Judaism, women learn to people silences with our own shadowy forms.

Rebekah, Bruriah, and other individual women, a class on women in the Bible or a panel at the Y, are not disproofs of women's silence in Judaism. These are names and occasions we need to turn to *after* we have listened to silence, not in order to fill or deny it. Otherwise we miss the jolts against whose background particular women and events emerge: "you shall not covet your neighbor's wife" (Exod. 20:14) (who is the community being addressed?); the absence of Miriam's prophecy or the record of Huldah's teaching (the hints in normative sources that there is so much more to women's leadership than the sources choose to tell us): a talmudic discussion of whether a girl penetrated before age three should receive her full *ketubah* [marriage contract] (*Ketubot* 11a, b) (would women scholars ever have asked this question?); *a contemporary discussion of this talmudic debate that assumes this is a reasonable question.* Women were agents throughout Jewish history, fashioning and responding to Jewish life and carrying its burdens. But women's perceptions and questions did not give form and content to Scripture, shape the direction of Jewish law, or find expression in liturgy.

The second stage is *making a space to name silence*. Both hearing and naming silence can refer to the large silences of Jewish history or the smaller silences within any particular movement or community. Hearing silence is often a private experience. Whether a community will move beyond egalitarianism is in part determined by whether or not it creates the space for people to name the silences they hear. Often in particular egalitarian communities women's silence is interpreted either as accidental or as personal choice, or it simply leaves people resentful or befuddled. "We just don't happen to have many women who feel competent to lead Torah discussions." "I don't know why more men than women speak. A woman is leading the discussion; anyone can participate." The historical and structural impediments to women's speech thus get dismissed or overlooked, and the community is absolved from responsibility.

Communities need to set aside the time for members to speak the silences they hear. This might happen in an open meeting specifically called for the purpose. Participants might be asked to name the places where they feel silenced or hear women's silence. Discussion must take place initially without judgment and without challenge or cross talk, simply as an opportunity for people to speak their pain and their experience. Sometimes it helps to go around and give each person a chance to say something. Certainly, no one should speak for a second time until everyone who wants to has spoken once. The list of silences would provide a concrete agenda for a community to address.

The third stage is *creating the structures that allow women to speak*. What these structures are in particular contexts will emerge from the list of silences. In congregations where men dominate the Torah discussions, it might be decided that men and women will call on each other in alternation. In a Talmud class where women feel that the text ignores their questions and experiences, it might be agreed that women will lead the discussions for a certain period, with the understanding that the class is there precisely to hear women's questions of and responses to the text. In any context in which women are apparently free to speak but seldom take the opportunity, a program on gender differences in socialization, discourse, and learning styles may help both men and women to understand the personal and institutional barriers to women's participation, and to analyze the gender style of their own institution and events.

Crucial to allowing women to speak are women-only spaces—not women-only spaces that are auxiliaries to male ones, but spaces in which women meet to discuss and explore their experiences as women. Men can listen to women, but, by definition, they cannot be the ones to end women's silence, and there are many forces that prevent women from finding their voices in situations in which men are present.

Women's discussion groups, Rosh Hodesh groups, retreats, and spirituality collectives are spaces in which, to use Nelle Morton's phrase, women "hear each other into speech." These spaces are sources of energy, empowerment, and creativity that potentially enrich the whole Jewish community.

The fourth phase is *taking the authority to fill in silence*. Once silence is named and space created, there is nothing to do but to take courage to speak. This is what is happening all over the country as women compose new blessings and liturgies, create rituals to celebrate important turning points in our lives, research our history and write new midrashim, reclaim our sexuality and explore our concepts of God. This is the phase where we create the *content* of feminist Judaism, and its timeframe is open-ended, its agenda sufficiently broad to include every facet of Judaism.

Much of this exploration and creativity, however, is taking place outside the boundaries of particular Jewish movements or institutions. Whether feminist innovations will ultimately be integrated into the tradition depends to some extent on the earlier phases we have discussed. It is difficult for women to dare to take the authority to speak. But that authority will be acknowledged and welcomed only when members of the larger community open themselves to hearing silence and thus recognize the need for the inclusion of women's voices. Thus, to take one concrete example, through midrash, story-telling, and historiography, women are creating women's Torah. But women's Torah will be accepted and taught as Torah only as Jews acknowledge that at least half of Torah is missing. Will Hebrew Union College or the Jewish Theological Seminary confront the contradiction of educating women in institutions in which Torah is still defined entirely on male terms? That depends on whether they hear the silence built into their curricula.

The last phase is *checking back*. Speaking into silence entails enormous risk. It involves changes that are uncharted and whose direction is finally unpredictable. Not everything spoken into silences will be true or worth saying, and not everything said will finally feel Jewish. Any change that a community takes in the direction of transforming Judaism will necessarily involve feedback and evaluation. Did a particular liturgical or curricular change work? Whom did it empower? Did it create new areas of silence? Did it open new areas of Jewish experience and exploration? Did it feel Jewish? Why or why not? What is our operative understanding of "Jewish," and does it need to be expanded? Would we want to continue our change or experiment again? Would we want to teach the change to our children?

While such evaluation is crucial, it is equally crucial that it *follow* speaking into silence rather than precede it. Too often, questions concerning the appropriateness and boundaries of change are the first ones raised when feminists begin to alter tradition. Judgment is demanded in advance of any real experimentation. Will it be Jewish? is asked as a way of maintaining silence and continuing the status quo. But once we hear the silence of women, it becomes clear that repairing that silence will take all the creativity Jews can muster. Experiments in form, in content, in new relationships between women and men will all be necessary to make Judaism whole. There is time to decide the shape of the Jewish future—but that time is after those who have been silent have spoken.

Document 9. Shaina Sara Handelman, Excerpts from "Modesty and the Jewish Woman": Seeking Holiness Within

The traditional Jewish woman's path to spirituality, emphasizing modesty and inward sanctity, appeals to many women as an alternative to the sexual objectification of modern society. In this document, written for the *Ufrotzo Journal,* a journal of the Lubavitcher Chassidim, Dr. Shaina Sara Handelman criticizes advocates of women's equal participation in Jewish ritual for failing to understand the spirit of the Torah. The author, now known as Susan Handelman, is professor of English and Jewish Studies at the University of Maryland.[39]

In the value-system of Torah, that which is most precious, most sensitive, most potentially holy is that which is most private—in the spiritual as well as the physical realms. The holiest objects, such as the scrolls of Torah, are kept covered. In Torah, "modesty," "inwardness" is a prime spiritual value in contrast to the prevailing norms of contemporary culture, where self-advertisement and public recognition are emphasized. "He has told you, man, what is good and what the L-rd demands from you, but to do justice, love kindness, and to walk *privately* with you G-d" (Michah 6:8). Modesty of dress is an aspect of spiritual modesty, not of shame. The woman who claims that it is liberated to parade her body to anyone, anywhere, is in effect advertising herself as only body—not as a human person. In truth, she shows less sensitivity to the preciousness of her body than one who is "modest."

The desire to fulfill any public role in Jewish life—be it rabbi, cantor, communal leader and so forth—precisely because it is public and one gains recognition thereby is, of course, a most unworthy motive. Today, when for so large a part of the Jewish community, Torah has unfortunately been reduced to little more than a public performance of the most public rituals, and there is so little other content, especially in regard to the cultivation of true inner spirituality, thirsting women have sought to take a greater part in these public actions.

Those women who seek *aliyahs* to the Torah, or to don *tallis* and *tefillin,* etc. must also ask themselves, however, if they are motivated by a desire for a more inward spirituality, or for public recognition, display, and advertisement of self—albeit "spiritual" self. As M. Meiselman writes in *Jewish Women in Jewish Law* (New York: Ktav, 1978, pp. 11–12): "When anyone, male or female, serves G-d, he must concentrate on the inner dimensions of his personality. *Tznius* (modesty) is the inner-directed aspect of striving, the essence of the Jewish heroic act. Women are enjoined to develop this trait of personality to the highest degree." It is not public display in either the physical or spiritual realms that Torah values, but rather one's private actions for the eyes of G-d alone.

Aliyahs to the Torah, *tallis* and *tefillin,* have attracted so much attention because in many instances they are all that has remained of Jewish observance. In truth, however, for the observant Jew, there are 613 commandments, which encompass *every* aspect of life, including life outside the synagogue. Of these 613, 248 commandments are "positive" and 365 are "negative." According to the Talmud, women are equally obligated with men in all the negative *mitzvos,* and in all the positive *mitzvos* which are independent of time. They are, however, exempted (not barred) from those positive *mitzvos* which do depend on time. While no specific reason is given for this, there are many interpretations, among which are that woman's familial duties, because of their high priority, exempt her from time-bound commandments which would be difficult to perform—and that women, because their nature is innately more "in accordance with His will" (as a woman says every morning in her daily blessings), do not need these external reminders: they can achieve the same levels without them. In practice, the number of positive *mitzvos* dependent on time from which women are exempted amounts to about seven, but Jewish women have taken upon themselves almost all of these but *tallis* and *tefillin*. At the same time, women have three *mitzvos* which especially pertain to and are performed by them: the lighting of Shabbos candles, the separation of dough from *challah* for the "priestly portion," and the laws of *mikvah* and Family Purity in the Jewish marriage.

Though men and women are both obligated in prayer, men's obligation is more rigidly and communally defined and required at certain times, and consequently the public functions of the synagogues are more men's province, for the synagogue is the place of communal worship. The synagogue, notwithstanding its importance, has not been, however, the center of Jewish life. Today in America, though, when so little of the practice of Judaism is left in the home—which has been as much if not more the "spiritual center" of Jewish life and is called a "Miniature Temple"—and when the day-to-day lives of so many Jews are devoid of Jewish observance, the synagogue has been made into the only place where Torah can be found, certainly a mistaken idea and one all too similar to non-Jewish ideas about "Houses of Worship."

Though its nature is communal, the synagogue is not a place where there should be competition for public recognition, between men or between men and women. The greatest rabbis of the past had to be begged to assume synagogue positions, so much did they shy away from all manner of public recognition. *Chazzanim* (Cantors) who sought to show off their voices were ridiculed. Indeed, the culmination of the prayer service is *not* the *aliyah* to the Torah, but the most elevated prayer in the Jewish liturgy, the *Shemoneh Essray,* or *Amidah,* the "Silent Prayer" where each Jew stands most *intimately* and *privately* before G-d. And this prayer, which is the very center and core of Jewish worship—is modelled after the prayer of a woman, Chanah, as related in Samuel I.1:13, one of the most impressive examples of the power of her modesty. In the same vein, the reason that men and women are separated in prayer has nothing to do with the "exclusion" of women. Rather it is precisely because the essence of prayer is the private communion of the individual with G-d that there must be no distractions of any kind for either men or women. In truth, intimacy and separation are corollaries, not opposites.

Indeed, if we are to speak of the central purpose of the Jew as bringing *kedushah* into the world, it is important to note that a primary meaning of the word *kadosh* is "apart," "separate." "Sanctify yourselves therefore, and be holy, for I am holy," G-d says (Lev. 11:44). Just as G-d is holy, "apart," separate, private, mysterious, so, too, we are to be holy. The ultimate mystery of divinity is something withheld from us. But as Chassidus explains, it is only by G-d's "withholding," "withdrawing" of Himself, so to speak (*tzimtzum*), that creation comes about, that there is made a "place" for the world to exist so that the revelation of His being does not overwhelm and nullify finite creatures. Thus, in truth, withdrawal and separation are ultimately deeper, subtler *modes of revelation,* modes through which the most profound intimacy and union is made possible, be it between G-d and the world, or woman and man. Indeed G-d's relation to the Jewish people is compared to that of husband and wife.

The Torah's laws of Family Purity and *mikvah* reflect this concept of a rhythm of intimacy and separation between man and woman corresponding to the times of the month when the potential for new life is most real, and when that potential is lost. The laws of Family Purity are a profound reflection of the concept of the holiness of the physical, and not the reverse, as is so often not understood. Though the subject requires much further explanation and study, briefly stated, man and wife are forbidden to each other during the woman's menstrual period and for a week thereafter. After her immersion in a *mikvah* (ritual bath), they are permitted to resume relations. These laws were never meant to ostracize women or make them feel unclean. On the contrary, in part they demand that the couple be able to relate on a non-physical as well as physical level, to relate to each other as people rather than objects for the satisfaction of each other's drives. They often have the effect of avoiding monotony in marriage, and of making each partner dearer and more precious to the other, as they consecrate themselves anew every month. The laws of Family Purity ensure that even the most powerful of physical drives be touched with an awareness of holiness, and, as has been seen, holiness does not mean shame and contempt for the flesh, but rather its refinement—that it, too, may become invested with the spiritual. The physical separation of husband and wife at certain prescribed times is the counterpart of their intimacy and leads, ultimately, to a deeper union.

G-d's *kedushah,* finally, is an aspect of His Kingship. For the greatness of a king lies as much in his apartness from his people as his revelation of himself to them—and in the closeness and devotion his subjects feel even when he is not physically present. His divinity and power are manifest as much in his withholding of himself as in his open display of his wealth, power, and so forth. And the same is true of the queen—the Jewish woman. Shabbos, the holiest day, is also called a "queen" and reflects this idea of "withdrawal" from the public to the private realm—from the world of work to that of home and family, study and prayer. And through Shabbos, all the other days of the week and all our doings therein are blessed. Through the power of this "withdrawal," this privacy, we gain strength for our public pursuits. Hence when the Torah says that "The entire glory of the daughter of the King lies on the inside" it is not an expression of her inferiority, but on the contrary of her higher, more sensitive and elevated spiritual status. Instead of turning to the "outside" and seeking more public roles and more recognition, perhaps both women and men would find all that they seek by turning "in"—to that private, mysterious, divine core of the soul which is the source of one's true identity, integrity, and holiness as a Jew.

Document 10. Elyse Goldstein, "Take Back the Waters": A Feminist Reappropriation of Mikvah

The requirement that women purify themselves in a ritual bath following menstruation is among the most challenging traditions for Jewish feminists. Rabbi Elyse M. Goldstein (b. 1955), of Holy Blossom Temple in Toronto, advocates reinterpreting the mikvah to remove the associations many women find degrading.[40]

As a feminist, I have struggled with the Jewish menstrual taboos for many years. Leviticus 25 prohibits a menstruating woman from touching her husband or even his things for seven days; while at the same time it proscribes her husband from even sitting on the same chair upon which she has sat. . . .

There can be no doubt that the mikvah has been tied to menstruation since the destruction of the Temple and the subsequent end of other types of "impurities." Therefore, while men may occasionally go to mikvah to prepare for Shabbat or festivals, or even, among the ultra-observant, after an involuntary nocturnal emission, they are never predictably and cyclically in need of cleansing. For men, mikvah is non-obligatory and going is an act usually unconnected to their biologies or their marital status. Add to this the dirty and dark atmosphere of mikvaot in poor immigrant neighborhoods when our mothers grew up, fostering in them a fear and loathing of the whole process which we have inherited. Now add the English Biblical translation of a menstruating woman as "unclean" or "impure." Add our grandmother's "meises" about not touching a Torah during that time of month. (This has absolutely no *halachic* basis. R. Yehudah ben Batera in Tractate Brachot and also the Tosefta of Brachot (22a) state that a menstruating woman may even go up to the Torah. A Torah scroll is supra-holy: it is too holy to be defiled by any person or any object at all.) Then add one more piece of fuel to the fire: that mikvah has been the domain of married women only. It is inexorably linked to having a husband, to making oneself ready to return to sexual relations with one's male partner, to being connected to a man. Divorced and single women, even though menstruating, are not to go to mikvah, according to tradition—because no matter how we try to skirt the issue, no matter how we rewrite history or remake images, the bottom line is that mikvah is seen as the last necessary step before resuming sexual relations within a heterosexual marriage, a step commanded by God. Any other reason for going—to spiritually renew oneself after one's cycle, to cleanse from this "whisper of death," to link oneself to Jewish women's history, to reground after feeling crampy and bloated—all these are lovely, interesting and unique. But according to tradition these reasons are ultimately secondary and even superfluous. All of these factors add up to a great deal of resentment toward the mikvah among modern women.

Why then was I, a Reform rabbi and committed feminist, splashing around in the mikvah? Was I going to make myself "kosher" for my new husband? Hardly. For me, it was an experience of reappropriation.

The mikvah has been taken from me as a Jewish woman by sexist interpretations, by my experiences with Orthodox "family purity" committees who run communal mikvaot as Orthodox monopolies, by a history of male biases, fears of menstruation and superstitions. I was going to take back the water.

To take back the water means to see mikvah as a wholly female experience: as Miriam's well gave water to the Israelites so too will the mikvah give strength back to Jewish women. Water is the symbol of birth—now it can be a symbol of rebirth. To take back the water means to open the mikvah up to women not attached to men. In order to do that we may have to build alternative mikvaot, run by women, for women, following women's rules, not funded or run "behind the scenes" by male rabbis with family purity laws or their own denominational territories to protect. To take back the waters means to dip on Rosh Chodesh, when the moon and the sea and women's cycles become one. To take back the water means to open the mikvah during the day, so women don't have to sneak in under cover of darkness. (If we aren't ashamed of our bodies, why do we need to hide our immersions? If we reject the notion that mikvah is only for the right to resume sex with our husbands, we won't have to be modest about going.) To take back the water means to turn the mikvah into a Jewish women's center: with Torah learning and books available, maybe even feminist shiurim, not just sheitl advertisements and pamphlets on keeping a kosher home.

But why bother at all to take back the water? Why not simply abandon an institution which has been used to debase us? Because we have so little that is ours. We put on a *tallis* but in doing so we share a man's ritual garb. The water is ours: it is the fluid of our own bodies and a deeply moving experience of connection to Mother Earth. We climb the top of Masada in Israel and there we see a mikvah. It is our Jewish history.

So there we were: washing away past relationships, past hurts. As we prepared, we sang; one friend washed my hair, another rubbed my feet. when I entered the water, they all entered with me. I began with a chant: May my *tevilah* (immersion) cleanse me of past wrongs. . . . May it cleanse me of grudges toward past loves. . . . May it cleanse me of pain from past loves. . . . May it cleanse me of the times I have hurt past loves. . . . May it move me in the future. . . . May my *tevilah* connect me to other women. . . . May it strengthen my commitment to women's causes. . . . May it bring out the goodness of woman in me. I dipped and sang out the traditional blessing, not meekly and with arms covering my breasts as the attendant would have liked, but in a clear, loud song. And I dipped again and again, saying "Amen, May it be Your will," as each friend offered her prayer, her wish for my future life. The attendant grew weary of what she thought were antics—yet we continued in this deeply spiritual vein long after she left. It was a moment which inspired me. It was a moment I shall never forget. It was a moment of taking back what was mine a long time ago, offering a new wisdom of the water which can be uplifting for all women.

Document 11. Susan Grossman, "Finding Comfort After a Miscarriage": Creating New Rituals

Jewish women who find that the tradition does not provide rituals to sacralize the events of their lives have turned back to the tradition for the tools to create new rituals. Rabbi Susan Grossman, of Genesis Agudas Achim Congregation, in Westchester, New York, used the *birkat ha-gomel,* the prayer said after safely surviving a dangerous experience, as the point of departure for this new liturgy.[41]

When I miscarried during my sixth week of pregnancy, I felt a great sense of pain and loss. As a committed Jew who lives her life around the Jewish calendar and steeped in Jewish ritual, I naturally sought to find comfort in Jewish prayer and ritual. However, I felt myself abandoned by the tradition with which I normally feel so much at home. There are no traditional prayers to recite over a miscarriage. There is no funeral or mourning ritual to follow. After suffering a miscarriage, a woman does not even routinely recite the prayer said after coming safely through a dangerous experience, *birkat ha-gomel,* something all women can do after giving birth.

Until I had suffered a miscarriage, I had never understood what had motivated European women to seek all those amulets arrayed on exhibit in the Israel Museum in Jerusalem—amulets against the Evil Eye and the much maligned Lilith, amulets calling on various angels for protection of the mother and unborn child. Now I understand. The feeling of helplessness is overwhelming during and after a miscarriage. The actual miscarriage is terrifying. As the body begins to bleed uncontrollably, one fears—at least a little—for one's own health and life. After recovering physically, one is often left without answers to that fundamental question: Why did it happen? Even modern science often cannot point to a cause, so as to reassure the mother it will not happen again, although friend and scientific statistics both assure her that the next pregnancy should come to term and bring forth a healthy child.

My strong feelings led me to seek in liturgy a way to turn to God in my pain and fear and sense of helplessness, to seek comfort in the protection of God's grace. Yet, I found no prayer in the standard prayer books of any of the movements that seemed to meet my needs. If such prayers exist in the Yiddish *tehinot* literature, they are not easily accessible.

Below is the meditation I composed for myself to introduce my recitation of *birkat ha-gomel* after receiving an *aliyah* during the Torah reading in the synagogue. I found that, while not obligatory, the recitation of *birkat ha-gomel* after a miscarriage should be encouraged, because a miscarriage does pose a danger to a woman's health.[42]

Meditation After a Miscarriage

"He blossoms like a flower and withers; he vanishes like a shadow and does not endure" (Job 14:2).

"Seeing his days are determined, the number of his months are with You, You set him limits that he *could* not pass" (on Job 14:5).

O God, I commend back to Your safe keeping the potential life entrusted to me for so short a time.

For first pregnancies terminated before 40 days:

Not yet having reached 40 days of life, this fetus did not open my womb, it was not my *bakhor,* still I grieve its passing out of the protection of my body.

For pregnancies terminated after 40 days:

Having reached _____ weeks, this fetus was my *bakhor,* opening my womb. I grieve its passing out of the protection of my body.

If not first pregnancy:

Having reached _____ weeks, this fetus would have been my (number) child. I grieve its passing out of the protection of my body.

"You know when the wild goats of the rock give birth, You mark when the hinds calve" (on Job 39:1).

You created the miracle of birth and the wonder of the body that cares for mother and child.

Dayyan Ha-Emet, Righteous Judge, You care for Your creatures even when such care tastes bitter.

Who are we to understand Your ways, to know what future would have lain ahead for myself and my child had it come to term?

"But her flesh upon her shall have pain and her soul within her shall mourn" (adapted from Job 14:22).

Ha-Rahaman, O Merciful One, heal my body and my soul; heal my womb so that I may carry to term a healthy soul, that I may come to sing Your praises as a happy mother surrounded by her children in the courtyards of a Jerusalem at peace.

Recite Birkat ha-gomel:

Blessed are You, Almighty God, Sovereign of the Universe, Who bestows kindness on the undeserving, and has shown me every kindness.

Congregation responds:

May the One who has shown you every kindness, ever show kindness to you, sela. Amen.

CHAPTER FOUR

Black Women

From Slavery to Womanist Liberation

Emilie M. Townes

Documents

THE COLONIAL ERA

1. Phillis Wheatley: Colonial Evangelical Piety

THE NINETEENTH CENTURY

2. Amanda Berry Smith: Conversion Through Wrestling with the Devil
3. Sojourner Truth: The Conversion of a Female Slave
4. Ida B. Wells-Barnett: Living in the New Jerusalem
5. Anna Julia Cooper: Women and the Regeneration and Progress of the Race

THE TWENTIETH CENTURY

6. Mary McLeod Bethune: Leaving a Legacy
7. Sara Duncan: Vital Questions
8. Church of God in Christ: 1941 Annual Convocation Minutes
9. National Black Sisters' Conference: Statement of Purpose
10. Nannie Helen Burroughs: "The Slabtown District Convention"
11. Zora Neale Hurston: "The Wounds of Jesus"

MOVING INTO THE TWENTY-FIRST CENTURY

12. Toni Morrison: Loving the Heart
13. Katie Geneva Cannon: Black Women's Stories and Moral Wisdom
14. Delores S. Williams: Speaking Black Women's Tongue?
15. Jacquelyn Grant: The Bible and Jesus in Womanist Tradition
16. Cheryl Townsend Gilkes: Afrocentric Appropriation of the Bible

IN 1619, when Africans first arrived on the shores that would become the United States, they came with a religious world far different from that of their white masters and mistresses.[1] Until the next century, however, Africans brought to the New World had little or no contact with Christianity. A few Blacks did convert to Christianity, but their conversions had little positive effect on white attitudes toward Africans. Like Black men, Black women were excluded from worship by their white masters and mistresses. Virginia's laws made a distinction between servants from Europe who were called Christians and servants from Africa who were Negro servants. Colonists did not seek to convert Negro servants, and sometimes legislation forbade attending church and discouraged conversions. However, in his memoirs, John Winthrop noted that a Black woman was baptized and communed into the Puritan congregation in 1641. This, he notes, was only after she proved her faithful commitment to God over many years. In 1662 the Virginia legislature decreed that children inherited their mother's social status, not her religious station. The witchcraft hysteria that swept through the colonies from 1647 to 1692 touched the lives of Blacks. A Black woman servant, Marja, was among the first to fall victim to the frenzy of the colonists.

In 1701 the Society for the Propagation of the Gospel in the Foreign Parts began to Christianize slaves. Even so, slaves did not convert to Christianity in any significant or recorded numbers until the 1740s, during the First Great Awakening. However, slaves in the South and free Blacks in the North were not without a religious life. The constant influx of Black Africans through the slave trade meant a continual renewal and revitalization of the traditions and religions of Africa in the Americas.[2] Slaves maintained links with their African heritage through oral history, drumming at funerals and dances, preserving the art of wood carving, and making reed baskets and mats.

The cosmology of the slaves during the 1600s and 1700s was a universe crafted from a blend of West African religions with Christianity. White missionaries and ministers prohibited religious dancing and shouting, but the slaves did so in their religious life beyond the watchful eye of white religious authorities.[3] When left alone, slave worship contained the West African notion of the forces of the universe, both evil and good. Both were at hand and available for consultation and for protection.[4] Also present was the Christian God who would send a man to set the slaves free as Moses had confronted Pharaoh to set the Hebrew slaves free. This was a God who was not wholly transcendent but immanent as well.

In this period, Black women converted to Christianity in greater numbers than Black men. One of the first free Black women to present her child for baptism in 1683, Ginney Bess, was among the number of women who joined churches. Their hope, in part, was to provide an asylum from the harshness of slavery in the South and white prejudice in the North. However, the evangelical fervor many of these women found in the First Great Awakening should not be overlooked. The writings of Phillis Wheatley near the close of the eighteenth century reflect this deep religious enthusiasm (document 1). Writing from a Northern context in Boston, Wheatley did not question her servitude. Rather, she sought personal moral rectitude and salvation. Her concern for "true felicity" extended to others as well.

The evangelical religion of the Second Awakening in the early decades of the nineteenth century provided a refuge for people who relied on their subjective knowledge of God (experiential and emotional) rather than on objective knowledge (reason and logic). The Second Awakening was more secular and more optimistic than the first. It popularized religion while at the same time being larger than merely a manifestation of religion. This new evangelical fervor came at a crucial time in the social life of the country. The United States was emerging from a period of anticlericalism and into one of social and cultural disintegration.

Religion, evangelical and indigenous, helped to instill and strengthen a sense of identity among marginal groups in American society. Among Blacks, the folk beliefs and fetishes that had developed in the African American religious worldview blended with the evangelical enthusiasm that the revivalist movement brought to the early nineteenth century. Evangelical religion was felt personally and bodily, and this was particularly true for African Americans.[5] Although by 1790 the number of slaves raised within a fully developed African culture made up only a small percentage of the total slave population, Black slaves who were religious had a legacy of an African cosmology, which stressed body and spirit, that ordered their religious and social worlds.[6] Yet more slaves were employing Jewish and Christian symbols to formulate their conceptions of their origin and destiny.[7]

The burst of revivalism in the early nineteenth century helped African Americans and whites alike to gain reference points in a society that was undergoing drastic changes through immigration, the closing of the slave trade, and growing technology. On some levels, Black churches embraced a theology of liberation, self-determination, and African American autonomy.[8] Slaves who gathered to worship could not reflect a concrete millennial impulse openly.[9] With whites keeping a watchful eye on slave religious gatherings, slaves were forced to be careful in their eschatological impetus. The untrained or ignorant eye and ear could not catch the this-worldly implications of spirituals drawn from the Bible, Protestant hymns, sermons, and African styles of singing and dancing.[10]

African American evangelicalism was a communal celebration, not an "isolating experience of awakening to a deep sense of guilt and sinfulness." This was contrary to white evangelicalism, which stressed a polarization between individualism and communitarianism. Also, white evangelicalism had a need to create powerful symbols of sinful worldliness. Whites felt a need to find signs of redemption in abstinence, bodily inhibition, and withdrawal from the world. Such needs were not shared by slaves, who lived in a world of sacred meaning and collective redemption.[11]

Salvation was the central focus for Black evangelicalism. Human repentance and faith were not sufficient to guarantee salvation (document 2). Slaves prayed to be released from sin in the midst of a physical bondage that could be objectified and cast outside their souls in a way that was unavailable to their white masters.[12] The historian Donald Mathews notes that "the emotional toll of slavery was much more effective than the doctrine of original sin in creating self-contempt."[13]

From evangelicalism, Blacks inherited a belief system that valued a disciplined person who lived within a disciplined community. African Americans believed that by submitting to such discipline they could demand that whites deal with them according to standards that transcended the master-slave relationship.[14]

Protest and accommodation were the two poles open to slaves in their religious as well as secular lives. Evangelical Christianity supported both, at times enabling slaves to choose protest and at other times calling slaves to accept their fate.[15] The protest tradition of the Black Church faded as the nineteenth century wore on. The militancy represented by

African Americans such as David Walker and Henry Highland Garnet diminished as the independent Black evangelical churches began to institutionalize and take on many characteristics of their white evangelical counterparts.[16]

The primary responses of the late-nineteenth-century African American woman to her struggle with the narrow space and dark enclosure of racial and economic subordination were expressed through her commitments to religious and social organizations. African American women of this era espoused a profound spirituality forged from the twin hearths of African cosmology and evangelical piety. This spirituality was distinct from white evangelical Christianity in form and practice. However, both Black and white spiritualities provided the framework for women's participation in social and moral reform in the public realm.

African American and white women's religious expression and their spirituality were intensely personal matters. Yet they took their concern for their moral development, expanded it to their families, and ultimately presented their concerns to the larger society through associational work and moral reform societies as well as preaching and exhorting (document 2).

Black women who were active in the church had a deep, personal relationship with God and Jesus. This was not unlike the experience of Black men who were active in the church. Jesus was not only Lord and Savior; he was brother and friend. Through this personal relationship with Jesus, Black women could transcend the inhuman structures that surrounded them in the slave South and repressive North.

At the beginning of the nineteenth century, religious worship and spirituality were expressed in groups, as people gathered to worship in a blending of African survivalisms and white evangelical Christianity. One's spiritual life was shared through conversion, baptism, and communion. Increasingly, the joy and release of the ring shout, the spontaneity of spirituals, and the appeal to the interrelatedness of humans with nature were lost. African American Christians began a personal journey in their faith.

African American women, however, took an intriguing avenue in expressing their spirituality. Black women in religious circles did not depict themselves as the larger society portrayed white women—fragile and impressionable with little capacity for rational thought.[17] Black women viewed themselves as having a capacity to influence men and consistently described their power of persuasion over men as historically positive. African American women's biblical hermeneutics reveal women in dual image, just as men were portrayed, and they affirmed their likeness to men and their oneness with men in a joint quest for salvation.[18]

Black women took pride in the mothers of the Bible, who became their role models for motherhood. The mothers of Isaac, Moses, Samson, and others gave Black women a view of women as more than bodily receptacles through which great men were born. They saw these mothers as responsible for raising sons who would deliver Israel from its oppressors.[19] They drew the obvious parallels for their lives and the lives of Black people in the nineteenth century.

African American women did not break from the orthodoxy of the Black Church but restated that orthodoxy in what historian Evelyn Brooks Higginbotham characterizes as a "progressive and liberating language for women."[20] Black women took the roles of wife, sister, daughter, and mother; combined them with a personal spiritual experience of God in Christ; and understood themselves to be ministers in their homes. With that step, Black women moved on from their image of domestic comforter to a greater call. This was possible through their intense evangelical spiritual drive to live a higher and better life and their concern to shape families and a society that reflected Christian morals and precepts. Black women took the biblical images of Phoebe, Priscilla, and Mary as co-workers with Paul and translated them into their own work. Their stress was an ultimate allegiance to God and not to men.[21] This drive toward Christian moral perfection by Black women did not readily translate into ordination. Jarena Lee traveled well over two thousand miles and delivered 178 sermons to spread the gospel, yet she was never ordained (see document 10 of chapter 7).[22]

Black women's religious experience in the nineteenth century combined the idealization of the home and motherhood with the attack of the secular woman's movement against sexually exclusive spheres. Brooks notes that the dual image of Christ as "feminine and masculine, passive and aggressive, meek and conquering," emerged to inform "their self-perceptions and self-motivations." Brooks observes that these women shifted back and forth from feminine to masculine imagery as they described their role in the evangelical crusade of the period: they described themselves both as homemakers and as soldiers.[23]

African American women, like white women, could not remain within their homes and see themselves as fully answering God's call to repentance and salvation. Women's associational activities were in direct response to the Great Awakening, in which Protestants tried to counteract the influence of Catholicism and the religious indifference and rationalism of the day to create an enduring and moral social order.[24]

Black and white women developed a spirituality that took them outside their daily prayer and reflection time and into the world. Their public work was deeply wedded to their inner and intense reflection. The goal was salvation on earth. Because of their unique role in shaping the moral fiber of society through the family, women took up the challenge to spread the promise of salvation. Religion provided a way to order one's life and priorities. It also enabled women to rely on an authority beyond the world of men (document 5).[25]

African American and white women formed maternal societies in response to the cultural and religious elevation of the role of motherhood. Their members gathered to prepare themselves to guide children properly and to raise a generation of Christians. Moral reform societies were begun to eliminate the sin of licentiousness that appeared in the lust of men and the prostitution of women. These societies sought to reform and resurrect fallen women and to publicize and ostracize men who visited prostitutes. The focus of moral reform societies was on the family as an arena for solving larger social problems. The women of these societies often portrayed females as sacrificial victims to male lust, and they decried prostitution in language evoking women's power to avenge.[26]

African American women began with an intense personal experience of the divine in their lives and took that call to salvation into the public realm to reform a corrupt moral order. Their spirituality, which at first viewing resembles a self-centered piety with little relation to the larger context, exemplifies the linking of personal and social transformation to effect salvation. These women sought perfection and advocated social reform in the framework of a spirituality that valued life and took seriously the responsibility to help create and maintain a just and moral social order. These women of the nineteenth century lived their spirituality (document 4). They accepted the traditional roles handed to them yet began to shape and bend them through their understandings of their ultimate relationship to God.

The brutal reality of Jim Crow laws that legalized segregation in the United States placed a heavy burden on African Americans. This separate but equal decree of 1896 ushered in what W. E. B. DuBois called the problem of the twentieth century—the color line. Black men and women found the indignities of slavery replaced with the perniciousness of racism. For Black Christians, 95 percent of whom lived in the South, legalized segregation and unchecked racism became the fodder for their witness against injustice. Most of these Black Christians were women who understood that their Christian duty called them to oppose Jim Crow with every moral fiber of their being.

In the secular arena, Black churchwomen turned to the club movement to alleviate Black suffering and agitate for social equality. Black club women, like their white sisters, placed a great emphasis on the sanctity of the home and the woman's place in it. There was little direct contradiction of the church's doctrine that females were essentially domestic beings. Both within and outside the club movement, motherhood enjoyed the greatest sanctity. Black women saw Mary, the mother of Jesus, as the personification of the highest expression of womanhood.[27] Although motherhood was dominant, these women also referred to their roles as wives, sisters, and daughters. Men's conversions and the minister's moral rectitude were attributed to "a mother's influence, a sister's guidance, or to the tender persuasion of a devoted wife or daughter."[28]

Like white women active in the club movement, Black women too enlarged the concept of domesticity to include area interests of club women.[29] They held mothers' meetings involving discussions on "child culture" and "social purity." They believed that a "woman's true calling is to make peoples' lives better."

The combined efforts of Black and white women were essential for the progress of Blacks and peaceful race relations. Women believed that Christianizing the home and education were key to solving the race problem.[30] Black women identified with Esther, who acted as an intermediary for her race. Through them, as through Esther, the race would be saved and lifted to greater heights; African Americans would receive deliverance.

A clear, strong, voice within the Black Church carried the mild rhetoric of Black women to its furthest extension. For women like Mrs. G. D. Oldham of Tennessee, women were to be ministers, not slaves to their homes.[31] Lucy Wilmot Smith, speaking in 1886 to a predominantly male audience in a church, stated, "It is one of the evils of the day that from babyhood girls are taught to look forward to the time when they will be supported by a father, a brother, or somebody else's brother."[32]

The image of woman as loyal and comforting spouse from the cult of true womanhood was transcended as Black women embraced Jesus. The stress was on an ultimate allegiance to God, not to men. In a strictly biblical appeal, women yoked their faith, with its requirement for support and kindness, with women's domestic image as comforter to support a public responsibility to prophesy and spread the gospel.[33]

Most club members were active church workers or at least attended church. Churches were the major benevolent, spiritual, and social institutions of the African American community.[34] The Black Church opened its doors for the women of the club movement. The first national organization for club women, the 1896 convention of the National Association of Colored Women, was held at Nineteenth Street Baptist Church in Washington, D.C. Of the following fifteen national meetings between 1901 and 1930, eight were held in churches.

The second organization affecting Black club women on a national level was the National Association of Colored Women. This organization focused on the uplift of the Black peasant woman and the improvement of Negro family life.[35] As Wilson Moses notes, one of its goals was to introduce the standards of Victorian domesticity into the cabins of Georgia and Alabama sharecroppers. There was a decided class bias in the organization, with the most influential and dominant members coming from the emerging Black middle class.

Josephine St. Pierre Ruffin was a major force in this organization and in the Black woman's club movement in general. Ruffin founded the Women's Era Club on the belief that the Black women's club movement should be involved in temperance, morality, higher education, and hygienic and domestic questions.[36] The club founded a newspaper, The Woman's Era. The paper reflected concerns of the club and, in particular, Ruffin's concerns. It was uncompromising in its defense of Black womanhood and in its condemnation of lynching.

The club movement gave Black women an outlet to express their social witness based on their Christian faith. Their passion for social change and racial uplift revitalized the Black community. The organizations women created addressed specific yet universal problems in the Black community. The women did not allow denominational differences to prevent their uniting to form the National Association of Colored Women's Clubs. Indeed, the women were so effective in their work that W. E. B. DuBois called for Black men to support women's suffrage because of the emerging role Black women were playing as "the intellectual leadership of the race."[37] The work Black women took on was a frontal assault on Jim Crow, blending secular and religious concerns into effective social action.

From this vital base, Black women in the churches have moved into the late twentieth century refining, adopting, discovering, and acting on strategies for effective social change and religious transformation. This, at times, has been an uphill struggle, given the deep structural sexism of the Black Church. The distinction between speaking and teaching as feminine activities and preaching as a masculine one remains a stubborn stumbling block to creating an effective Black Church witness. However, many women and men refuse to allow such an inefficient and ineffective sexual division of labor to cut short the variety of gifts women have to offer. Educators such as Mary McLeod Bethune (document 6), Anna Julia Cooper (document 5), Ida B. Wells-Barnett (document 4), and Nannie Helen Burroughs (document 10) grounded their teaching in a deep faith that demanded they share their gifts with other African Americans. Even in churches that refuse to ordain women, women serve in roles and offices that afford them the same ministries as men—the major distinction being the title.

Black women offered an internal critique of their subordinate roles in the church. Sara Duncan was forthright in her defense of women's missionary efforts (document 7). Her refusal to bow to male opinion about the proper missionary work for Black women pointed the way to a growing resistance by many religious Black women to confine their ministry to accepted roles and expectations. Duncan's defense came in the midst of the late-nineteenth- and early-twentieth-century Holiness movement in the South. The Holiness movement produced denominations that ordained women to all of the functions of ministry. The Church of God in Christ has its origins in this movement.

When a disagreement concerning the doctrine of the Pentecost split the Church of God in Christ, the pro-Pentecost faction remained in control of the original church charter and the legal right to use the name Church of God in Christ. The first legally organized Pentecostal denomination arose from this split. Among Blacks, Holiness and Pentecostal churches are called "the Sanctified Church."

Women in the Church of God in Christ developed strong women's departments that functioned with near autonomy, since the women were subordinate to and cooperative with their bishops. Although generally regarded as otherwordly theologically, Sanctified Church women participated in the movement for racial uplift (document 8) alongside their Baptist and Methodist sisters.

Black Roman Catholic women were faced with many of the same obstacles to practicing the fullness of their call as their Protestant sisters. The National Black Sisters' Conference (document 9) has played an important role for Black Catholic women. Black sisters and nuns are active participants in the ministry of the Catholic Church in the United States. The National Black Sisters' Conference has worked with the National Office of Black Catholics to help shape a more relevant and responsive Catholic Church to the needs of Black Catholics.

As Black women move into the twenty-first century, the experiences of Black women, men, and children are the grist for the mill of religious and theological reflection. A key source for this is found in the writings of Black women authors. Novels written by Black women often have a deep spiritual and moral undergirding. Zora Neale Hurston's character the Reverend John Buddy Pearson in *Jonah's Gourd Vine* preaches a powerful sermon entitled "The Wounds of Jesus," based on Zechariah 13:6 and Isaiah 53 (document 11). The sermon in the Clearing in Toni Morrison's novel *Beloved* is on the nature of grace (document 12). The writings of Black women novelists echo the work Black women do in their faith communities and in society. The African American woman of this era, like her foremothers, refuses to bend to the yoke of silence. The work of God is too important in a land in which there is no hiding place from injustice.

The late twentieth century has also seen the rise of African American women as scholars in theological academic discourse. Black women scholars are active in shaping the direction and content of all the major theological disciplines. The same activism found in the life of the church is also at the heart of the emerging body of womanist theological reflection.

The womanist witness arises out of Alice Walker's four-part definition, in which she describes the origins of the term *womanist*[38] from the Black folk expression "You're acting womanish!" This signals, first, a young Black girl's proclivity for inquiring about the nature and fairness of life. Second, Black women exercise concern and responsibility for the survival of the African American community—male, female, young, old, gay, lesbian, straight, rich, poor. The third part of the definition celebrates and affirms the beauty of the Black woman as an individual and her love of the Spirit—regardless. The final part of the definition—"Womanist is to feminist as purple is to lavender"—is a critique of the incomplete analysis of traditional white feminism, which neglects a rigorous race, gender, and class analysis.

Ethicist Katie Geneva Cannon provides an important link between Walker's literary work and formal theo-ethical reflection. Cannon is an early voice in womanist religious thought. Her essay "Moral Wisdom in the Black Women's Literary Tradition" (document 13) explores how Black women's literature can help explain and interpret Black sociocultural patterns. From this, ethical values will emerge. The work of theologians Delores Williams (document 14) and Jacquelyn Grant (document 15) are foundational voices as well. Each situates womanist theological reflection in the context of Black women's struggles for the survival of the community. Williams offers a helpful critique and reinterpretation of feminism in the "Black woman's tongue." Grant provides a rigorous argument for Black women's experience as the crucible for womanist theology. The work of sociologist Cheryl Townsend Gilkes is an excellent representative of the interdisciplinary nature of womanist religious thought. Her essay "'Mother to the Motherless, Father to the Fatherless': Power, Gender, and Community in an Afrocentric Biblical Tradition" (document 16) is a theological and sociocultural study of the way African Americans use the Bible as an interpretive tool for religious reflection and survival under oppression.

These early voices have been joined by womanist scholars in various theological disciplines. In biblical interpretation, Clarice Martin and Renita Weems explore womanist implications in the New Testament and

Elizabeth Freeman (Mumbet), a slave in Massachusetts, won her suit for freedom under the United States Constitution, which says that all *men* are created free and equal.

Abolitionist, reformer, and women's rights advocate Sojourner Truth (1797–1883) was one of the most famous Black women of the nineteenth century. Her social commitments were based on a deep religious faith.

Phillis Wheatley (1753–1784), poet. This portrait appeared as the frontispiece of her poems published in 1773.

Mary McLeod Bethune (1875–1955), a leading Black educator, founded Daytona Normal and Industrial School for Negro Girls, which became Bethune-Cookman College. Active in the Black women's club movement, she founded the National Council of Negro Women.

Bishop Ida Robinson, founder of Mt. Sinai Holy Churches of America, Inc.

Nannie Helen Burroughs (1883–1961), educator and Baptist leader, founded the Women's Day in Baptist churches, which spread to other denominations. The Women's Auxiliary of the National Baptist Convention and the Progressive National Baptist Convention are inheritors of her legacy.

Black preacher Amanda Berry Smith (1837–1915) was one of the most powerful evangelists and effective missionaries of the nineteenth century. James Thoburn, Methodist Episcopal bishop, testified that he had learned more of actual value to him from Amanda Smith than from any other person.

Ida B. Wells-Barnett (1862–1931), a crusading journalist, lecturer, and club woman, campaigned for rights of Black people, particularly Black women. She fought against lynching and racial segregation, organized the first Black women's suffrage organization, and was active in the settlement house movement.

168

Hebrew Bible, respectively. Ethicists such as Toinette Eugene, Marcia Riggs, and Cheryl Saunders offer new ways to understand the interstructured nature of oppression. Theologians Karen Baker-Fletcher, M. Shawn Copeland, Kelly Brown Douglass, and Diana Hayes expand the womanist theological canon. Each womanist scholar builds on the Black Church tradition and critiques it. They are engaged in work our souls must have to survive in times such as these and beyond. They are inheritors of a centuries-old dynamic witness for the personal and corporate liberation of a whole people.

Documents

THE COLONIAL ERA

Document 1. Phillis Wheatley: Colonial Evangelical Piety

Phillis Wheatley (1753–1784) was the property of the wealthy Boston merchant John Wheatley. Because the young Phillis was bright, John Wheatley educated her and treated her as more a daughter than a slave. Her intellectual prowess and her race won her the label of prodigy in her youth. The Countess of Huntingdon in England was so impressed with Phillis after being entertained by her that she arranged for the publication of her verses. Phillis died in poverty after the Wheatley household dispersed due to marriage and death. In the letter written to her friend Arbour Tanner, the nineteen-year-old Wheatley reveals her evangelical Christianity.[39]

Boston, May 19th, 1772

Dear Sister,—I rec'd your favour of February 6th for which I give you my sincere thanks. I greatly rejoice with you in that realizing view, and I hope experience, of the saving change which you so emphatically describe. Happy were it for us if we could arrive to that evangelical Repentance, and the true holiness of heart which you mention. Inexpressibly happy should we be could we have a due sense of the beauties and excellence of the crucified Saviour. In his Crucifixion may be seen marvellous displays of Grace and Love, sufficient to draw and invite us to the rich and endless treasures of his mercy; let us rejoice in and adore the wonders of God's infinite Love in bringing us from a land semblant of darkness itself, and where the divine light of revelation (being obscur'd) is as darkness. Here the knowledge of the true God and eternal life are made manifest; but there, profound ignorance overshadows the land. Your observation is true, namely, that there was nothing in us to recommend us to God. Many of our fellow creatures are pass'd by, when the bowels of divine love expanded towards us. May this goodness & long suffering of God lead us to unfeign'd repentance.

It gives me very great pleasure to hear of so many of my nation, seeking with eagerness the way of true felicity. O may we all meet at length in that happy mansion. I hope the correspondence between us will continue, (my being much indispos'd this winter past, was the reason of my not answering yours before now) which correspondence I hope may have the happy effect of improving our mutual friendship. Till we meet in the regions of consummate blessedness, let us endeavor by the assistance of divine grace, to live the life, and we shall die the death of the Righteous. May this be our happy case, and of those who are travelling to the region of Felicity, is the earnest request of your affectionate

Friend & humble servant. Phillis Wheatley

THE NINETEENTH CENTURY

Document 2. Amanda Berry Smith:
Conversion Through Wrestling with the Devil

Amanda Berry Smith (1837–1915) received sanctification in 1868 and dedicated herself to a life of evangelical piety. Her vivid conversion came after a life that featured two unhappy marriages and work as a washerwoman. Her conversion led her to a ministry of preaching at Holiness camp meetings in the United States and Britain. She also led evangelical crusades to Africa and India. This she did although never ordained. In this excerpt from her autobiography, Smith describes her own conversion through a struggle with the devil and God.[40]

. . . On Tuesday, the 17th day of March, 1856, I was sitting in the kitchen by my ironing table, thinking it all over. The Devil seemed to say to me (I know now it was he), "You have prayed to be converted."

I said, "Yes."

"You have been sincere."

"Yes."

"You have been in earnest."

"Yes."

"You have read your Bible, and you have fasted, and you really want to be converted."

"Yes, Lord. Thou knowest it; Thou knowest my heart, I really want to be converted."

Then Satan said, "Well, if God were going to convert you He would have done it long ago; He does His work quick, and with all your sincerity God has not converted you."

"Yes, that is so."

"You might as well give it up, then" said he, "it is no use, He won't hear you."

"Well, I guess I will just give it up. I suppose I will be damned and I might as well submit to my fate." Just then a voice whispered to me clearly, and said, "Pray once more." And in an instant I said, "I will." Then another voice seemed like a person speaking to me, and it said, "Don't you do it."

"Yes, I will."

And when I said, "Yes, I will," it seemed to me the emphasis was on the "will," and I felt it from the crown of my head clear through me, "I WILL," and I got on my feet and said, "I will pray once more, and if there is any such thing as salvation, I am determined to have it this afternoon or die."

I got up, put the kettle on, set the table and went into the cellar and got on my knees to pray and die, for I thought I had made a vow to God and that He would certainly kill me, and I didn't care, I was so miserable, and I was just at the verge of desperation. I had put everything on the table but the bread and butter, and I said, "If any one calls me I won't get up, and if the bread and butter is all that is to go on the table, Miss Sue [the daughter] can finish the supper, and that will save them calling for me, and when they come down cellar after it they will find me dead!" . . .

I prayed the third time, using these same words. Then somehow I seemed to get to the end of everything. I did not know what else to say or do. Then in my desperation I looked up and said, "O, Lord, if Thou wilt help me I will believe Thee," and in the act of telling God I would, I did. O, the peace and joy that flooded my soul! The burden rolled away; I felt it when it left me, and a flood of light and joy swept through my soul such as I had never known before. I said, "Why, Lord, I do believe this is just what I have been asking for," and down came another flood of light and peace. And I said again, "Why, Lord, I do believe this is what I have asked Thee for." Then I sprang to my feet, all around was light, I was new. I looked at my hands, they looked new. I took hold of myself and said, "Why, I am new, I am new all over." I clapped my hands; I ran up out of the cellar, I walked up and down the kitchen floor. Praise the Lord! There seemed to be a halo of light all over me; the change was so real and so thorough that I have often said that if I had been as black as ink or as green as grass or as white as snow, I would not have been frightened. I went into the dining room; we had a large mirror that went from the floor to the ceiling, and I went and looked in it to see if anything had transpired in my color, because there was something wonderful had taken place inside of me, and it really seemed to me it was outside too, and as I looked in the glass I cried out, "Hallelujah, I have got religion; glory to God. I have got religion!" I was wild with delight and joy; it seemed to me as if I would split! I went out into the kitchen and I thought what will I do, I have got to wait till Sunday before I can tell anybody. This was on Tuesday; Sunday was my day in town, so I began to count the days, Tuesday, Wednesday, Thursday, Friday, Saturday, Sunday. O, it seemed to me the days were weeks long. My! can I possibly stand it till Sunday? I must tell somebody, and as I passed by the ironing table it seemed as if it had a halo of light all around it, and I ran up to the table and smote it with my hand and shouted, "Glory to God, I have got religion!"

Document 3. Sojourner Truth:
The Conversion of a Female Slave

Sojourner Truth (1797–1883) was born a slave in New York State. Until 1843 she was known as Isabella, but she changed her name to reflect her changed heart and mission. She gained her freedom in 1827 and wandered the country in response to mystical voices and preached that God was loving and kind. Truth is the most famous Black female religious figure in the antebellum period. Her narrative, penned by Olive Gilbert in 1850, is one of the few accounts of Black women's religious experience in the nineteenth century. The following excerpt relates her conversion, which took place when she was in her twenties.[41]

She talked to God as familiarly as if he had been a creature like herself; and a thousand times more so, than if she had been in the presence of some earthly potentate. She demanded, with little expenditure of reverence or fear, a supply of all her more pressing wants, and at times her demands approached very near to commands. She felt as if God was under obligation to her, much more than she was to him. He seemed to her benighted vision in some manner bound to do her bidding. . . .

. . . She says that God revealed himself to her, with all the suddenness of a flash of lightning, showing her, "in the twinkling of an eye, that he was *all over*"—that he pervaded the universe—"and that there was no place where God was not." She became instantly conscious of her great sin in forgetting her almighty Friend and "ever-present help in time of trouble." All her unfulfilled promises arose before her, like a vexed sea whose waves run mountains high; and her soul, which seemed but one mass of lies, shrunk back aghast from the "awful look" of Him whom she had formerly talked to, as if he had been a being like herself; and she would now fain have hid herself in the bowels of the earth, to have escaped his dread presence. But she plainly saw there was no place, not even in hell, where he was not: and where could she flee? Another such "a look," as she expressed it, and she felt that she must be extinguished forever, even as one, with the breath of his mouth, "blows out a lamp," so that no spark remains.

. . . [She said,] "Oh, God, I did not know you were so big," walked into the house, and made an effort to resume her work. But the workings of the inward man were too absorbing to admit of much attention to her avocations. She desired to talk to God, but her vileness utterly forbade it, and she was not able to prefer a petition. "What!" said she, "shall I lie again to God? I have told him nothing but lies; and shall I speak again, and tell another lie to God?" She could not; and now she began to wish for someone to speak to God for her. Then a space seemed opening between her and God, and she felt that if some one, who was worthy in the sight of heaven, would but plead *for* her in their own name, and not let God know it came from *her,* who was so unworthy, God might grant it. At length a friend appeared to stand between herself and an insulted Deity; and she felt as sensibly refreshed as when, on a hot day, an umbrella had been interposed between her scorching head and a burning sun. But who was this friend? became the next inquiry. Was it Deencia, who had so often befriended her? She looked at her with her new power of sight—and, lo! she, too, seemed all "bruises and putrefying sores," like herself. No, it was some one very different from Deencia.

"Who *are* you?" she exclaimed, as the vision brightened into a form distinct, beaming with the beauty of holiness, and radiant with love. She then said, audibly addressing the mysterious visitant—"I *know* you, and I *don't* know you." Meaning, "You seem perfectly familiar; I feel that you not only love me, but that you *always* have loved me—yet I know you not—I cannot call you by name." When she said, "I know you," the subject of the vision remained distinct and quiet. When she said, "I don't know you," it moved restlessly about, like agitated waters. So while she repeated without intermission, "I know you, I know you," that the vision might remain—"Who are you?" was the cry of her heart, and her whole soul was in one deep prayer that this heavenly personage might be revealed to her, and remain with her. At length, after bending both soul and body with the intensity of this desire, till breath and strength seemed failing, and she could maintain her position no longer, an answer came to her, saying distinctly, "It is Jesus." "Yes," she responded, "it is *Jesus.*"

Previous to these exercises of mind, she heard Jesus mentioned in reading or speaking, but had received from what she heard no impression that he was any other than an eminent man, like a Washington or a Lafayette. Now he appeared to her delighted mental vision as so mild, so good, and so every way lovely, and he loved her so much! And, how strange that he had always loved her, and she had never known it! And how great a blessing he conferred, in that he should stand between her and God! And God was no longer a terror and a dread to her.

Document 4. Ida B. Wells-Barnett:
Living in the New Jerusalem

Ida B. Wells-Barnett (1862–1931) was a turn-of-the-century social reformer. She led the antilynching crusade in this country, agitated for women's suffrage, was active in the club movement, and worked in the settlement house movement in Chicago. Her pen as a journalist was swift and incisive. In the following excerpt, Wells-Barnett is visiting twelve Black men unfairly jailed in Elaine, Arkansas, on the charge of inciting a riot.[42]

When we came into the building in which these twelve men were incarcerated, we were readily admitted. Mrs. Moore, the leading spirit among the wives, who was well known because of her frequent visits, said, "Boys, come and shake hands with my cousin who has come from Saint Louis to see me." The iron bars were wide enough apart to enable us to shake hands. The one guard on duty sat about fifty feet away reading the Sunday paper. When he looked up, he saw only a group of insignificant looking colored women who had been there many times before so he went on reading his paper.

When we got up close to the bars, Mrs. Moore whispered, "This is Mrs. Barnett from Chicago." An expression of joy spread over their faces, but I put my finger to my lips and cautioned them not to let on, and immediately a mask seemed to drop over the features of each one. I talked with them about their experiences, asking them to write down everything they could recollect about the rioting, and what befell each of them. . . .

Then Mrs. Moore said, "Boys, don't you want to sing for my cousin?" Whereupon they sang a song of their own composition and many others. . . . I listened to those men sing and pray and give testimony from their overburdened hearts, and sometimes the women would take up the refrain. They shed tears and they got "happy," and the burden of their talk and their prayers was of the hereafter.

Finally I got up and walked close to the bars and said to them in a low tone, "I have been listening to you for nearly two hours. You have talked and sung and prayed about dying, and forgiving your enemies, and of feeling sure that you are going to be received in the New

Jerusalem because your God knows that you are innocent of the offense for which you expect to be electrocuted. But why don't you pray to live and ask to be freed? The God you serve is the God of Paul and Silas who opened their prison gates, and if you have all the faith you say you have, you ought to believe that he will open your prison doors too.

"If you do believe that, let all of your songs and prayers hereafter be songs of faith and hope that God will set you free; that the judges who have to pass on your cases will be given the wisdom and courage to decide in your behalf. That is all I've got to say. Quit talking about dying; if you believe your God is all powerful, believe he is powerful enough to open these prison doors, and say so. Dying is the last thing you ought to even think about, much less talk about. Pray to live and believe you are going to get out."

I went away and spent nearly all night writing down the experiences of the women who were also put in prison in Helena, and within two days I had written statements of each of those twelve men and the facts I had requested. It is a terrible indictment of white civilization and Christianity. It shows that the white people did just what they accused the Negroes of doing: murdered them and stole their crops, their stock, and their household goods. And even then they were invoking the law to put the seal of approval on their deeds by legally (?) executing those twelve men who were found guilty after six minutes' deliberation!

Document 5. Anna Julia Cooper: Women and the Regeneration and Progress of the Race

Anna Julia Cooper (1858–1964) was one of the most highly educated and intellectual Black women of the late nineteenth and early twentieth centuries. She served as principal for the M Street School in Washington, D.C., from 1901 to 1906. There she introduced college preparatory subjects to the curriculum. In 1925 Cooper received her Ph.D. from the Sorbonne in France. She returned to Washington to serve as principal of Dunbar High School. In her retirement, she served as president of Frelinghuysen University, a school for Black working adults in Washington, D.C. The following excerpt, from her book, *A Voice from the South,* was read at a convocation of the Black clergy of the Protestant Episcopal Church in 1886.[43]

By laying down for woman the same code of morality, the same standard of purity, as for man; by refusing to countenance the shameless and equally guilty monsters who were gloating over her fall,— graciously stooping in all the majesty of his own spotlessness to wipe away the filth and grime of her guilty past and bid her go in peace and sin no more; . . . throughout his life and in his death he has given to men a rule and guide for the estimation of woman as an equal, as a helper, as a friend, and as a sacred charge to be sheltered and cared for with a brother's love and sympathy, lessons which nineteen centuries' gigantic strides in knowledge, arts, and sciences, in social and ethical principles have not been able to probe to their depth or to exhaust in practice.

. . . Only the BLACK WOMAN can say "when and where I enter, in the quiet, undisputed dignity of my womanhood, without violence and without suing or special patronage, then and there the *whole Negro race enters with me.*" Is it not evident then that as individual workers for this race we must address ourselves with no half-hearted zeal to this feature of our mission. The need is felt and must be recognized by all. There is a call for workers, for missionaries, for men and women with the double consecration of a fundamental love of humanity and a desire for its melioration through the Gospel; but superadded to this we demand an intelligent and sympathetic comprehension of the interests and special needs of the Negro. . . .

. . . It is a mistake to suppose that the Negro is prejudiced against a white ministry. Naturally there is not a more kindly and implicit follower of a white man's guidance than the average colored peasant. What would to others be an ordinary act of friendly or pastoral interest he would be more inclined to regard gratefully as a condescension. And he never forgets such kindness. Could the Negro be brought near to his white priest or bishop, he is not suspicious. He is not only willing but often longs to unburden his soul to this intelligent guide. There are no reservations when he is convinced that you are his friend. It is a saddening satire on American history and manners that it takes something to convince him.

That our people are not "drawn" to a church whose chief dignitaries they see only in the chancel, and whom they reverence as they would a painting or an angel, whose life never comes down to and touches theirs with the inspiration of an objective reality, may be "perplexing" truly (American caste and American Christianity both being facts) but it need not be surprising. There must be something of human nature in it, the same as that which brought about that "the Word was made flesh and dwelt among us" that He might "draw" us towards God.

Men are not "drawn" by abstractions. Only sympathy and love can draw, and until our Church in America realizes this and provides a clergy that can come in touch with our life and have a fellow feeling for our woes, without being imbedded and frozen up in their "Gothic antipathies," the good bishops are likely to continue "perplexed " by the sparsity of colored Episcopalians. . . .

. . . The institution of the Church in the South to which she mainly looks for the training of her colored clergy and for the help of the "Black Woman" and "Colored Girl" of the South, has graduated since the year 1868, when the school was founded, *five young women;*[44] and while yearly numerous young men have been kept and trained for the ministry by the charities of the Church, the number of indigent females who have here been supported, sheltered and trained, is phenomenally small. Indeed, to my mind, the attitude of the Church toward this feature of her work is as if the solution of the problem of Negro missions depended solely on sending a quota of deacons and priests into the field, girls being a sort of *tertium quid* whose development may be promoted if they can pay their way and fall in with the plans mapped out for the training of the other sex. Now I would ask in all earnestness, does not this force potential deserve by education and stimulus to be made dynamic? Is it not a solemn duty incumbent on all colored churchmen to make it so? Will not the aid of the Church be given to prepare our girls in head, heart, and hand for the duties and responsibilities that await the intelligent wife, the Christian mother, the earnest, virtuous, helpful woman, at once both the lever and the fulcrum for uplifting the race?

THE TWENTIETH CENTURY

Document 6. Mary McLeod Bethune:
Leaving a Legacy

Mary McLeod Bethune (1875–1955) was one of the most powerful national Black leaders. She embodied service to the community through a deep sense of Christian duty and calling. In her early years she held several teaching positions in the United States and Africa. She founded the Daytona Normal and Industrial School for Negro Girls in Daytona Beach, Florida (1904), which later became Bethune-Cookman College. She was active in the club movement and founded the National Council of Negro Women (NCNW) in 1935, which served as an umbrella organization for most of the Black women's clubs of the era. Bethune was ecumenical and interfaith as she was educated by the Presbyterians, an active and committed Methodist, a member of the Executive Board of the Council of Church Women, and an honorary member of Hadassah. This excerpt is a "Last Will and Testament" for her people.[45]

Sometimes I ask myself if I have any legacy to leave. My worldly possessions are few. Yet, my experiences have been rich. From them I have distilled principles and policies in which I firmly believe. Perhaps, in them there is something of value. So as my life draws to a close, I will pass them on to Negroes everywhere in the hope that this philosophy may give them inspiration. Here, then, is my legacy:

I LEAVE YOU LOVE. Injuries quickly forgotten quickly pass away. Personally and racially, our enemies must be forgiven. Our aim must be to create a world of fellowship and justice where no man's color or religion is held against him. "Love thy neighbor" is a precept which could transform the world if it were universally practiced. It connotes brotherhood and to me, brotherhood of man is the noblest concept of all human relationships. Loving your neighbor means being interracial, interreligious and international.

I LEAVE YOU HOPE. Yesterday, our ancestors endured the degradation of slavery, yet they retained their dignity. Today, we direct our economic and political strength toward winning a more abundant and secure life. Tomorrow, a new Negro, unhindered by race taboos and shackles, will benefit from this striving and struggling.

I LEAVE YOU A THIRST FOR EDUCATION. More and more, Negroes are taking full advantage of hard-won opportunities for learning, and the educational level of the Negro population is at its highest point in history. We are making greater use of the privileges inherent in living in a democracy. Now that the barriers are crumbling everywhere, the Negro in America must be ever vigilant lest his forces be marshalled behind wrong causes and undemocratic movements. . . . He must not lend his support to any group that seeks to subvert democracy.

I LEAVE YOU FAITH. Faith is the first factor in a life devoted to service. Without faith, nothing is possible. With it, nothing is impossible. Faith in God is the greatest power, but great faith too is faith in oneself. The faith of the American Negro in himself has grown immensely, and is still increasing. The measure of our progress as a race is in precise relation to the depth of the faith in our people held by our leaders.

I LEAVE YOU RACIAL DIGNITY. I want Negroes to maintain their human dignity at all costs. We, as Negroes, must recognize that we are the custodians as well as the heirs of a great civilization. As a race we have given something to the world, and for this we are proud and fully conscious of our place in the total picture of mankind's development.

I LEAVE YOU A DESIRE TO LIVE HARMONIOUSLY WITH YOUR FELLOW MEN. The problem of color is world wide, on every continent. I appeal to all to recognize their common problems, and unite to solve them. So often our difficulties have made us supersensitive and truculent. I want to see my people conduct themselves in all relationships, fully conscious of their responsibilities and deeply aware of their heritage. We are a minority of fifteen million living side by side with a white majority of 177 million. We must learn to deal with people positively and on an individual basis.

I LEAVE YOU FINALLY A RESPONSIBILITY TO OUR YOUNG PEOPLE. Our children must never lose their zeal for building a better world. They must not be discouraged from aspiring toward greatness, for they are to be leaders of tomorrow. We have a powerful potential in our youth, and we must have the courage to change old ideas and practices so that we may direct their power toward good ends.

Faith, courage, brotherhood, dignity, ambition, responsibility—
these are needed today as never before. We must cultivate them and use
them as tools for our task of completing the establishment of equality
for the Negro. We must sharpen these tools in the struggle that faces us
and find new ways of using them. The Freedom Gates are half a-jar. We
must pry them fully open.

If I have a legacy to leave my people, it is my philosophy of living
and serving. As I face tomorrow, I am content. I pray now that my philosophy may be helpful to those who share my vision of a world of
Peace.

Document 7. Sara Duncan: Vital Questions

By 1904 the Southern women of the African Methodist Episcopal
Church (AME) had begun a second missionary society designed to help
alleviate some of the social injustices and inhumane conditions Blacks
in the South had to endure. However, many in the denomination did
not believe that women could or ought to carry out this additional
missionary endeavor. Sara Duncan rose to the occasion and challenged
the opinion that the older Women's Parent Mite Missionary Society was
the suitable place for all AME women's work.[46]

1st. In perusing the different church papers accumulated during my
two months' absence, engaged in the missionary field, I find in the issue
of the *Christians Recorder* of December 3, an article from a brother on
"Vital Questions—Our Missionary Department." And I wish to say a
word to the good brother who seems not to have kept up with the correct records of the missionary department, though were it not for and in
defense of the dear sisters who have worked so very hard the past seven
years to keep alive the department of Home and Foreign Missions, I
should keep quiet, but for their dear sakes "can not hold my peace."

As one of the leaders in the missionary work in this section since
1897, I have traveled to some extent in the South and Southwest, with a
chance now and then to look in upon the workers in the North and
East. We have made a careful study of the same, perhaps more largely
than our brother, having done but little else during these seven years.

Some of the points made by our brother are well taken and others are not; we feel them an injustice.

In the second clause of his argument, "Parents' Mite Missionaries," he expresses himself, regretting that the General Conference was unable to so adjust matters as to bring them under one head, viz: Women's Mite Missionary Society. And the organization that was doing real work is the W. M. Missionary Society, even though it exists only in the first, second, third, fourth and fifth districts, and the other section which is by far the stronger—yea, five times as strong—being the domain of the southern Woman's Home and Foreign Missionary Society. If the W. M. M. Society was allowed to enter the strongholds of the South and take such well organized shape as it has in the Northern and Western sections of our church, where our memberships are not so large by virtue of the sections of the country, then we would behold an income of $15,000. in the women's department alone, which would make it such an important factor in the missionary work of our church that our department could meet every obligation with which it might be encumbered and plan for broadening its scope of activity, thus carrying the church in undeveloped regions at home and abroad.

We first ask a question, where peace reigns, why will some persist in stirring up strife?

Nothing good can come out of confusion.

Since the General Conference has and did arrange in 1896, to have two missionary societies, why can not we work more, strive harder, leaving the rest with God?

And since there are so many things of vital interest to the church to be brought before the General Conference, why not let the women alone, and let them be in harmony, doing the will of the Master as best they can.

1st. Our brother is quite mistaken when he says all but the district's is operated by the W. H. & F. M. [Women's Home and Foreign Missionary] Society. He must search the records closely.

2nd. We emphatically deny "that it is the W. M. M. Society that is doing the real work," as our report to the coming General Conference will show; we are proud to be able to agree with our brother and say the W. M. M. Society is a grand and noble organization, and we would and will always be an helper rather than a hindrance; yet, at the same time, look out for that placed in our hands by the church that it may be preserved and prosper.

In '96 we started out with hardly a constitution to work by and not an organization of any kind, subject to the general church, only a few Home Mission Societies in a few churches for the benefit of the immediate communities, and when pastored by a few ministers who had the spirit of missions, would send from two to three dollars to the Annual Conference, and thought something had been done.

We feel that we speak for the sisters of both organizations when we say that the General Conference of the A.M.E. Church settled the matter in 1900 once for all, and there is no dissension among them, they are each working with might and main to have good reports at each annual conference, and each General Conference, and have no time to wrangle over what the name of the society is, or should be.

Document 8. Church of God in Christ: 1941 Annual Convocation Minutes

Although subordinate, the women of the 1941 national convocation of the Church of God in Christ were not marginal to the proceedings. The minutes highlight the connection between the women's department and the National Council of Negro Women. This connection dispels the stereotypical notion that the Sanctified Church (Black Holiness and Pentecostal churches) shuns social change and racial uplift. Along with showing their efficiency in raising money, the minutes also show the role of the district missionary and the separation of these roles from marital ties. The Sanctified Church went further than other Black churches in separating women's leadership roles from their marital relationships. Among the tasks of the district missionary was to inform and remind the churches in the district of their responsibilities toward the local church, district, state, and national work. This task, to be done at least twice a year, held within it the potential for conflict of interest. Such conflicts were addressed in the National Convocation.[47] An interesting note about the convocation is that the United States entered World War II at this time; it is referred to in the minutes only in the women's concern for several missionaries.[48]

We had greetings from State Mother Hale, Southern California who came forth singing, "All Things in Jesus Supplied" for God wills his saints to live righteously in this world. She told of God's help as a physician in child-bearing when all other help had failed. Her message was both spiritual discernment and a help to expectant mothers. . . .

From our Assistant General Mother L. Coffey we received greetings and she thanked God for God's blessing on the Senior leaders, Eld. C. H. Mason and Mother Lizzie Roberson. "Many officials of this church have been stricken, yet their lives are tied up in their work. And all their energy is given to the uplift of the work. Promotion does not take one out of service. We should serve for there is plenty of service to render. I am a servant of the most high God. God gave me this appointment and no man can take it from me." Mother Coffey was blessed to have a consideration opened for her through Pres. [of Saints Academy] Arenia Mallory, to attend the National Federation of Negro Women's Clubs, as a representative of the Church of God in Christ; not as an invited guest but as a leader and a guest of the President's honored wife, Mrs. E. Roosevelt; together with Mrs. Bethune, as president of this organization and the many other women of national repute. We know of no one more eligible for such a position, and to embrace such an occasion, to express herself on "Religious Morale." Also, among the noble women present we were happy to hear of the presence in this meeting of Miss Arenia Mallory, Pres., Saints Industrial School, Lexington, Mississippi and Mrs. Alice Mason Amos, daughter of Bishop Mason. Each had a voice in this meeting. God has given them wisdom to come before rulers and magistrates.

Much praise was accorded the Sisters for attending the call of Gen. Mother Roberson. Over $17,000 was sent in to our Gen. Mother and it made the heart of the Senior Bishop glad in receiving. Financial support was promised by all.

God's favor was to us in that he touched the body of our General Mother and brought her as it were from the dead, and let her be at her post of duty. As she appeared in our midst, accompanied by her beautiful and loyal daughter, Sister Ida Baker, our hearts overflowed with joy. Just to see her, comforted hearts that had been in sorrow. Her appearance was made possible by the love extended to her by her executive board of women. Assistant General Mother L. Coffey asked for absolute quietness to reign, and the Saints of God to arise at her coming, in honor of her presence in the room. Great was the demonstration, in God. Tears of joy were shed. She wanted all to know that she was not dead. She is the National Mother exercising all the power invested in her by Senior Bishop Mason, in the organizing of the Women's work. . . . We listened to the touching testimony of her daughter, Sis. Baker, as to her untiring care of Mother. Questions were asked Mother concerning the power invested in District Missionaries and those excluded from serving. Those not serving are Minister's wives in the same district with the husband. They are privileged to work in any other district. All district missionaries are subject to the State Mother. No district Missionaries are to be called "Supervisors." Her appointments are under the supervision of her State Mother: both working in cooperation. Many instructions were given to State Mothers and Workers. . . .

We waited in high expectancy for Mothers Day Service. A beautiful program was arranged by our Assistant General Mother L. Coffey, one whom Mother styles as her "eyes, feet, hands, and ears"; and left this edict with all her daughters: "Do what she tells you to do because she speaks my words." At the appointed hour (Tues., Dec. 9) seated on the platform were 34 State Supervisors. We beheld our General Mother walking down the aisle in all the dignity of her office. Our hopes and prayers were realized. . . . Mother gave her daughters more instructions. Speaking, she said, that it was the part of the State Mother to defend the Overseer, and should the wife be serving with him in the capacity of District Missionary (in case of misunderstanding) it would become a husband and wife issue; for wife or husband will defend one another. People do not want all the church to be consolidated in one house. Go from this meeting and make the changes, then come back to a new appointment. . . .

Document 9. National Black Sisters' Conference: Statement of Purpose

In 1968 Black women from the several congregations of Black women religious organized the National Black Sisters' Conference. The following is from their statement of purpose.[49]

The members of the National Black Sisters' Conference pledge to work unceasingly for the liberation of black people. Black religious women see themselves as gifted with the choicest of God's blessings.

The gift of our blackness gives us our mandate for the deliverance of a special people, our own black people. And the gift of our religious vocation makes accessible to us that union with Christ which guides us to the task, strengthens our determination, and sustains our efforts.

Black sisters are fully aware of that great WEALTH OF PERSON which is the rich heritage of black people in America. The National Black Sisters' Conference appreciates most deeply that total black experience, that indefinable yet identifiable "soul" which is our proud possession.

The communal concern of black folk is our greatest asset. It is the cornerstone of our endeavor to deliver a people who will carry on the great work to which Christ has called us, the work of building the Kingdom of God.

The National Black Sisters' Conference is initiating programs that will enable the people to question the reality and validity of what has been presented to them by the Church, formal education, government and by big business: thereby having a greater part in shaping not only our environment but also our future and, most important, the future of our children and we will share this new determination with all who are interested.

Within this context, we believe it is necessary to express ourselves as black religious women.

Document 10. Nannie Helen Burroughs: "The Slabtown District Convention"

Nannie Helen Burroughs (1883–1961) casts a huge and faithful shadow on the work of Black Baptist women. Both the Women's Auxiliary of the National Baptist Convention and the Progressive National Baptist Convention are inheritors of her legacy. Burroughs, an educator who founded the Women's Day in Baptist churches that then spread to other denominations, wrote the following play to teach proper behavior to women in the church. The play pokes fun at every aspect of a typical convention, although she did not include prayers in the play.

This omission was due to her piety. These excerpts are from the address of welcome, response, president's address, and an "appeal for the redemption of Slabtown."[50]

. . . "Members of the Local Missionary Society, citizens and friends: On behalf of the delegates in attendance upon the Tenth Annual Session of the Slabtown Women's District Convention, I accept your welcome, such as it is. We shall hurry up and get through with our business and go home where we can get something to eat. We are sorry you are having such hard times here. Anybody who lived through the drought and the depression certainly can feed and sleep this handful of folks a few days. Of course, you all invited us. . . . But we shall do the best we can and leave as soon as we can. We thank you for your hard-time welcome." . . . "It is now time for our President's address. . . ."

. . . "Fellow officers, delegates, ladies and gentlemen. . . . I have traveled all over Slabtown visiting missionary societies and waking up sleepy leaders. . . . I have gone to a number of missionary societies where there is about as much spiritual life as you would find in a grave-yard. . . . Some of you missionary sisters are raising money for missions and paying church debts and making presents to yourselves and your pastors. The Bible asks, 'Will a man rob God?' I answer, yes. A man will not only rob God, but he will get the women to help him. Sisters, it is not right for you to raise money for missions and use it to make presents and pay church debts. . . ."

. . . "And now, to these brethren who come to these conventions to tell the sisters what to do and how to vote, I want to say to you that you are welcome to our meetings, and if you will appreciate the courtesy extended to you by this association, you will go down from this place without any mark of displeasure upon you. But if you come here to use some of these sisters as tools to carry points that will work to your advantage in the distribution of funds and other, we want you to look to the Lord and be dismissed right now. . . ."

. . . "It affords me great pleasure to present Mrs. Betsy Lizzard, to make 'An Appeal for the Redemption of Slabtown.'" . . .

. . . "Sister and Friends: . . . I come in behalf of the schools in our district. I ain't no educated woman, but I got plenty of mother wit and common sense, and I got plenty of old-fashioned pride. I know the value of education in building up people and in building up communities. We can't get very far in these days without it and I certainly don't want to live in these woods with this raft of children growing up in ignorance. It is dangerous; and, furthermore, it is expensive. . . . It don't mean nothing but disgrace and workhouses and jails to let children grow up uneducated. We've been talkin' about making decent citizens, and I want to know how in the name of common sense we are going to make them when these people don't give our children but a few months of schooling and pay such no 'count salaries that they can't get teachers with sense enough to teach. Sisters, we just got to get the right kind of moral teachers who is properly educated, for the schools. We done had enough of that kind that thinks they are better than anybody else because they got a little education. That's all they have got. They ain't got no common sense and they ain't got influence enough to change a run-down community. Anybody can put on airs. We want teachers who can lift up a community. . . .

. . . "We want people who'll 'sociate with us, show us how to live; how to organize our community work; build up our Sunday schools and missionary societies. Some of them comes to church late, dressed like a lot of peacocks, and sits back and look in pity or scorn on us poor, unlearned critters, and laugh and nudge each other when we make mistakes. . . . There are just a few real ones. There's dear Miss Georgia. . . . She ain't got half the 'plomas that some . . . got, but she's got more character and more sense. . . . She's what I call educated. These other folks are just schooled. She's a model. . . . Look how she speaks to us when she meets us. . . . Look how the boys and girls who go to her school talk her up, and look how many she's put ambition into to go to higher schools and get more education. . . . We want teachers with souls, heads and hands dedicated to the redemption of Slabtown. They are in the world and we must find 'um."

Document 11. Zora Neale Hurston:
"The Wounds of Jesus"

Zora Neale Hurston (1901?–1960) was a remarkable novelist, journalist, folklorist, anthropologist, and critic.[51] From 1920 to 1950 she was the most prolific Black woman writer in the United States. Her ability to report with clarity and accuracy the positive aspect of life for poor and marginalized Blacks is a wellspring for exploring the values and morals for our contemporary context. She was a meticulous collector of folklore, legends, superstitions, music, and dance of poor Blacks in the South. Her work helped bring to the fore the rich life of Blacks in the South. The following excerpt is a crucifixion sermon from her first novel, *Jonah's Gourd Vine* (1934), which was published before, but written after, her first folklore collection, *Mules and Men* (1935).[52]

> . . I can see Him step out upon the rim bones of nothing
> Crying I am de way
> De truth and de light
> . . . .
> I can see Him as He mounted Calvary and hung upon de cross
>   for our sins.
> I can see-eee-ee
> De mountains fall to their rocky knees when He cried
> "My God, my God! Why hast Thou forsaken me?"
> The mountains fell to their rocky knees and trembled like a
>   beast
> From the stroke of the master's axe
> One angel took the flinches of God's eternal power
> And bled the veins of the earth
> One angel that stood at the gate with a flaming sword
> Was so well pleased with his power
> Until he pierced the moon with his sword
> And she ran down in blood
> And de sun
> Batted her fiery eyes and put on her judgment robe
> And laid down in de cradle of eternity
> And rocked herself into sleep and slumber
> He died until the great belt in the wheel of time
> And de geological strata fell aloose
> And a thousand angels rushed to de canopy of heben
> With flamin' swords in their hands
> And placed their feet upon blue ether's bosom, and looked
>   back at de dazzlin' throne
> And de arc angels had veiled their faces
> And de throne was draped in mournin'

And de orchestra had struck silence for the space of half an
   hour
Angels had lifted their harps to de weepin' willows
And God had looked off to-wards immensity
And blazin' worlds fell off His teeth
And about that time Jesus groaned on de cross, and
Dropped His head in the locks of His shoulder and said, "It
   is finished, it is finished."
And then de chambers of hell exploded
And de damnable spirits
Come up from de Sodomistic world and rushed into de smoky
   camps of eternal night,
And cried, "Woe! Woe! Woe!"
And then de Centurion cried out,
"Surely this is the Son of God."
. . . .
I heard de whistle of de damnation train
Dat pulled out from Garden of Eden loaded wid cargo goin'
   to hell
Ran at break-neck speed all de way thru de law
All de way thru de prophetic age
All de way thru de reign of kings and judges—
Plowed her way thru de Jurdan
And on her way to Calvary, when she blew for de switch
Jesus stood out on her track like a rough-backed mountain
And she threw her cow-catcher in His side and His blood
   ditched de train
He died for our sins.
Wounded in the house of His friends.
That's where I got off de damnation train
And dat's where you must get off, ha!

MOVING INTO
THE TWENTY-FIRST CENTURY

Document 12. Toni Morrison: Loving the Heart

Toni Morrison (b. 1931), the 1993 recipient of the Nobel Prize for
Literature, is a writer of richly textured characters and lyrical story lines

that explore the horrors of racism and oppression on the individual and the community. Her novels include *Sula* (1973), *Tar Baby* (1981), *Song of Solomon* (1977), *The Bluest Eye* (1970), and *Jazz* (1992). The selection below is from her fifth novel, *Beloved* (1987),[53] which won the 1988 Pulitzer Prize. The novel tells of the ravages of slavery through the story of Sethe. *Beloved* has been characterized as both a holocaust novel and an apocalyptic novel.

It was in front of *that* 124 that Sethe climbed off a wagon, her newborn tied to her chest, and felt for the first time the wide arms of her mother-in-law, who had made it to Cincinnati. Who decided that, because slave life had "busted her legs, back, head, eyes, hands, kidneys, womb and tongue," she had nothing left to make a living with but her heart—which she put to work at once. Accepting no title of honor before her name, but allowing a small caress after it, she became an unchurched preacher, one who visited pulpits and opened her great heart to those who could use it. In winter and fall she carried it to AME's and Baptists, Holinesses and Sanctifieds, the Church of the Redeemer and the Redeemed. Uncalled, unrobed, unanointed, she let her great heart beat in their presence. When warm weather came, Baby Suggs, holy, followed by every black man, woman and child who could make it through, took her great heart to the Clearing—a wide-open place cut deep in the woods nobody knew for what at the end of a path known only to deer and whoever cleared the land in the first place. In the heat of every Saturday afternoon, she sat in the clearing while the people waited among the trees.

After situating herself on a huge flat-sided rock, Baby Suggs bowed her head and prayed silently. The company watched her from the trees. They knew she was ready when she put her stick down. Then she shouted, "Let the children come!" and they ran from the trees toward her.

"Let your mothers hear you laugh," she told them, and the woods rang. The adults looked on and could not help smiling.

Then "Let the grown men come," she shouted. They stepped out one by one from among the ringing trees.

"Let your wives and your children see you dance," she told them, and groundlife shuddered under their feet.

Finally she called the women to her. "Cry," she told them. "For the living and the dead. Just cry." And without covering their eyes the women let loose.

It started that way: laughing children, dancing men, crying women and then it got mixed up. Women stopped crying and danced; men sat down and cried; children danced, women laughed, children cried until, exhausted and riven, all and each lay about the Clearing damp and gasping for breath. In the silence that followed, Baby Suggs, holy, offered up to them her great big heart.

She did not tell them to clean up their lives or to go and sin no more. She did not tell them they were the blessed of the earth, its inheriting meek or its glorybound pure.

She told them that the only grace they could have was the grace they could imagine. That if they could not see it, they would not have it.

"Here," she said, "in this here place, we flesh; flesh that weeps, laughs; flesh that dances on bare feet in grass. Love it. Love it hard. Yonder they do not love your flesh. They despise it. They don't love your eyes; they'd just as soon pick em out. No more do they love the skin on your back. Yonder they flay it. And O my people they do not love your hands. Those they only use, tie, bind, chop off and leave empty. Love your hands! Love them. Raise them up and kiss them. Touch others with them, pat them together, stroke them on your face 'cause they don't love that either. *You* got to love it, *you!* And no, they ain't in love with your mouth. Yonder, out there, they will see it broken and break it again. What you say out of it they will not heed. What you scream from it they do not hear. What you put into it to nourish your body they will snatch away and give you leavins instead. No, they don't love your mouth. *You* got to love it. This is flesh I'm talking about here. Flesh that needs to be loved. Feet that need to rest and to dance; backs that need support; shoulders that need arms, strong arms I'm telling you. And O my people, out yonder, hear me, they do not love your neck unnoosed and straight. So love your neck; put a hand on it, grace it, stroke it and hold it up. And all your inside parts that they'd just as soon slop for hogs, you got to love them. The dark, dark liver—love it, love it, and the beat and beating heart, love that too. More than eyes or feet. More than lungs that have yet to draw free air. More than your life-holding womb and your life-giving private parts, hear me now, love your heart. For this is the prize." Saying no more, she stood up then and danced with her twisted hip the rest of what her heart had to say while the others opened their mouths and gave her the music. Long notes held until the four-part harmony was perfect enough for their deeply loved flesh.

Document 13. Katie Geneva Cannon:
Black Women's Stories and Moral Wisdom

Womanist ethicist Katie Geneva Cannon broke new ground in her critique of traditional ethical theory in her book *Black Womanist Ethics* (1988). In the following excerpt from an earlier essay,[54] Cannon begins to articulate the different worldview of traditional ethical theory, which she terms "dominant ethics," and the reality of African American life in the United States. She turns to the work of Black women writers to illuminate this reality. This use of African American women novelists as a methodological tool for ethical reflection moves contemporary ethics in challenging new directions.

I first began pondering the relationship between faith and ethics as a schoolgirl while listening to my grandmother teach the central affirmations of Christianity within the context of a racially segregated society. My community of faith taught me the principles of God's universal parenthood that engendered a social, intellectual, and cultural ethos embracing the equal humanity of all people. Yet my city, state, and nation declared it a punishable offense against the laws and mores for Blacks and whites "to travel, eat, defecate, wait, be buried, make love, play, relax and even speak together, except in the stereotyped context of master and servant interaction."[55]

My religious quest tried to relate the Christian doctrines preached in Black Church to the suffering, oppression, and exploitation of Black people in society. How could Christians who were white flatly and openly refuse to treat as fellow human beings Christians who had African ancestry? Was not the essence of the Gospel mandate a call to eradicate affliction, despair, and systems of injustice? Inasmuch as the Black Church expressed the inner ethical life of the people, was there any way to reconcile the inherent contradictions in Christianity as practiced by whites with the radical indictments of and challenges for social amelioration and economic development in the Black religious heritage? How long would the white church continue to be the ominous symbol of white dominance, sanctioning and assimilating the propagation of racism in the mundane interests of the ruling group?

In the 1960s my quest for the integration of faith and ethics was influenced by scholars in various fields who surfaced the historical contributions of Afro-Americans that had been distorted and denied. Avidly I read the analysis exposing the assumptions and dogmas that made Blacks a negligible factor in the thought of the world. For more than three and a half centuries, a "conspiracy of silence" rendered invisible the outstanding contributions of Blacks to the culture of humankind. From cradle to grave the people in the United States were taught the alleged inferiority of Blacks.

When I turned specifically to theological ethics, I discovered the dominant ethical systems implied that the doing of Christian ethics in the Black community was either immoral or amoral. The cherished ethical ideas predicated upon the existence of freedom and a wide range of choices proved null and void in situations of oppression. The real-lived texture of Black life requires moral agency that may run contrary to the ethical boundaries of mainline Protestantism. Blacks may use action guides that have never been considered within the scope of traditional codes of faithful living. Racism, gender discrimination, and economic exploitation, as inherited, age-long complexes, require the Black community to create and cultivate values and virtues in their own terms so that they prevail against the odds with moral integrity.

For example, dominant ethics makes a virtue of qualities that lead to economic success—self-reliance, frugality, and industry. These qualities are based on an assumption that success is possible for anyone who tries. Developing confidence in one's own abilities, resources, and judgments amidst a careful use of money and goods—in order to exhibit assiduity in the pursuit of upward mobility—have proven to be positive values for many whites. But the oligarchic economic powers, and the consequent political power they generate, own and control capital and distribute credit in a manner detrimental to Blacks. As part of a legitimating system to justify the supposed inherent inferiority of Blacks, the values so central to white economic mobility prove to be ineffectual. Racism does not allow all Black women and Black men to work and save in order to develop a standard of living that is congruent with the American ideal.

Theory and analysis demonstrate that to embrace work as a "moral essential" means that Black women are still the last hired to do the work that white men, white women, and men of color refuse to do, and at a wage that men and white women refuse to accept. Black women, placed in jobs proven to be detrimental to their health, are doing the most menial, tedious, and by far the most underpaid work, if they manage to get a job at all.

Dominant ethics also assumes that a moral agent is to a considerable degree free and self-directing. Each person possesses self-determining power. For instance, one is free to choose whether or not she or he wants to suffer and make sacrifices as a principle of action or as a voluntary vocational pledge of crossbearing. In dominant ethics a person is free to make suffering a desirable moral norm. This is not so for Blacks. For the masses of Black people, suffering is the normal state of affairs. Mental anguish, physical abuse, and emotional agony are all part of Black people's daily lives. Due to the white supremacy and male superiority that pervade this society, Blacks and whites, women and men are forced to live with very different ranges of freedom. As long as the white-male experience continues to be established as the ethical norm, Black women, Black men, and others will suffer unequivocal oppression. The range of freedom has been restricted by those who cannot hear and will not hear voices expressing pleasure and pain, joy and rage as others experience them.

In the Black community, qualities that determine desirable ethical values of upright character and sound moral conduct must always take into account the circumstances, paradoxes, and dilemmas that constrict Blacks to the lowest rungs of the social, political, and economic hierarchy. Black existence is deliberately and openly controlled. . . . The vast majority of Blacks suffer every conceivable form of denigration. Their lives are named, defined and circumscribed by whites.

The moral wisdom of the Black community is extremely useful in defying oppressive rules or standards of "law and order" that degrade Blacks. It helps Blacks purge themselves of self-hate, thus asserting their own validity. But the ethical values of the Black community are not identical with the obligations and duties that Anglo-Protestant American society requires of its members. Nor can the ethical assumptions be the same, as long as powerful whites who control the wealth, the systems, and the institutions in this society continue to perpetuate brutality and criminality against Blacks. . . .

Document 14. Delores S. Williams: Speaking Black Women's Tongue?

Delores S. Williams provides a provocative critique of white feminist theology in the following selection.[56] Her use of the term *demonarchy* as contrasted with patriarchy helps to illuminate the theological and sociopolitical differences between white and African American women's oppression. Her aim is exploring the implications of being a Black feminist mindful of dangers of co-optation and irrelevancy. She understands that a key task of the womanist theologian is to be accountable to the realities of Black Christian women's lives and the life of the Black community in general. Her most recent work, *Sisters in the Wilderness: The Challenge of Womanist God-Talk* (1993), explores the image and metaphor of the wilderness as a way to push current feminist and Black theology into deeper reflection on the nature of social oppression.

For feminist thinking, an important idea is that patriarchy is the major source of all women's oppression. However, this idea becomes limited and problematic when one attempts to use it to understand the Afro-American woman's *total* experience of oppression in North America.

In feminist literature, patriarchy is the power relation between men and women and between women and society's institutions controlled by men. White-American feminist Adrienne Rich describes it as:

> . . . the power of the fathers: a familial-social, ideological, political system in which men—by force, direct pressure, or through ritual, tradition, law and language, customs, etiquette, education, and division of labor, determine what part women shall or shall not play, and in which the female is everywhere subsumed under the male.[57]

While Mary Daly, in *Beyond God the Father,* reveals how the patriarchal religions (e.g., Judaism and Christianity) reinforce women's oppression and validate male supremacy, her understanding of patriarchy apparently concurs with Rich's definition. It is not reductionist, I think, to suggest

that most feminist writing on the subject does support Rich's understanding of the meaning of patriarchy.[58]

However, a simple interpolation of Rich's definition reveals its
limitation as far as black women are concerned. To be congruent with
the Afro-American woman's experience of oppression in this country,
patriarchy would have to be defined as:

> ,... the power of ... [white men and white women]: a familial-social,
> ideological, political system in which [white men and white women]—
> by force, direct pressure, or through ritual, tradition, law and language,
> customs, etiquette, education, and division of labor, determine what
> part [black women] shall or shall not play, and in which the [black
> female] is everywhere subsumed under the [white female] and white
> male.[59]

Thus defined, patriarchy loses its identity. It is no longer just the power
of fathers, or men, to oppress women. It is also the power of a certain
group of females to oppress other groups of females. This inclusion of a
group of women as oppressors—an assessment that speaks the truth of
the Afro-American woman's history in North America—renders the
feminist patriarchal critique of society less valid as a tool for assessing
black women's oppression *resulting from their relation to white-controlled
American institutions.* Therefore, one cannot claim that patriarchy, as it is
understood by feminists, is the major source of all women's oppression.

Another limitation of the feminist understanding of patriarchy is
that it fails to place emphasis upon what appears to be a positive side of
patriarchy with regard to the development of white-American women.
It is also the operation of this positive side that indicates a clear distinction between white women's and black women's oppression.

White American patriarchy, in its institutional manifestations,
affords many white female children and white female adults (as groups)
the care, protection, and resources necessary for intellectual development and physical well-being.[60] White American patriarchy has thus
provided white women with the education, skills, and support (and
often financial resources) they need to get first chance at the jobs and
opportunities for women resulting from the pressures exerted by the
civil rights movements in America. White American patriarchy, in its
private and institutional manifestations, also intends to support the life,

physical growth, intellectual development, and economic well-being of the female and male fruit of the white woman's womb—*When That Fruit Issues From Her Sexual Union With White Males.* From a black female perspective, then, it is possible to speak of *the productive patriarchal intent of white patriarchy* for the female and male fruit of the white woman's womb. And this productive patriarchal intent permeates the relation between white women (as a group) and the white-controlled institutions of American society.

However, the same institutions have no such productive intent for black women or for the fruit of black women's wombs (even if that fruit derived from sexual union between a black female and a white male).[61] Rather, these institutions intend the retardation of the intellectual, emotional, spiritual, economic, and physical growth of black women and the fruit of their wombs, male and female. This is partly demonstrated in the current operation of the white-controlled public school system in America. The black struggle for equality through integration into that system has exposed black children to a host of white male and white female teachers who daily undermine (often through ignorance of their own racism) the confidence, the intellectual stamina, the spirit, and the leadership development of black children. Convinced that black people are intellectually inferior to whites, many of these white teachers and school administrators "do not encourage black children to excel like they do white children," a black female student in my freshman English class once told me. "If you keep quiet, act nicely, and do a little work they will pass you," she said. "It doesn't matter that nobody taught you to read or write a theme." . . .

. . . The failure of white feminists to emphasize the *substantial difference* between their patriarchally-derived-privileged-oppression and black women's demonically-derived-annihilistic-oppression renders black women invisible in feminist thought and action. It is no wonder that in most feminist literature written by white-American women, the words "woman" and "women" signify only the white woman's experience. By failing to insert the word "white" before "woman" and "women," some feminists imperialistically take over the identity of those rendered invisible. Therefore, one can encounter instances in white feminist literature when feminists make appropriations from Afro-American culture without identifying the source of the appropriation and without admitting that American feminism has roots deep in black culture. . . .

... The implication of all the preceding discussion is that black women, *in their relation to white-controlled American institutions,* do not experience patriarchy.[62] It is necessary, then, for black women—when describing their own oppressed relation to white-controlled American institutions—to use new words, new language, and new ideas that fit their experience. These new words, language, and ideas will help black women develop an appropriate theoretical foundation for the ideology and political action needed to obtain the liberation of black women and the black family.[63]

Therefore, as a beginning, I suggest that there are at least two ways of institutional white-rule effecting the oppression of many American women. Certainly one of these is patriarchy as described by Adrienne Rich earlier in this paper. There is also the demonic way of institutional white-rule which controls black women's lives. This way can be named demonarchy.[64] Patriarchy, *in its white institutional form,* can also be understood as the systemic governance of white women's lives by white women's fathers, brothers, and sons using care, protection, and privilege as instruments of social control. Demonarchy can be understood as the demonic governance of black women's lives by white male and white female ruled systems using racism, violence, violation, retardation, and death as instruments of social control. Distinguished from individual violent acts stemming from psychological abnormalities on the part of the perpetrator, demonarchy is a traditional and collective expression of white government in relation to black women. It belongs to the realm of normalcy. It is informed by a state of consciousness that believes white women are superior to and more valuable than any woman of color and that white men are the most valuable and superior forms of life on earth. While sexism is a kind of women's oppression issuing from patriarchy, racist-gender oppression of black women issues from demonarchy. Black women cannot disjoin race and gender as they describe their oppression resulting from their relation to white-controlled American institutions. . . .

Document 15. Jacquelyn Grant:
The Bible and Jesus in Womanist Tradition

Jacquelyn Grant explores the nature of the Bible and Jesus in the womanist tradition.[65] Her work takes great care to place Black women's experience at the core of womanist theology. Her concern is to uncover the ways in which African American women of faith interpret the liberating message of the gospel to make sense out of race, gender, and class oppression. Her book, *White Women's Christ, Black Women's Jesus* (1990), includes a thorough survey of white feminist Christology. She then offers a critique and expansion based on Black women's understanding of Jesus.

Theological investigation into the experiences of Christian Black women reveals that Black women considered the Bible to be a major source of religious validation in their lives. Though Black women's relationship with God preceded their introduction to the Bible, this Bible gave some content to their God-consciousness.[66] The source for Black women's understanding of God has been twofold: first, God's revelation directly to them, and secondly, God's revelation as witnessed in the Bible and as read and heard in the context of their experience. The understanding of God as creator, sustainer, comforter, and liberator took on life as they agonized over their pain, and celebrated the hope that as God delivered the Israelites, they would be delivered as well. The God of the Old and New Testament became real in the consciousness of oppressed Black women. Of the use of the Bible, Fannie Barrier Williams quite aptly said:

> Though the Bible was not an open book to the Negro before emancipation, thousands of the enslaved men and women of the Negro race learned more than was taught to them. Thousands of them realized the deeper meanings, the sweeter consolations and the spiritual awakenings that are part of the religious experiences of all Christians.[67]

In other words, though Black people in general and Black women in particular were politically impotent, religiously controlled, they were able to appropriate certain themes of the Bible which spoke to their reality. For example, Jarena Lee, a nineteenth century Black woman preacher in the African Methodist Episcopal Church, constantly emphasized the theme "Life and Liberty" in her sermons which were always biblically based. This interplay of scripture and experience was exercised even more expressly by many other Black women. An ex-slave woman revealed that when her experience negated certain oppressive interpretations of the Bible given by white preachers, she, through engaging the biblical message for herself, rejected them. Consequently, she also dismissed white preachers who distorted the message in order to maintain slavery. . . .

The truth which the Bible brought was undeniable, though perception of it was often distorted in order to support the monstrous system of oppression. Sarcastically responding to this tendency, Fannie Barrier Williams admonished, "do not open the Bible too wide." Biblical interpretation, realized Williams, a non-theologically trained person, had at its basis the prior agenda of white America. She therefore argued:

> Religion, like every other force in America, was first used as an instrument and servant of slavery. All attempts to Christianize the negro were limited by the important fact that he was property of valuable and peculiar sort, and that the property value must not be disturbed, even if his soul were lost. If Christianity could make the negro docile, domestic and less an independent and fighting savage, let it be preached to that extent and no further.[68]

Such false, pernicious, demoralizing gospel could only be preached if the Bible was not opened wide enough, lest one sees the liberating message of Jesus as summarized in Luke 4:18. The Bible must be read and interpreted in the light of Black women's own oppression and God's revelation within that context. Womanists must, like Sojourner, "compare the teachings of the Bible with the witness" in them.[69]

To do Womanist theology, then, we must read and hear the Bible and engage it within the context of our own experience. This is the only way that it can make sense to people who are oppressed. Black women of the past did not hesitate in doing this and we must do no less. . . .

. . . Having opened the Bible wider than many White people, Black people, in general, and Black women in particular, found a Jesus who they could claim, and whose claim for them was one of affirmation of dignity and self-respect.

In the experience of Black people, Jesus was "all things."[70] Chief among these however was the belief in Jesus as the divine co-sufferer, who empowers them in situations of oppression. For Christian Black women in the past, Jesus was their central frame of reference. They identified with Jesus because they believed that Jesus identified with them. As Jesus was persecuted and made to suffer undeservedly, so were they. His suffering culminated in the crucifixion. Their crucifixion included rapes, and husbands being castrated (literally and metaphorically), babies being sold, and other cruel and often murderous treatments. But Jesus' suffering was not the suffering of a mere human, for Jesus was understood to be God incarnate. As Harold Carter observed of Black prayers in general, there was no difference made between the persons of the trinity, Jesus, God, or the Holy Spirit. All of these proper names for God were used interchangeably in prayer language. Thus, Jesus was the one who speaks the world into creation. He was the power behind the Church.[71] Black women's affirmation of Jesus as God meant that White people were not God. . . .

Document 16. Cheryl Townsend Gilkes:
Afrocentric Appropriation of the Bible

The work of sociologist Cheryl Townsend Gilkes represents the best of the interdisciplinary enterprise of womanist thought. An expert on the Sanctified Church (Black Holiness and Pentecostal churches), Gilkes explores how the Bible was an important interpretative tool for Africans as they developed a distinctive Afro-Christian tradition.[72] In the following excerpt, Gilkes looks at the King James Bible as an Afrocentric matrix as she develops the theme "mother to the motherless, father to the fatherless."

. . . An Afrocentric reading of the Bible is a reading that incorporates the events that are central to the black experience and affirms the dignity of the African personality in the face of the forces of degradation; such a reading rejects the use of Bible as an apology for oppression and it is quick to point out the categorical inclusion of Africans. This inclusion becomes the basis upon which the text can be expanded upon and augmented to include the range of experiences that are peculiarly African and African-American and yet affirm the universality of the good news. Through a variety of folktexts, the Afrocentric reading captures the multivalent dimensions of the oppression. Ultimately an Afrocentric reading of the Bible is an important contribution to an ever expanding hermeneutic of suspicion growing out of many theologies of liberation and to a hermeneutic of affirmation and of creative actualization that have roots in the preaching traditions of black churches.

The problems of powerlessness and injustice are central themes in the Bible. The category "fatherless" is extremely large and God as "father to the fatherless" is reinforced in the Anglican prayer tradition, something the Africans and their descendants borrowed in spite of their rejection of the worship tradition. The genius of this Afrocentric reading of the Bible is its recognition of the central issues of powerlessness, justice, and theodicy in a context where the dominant "canon within the canon" did not. Hanks[73] described his response when he noted this omission in the dominant exegetical tradition. He reflected "Imagine my shock when I consulted work after work of First World biblical erudition . . . and found almost nothing! My initial reaction was one of perplexity, frustration, and indignation." The Afrocentric reading discerned what Hanks[74] discovered: that "oppression [is] *a basic structural category of biblical theology.*"

Biblical definitions of oppression embraced the slaves' experience. The Bible identified multiple "forms and methods of oppression." Tamez,[75] summarizing this biblical perspective, writes:

> The oppressors are thieves and murderers, but their ultimate purpose is not to kill or impoverish the oppressed. Their primary objective is to increase their wealth at whatever cost. The impoverishment and death of the oppressed are a secondary consequence. There are two levels of oppression: the international and the national. Black people experienced both and they observed this in their close relationship with Native peoples in the South. At the international level that oppression described in the Bible consists of "the enslavement and exploitation of . . . workers, . . . genocide, [ideologies and] myths of idleness, . . . deceitful concessions, [crushing violent force], . . . plunder and slaughter, . . . the imposition of tribute, . . . and exile."[76]

Slaves knew they were exploited workers. They experienced the genocidal dimensions through the murders and tortures of slavery and the Middle Passage. They were victimized by the myths of idleness embedded in such stereotypes as Sambo.[77] Story after story of slaves cheated out of their opportunity to buy their own or their family members' freedom spoke to the problem of deceitful concessions. The excessively brutal responses to slave revolts and the decades of post-bellum terror reinforced biblical images of plunder and slaughter. Even the problem of exile—the legal and customary inability to live as free persons in slave areas—was prominent in slave consciousness. Manumission could mean the loss of family and community. Women's low rates of escape reflect these constraints of family and community.

Even the "national" dimensions of biblical oppression, "exploitation of workers, . . . fraud, and . . . [violence], murder," were evident in the black experience. The Bible also counseled against lending systems or "usury" that perpetuated an oppressed state and southern sharecroppers of the late nineteenth and early twentieth centuries had no trouble recognizing the biblical opposition to their plight. The Bible also cited "sexual violation of women" as one of the central "methods" of oppression. The disparity of strength was so great that rape was sometimes imaged as a form of murder.[78]

In their reading of Psalm 68 and by extension the other psalms that speak directly of the "poor," the "fatherless," the "widow," "the weak," and the "captive," slaves understood that they were poor and in need of liberation. In recognizing their "fatherlessness" black people grappled with their "natal alienation" or "social death."[79] Their humanity was legally stripped from them and their only realistic challenge was moral and religious in a society where ideologies of freedom and citizenship abounded. Psalm 68 as part of their Afrocentric reading became a promise of ultimate empowerment. As the biblical "fatherless" and therefore God's people, they were endowed with rights and privileges. Their emphasis on "Jubilee" as an aspect of liberation and freedom perceived that even in biblical slavery, a challenge existed to the injustice they experienced. The Bible offered a vision of economic equity and citizenship. Redemption or salvation incorporated economic and political empowerment and a restoration to civil status.

Slaves' view of themselves as motherless addressed the powerlessness of their family and community systems. That view recognized the devastating assault on women within the system of racial oppression. Black men wrote most of the slave narratives that account for the suffering of women, usually their mothers or other relatives. They lamented the neglect that stemmed from slave women's exploitation as nurses and caretakers of white children. They described the pervasive violence and sexual abuse in the slave system. The physical and ideological assaults on black mothers were major manifestations of cultural humiliation. The powerlessness of women to withstand sexual victimization was an emblem of group oppression.

By connecting motherlessness and fatherlessness, the Afro-Christian tradition provided a comprehensive portrait of powerlessness. It was a civil, economic, political, and cultural problem combined. Fatherlessness linked with motherlessness apprehended the particularities of the black situation. The theological perspective in the Afrocentric reading assesses the morality of oppression, particularly the morality of the oppressors themselves. Intuitively, this Afrocentric approach recognized what Tamez describes as a basic characteristic of oppressors: "The oppressors are rich and influential people . . . ; their basic concern is to accumulate wealth. They . . . are idolaters who follow false gods that can lend an aura of legitimacy to their actions. . . ."[80] Since Psalm 68 spoke of the necessity for all to turn to God, oppressors were brought under its judgment. In opposition to the oppressors' attempts to ideologize the Bible, this reading upheld the Bible's original judgment of power and oppression.

CHAPTER FIVE

Evangelical Women

Nancy A. Hardesty

Documents

REVIVALS and the denominations they spawned are the sources of evangelicalism. Revivals are a relatively modern phenomena growing out of the Puritan emphasis on conversion as evidence and experience of salvation. The Reformation emphasis on Scripture and a commitment to social involvement are also important to evangelical Christianity.

In the United States the preaching of Jonathan Edwards (1703–1758) and Englishman George Whitefield (1715–1770) ignited the First Great Awakening in the 1730s and 1740s among New England Puritans. In England John Wesley (1703–1791) read Edwards's *Faithful Narrative* (1737) and teamed up with Whitefield to preach among the miners, farmers, and urban poor. Out of their efforts grew the Methodists. At his mother Susanna's urging, Wesley encouraged lay male preachers and eventually women preachers, teachers, and class leaders.

English and Irish immigrants brought their Methodist faith and practice to the colonies. Although some believe that the first Methodist Church in America was founded by Robert Strawbridge in Maryland, others point to Barbara Ruckle Heck (1734–1804) in New York City, who in 1766 urged her cousin Philip Embury to renew his work as a class leader and local preacher. That first congregation included Heck, her husband, Paul, their African American servant, Betty, and a hired man, John Lawrence. Heck was also instrumental in forming the first Methodist society in Canada.

After the First Great Awakening the colonies concentrated on revolution and then the formation of a new type of government. Religion appeared to take a declining role. Again the call came for revival.

This time it began on the Kentucky frontier in August 1801. A "sacramental season" camp meeting convened at Cane Ridge in Bourbon County. The crowd of more than ten thousand was exhorted by Presbyterian, Baptist, and Methodist preachers. Listeners responded with an outpouring of religious fervor accompanied by various physical "exercises" described as falling, "the jerks," dancing, barking, running, and singing. Some women swayed backward and forward so rapidly that their hair snapped like a whip. The weeklong meeting led to a wave of similar meetings across the South for the next several years.

In the Northeast there was a tidal wave of organizing for the social good. The American Board of Commissioners for Foreign Missions was founded in Boston in 1810. Soon every hamlet had both men's and women's missionary societies, "mite" or "cent" societies. The American Education Society, founded in 1815, and the American Home Missionary Society (1826) supported the education and deployment of ministers for the frontier. The American Bible Society (1816) and the American Tract Society (1826) supplied written materials for missions and frontier churches. Women began to gather poor children and teach them reading and writing as well as the gospel; the American Sunday School Union was born in 1817. The list of benevolent societies was endless, aiding the poor, supporting mothers, caring for the aged and infirm, helping the blind and mentally ill. Evangelicals were involved on every front.

Widespread revival did not break out until 1826 when Presbyterian evangelist Charles Grandison Finney (1792–1875) began preaching in upstate New York. In that area Calvinist Presbyterians and Congregationalists taught that conversion was something to wait for. One usually attended church and tried to live a devout life, but opinion was divided about whether any of these "means" were of any consequence if one was not "elected" to salvation. Election was evidenced by a conversion experience brought about by a spontaneous outpouring of God's grace (document 1). Finney, trained as a lawyer, declared that one could make a choice and settle the matter. "Religion is not something to wait for but something to do!" he said. One woman converted under his ministry was Elizabeth Cady Stanton (1815–1902) (document 2).

Finney instituted a new form of revivalism outlined in his 1835 *Lectures on Revivals of Religion.* His "new measures" included "protracted" meetings lasting weeks or months, colloquial preaching, praying for people by name, asking people concerned about the state of their souls to attend "anxious meetings" or to sit on an "anxious bench," and allowing women to pray and testify in public. This latter innovation caused great controversy.[1]

Finney also strongly linked revival with social reform such as temperance, moral reform, and abolition. In 1835 Finney became professor of theology at Oberlin College, the first school to admit women and Blacks on a par with white men. Among his students at Oberlin were Antoinette Brown, who became in 1853 the first woman fully ordained in this country (document 4), and Lucy Stone, who became an abolition lecturer and founder of a major woman's rights organization.

Finney advocated abolition of slavery, and his followers campaigned for it. Many of his most ardent male converts, including Theodore Weld (1803–1895) and Henry Stanton (1805–1887) began to evangelize for abolition and then train others to do the same. Among "the Seventy" they trained in 1836 were Sarah (1792–1873) and Angelina (1805–1879) Grimke, South Carolina sisters who had seen first-hand the degradation of slavery. In order to speak out on behalf of the slaves, the Grimke sisters found themselves defending woman's rights against the Congregational clergy of Connecticut (document 3).

The first woman's rights convention was organized by Elizabeth Cady Stanton and Quaker preacher Lucretia Mott (1793–1880). The Stantons' wedding trip in 1840 was to the World's Anti-Slavery Convention in London. There Mott and other elected women delegates were forced to observe from the balcony. Stanton and Mott decided to organize for woman's rights. The first convention was held in 1848 at Seneca Falls, New York. At many of the early conventions Antoinette Brown interpreted the Bible in support of their actions.

Finney also supported his wife Lydia's work in moral reform. While male Finneyites first tried to start a Magdalene home to convert prostitutes, evangelical women immediately realized that the problem was not in the moral laxity of the prostitute but in her economic need and her ready market. Moral reform societies sought to offer economic help (training, equipment, job placement, work collectives, childcare, and so forth) and to discourage male patrons by publishing their names in society journals.

Finney also advocated temperance. Many of his followers were active in antebellum temperance societies. Frances Willard (1839–1898) grew up in a temperance and reform household. Her parents, born in the "burned-over district" of upstate New York (an area repeatedly swept by the wildfire of revival and reform movements) and influenced by Finney's revivals, spent several years at Oberlin College. Eventually they moved to Evanston, Illinois, where Frances and her sister Mary attended school. A committed Methodist, Frances raised money throughout the church to build Heck Hall at Garrett Seminary in Evanston. She served as the first woman college president (1871–73) at the fledgling Evanston College for Ladies, which soon merged into Northwestern University. In 1877 she served as an assistant to revivalist Dwight L. Moody in Boston.

When temperance reemerged in 1874 as a woman's cause, Willard served as president of the Chicago and Illinois Woman's Christian Temperance Unions (1874–77) and as the first corresponding secretary of the national WCTU in 1874. She was elected national president in 1879 and served until her death. She was an outspoken advocate of woman's rights and suffrage in church and state (document 5). She defended women's ministry in *Woman in the Pulpit* and always encouraged women preachers by showcasing them at WCTU conventions.

In the midnineteenth century, evangelical Christianity seemed the dominant force in American Christianity. An Evangelical Alliance was formed in London in 1846, representing more than fifty American and European groups. The Evangelical Alliance in the U.S. began in 1867 to further cooperative enterprises among Protestant denominations. The Methodist Episcopal Church and its African American counterparts (such as the African Methodist Episcopal Church and the African Methodist Episcopal Church, Zion) formed the largest group. Presbyterians, Baptists, and Congregationalists were numerous. Protestant hegemony was at its peak. However, as the century progressed the alliance waned, its power diluted by the massive influx of Roman Catholic and Jewish immigrants toward the end of the century and the rise of biblical criticism, science, and secularism.

Both Charles Finney and Frances Willard experienced and advocated holiness or entire sanctification. John Wesley had talked about "perfect love" and wrote a *Plain Account of Christian Perfection.* He thought of it as a lifetime process subsequent to conversion, rarely completed before death. However, some of his associates began to claim that they had already achieved a state of sinless perfection.

American Methodist laywoman Phoebe Palmer (1807–1874) followed Finney's lead and discovered a "shorter way." Just as Finney had condensed the Puritan process of conversion into a crisis experience of commitment, so Palmer declared that sanctification was a matter of commitment and claiming God's promise. In the 1840s she published a series of books developing her "altar terminology." She argued that all one needed to do was to lay one's all "on the altar." Since according to God's promise "the altar sanctifies the gift" and we can believe God's promises, we can then claim our holiness by faith (documents 6 and 7). Palmer and her husband Walter, a physician, preached this message at summer camp meetings from New Jersey to Nova Scotia and in the British Isles. Her books and their magazine, *Guide to Holiness,* circled the globe. For nearly sixty years the Palmer home was the site of the Tuesday Meeting for the Promotion of Holiness, attended by women, laymen, ministers, and bishops from across the country and around the world.

Eventually holiness advocates organized the National Campmeeting Association for the Promotion of Holiness in 1866 and then state-level associations. Members were increasingly alienated from their local churches and gradually formed a whole family of denominations: the Wesleyan Methodist Church, the Free Methodist Church, Church of God (Anderson, Indiana), Church of the Nazarene, Christian and Missionary Alliance, the Pilgrim Holiness Church, the Salvation Army, and others.

In the late nineteenth century many Holiness people were increasingly radicalized and marginalized. Many adopted a belief in faith healing (healing through prayer and without recourse to doctors or drugs). Initially sick persons were encouraged to "pray the prayer of faith" (document 8), but eventually certain people came to be seen as having a "gift of healing," and they began to "lay hands" on the sick and heal them (document 9).

Holiness advocates and others also adopted certain interpretations of biblical prophecy recently devised by a British preacher named John Nelson Darby (1800–1882) and popularized by his Plymouth Brethren. Darby read 1 Thessalonians to say that at any moment Christ might return to claim all true Christians, catching them up in the "rapture" to be with him in the clouds. On earth life would deteriorate under the seven-year rule of an Antichrist (the "Great Tribulation") until Jesus came again to earth to fight Satan at the Battle of Armageddon. Christ's victory would inaugurate the "millennium," Christ's thousand-year reign of peace and prosperity.

As Donald W. Dayton has argued in his *Theological Roots of Pente-costalism,*[2] within the Holiness movement language had been shifting from "entire sanctification" or "Christian perfection" to "baptism of the Holy Spirit," a movement from a more internal understanding of spirituality to an external one. When people began to look for that concept in Scripture, they focused on Acts 2, the account of Pentecost.

One group to do so was Charles Fox Parham's (1873–1929) Bethel Bible School in Topeka, Kansas. In late 1900 he asked students to research the subject while he went on a preaching mission. When he returned after Christmas, they told him it was obvious that when one was baptized with the Holy Ghost, one spoke in tongues. During a New Year's Day service on January 1, 1901, a student, Agnes Osman, asked him to lay hands on her and pray that she might receive the experience. Suddenly she began to speak in tongues (document 10). Although a few other students followed suit, the phenomena did not last long.

Parham continued to preach and teach the doctrine. William Joseph Seymour (1870–1922), an African American Holiness preacher, and Neeley Terry, an African American woman from Los Angeles, were students of Parham in Houston. After she returned to Los Angeles in 1906, Terry invited Seymour to come preach in her church, which he did. At first the congregation resisted, but eventually some members were baptized by the Spirit and began to speak in tongues. Their meeting place on Azusa Street became famous around the world as ground zero for the Pentecostal revival.

Florence Crawford (1872–1936) visited Azusa Street and said that "a sound like a rushing, mighty wind filled the room, and I was baptized with the Holy Ghost and fire. Rivers of Joy and love divine flooded my soul."[3] She spoke in tongues and was healed. In 1907 she moved to Portland, Oregon, where she founded the Pentecostal Apostolic Faith movement. Other leaders across the country moved to form such denominations as the Pentecostal Holiness Church, the Church of God in Christ, the Assembly of God, the Church of God (Cleveland, Tennessee), and many other smaller groups.

Alma White (1862–1946) founded the Pillar of Fire denomination and published a magazine titled *Woman's Chains.*[4] She combined a keen sense of woman's rights and the need for political action. Aimee Semple McPherson (1890–1944) founded the International Church of the Foursquare Gospel after embracing Pentecostalism in 1908. She proclaimed Jesus Christ as Savior, Baptizer in the Holy Spirit, Healer, and Coming King. Her theatrical style gained national attention. She was also a pioneer in the use of radio to spread the gospel.[5]

In both Holiness and Pentecostal groups women played major roles. In many denominations they were allowed to travel as evangelists and to pastor local churches. Some Holiness and Pentecostal churches gave women full ordination while mainline churches were still vigorously resisting the idea.

On the other hand, women played very little role in the development of Fundamentalism. That movement can be traced back to the influence of John Nelson Darby on revivalist D. L. Moody (1837–1899), a shoe salesman before he began to preach the gospel. Moody promoted "dispensationalism," as Darby's premillennial views were labeled by theologians, through a series of Bible and prophecy conferences at his home in Northfield, Massachusetts, and at Niagara Falls in Canada.

Although Moody had also at one time accepted the Methodist view of holiness as it was presented to him by a Methodist woman, he later promoted what came to be known as Keswick Holiness, the "higher Christian life" or the "victorious life." Although the movement is named for a place in England, the concepts were initially presented by Americans, two married couples. William Boardman (1810–1886) first wrote *The Higher Christian Life* in 1858. He and his wife Mary were joined by Robert Pearsall Smith (1827–1899) and Hannah Whitall Smith (1832–1911) at meetings in England in 1873 and 1874. Hannah published her classic *The Christian's Secret of a Happy Life* in 1875 (document 11). Their teaching of full surrender to God leading to a perfection of the will was welcomed by a number of upper-class Britons. Robert Smith also made a very successful speaking tour in Europe.

However, in 1875 rumors of improprieties by Robert Smith forced him and Hannah to return to the United States. Although American friends tried to encourage their continued ministry, Robert became morose and never again took up a public ministry. Hannah's book continued to have a life of its own, and after rearing her children and moving the family to England, Hannah continued her public and private ministries. Keswick Holiness became institutionalized at annual summer meetings at Keswick, England, and Keswick, New Jersey.

The third and key element in Fundamentalism was the adoption of a particular view of the Bible developed at Princeton Seminary in response to German higher criticism. Based on a seventeenth-century philosophical notion called Scottish Common Sense Realism, Princeton theologians Charles Hodge (1797–1878), his son A. A. Hodge (1823–86), and B. B. Warfield (1851–1921) argued for the verbal and plenary inspiration of the Bible. They then declared that this produced a book that was inerrant, at least in the original autographs. These novel doctrines became the basis of the Fundamentalist defense of Scripture against the "modernists." Both Princeton and Dispensational views were enshrined in the notes of the Scofield Reference Bible, published in 1909.[6]

In 1910 a group of men collaborated to publish twelve volumes of *The Fundamentals,* essays on Scripture, the Second Coming, evolution, and personal testimony. These books were sent to every American pastor, church worker, missionary, Young Men's Christian Association director, and so forth, around the world. Controversy over these issues began to trouble especially the northern Presbyterian Church and the Northern (American) Baptist Convention. Eventually Fundamentalists split from both of these groups and formed their own denominations and para-church organizations. Such denominations included the General Association of Regular Baptists (GARB), the Conservative Baptist Church, the Orthodox Presbyterian Church, and thousands of independent Baptist and Bible churches. The World's Christian Fundamentals Association was formed in 1919 and the American Council of Christian Churches in 1941. Fundamentalists also formed their own mission organizations.

Researchers have found rather distinct differences in attitudes toward women among Fundamentalists. Betty DeBerg has argued that in many ways the theological stances of Fundamentalists were handy rationales for their vehement attempts to retain distinct Victorian gender roles.[7] Independent Baptist preacher and editor of *The Sword of the Lord,* John R. Rice (1895–1980), wrote an essay on "Bobbed Hair, Bossy Wives, and Women Preachers," which has become a classic (document 12).

On the other hand, Janette Hassey, Virginia Lieson Brereton, and Margaret Bendroth have found that particularly those Fundamentalists involved in creating and administering Bible schools welcomed women students and fostered women's ministries as home and foreign missionaries and even as local pastors.[8] Although virtually all Fundamentalist denominations barred women from public ministry, many women circumvented this restriction by establishing parachurch ministries of their own.

In the 1930s and 1940s Fundamentalism became increasingly withdrawn from national public life. In 1943 a number of conservative denominations banded together to form the National Association of Evangelicals. Toward the end of the 1940s some leaders became disenchanted with the increasingly militant separatism of Fundamentalism. Carl Henry (1913–) wrote of *The Uneasy Conscience of Modern Fundamentalism* (1947). In 1948 he moved to Pasadena, California, to become part of the original faculty of Fuller Seminary, and in 1955 he was invited by Billy Graham to become editor of the new magazine *Christianity Today*. All were elements in a broadening movement that came to be termed "evangelicalism" or "neoevangelicalism." The movement was typified by evangelist Billy Graham's openness in cooperating with all pastors, including Roman Catholics, who were willing to support his urban crusades.

In the 1940s and 1950s women leaders within the Holiness and Pentecostal churches went into eclipse. Almost a lone exception was healing evangelist Kathryn Kuhlman (1907–1976) (document 13). Within Fundamentalism and evangelicalism, women were confined to very traditional roles of wife and mother. However, women were still encouraged to gain education in Bible schools, which were rapidly joining the ranks of "Christian liberal arts colleges."

In the 1960s evangelical women were exposed to the nascent secular woman's liberation movement. In 1973 a group of evangelical men unhappy with the identification of conservative theology with conservative and complacent politics gathered in Chicago for a Thanksgiving Workshop on Evangelicals and Social Concern (they invited three or four women).[9] Their "Chicago Declaration" contained an acknowledgment that conservative Christians "have encouraged men to prideful domination and women to irresponsible passivity. So we call both men and women to mutual submission and active discipleship."[10]

The following year a slightly larger group (increased by a quota of invited women and African American men) broke into interest groups, one of which became the Evangelical Women's Caucus International. The EWCI soon became a separate organization, holding its own conference Thanksgiving weekend 1975 in Washington, D.C. The group, now called the Evangelical and Ecumenical Women's Caucus,[11] has continued to struggle with such issues as sexism, racism, heterosexism, inclusive language, militarism, family abuse and violence, the environment, and imperialism. A crisis came in 1986 when the group adopted a resolution stating, "Whereas homosexual people are children of God, and because of the biblical mandate of Jesus Christ that we are all created

Antoinette L. Brown Blackwell (1825–1921) was the first American woman to be fully ordained to the Christian ministry. The ordination service was held in the Congregational Church of South Butler, New York, on September 15, 1853.

Frances E. Willard (1839–1898), leader of the Woman's Christian Temperance Union from its founding, served as its national president from 1879 until her death. She was also a pioneer for the rights of laywomen and clergywomen in the church.

Kathryn Kuhlman (1907–1976), faith healer, took her ministry to hundreds of thousands beginning in 1946. She was virtually the only female leader in the Holiness and Pentecostal churches during the 1940s and 1950s.

Evangelical and Ecumenical Women's Caucus leaders, Nancy Hardesty, Judy Jahnke, Jeanne Bailey, and Virginia Mollenkott, gathered at the group's twentieth anniversary celebration in Chicago, 1994.

Aimee Semple McPherson (1890–1944) embraced Pentecostalism in 1908 and founded the International Church of the Four-square Gospel. She became a famous evangelist and pioneer of radio gospel broadcasting.

Hannah Whitall Smith (1832–1911) was one of the few women of prominence within Fundamentalism. Her 1875 classic, *The Christian's Secret of a Happy Life,* is still a major seller.

Alma Bridewell White (1862–1946) founded the Pillar of Fire Church in 1901 and held the rank of bishop in the church. She also published the magazine *Woman's Chains.*

Phoebe Palmer (1807–1874), prominent lay evangelist in the Holiness movement in the midnineteenth century, wrote the strongest early defense of women's right to preach the gospel in *The Promise of the Father* (1859).

equal in God's sight, and in recognition of the presence of the lesbian minority in EWCI, EWCI takes a firm stand in favor of civil rights protection for homosexual persons."

In response, however, some members broke away to form Christians for Biblical Equality.[12] Their statement of faith contains the following paragraph: "We believe in the family, celibate singleness, and faithful heterosexual marriage as the patterns God designed for us."

In reaction to the feminist commitments of both organizations, the Council on Biblical Manhood and Womanhood produced the Danvers Statement (document 14), affirming separate gender roles in home, church, and society.[13] Fundamentalist women organized politically through Concerned Women for America, founded by Beverly LaHaye.

Many evangelical women and men have eschewed their former antagonism to Roman Catholicism and formed alliances with them and others to oppose abortion. Feminist evangelicals, while supporting alternatives to abortion, feel that women should be free to make their own difficult decisions. Fundamentalists and many conservative evangelicals are very concerned about public education, opposing new teaching techniques in schools and supporting voucher systems or home schooling. They have also been politically active in opposing sexually explicit and exploitive materials in books, magazines, and the media, and in opposing violence on television. Many have supported boycotts of sponsors of programs they deem objectionable.

The oldest publication of "biblical feminism" is *Daughters of Sarah*,[14] founded in Chicago in 1974 (document 15). It has wrestled with issues such as violence, peace and war, racism, sexuality, poverty, aging, views of the atonement, family relationships, work, and food. It has developed an increasingly ecumenical readership of women and men interested in studying issues from biblical and feminist perspectives.

Down through the centuries the faith of evangelical women has encouraged them to speak out and reach out—in testimony, evangelism, various forms of ministry, and social reform.

Documents

Document 1. Osie M. Fitzgerald:
"The Joy of the Lord Filled My Heart"

Every evangelical spiritual pilgrimage begins with a story of conversion. This is the story of Osie M. Fitzgerald, written in Newark, New Jersey, dated June 18, 1887, and published in *Forty Witnesses*.[15]

I was born in Bernardsville, New Jersey, in 1813. When I was about six years old, thinking I would have a nice time, I took a watermelon from my uncle's farm nearby and divided it with two cousins. My oldest brother, nearly twelve years of age, heard what I had done. In the evening he took me aside and asked me if I knew I had been stealing. He said that, having taken it without my uncle's consent, it was stealing. What he said made no impression upon me at the time; but the next April that dear brother died. Some time after his death I became deeply convicted of sin. My brother had told me that no one who stole could enter heaven. So I felt that I was lost. My convictions were so keen they destroyed my appetite, and I stayed away from my dinner. My father missed me and sent a servant for me. I told her I did not want any dinner, but wanted to see my father. I was in the garden weeping bitterly. The dinner was given up by my father. I was taken into the sitting-room, and he took me on his lap. Then I told him all—how I had taken the melon, and that I should be lost. He told me to stop crying and listen to him. He said Jesus had died for my sins, and if I would trust Jesus to save me He would do it. I think I believed because my father said so. As soon as I believed that Jesus pardoned my sins, in the twinkling of an eye the joy of the Lord filled my soul, so that I went skipping from sitting-room to parlor, from parlor to kitchen, like a bird of the air. My parents were delighted, for I had been under that weight of sin for weeks, till they began to fear for my health, not knowing what ailed me. At this time I was seven years old, and was thought too young to join the Church, so I was left out in the cold until I was nearly frozen to death.

Some years afterward the Lord graciously visited the Presbyterian Church (to which my parents belonged) and gave me a fresh token of my acceptance with Him. I was then taken into the Church with my older brother and sister. At that time I was fifteen years of age.

Document 2. Elizabeth Cady Stanton:
"The Way to Salvation Was Short and Simple"

Although Elizabeth Cady Stanton (1815–1902) rejected the evangelical tradition, she was very much a product of it. Her description of her conversion under the ministry of Charles Finney fits with the experiences of other women in the period.[16]

The next happening in Troy [New York] that seriously influenced my character was the advent of the Rev. Charles G. Finney, a pulpit orator, who, as a terrifier of human souls, proved himself the equal of Savonarola. He held a protracted meeting in the Rev. Dr. [Nathaniel] Beaman's church, which many of my schoolmates [at Emma Willard's Troy Female Seminary] attended. The result of six weeks of untiring effort on the part of Mr. Finney and his confreres was one of those intense revival seasons that swept over the city and through the seminary like an epidemic, attacking in its worst form the most susceptible. Owing to my gloomy Calvinistic training in the old Scotch Presbyterian church, and my vivid imagination, I was one of the first victims. We attended all the public services, beside the daily prayer and experience meetings held in the seminary. Our studies, for the time, held a subordinate place to the more important duty of saving our souls.

To state the idea of conversion and salvation as then understood, one can readily see from our present standpoint that nothing could be more puzzling and harrowing to the young mind. The revival fairly started, the most excitable were soon on the anxious seat. There we learned the total depravity of human nature and the sinner's awful danger of everlasting punishment. This was enlarged upon until the most innocent girl believed herself a monster of iniquity and felt certain of eternal damnation. Then God's hatred of sin was emphasized and his irreconcilable position toward the sinner so justified that one felt like a miserable, helpless, forsaken worm of the dust in trying to approach him, even in prayer.

Having brought you into a condition of profound humility, the only cardinal virtue for one under conviction, in the depths of your despair you were told that it required no herculean effort on your part to be transformed into an angel, to be reconciled to God, to escape endless perdition. The way to salvation was short and simple. We had naught to do but to repent and believe and give our hearts to Jesus, who was ever ready to receive them. How to do all this was the puzzling question. Talking with Dr. Finney one day, I said:

"I cannot understand what I am to do. If you should tell me to go to the top of the church steeple and jump off, I would readily do it, if thereby I could save my soul; but I do not know how to go to Jesus."

"Repent and believe," said he, "that is all you have to do to be happy here and hereafter."

"I am very sorry," I replied, "for all the evil I have done, and I believe all you tell me, and the more sincerely I believe, the more unhappy I am."

With the natural reaction from despair to hope many of us imagined ourselves converted, prayed and gave our experiences in the meetings, and at times rejoiced in the thought that we were Christians—chosen children of God—rather than sinners and outcasts.

Document 3. Sarah Grimke: "Solely on the Bible"

When Quaker sisters Sarah (1792–1873) and Angelina (1805–1879) Grimke became antislavery lecturers, they were condemned in a *Pastoral Letter* by the Congregational clergy of Massachusetts for speaking to "promiscuous" assemblies (containing both women and men—the men had sneaked in to see what was being said). Sarah answered the accusations in 1838 with a series of *Letters on the Equality of the Sexes and the Condition of Woman*.[17]

In examining this important subject, I shall depend solely on the Bible to designate the sphere of woman, because I believe almost every thing that has been written on this subject, has been the result of a misconception of the simple truths revealed in the Scriptures, in consequence of the false translation of many passages of Holy Writ. My mind is entirely delivered from the superstitious reverence which is attached to the English version of the Bible. King James's translators certainly were not inspired. I therefore claim the original as my standard, *believing that to have been inspired,* and I also claim to judge for myself what is the meaning of the inspired writers, because I believe it to be the solemn duty of every individual to search the Scriptures for themselves, with the aid of the Holy Spirit, and not to be governed by the views of any man, or set of men. . . .

The New Testament has been referred to, and I am willing to abide by its decisions, but must enter my protest against the false translation of some passages by the MEN who did that work and against the perverted interpretation by the MEN who undertook to write commentaries thereon. I am inclined to think, when we are admitted to the honor of studying Greek and Hebrew, we shall produce some various readings of the Bible a little different from those we have now. . . .

Men and women were CREATED EQUAL; and they are both moral and accountable beings, and whatever is *right* for man to do, is *right* for woman.

But the influence of woman, says the Association, is to be private and unobtrusive; her light is not to shine before man like that of her brethren; but she is passively to let the lords of the creation, as they call themselves, put the bushel over it, lest peradventure it appear that the world has been benefitted by the rays of *her* candle. . . . How monstrous, how anti-Christian, is the doctrine that woman is to be dependent on man! Where, in all the sacred Scriptures, is this taught? Alas! she has too well learned the lesson which MAN has labored to teach her. . . . "Rule by obedience and by submission sway," in other words, study to be a hypocrite, pretend to submit, but gain your point, has been the code of household morality which woman has been taught. . . . This doctrine of dependence upon man is utterly at variance with the doctrine of the Bible. . . .

But woman may be permitted to lead religious inquirers to the PASTORS for instruction. Now this is assuming that all pastors are better qualified to give instruction than woman. This I utterly deny. I have suffered too keenly from the teaching of man, to lead any one to him for instruction. The Lord Jesus says,—"Come unto me and learn of me." He points his followers to no man; and when woman is made the favored instrument of rousing a sinner to his lost and helpless condition, she has no right to substitute any teacher for Christ; all she has to do is, to turn the contrite inquirer to the "Lamb of God which taketh away the sins of the world." More souls have probably been lost by going down to Egypt for help, and by trusting in man in the early stages of religious experience, than by any other error. . . . That woman can have but a poor conception of the privilege of being taught of God, what he alone can teach, who would turn the "religious inquirer aside" from the fountain of living waters, where he might slake his thirst for spiritual instruction, to those broken cisterns which can hold no water, and therefore cannot satisfy the panting spirit. The business of men and women, who are ORDAINED OF GOD to preach the "unsearchable riches of Christ" to a lost and perishing world, is to lead souls to Christ, and not to Pastors for instruction. . . .

Ah! how many of my sex feel in the dominion, thus unrighteously exercised over them, under the gentle appellation of *protection,* that what they have leaned upon has proved a broken reed at best, and oft a spear.

Document 4. Antoinette Brown (Blackwell): "The Propriety of the Expedience of Woman's Becoming a Public Teacher"

While Antoinette Brown (1825–1921) was just a student at Oberlin College, her professors encouraged her to publish an exegesis of 1 Corinthians 14:34–35 and 1 Timothy 2:11–12 in the *Oberlin Quarterly Review.*[18] In 1853 she became the first woman to be officially ordained in this country. Later she left the Congregational Church to be a minister in the Unitarian-Universalist Fellowship.

If it *is wrong per se* [for woman to engage in public teaching], then God Himself could not make it *right;* and we are driven to the necessity of maintaining that none of the ancient prophetesses were called of the Lord to become teachers of Israel. That is a proposition which no believer in revelation would think of assuming. . . .

To assume that the apostle commanded those women to abstain from public teaching, lest it should prove a stumbling block on account of the Jewish and Gentile prejudices of the surrounding nations, is entirely unwarrantable; for degraded as was the social position of women in most respects, there were and always had been prophetesses in the Jewish church, and the priestesses of the heathen deities had been uttering their mysterious oracles from time immemorial. . . .

On entering upon this exegesis, it will be proper to enquire into the meaning of some of the terms here employed, as used in the original. First, let us look at the word *lalein,* translated "to speak" [in 1 Cor. 14:34]. What is its use in classic Greek? It is defined in Liddell and Scott's Lexicon, "to talk, chatter, babble; strictly to make a babbling, prattling sound, as monkeys and dogs; hence also of birds, locusts, to twitter, chirp." . . .

Now what do Robinson, and the commentators of the old school find in the context of this 14th chapter, which compels them to attach to this word the idea of teaching or preaching? . . . Again, if the connection plainly shows that the word here means simply to speak, to use the voice, without any reference to the words spoken, then all the vocal exercises of the church must be unlawful to females, and a manifest violation of this precept. . . .

What is the subject treated of in this connection? and what abuses is the apostle here laboring to rectify? The whole chapter is taken up with spiritual gifts, and the improper exercise of the liberty connected with those gifts, occasioning noise and confusion in the church, and thus bringing disgrace and reproach upon the cause of Christ. . . .

In the 35th verse, the apostle says, "If they will learn any thing, let them ask their husbands at home, for (because) it is a shame for women to speak in the church." Here then is a *clew,* which will guide us to the meaning of the word *lalein.* The women are represented as ignorant, and desiring to be instructed. It is assumed also that their husbands and male friends are capable of giving this instruction, and they are directed not to ask for the desired information in the church, but to wait till an opportunity is afforded for doing so in private. . . .

The apostle does not reprove them for being desirous to obtain information. He only tells them kindly to wait and ask their husbands at home. This was demanded by the greatest good of the church, and therefore required by the law of disinterested benevolence.

Asking ill-timed questions, then, certainly was one thing which was prohibited—prohibited too, for the same reason that he censured them for the improper use of spiritual gifts. It was a stone of stumbling to strangers, not calculated to do them good; and it made God the author of confusion. . . .

We will now turn to a consideration of the remaining passage [1 Tim. 2:11–12].

If [the apostle] has directed her not to instruct a public assembly, he has also commanded her not to teach in the Sabbath school—in the social circle, or in the nursery. Shall we then admit the supposition that the inspired writer has forbidden woman to instruct even her own children? . . .

Let us look more carefully at the phrase, Let your women learn in silence. This certainly can not be a silence which prohibits the asking of questions, as the apostle expressly declared this to be a privilege of females; and it is ridiculous to suppose it requires them to be perfectly still and noiseless, as though they were hardly to be permitted to draw a long breath during the time they were allowed this unspeakable privilege of receiving instruction. . . .

This silence then, must refer to a quiet teachable spirit—that state of mind which is attentive, willing to listen and learn. . . . In 2 Thess. 3: 11, 12 . . . the word is used in opposition to all kinds of disorderly conduct, and evidently refers to a state of tranquility. . . .

The word *didaskein* must . . . be opposed to *esuchia,* or that quiet, tranquil, peaceful state of mind which indicates true Christian subjection. It is connected with usurping authority, and evidently includes a dictatorial, self-important, overbearing manner of teaching, which was far from salutary in its influence. . . .

The apostle does strictly prohibit *that* kind of teaching . . . but in what portion of the inspired volume do we find any commandment forbidding woman to act as a public teacher *provided* she has a message worth communicating, and will deliver it in a manner worthy of her high vocation?

Document 5. Frances Willard:
"Christ Hath Made Woman Free"

Frances Willard used her 1888 Presidential Address to the Woman's Christian Temperance Union to castigate the church's injustice to women. Having been duly elected as a delegate to the Methodist

Episcopal Church's General Conference, she herself had been denied a seat, along with five other women delegates.[19]

By a strange and grievous paradox, the Church of Christ, although first to recognize and nurture woman's spiritual powers, is one of the most difficult centers to reach with the sense of justice toward her, under the improved conditions of her present development and opportunity. . . . *Woman, like man, should be freely permitted to do whatever she can do well.*

Who that is reasonable doubts but that if we had, in every church, a voice in all its circles of power, it would be better for the church, making it more homelike and attractive, more endeared to the people, and hence more effective in its great mission of brotherly and sisterly love? By what righteous principle of law or logic are we excluded from church council when we so largely make up the church's membership? Who that did not know it beforehand would believe that good men actually desire to keep us out? . . . We have not ourselves rightly understood the liberty wherewith Christ hath made woman free. . . .

"What shall be done about it?" is everywhere the question.

"Stay in the church and help reform it," says one. "No that is impossible; old churches and old parties are equally crystalized," comes the reply. "Let the W.C.T.U. organize a church, and we will join it every man of us," is the declaration of an influential group of earnest men. "No, we have too many churches already," objects a listener. . . .

But for myself, I love my mother-church so well and recognize so thoroughly that the base and body of the great pyramid she forms is broader than its apex, that I would fain give her a little time in which to deal justly by the great household of her loving, loyal, and devoted daughters. I would wait four years longer, in fervent hope and prayer, that the great body of her ministers and her membership may make it manifest to all the world, that the church of Lady Huntingdon, Barbara Heck, and Phoebe Palmer does not hesitate to march with the progressive age it has done so much to educate, nor fear to carry to their logical sequence its lifelong teachings as to woman's equality within the house of God. . . . The time will come, however, and not many years from now, when if representation is still denied us, it will be our solemn duty to raise once more the cry, "Here I stand, I can do no other," and step out into the larger liberty of a religious movement, where majorities and not minorities, determine the fitness of women as delegates and where the laying on of hands in consecration, as was undoubtedly done in the early church, shall be decreed on a basis of "gifts, graces and usefulness," irrespective of sex.

Document 6. Phoebe Palmer: Lay Your All upon the Altar

John Wesley taught that entire sanctification was a lifelong process. In the 1840s Methodist evangelist Phoebe Palmer was challenged by the question, "Is there not a shorter way?" She concluded that there was. She explained it, using the images of altar and sacrifice.[20]

In the simplicity of my heart I expressed my desires as nearly as I can remember thus: "Let me have the blessing in some such tangible form, that the enemy may never be successful in the insinuation, that I believe merely because I will believe, without a reasonable foundation for my faith to rest upon." . . .

My prayer was answered; . . . The Holy Spirit took of the things of God and revealed them unto me, by opening to my understanding Rom. xii, 1: "I beseech you, brethren, by the mercies of God that ye present your bodies a living sacrifice, holy, acceptable unto God, which is your reasonable service." . . . I saw that nothing less than the omnipotence of grace could have enabled me thus to present my whole being to God. That the power to do so was of itself a miracle. That while I was thus empowered to present every faculty of soul and body a *living* or, as Dr. [Adam] Clarke says, a *continual,* sacrifice, it was an express declaration—a truth to be *believed,* and therefore not to be doubted without sin, that the blood of Jesus *cleanseth* the offering thus presented from all unrighteousness.

This, I was given to see, was in verity placing all upon that altar which sanctifieth the gift. So long as my heart assured me that I offered all, I saw it was not only my privilege, but my solemn *duty,* to believe that the blood of Jesus *cleanseth,* at the present and each succeeding moment, so long as the offering be presented. . . . Should I discontinue the entire abandonment of every power and faculty to God, by shrinking from some duty because the flesh is not willing, it would be at the forfeiture of a state of holiness.

Document 7. Osie M. Fitzgerald:
"The Holy Ghost Sanctified Me Wholly"

In *Forty Witnesses* Osie M. Fitzgerald goes on to describe her experience of entire sanctification.[21]

The Lord sent the Rev. James Caughey to the Central Methodist Episcopal Church for a few weeks, and he preached clearly the doctrine of entire sanctification. I had not thought that I could ever live without daily committing sin. But when he took his text, "Be ye holy for I am holy," and said we are not only invited but commanded to be holy, the words struck deep into my heart. . . . We were invited forward to the altar. I went to get a clean heart; but when asked what I came for I said, "A deeper work of grace." . . . Then it came to me, "Will you give your children to the Lord?" It was suggested, "If you do He will take them out of the world." At last I surrendered them to God. Then came a still greater struggle. The Spirit said, "Will you give up your husband to me?" I said, "Lord, I will die willingly if Thou wilt let him live. I am not of much account, but I cannot live and let him die, for my health is so poor I will be unable to take care of my family." It was also suggested that we might lose all our property, and I would at last have to go to the alms-house. That struggle lasted for two days or more. Then it was whispered to me, "You may be the means of saving some soul in the alms-house." Then came the passage, "No good thing will he withhold from them that walk uprightly." I yielded all to God. Saturday night came. I went forward for prayers. The Spirit said to me, "If I give you a clean heart, and sanctify you wholly, will you speak before this people and tell them what I have done for you?" Having been brought up a Presbyterian I was very much opposed to women speaking in the church. I thought no one but a bold Methodist woman would speak in church. Consequently I said, "No; it is not the place for a female to speak." Again the question was repeated. I then said, "I will do it if the Lord requires it, but He does not, for there are plenty of men to speak." My agony of soul increased, and as I continued to plead the question continually recurred. My agony of soul was so intense that it seemed to me it must soon be victory or death, and I cried out, "Yes, Lord, though it be before a thousand people." Then there was a great calm in my soul. And I said, "What now, Lord?" . . . I saw clearly I must believe before I could receive. . . .

Some time after a good brother said to me, "You do believe that God cleanseth you now from all sin." If I had had a thousand bodies and souls I could have thrown them all into that "Yes." The moment I confessed it the Holy Ghost with lightning speed came into my heart and cleansed it from all sin, and took up His abode in my heart and filled me with such unspeakable joy that for three days I scarcely knew whether I was in the body or out of it. . . .

God pardoned my sins in the winter of 1820–21. On the 27th of December, 1856, in the evening in Central Methodist Episcopal Church in Newark, N.J., through the blood of Jesus Christ, God cleansed my heart from all sin, and the Holy Ghost sanctified me wholly, I think. . . . For I have never lost it, and I have no recollection of ever feeling the stirrings of anger, jealousy, pride, self-will, or bitterness, since the day God cleansed my heart from all sin and the Holy Ghost came in and filled me.

Document 8. Carrie Judd Montgomery: The Prayer of Faith

Within the Holiness movement, many adopted a belief in faith healing. Initially the object was to enable the sick person to "pray the prayer of faith." Here Carrie Judd Montgomery (1858–1946), a leader in the movement, talks about her own healing.[22]

My disease was now accompanied with blood consumption; I was emaciated to a shadow, and my largest veins looked like mere threads. Nothing could keep me warm, and the chill of death seemed upon me. A great part of the time I lay gasping faintly for breath, and I suffered excruciatingly. . . . I have no doubt that it was ordered by Providence that, just at this time, there should appear in the daily paper a short account of the wonderful cures performed in answer to the prayers of Mrs. Edward Mix, a colored woman, of Wolcottville, Conn. . . . She had, herself, been cured after years of ill health, by the prayers and laying on of hands. . . . Mother mentioned these facts to me, and the more I thought on the subject, the more I felt that a letter must be written her in regard to my own case. . . . [I] then requested my sister to write her that I believed her great faith might avail for me, if she would pray for my recovery, even if she were not present to lay her hands upon me. On Tuesday February 25th, her answer came as follows

Wolco[t]tville, Conn., Feb. 24, 1879.

Miss Carrie Judd:

I received a line from your sister stating your case, your disease, and your faith. I can encourage you, by the Word of God, that "according to your faith" so be it unto you; and besides you have this promise, "The prayer of faith shall save the sick, and the Lord shall raise him up." Whether the person is present or absent, if it is a "prayer of faith" it is all the same, and God has promised to raise up the sick ones, and if they have committed sins to forgive them. Now this promise is to you as if you were the only person living. Now if you can claim that promise, I have not the least doubt but what you will be healed. You will first have to lay aside all medicine of every description. Use no remedies of any kind for anything. Lay aside trust in the "arm of flesh," and lean wholly upon God and His promises. When you receive this letter I want you to begin to pray for faith, and Wednesday afternoon the female prayer-meeting is at our house. We will make you a subject of prayer, between the hours of three and four. I want you to pray for yourself, and pray believing and then *act faith*. It makes no difference how you feel, but get right out of bed and begin to walk by faith. Strength will come, disease will depart and you will be made whole. We read in the Gospel, "Thy faith hath made thee whole." Write soon.

Yours in faith,
Mrs. Edward Mix.

. . . At the hour appointed by Mrs. Mix, members of our own family also offered up prayer, though not in my room. . . .

There was no excitement, but, without the least fear or hesitation, I turned over and raised up alone, for the first time in over two years. My nurse, Mrs. H., who had taken care of me for nearly a year was greatly affected, and began praising God for His wonderful power and mercy.

Document 9. Maria Woodworth-Etter:
The Laying On of Hands

As Holiness doctrine began to shade into Pentecostal teaching, healing through the "prayer of faith" began to shift toward healing through the "laying on of hands." Maria Woodworth-Etter (1844–1924) began as a Holiness evangelist and eventually became a Pentecostal preacher and faith healer.[23]

The Lord showed me while here [conducting a revival in Columbia City, Indiana, in March 1885] that I had the gift of healing, and of laying on of hands for the recovery of the sick. I had been working day and night for many months and had no strength only as God gave me each meeting. It would be two o'clock often before I would get to sleep. When God began to show me I must preach divine healing I could not understand that it was the spirit of God leading me. For three nights when I was most dead for rest I lay awake. God was teaching me a lesson I could not or would not learn. I said: Lord, you know I started out to win souls for heaven, and I have been busy all the time. I have tried to be faithful in everything you have given me to do. I am so exhausted with constant labor that I have to be helped many times to rise from my bed.

I thought if I would preach divine healing they would bring all the cripples in the country, and I would neglect the salvation of souls. The Lord showed me he would take care of the work. I told the Lord if he wanted me to pray for the sick to send them to the meetings, and show me he wanted me to pray for them, and I would. When I made this promise I had perfect rest of mind and soul. From this time God began to lead me to teach divine healing and pray for the sick. It is now nine years since, and God has healed thousands of all manner of diseases. Thousands have been brought to Christ by seeing the people healed.

Document 10. Agnes Osman (LaBerge):
The Gift of the Holy Spirit

Agnes N. Osman (LaBerge) was the first person in modern times to speak in tongues and to understand it as the gift of the Holy Spirit spoken of in Acts. Her account is quoted from Sarah Parham's biography of her husband, Pentecostal founder Charles F. Parham.[24]

I had been a Bible student for some years and had attended T. C. Horton's Bible School at St. Paul, Minn., and A. B. Simpson's Bible School at New York City. For some time I had been doing mission work. In the fall of 1900 I was in Kansas City and heard that a Bible School was to be opened at Topeka, Kans. I had a desire to go to this school, and asked the Lord that if it was His plan for me to go, to provide the fare. A sister gave me more than enough to pay for my fare and so I felt assured it was God's will for me to go. I was living by simple faith in the Lord, trusting Him to supply all my needs according to Phil. 4:19.

It was in October 1900, that I went to this school which was known as Bethel College. We studied the Bible every day and did much work down town at night. Prayer was offered night and day continually in a special upper room set apart as a prayer tower. I had many blessed hours of prayer in this upper room during the night watches. As we spent much time in the presence of God, He caused our hearts to be opened to all that is written.

I had some experience with the Lord, and tasted the joy of leading some souls to Christ, and had some marvelous answers to prayer for guidance and in having my needs supplied. I was blessed with the presence of the Lord, who, in response to my prayer, healed some who were sick. Like some others, I thought that I had received the baptism of the Holy Ghost at the time of consecration, but when I learned that the Holy Ghost was yet to be poured out in greater fullness, my heart became hungry for the promised Comforter and I began to cry out for an enduement with power from on high. At times I longed more for the Holy Spirit to come in than for my necessary food. At night I had a greater desire for Him than for sleep. . . .

As the end of the year drew near some friends came from Kansas City to spend the holidays with us. On watch night we had a blessed service, praying that God's blessing might rest upon us as the New Year came in. During the first day of 1901 the presence of the Lord was with us in a marked way stilling our hearts to wait upon Him for greater things. The spirit of prayer was upon us in the evening. It was nearly seven o'clock on this first of January that it came into my heart to ask

Bro. Parham to lay his hands upon me that I might receive the gift of the Holy Spirit. It was as his hands were laid upon my head that the Holy Spirit fell upon me and I began to speak in tongues, glorifying God. I talked several languages, and it was clearly manifest when a new dialect was spoken. I had the added joy and glory my heart longed for and a depth of the presence of the Lord within that I had never known before. It was as if rivers of living water were proceeding from my innermost being.

The following morning I was accosted with questions about my experience the night before. As I tried to answer I was so full of glory that I pointed out to them the Bible references, showing that I had received the baptism according to Acts 2:4 and 19:1–6. I was the first one to speak in tongues in the Bible school and it seemed to me that the rest were wanting to speak in tongues too. But I told them not to seek for tongues but to seek for the Holy Ghost. I did not know at that time that anyone else would speak in tongues. I did not expect the Holy Spirit to manifest Himself to others as He did to me.

On January 2, some of us went down to Topeka to a mission. As we worshipped the Lord I offered prayer in English and then prayed in another language in tongues. A Bohemian who was present said that he understood what I said. Some months later at a school house with others, in a meeting, I spoke in tongues in the power of the spirit and another Bohemian understood me. Since then others have understood other languages I have spoken.

Document 11. Hannah Whitall Smith:
The Christian's Secret

Because of its roots in Presbyterian and Baptist circles, Fundamentalism adopted the British Keswick Holiness or "victorious life" piety rather than the more Wesleyan teachings of the Holiness movement. Keswick Holiness was rooted in the teaching of American Quaker Hannah Whitall Smith. Her classic, *The Christian's Secret of a Happy Life,* is still a bestseller.[25]

A great many Christians seem practically to think that all their Father in heaven wants is a chance to make them miserable and to take away all their blessings; and they imagine, poor souls, that if they hold on to things in their own will they can hinder Him from doing this. . . .

A Christian lady who had this feeling was once expressing to a friend how impossible she found it to say, "Thy will be done," and how afraid she should be to do it. She was the mother of an only little boy, who was the heir to a great fortune, and the idol of her heart. After she had stated her difficulties fully, her friend said, "Suppose your little Charley should come running to you to-morrow and say, 'Mother, I have made up my mind to let you have your own way with me from this time forward. I am always going to obey you, and I want you to do just whatever you think best with me. I will trust your love.' How would you feel towards him? Would you say to yourself, 'Ah, now I shall have a chance to make Charley miserable. I will take away all his pleasures, and fill his life with every hard and disagreeable thing that I can find. I will compel him to do just the things that are the most difficult for him to do, and will give him all sorts of impossible commands.'" "Oh, no, no, no!" exclaimed the indignant mother. "You know I would not. You know I would hug him to my heart and cover him with kisses and would hasten to fill his life with all that was sweet and best." "And are you more tender and more loving than God?" asked her friend. "Oh, no!" was the reply. "I see my mistake. Of course, I must not be any more afraid of saying, 'Thy will be done,' to my Heavenly Father than I would want my Charley to be of saying it to me."

Better and sweeter than health, or friends, or money, or fame, or ease, or prosperity, is the adorable will of our God. . . . Surely, then, it is only a glorious privilege that is opening before you when I tell you that the first step you must take in order to enter into the life hid with Christ in God is that of entire consecration. . . .

Faith is the next thing after surrender. Faith is an absolutely necessary element in the reception of any gift, for let our friends give a thing to us ever so fully, it is not really ours until we believe it has been given, and claim it as our own. Above all, this is true in gifts which are purely mental or spiritual. Love may be lavished upon us by another without stint or measure, but until we believe that we are loved, it never really becomes ours. . . .

I mean all this, of course, experimentally and practically. Theologically and judicially I know that every believer has everything as soon as he is converted; but experimentally nothing is his until by faith he claims it. . . .

But this faith of which I am speaking must be a present faith. No faith that is exercised in the future tense amounts to anything. A man may believe forever that his sins will be forgiven at some future time, and he will never find peace. He has to come to the *now* belief, and say by a present appropriating faith, "My sins are now forgiven," before his soul can be at rest. And similarly, no faith that looks for a future deliverance from the power of sin will ever lead a soul into the life we are describing. The enemy delights in this future faith, for he knows it is powerless to accomplish any practical results. But he trembles and flees when the soul of the believer dares to claim a present deliverance, and to reckon itself *now* to be free from his power.

Perhaps no four words in the language have more meaning in them than the following, which I would have you repeat over and over with your voice and with your soul, emphasizing each time a different word:—

Jesus saves me now.—It is He.
Jesus *saves* me now.—It is His work to save.
Jesus saves *me* now.—I am the one to be saved.
Jesus saves me *now.*—He is doing it every moment.

To sum up, then, in order to enter into this blessed interior life of rest and triumph, you have two steps to take,— first, entire abandonment; and second, absolute faith.

Document 12. John R. Rice: "Bobbed Hair, Bossy Wives, and Women Preachers"

The writings of John R. Rice (1895–1980), Baptist preacher and editor of *The Sword of the Lord,* are typical of the harsh tone with which some Fundamentalist leaders addressed the roles and relationships of women and men.[26]

"Thy desire shall be to thy husband, and he shall rule over thee" [Gen. 3:16]. Wives must be subject to the rule of their husbands if they fit into God's order of things. Does some wife who reads this find her heart rebellious against her husband? You do not want him to rule you?

You do not want to obey? Then you feel just like all the criminals in the penitentiaries and jails feel. They, too, are rebels against God-given authority. They, too, want to be independent and have their own way. The very heart of the crime question is rebellion against authority. And most criminals were first allowed to get away with rebellion against the rule of parents in their own homes. Not being disciplined and con- trolled and conquered as children, they were not willing to be subject to the next authority God put over them, the authority of government. Criminals are simply rebels against authority and every rebellious wife has the same attitude of heart. You who read this do not want to have this attitude and I trust you will carefully search your heart and ask God to take away any rebellion against His will or against those to whom He commands you to have obedience. . . .

"But my husband wants me to have bobbed hair, and you said for me to obey my husband," some woman says. No, you are mistaken. It was not I who said you were to obey your husband. It was the Lord, and the Lord plainly promised that your husband would be won to God by your obedience (1 Peter 3:1, 2), and not that you would be led into sin. And any woman who obeys her husband reverently and lovingly in other matters, and explains her Christian convictions on matters of pleasing God, will find that her husband will not want to lead her into sin. I know that God's way always works, and any Christian woman can have God's help in doing right. If you explain why you should have long hair, and obey your husband in other matters, he will not want you to lose your glory by sinning in having bobbed hair.

From a sermon to men only:[27]

. . . God is a masculine God.

A man, then, is nearer like God than a woman, and in a sense, man is in the image of God. . . .

Am I Christ's own personal representative? Do I represent Jesus Christ in my home? The wife is to come to her husband to find God's will. The wife is to glorify her husband and look to him as if in some sense Christ dwells in your body in the home. I am, in my home, the image of God Almighty. . . .

The Bible plainly says that Eve was deceived but that Adam was not deceived [1 Tim. 2:14]. He knew better. He knew it would not make him wise. God never intended women to lead men around by their noses. . . .

Men, do you see how serious is your responsibility? If God is going to win this country, He must do it through men. It is a strange thing that people have got more sense in matters of government and business than in matters of religion. We would not elect a woman president, nor follow a woman in business, but we leave church work to the women! No wonder the Bible said, "The children of this world are in their generation wiser than the children of light" (Luke 16:8).

Preachers, are you willing for your church to be run by a handful of critical old hens who want to tell you where to head in? They have got to have their own announcements. You must not run past twelve o'clock or the dinner will burn! God bless women, but He never intended any preacher to be run by a bunch of women. God never intended the home to be run by women, and God never intended Christian work to be run by women.

Men are to lead out in music, in Bible teaching in the church, in personal soul winning in the church. God depends on men for leadership. Go to your Bible and try to find any contradictions to that. You can't do it. God has reserved the main place in the church for men.

Document 13. Kathryn Kuhlman:
The Holy Spirit Was the Answer

Kathryn Kuhlman (1907–1976) was the most widely known woman evangelist in the twentieth century. She began her ministry at sixteen, soon itinerating throughout the West. Her healing ministry began in the 1940s when people began to be spontaneously healed during her services. She maintained an effective radio, television, and personal ministry until her death.[28]

In the early part of my ministry, I was greatly disturbed over much that I observed occurring in the field of Divine Healing. I was confused by many of the "methods" I saw employed, and disgusted with the unwise "performances" I witnessed. . . .

I remember well the evening when I walked from under a big tent where a Divine Healing service was being conducted. The looks of despair and disappointment on the faces I had seen, when told that only their lack of faith was keeping them from God, was to haunt me for weeks. . . .

Fortunately I had learned a valuable spiritual lesson early in my ministry—one which was to come to my aid now: I had learned that the only way to get the truth is to come in sincerity and absolute honesty of heart and mind, and let the Lord Himself give one the blessed revelations of His Word, and *through* the Word, make His Presence real and His Truth known. . . .

I waited expectantly for the answer, and it came.

One night during a series of services that I was conducting, a very fine Christian lady arose from where she was sitting in the audience and said, "Please—before you begin your sermon, may I give a word of testimony regarding something that happened last evening while you were preaching?"

I nodded, and quickly recalled what I had said the night before. There had not been anything unusual about the sermon: it had been a very simple message regarding the Person of the Holy Spirit. . . .

"As you were preaching on the Holy Ghost," she said, "telling us that in Him lay the Resurrection power, I felt the Power of God flow through my body. Although not a word had been spoken regarding the healing of the sick, I knew instantly and definitely that my body had been healed. So sure was I of this, that I went to the doctor today and had my healing verified."

The Holy Spirit, then, was the answer: an answer so profound that no human being can fathom the full extent of its depths and power, and yet so simple that most folk miss it!

I understood that night why there was no need for a healing line; no healing virtue in a card or a personality; no necessity for wild exhortations "to have faith."

That was the beginning of this healing ministry which God has given to me.

Document 14. The Danvers Statement: "Distinctions in Masculine and Feminine Roles Are Ordained by God"

The Danvers Statement was issued in November 1988 by the Council on Biblical Manhood and Womanhood, a group of

Fundamentalist and evangelical men and women alarmed by the growth of biblical feminism. Their stated purpose was "to set forth the teachings of the Bible about the complementary differences between men and women, created equal in the image of God, because these teachings are essential for obedience to Scripture and for the health of the family and the Church."[29]

Rationale

We have been moved in our purpose by the following contemporary developments which we observe with deep concern:

1. The widespread uncertainty and confusion in our culture regarding the complementary differences between masculinity and femininity;

2. the tragic effects of this confusion in unraveling the fabric of marriage woven by God out of the beautiful and diverse strands of manhood and womanhood;

3. the increasing promotion given to feminist egalitarianism with accompanying distortions or neglect of the glad harmony portrayed in Scripture between the loving, humble leadership of redeemed husbands and the intelligent, willing support of that leadership by redeemed wives;

4. the widespread ambivalence regarding the values of motherhood, vocational homemaking, and the many ministries historically performed by women;

5. the growing claims of legitimacy for sexual relationships which have Biblically and historically been considered illicit or perverse, and the increase in pornographic portrayal of human sexuality;

6. the upsurge of physical and emotional abuse in the family;

7. the emergence of roles for men and women in church leadership that do not conform to Biblical teaching but backfire in the crippling of Biblically faithful witness;

8. the increasing prevalence and acceptance of hermeneutical oddities devised to reinterpret apparently plain meanings of Biblical texts;

9. the consequent threat to Biblical authority as the clarity of Scripture is jeopardized and the accessibility of its meaning to ordinary people is withdrawn into the restricted realm of technical ingenuity;

10. and behind all this the apparent accommodation of some within the church to the spirit of the age at the expense of winsome, radical Biblical authenticity which in the power of the Holy Spirit may reform rather than reflect our ailing culture. . . .

Affirmations

Based on our understanding of Biblical teachings, we affirm the following:

1. Both Adam and Eve were created in God's image, equal before God as persons and distinct in their manhood and womanhood.

2. Distinctions in masculine and feminine roles are ordained by God as part of the created order, and should find an echo in every human heart.

3. Adam's headship in marriage was established by God before the Fall, and was not a result of sin.

4. The Fall introduced distortions into the relationships between men and women.

   • In the home, the husband's loving, humble headship tends to be replaced by domination or passivity; the wife's intelligent, willing submission tends to be replaced by usurpation or servility.

   • In the church, sin inclines men toward a worldly love of power or an abdication of spiritual responsibility, and inclines women to resist limitations on their roles or to neglect the use of their gifts in appropriate ministries.

5. The Old Testament, as well as the New Testament, manifests the equally high value and dignity which God attached to the roles of both men and women. Both Old and New Testaments also affirm the principle of male headship in the family and in the covenant community.

6. Redemption in Christ aims at removing the distortions introduced by the curse.

   • In the family, husbands should forsake harsh or selfish leadership and grow in love and care for their wives; wives should forsake resistance to their husbands' authority and grow in willing, joyful submission to their husbands' leadership.

• In the church, redemption in Christ gives men and women an equal share in the blessings of salvation; nevertheless, some governing and teaching roles within the church are restricted to men.

7. In all of life Christ is the supreme authority and guide for men and women, so that no earthly submission—domestic, religious or civil—ever implies a mandate to follow a human authority into sin.

8. In both men and women a heartfelt sense of call to ministry should never be used to set aside Biblical criteria for particular ministries. Rather Biblical teaching should remain the authority for testing our subjective discernment of God's will. . . .

10. We are convinced that a denial or neglect of these principles will lead to increasingly destructive consequences in our families, our churches, and the culture at large.

Document 15. *Daughters of Sarah:*
"Christianity and Feminism Are Inseparable"

Daughters of Sarah, "the Magazine for Christian Feminists," was founded in 1974 about the same time as the Evangelical Women's Caucus. It has been published since then by a group of women, mostly volunteers, in Chicago. This statement of purpose appeared in the Fall 1993 issue.

WHO WE ARE
We are Christians.
We are also feminists.
Some say we cannot be both,
but for us
Christianity and feminism
are inseparable.
DAUGHTERS OF SARAH
　　is our attempt
　　to share our discoveries,
　　our struggles, and our growth
　　as Christian women.
We are committed to Scripture
　　and we seek to find in it
　　meaning for our lives.

We are rooted in a historical tradition
    of women who have served God
    in innumerable ways,
    and we seek guidance
    from their example.
We are convinced that Christianity
    is relevant to all areas
    of women's lives today.
We seek ways to act out our faith.

Why Sarah?

Sarah was a strong woman,
    equally called by God
    to a new land of promise.
We are Daughters of Sarah,
    not of the flesh,
    but of the promise,
    as Scripture says,
    co-heirs of God's grace and life.

CHAPTER SIX

Protestant Women and Social Reform

Joanne Carlson Brown

Documents

A WOMAN'S PLACE

1. Lucretia Mott: Why Shouldn't a Woman Be a Reformer?
2. Mrs. J. T. Gracey: Evangelical Organizing

REFORM AS AWAKENING

3. Abigail Abbot Bailey: Reform as Individual Empowerment in the Eighteenth Century
4. Mary Lyon and Mount Holyoke: Educating for Reform

TO REFORM THE NATION

5. Angelina Grimke: Abolition
6. New York Female Moral Reform Society: Prostitution

REFORM AS CHALLENGE

7. Elizabeth Cady Stanton: Christianity as Oppressor

REFORM AS VISION

8. Anna Howard Shaw: Freedom and Rights for the Oppressed
9. Frances E. Willard: The New Woman

FAITH, FEMINISM, AND THE FUTURE

10. National Association of Colored Women: Racism and Rights
11. Vida Dutton Scudder: Christian Radicals and Revolutionary Forces
12. Georgia Harkness: Peace
13. Religious Coalition for Abortion Rights: The Right to Choose
14. CLOUT, Christian Lesbians Out Together: Celebrating Identity

THIS was their vision: America—God's holy experiment, the promised land. Americans had entered into a covenant with God. They would be God's people and that One would be their God. God promised land and prosperity, and the people promised obedience and faithfulness. This is the rhetoric of the new Israel that helped to shape the American mythos, a myth that was to push the lives, thoughts, and actions of the people who lived in that land from the eighteenth to the twentieth centuries: God's chosen, covenanted people spreading out into the land their God had given.

But America was not paradise. Covenants were broken, between people and people, and between people and God. But as often as people drifted from their commitment, as often as they turned their backs on their promises, their God, and their neighbor, just as often some arose who remembered and called the people and the nation back, who reminded them to do what God required and who were not above telling their wayward generation just what that was.

From the Puritans to the Victorians, from the frontier to the slums of the cities, from the squalor of poverty to the drawing rooms of the rich, from the factory to the church, cries were raised to do justice and to seek mercy and to walk humbly with God. Throughout the history of America, the voice of the reformer has been heard, even if it was at times only a whisper.

While not all reform was religiously motivated, all reform movements had within them religious elements, rhetoric, and most importantly people who were engaged in the reform because God had called them to the work. Religious reformers were clear that God was leading them in their cause. This conviction strengthened their work and enabled many to persevere even when others gave up, their initial excitement dampened by the lack of immediate success. A number of scholars, Timothy Smith and Perry Miller among them, have identified strong links between revivals and various reform movements.[1] Revivals provided the impetus and methods of organization for the religious reformers. Their methods differed and their foci diverged, but religious reformers, whether concentrating on converting an individual sinner or transforming the whole society, were the main voices crying in the wilderness of broken covenants.

A WOMAN'S PLACE

Women have been among those voices from the beginning. In order to do so, they often had to defend their very right to speak. Women from all walks of life worked and spoke for reform, even if they did not label it as such at the time. Women were especially active in the group known as religious reformers. This is ironic since often it was religious people who most strongly rejected women's right or ability to engage in the work. There is much debate as to whether women brought something to the reform movements that men did not. This debate raged in the eighteenth and nineteenth centuries and continues into our own time. Are women innately more caring, more empathic? Are the motherly instincts called forth by a hurting world? Should women be engaged in work that is either beyond their sphere or in conflict with the values of that sphere (document 1)? Women themselves were not agreed on the approach or the methods. Especially in the nineteenth century, with the development of what historian Barbara Welter has called the "cult of true woman-hood,"[2] the way reform was carried out was a major issue. Some women's historians have argued that the cult ultimately kept women in their place and either rendered them ineffective or made them pawns or, as historian Ann Douglas argues, "slaves to an unappreciative master."[3]

Religious feminist reformers did not sacrifice their cause on the altar of the cult of true womanhood. They were neither exalted nor ignored. They were effective precisely because of their conviction that God, not man, had called them to this work. They were not blind idealists. These women acknowledged the spheres within which they worked, but they also challenged them from a religious basis. These women were clear that they had only one Lord and Master, and no man or organization had the right to try to usurp that place. Their religious experience enabled them to work no matter what the opposition, even if it came from other reformers.

Religious women reformers often began with mission work. God called workers for the harvest, and whether they went to the foreign field or supported from home, the response to the call transformed not only those to whom missions were directed but also those who were engaged in the mission work. Many women got their first taste of organizing through mission societies (document 2).

REFORM AS AWAKENING

Reform in America has operated under many guises and in many forms. It has followed a process that is closely linked with the development of theological and societal values and views. The eighteenth century was a time of religious convictions and challenge. The Puritan values came into confrontation with the more radical ideas of the Enlightenment. These values and ideas, in spite of and at times because of this confrontation, spurred on reforms modeled on newly emerging worldviews.

The New England Puritans understood themselves to be a people of the covenant, God's chosen or elect people, whose purpose was to establish God's commonwealth on earth for all to see and imitate. Puritans spoke a rhetoric of liberty, but it did not mean religious freedom. People were free to obey the will of God only in a community structured according to God's ordinances and desires. This resulted in a highly ordered society where all knew their place and stayed there, beginning in the family, the foundation of Puritan society. This kind of social order was unlikely to foster reform movements, since the community itself was to be the agent of God. But the values of election and of lay participation, also held by Puritans, helped to foster the seeds of reform on an individual basis. An example of this awakening can be seen in the memoirs of Abigail Abbot Bailey. She recorded her struggle with the realization that her husband was abusing herself and her children. She had few societal resources to challenge his behavior, but she finally gained strength from her convictions that God was moving her toward liberty and freedom as an individual (document 3). Reform here was spelled out in individual rather than societal terms.

This individualistic idea of reform found fertile soil in the Enlightenment and movements such as liberal New England theology, the Quakers, and the transcendentalists, all of which grew from it. At the same time, a new evangelicalism was developing on the heels of the Great Awakening. While the Enlightenment and evangelicalism differed in significant ways, both awakened in American society a sense of optimism and possibility. This was a society based on the understanding of covenant. The God of their covenant was a God vitally concerned with this world and the people in it. People could accomplish what God intended, and what God intended was the salvation of all people and the world that they inhabited. This theology, coupled with the tool of democracy, could shape and reform America.

The late-eighteenth-century movement from individual reform to the possibility of a reformed nation paved the way for the nineteenth-century scrutiny of society. Known as the age of reform, the nineteenth century would see societal as well as individual reform. The reforming eye, turned on every aspect of society, found plenty to improve. The covenant had experienced breaks that now needed to be healed.

The first awakenings of reform came through education. The evangelical reformers believed that if people saw what they were doing as a sin, they would repent and turn and follow God's will. The way to alert them to their sin was through education. Women were involved in educational reform from the beginning. For them it was a personal as well as a societal issue. Since avenues of education for women were limited, reform meant increasing those opportunities so that women could contribute to the improving of society. Emma Willard, Mary Lyon, and Catherine Beecher were early advocates of higher education for women. In 1837 Mary Lyon founded Mount Holyoke Female Seminary to train young women as teachers and missionaries, a conscious enterprise of Christian reform (document 4). Lyon exemplifies women reformers' attitudes. On her grave at the center of the Mount Holyoke campus is written this Lyon quote: "There is nothing in the universe that I fear, but that I shall not know my duty, or shall fail to do it." Through education all, but especially women, would know their duty and, God willing, would not fail to do it. These institutions educated many of the generation of reformers who shaped American society in the nineteenth and twentieth centuries.

TO REFORM THE NATION

From the foundation of education rose a complex of reforms constructed by women who saw themselves as restorers of the covenant, builders of the new heaven and new earth, following the direction and call of Mary's son, Jesus, the carpenter. No aspect of society was left untouched by these nineteenth-century reformers. Many entered into reform through abolition. The plight of slaves was held before all as a most despicable sin, one that both North and South had the responsibility to redress (document 5).

Temperance was another catalyzing reform. Combining individual and societal aspects, temperance work epitomized nineteenth-century understandings of reform. The drunkard himself was one target, but so was the environment that drove him to drink. Reformers critiqued politicians, businessmen who paid low wages, and saloon owners who grew rich from the misery of others. Reformers offered a social analysis to support their critique. Frances Willard and the Woman's Christian Temperance Union were clear that men drank to forget they could not earn enough to support their families. Then, after drinking away what little pay they had received, men went home and beat their wives and children out of frustration and guilt. The WCTU knew that merely exhorting people not to drink would not solve the problem; one had to address the conditions that drove people to drink in the first place. The language used in temperance reform was that of a crusade, and women were confident of victory.

Nineteenth-century women reformers were concerned about women as well, especially women's vulnerability in the face of similar economic oppression. Moral reform (the elimination of prostitution) was a major concern. It enabled the reformers not only to address prostitution but also to critique the sexism and double sexual standard that they saw operating within their communities. They also called for economic reforms to pay women a fair wage and to provide them with decent and safe working environments (document 6).

Women reformers worked on myriad reforms: better treatment for native peoples, freedmen's aid, prison reform, improved care for the insane, charitable work among the poor, peace, and women's rights. Through their work they hoped to create an America true to God's calling, a nation that lived and was governed by the law of justice, love, and equality—in short, a nation that lived out its covenantal commitment to God and to God's people.

One of the characteristics marking nineteenth-century women's reform is that the work was done mainly through organizations rather than through individuals, as had been the case in the eighteenth century. Women tended to create their own societies separate from the organizations begun by men. Often these women's societies were formed out of necessity because women were barred from full participation in the "general" (male) societies, but through organizing women also discovered women's strength in bonding together. The women carefully guarded their societies against takeover, particularly financial takeover, by the "general" societies that were addressing their issue. These women proved themselves to be consummate fund-raisers, administrators, and organizers.

What particularly motivated women reformers were the needs of other women. They wrote passionately of women in foreign lands and at home; of the drunkard's wife, the working girl, the slave woman, the prostitute, the immigrant girl; of the mother's heartbreak at losing a son in war. It was the pain and cries of other women that most deeply moved these reformers and that kept them at their task.

As historian Carolyn DeSwarte Gifford has pointed out, for many women "reform became their religion, a position of faith as much as a cause espoused."[4] Gifford uses Elizabeth Cady Stanton's assessment of her close friend Susan B. Anthony to illustrate many nineteenth-century women reformers' awareness that this union of religion and reform was appropriate for their time:

> Every energy of her soul is centered upon the needs of the world. To her work is worship. She has not stood aside shivering in the cold shadows of uncertainty; but has moved on with the whirling world, has done the good given her to do, and thus in the darkest hours has been sustained by an unfaltering faith in the final perfection of all things. Her belief is not Orthodox, but it is religious,—based on the high and severe moralities. In ancient Greece she would have been a Stoic; in the era of the Reformation a Calvinist; in King Charles' time, a Puritan; but in this nineteenth century, by the very laws of her being, she is a Reformer.[5]

The nineteenth-century women reformers blended and combined reforms, seeing "practical Christianity" as a whole as an expression of their most cherished ideals. While many of these reformers would engage in theological and biblical discussions, particularly around their right to be involved in reform, their convictions and work were grounded in everyday living out of the ethics of Jesus. They saw their work as a response to the call of Jesus to go into the world to make disciples and to help bring in the kingdom of God. It was a call to which they dedicated their lives.

REFORM AS CHALLENGE

In the midst of both reform work and arguing their right to be involved in reform, some women began to turn the critique they were leveling at society upon the church. A great deal of opposition to women reformers came from the same institution from which they drew their charge and their strength. Many argued with their opponents in order to justify their participation or to try to reform the church's message and practices toward what they saw as the message of the Galilean. For others the contradiction was too devastating for them to remain within the confines of the church and even of Christianity. One such critic was Elizabeth Cady Stanton. Together with a group of women scholars, she wrote *The Woman's Bible,* a scathing critique not only of the scriptural passages relating to women but of the very religion itself (document 7). This was not a popular stand even among most women reformers themselves, and many dissociated themselves from Stanton's project. Matilda Joslyn Gage's *Woman, Church and State,* an equally scathing critique of Christianity, suffered similar rejection by all but the most radical women reformers.

REFORM AS VISION

For most of the women reformers, though, Christianity was the foundation of, not the impediment to, their work. When challenged, they used the principles they found in the Gospels to support their work. They argued from the Scriptures that women and men were created equal. Though women might be endowed with different gifts than men, women's gifts were not inferior and women were not to be placed in a subordinate position. Women were created to be useful, not as ornaments. They had been created in the image of God and were answerable to God for the use to which they put their gifts. Their intellect, their reason, their hearts, and their bodies were all to be at the disposal of God, and woe to the man who tried to impede God's servants. Despite opposition, women were called to remain true to the heavenly vision to which they had been called by God (document 8).

As a result of their work for reform, women in the nineteenth century came to have a new understanding of themselves and of their society. They had enlarged the sphere that had been assigned them. While home and family were clearly still of central importance, these women carried family symbols into the world, making the world their home and all of humanity their family. They claimed the right to do some global housecleaning. These women have often been misunderstood by twentieth-century historians because of the language they used. Because they talked of motherhood, home, and family in describing and justifying their reform work, these nineteenth-century religious reformers have been labeled "maternal" or "soft" feminists. These women were caught on the cusp between concepts and words. They had new visions and understandings, but they did not yet have the language to express them. They used old words for new understandings and have been misheard ever since. Yet they glimpsed the new heaven and the new earth and the new woman who would live there, and that vision sustained them (document 9).

Despite these women's efforts, many of the reforms for which they worked did not come to fruition by the end of the nineteenth century. Slavery had been abolished, only to be replaced by an even more insidious racism. Prohibition was not the law of the land. Women did not have the vote. Despite the push for women to enter higher education and the professions, few were practicing in the professions and even fewer getting recognition for the quality of their work. The reformers believed that the new century would make these hopes a reality.

FAITH, FEMINISM, AND THE FUTURE

The twentieth century saw many changes. Some of the reforms for which the nineteenth-century women had worked came to fruition, such as women's suffrage and Prohibition. Women moved into many forms of business and the professions. Higher education became accessible. But was this all for which the women of the nineteenth century had hoped? When one looks at reform in the twentieth century, a number of issues must be discussed. One major problem is the very success of the women's efforts. What happens when a movement's goal has been achieved? In the twentieth century the stated goal of women's suffrage was met, but the overarching issues remained unresolved. With the passage of the Nineteenth Amendment in 1920, many felt their job was done. The women who disagreed found themselves isolated in a small group trying in vain to persuade others that this one success was not enough. Alice Paul's pleas for the Equal Rights Amendment immediately following the passage of the Nineteenth Amendment fell on mostly deaf ears. The same can be seen in the work surrounding temperance. Once Prohibition was passed, many felt the task was finished. But the woman's temperance movement had been concerned about much more than drink.

Another factor affecting the discussion of reform in the twentieth century is professionalism. The reforms of the nineteenth century were run mainly by voluntary associations and societies. The twentieth century saw the professionalization of much of this work. Paid social workers took the place of volunteer reformers. This shift happened because of the success of some of the very reforms for which the nineteenth-century women worked, especially education at the college and professional school levels. Many of these paid professionals viewed themselves as reformers and carried on the work and the ideals of their foremothers. They wrote and spoke and worked for reform from within their new professional sphere. The work was continuing, but an important shift in the focus and the self-understanding of the women doing it had taken place.

Another issue that needs to be taken into account is the secularization of American society that has occurred during the twentieth century. While the nineteenth-century women saw themselves firmly rooted in a religious conviction and having the goal of creating God's commonwealth on this earth, twentieth-century women faced a society that no longer understood itself to be essentially Christian or even religious. Twentieth-century reformers found themselves working within a pluralistic society, where the old language was simply no longer adequate. The covenant was broken, and the resources to restore it were no longer there. No longer did people share a vision of what America could and should be. The time of the collective understanding of what it meant to be God's people in this land had vanished, replaced by what were at times discordant claims and values.

Despite these shifts, women religious reformers were and are a vital part of American life. Many issues still need to be addressed, and women have taken up the challenge in this century. Many of these reforms have nineteenth-century foundations, even if the tactics are different.

The question of race has been a long-standing one in America. The nineteenth century's work for abolition was successful in freeing the slaves, but racism continued as strong as ever. Despite efforts in education and suffrage, overt discrimination and poverty were the norm for most African Americans at the turn of the century. Jim Crow laws reinforced a sense of inferiority, and the Ku Klux Klan added the threat of mortal danger. Many women, both black and white, worked to put an end to this terrorized existence (document 10). Women such as Ida B. Wells and Dorothy Rogers Tilley worked against lynching. Organizations such as the Young Women's Christian Association openly grappled with racism. This work has continued on into the late twentieth century. Women's groups are still actively fighting against the Klan and other forms of white supremacy. Groups of women of all colors are getting together to wrestle honestly with what it means to live and work and be friends in a racist society.[6]

The early part of the century saw women deeply involved in the struggle for economic justice. The Social Gospel movement led both women and men to call for labor reform and economic equality for all. Women such as Jennie Fowler Willing, Winnifred Chappel, and Vida Scudder approached these issues as Christians and as socialists, braving the tide of increasing hostility toward that particular brand of politics (document 11).

The work for peace was carried over into this century. Pacifism often has not been a popular stance, but women have been involved in many ways and through many wars, writing petitions, counseling conscientious objectors, working for disarmament, and urging a global solution to conflict, first through the League of Nations and later through the United Nations (document 12).

While the rhetoric justifying involvement in reform may no longer be of home and motherhood, much real housecleaning remains to be done. Twentieth-century women reformers are challenging every aspect of this complex society, continuing work begun in the nineteenth century and earlier on issues such as prison reform, prostitution, violence against women, sanctuary for refugees, ecological concerns, and, of course, women's rights.

The 1960s saw a resurgence of the women's movement. Calls for women to have a role beyond the home, renewed work for the ERA, consciousness-raising groups, and the formation of the National Organization of Women echoed the voices of their foremothers. Issues such as abortion have caused a great deal of debate and action (document 13). Along with the issue of control of one's own body comes control over one's own sexual activity and identity. Lesbians began "coming out" and demanding their rights both in society and in the church (document 14).

Twentieth-century women also turned the critique they were directing at society on the church. Many women became convinced that the church and Christianity were oppressive to women. Some chose to remain within the church and work for reform from within. These feminist theologians, such as Rosemary Radford Ruether, Carter Heyward, Jacquelyn Grant, Rita Brock, Susan Thistlethwaite, Virginia Mollenkott, and Delores Williams, are radically changing the face of Christian theology and the way women perceive God, the Christ, and themselves. Other women, such as Mary Daly, have chosen to leave the tradition and, echoing Elizabeth Cady Stanton, claim a post-Christian identity. Others, such as Carol Christ and Starhawk, have turned to the Goddess, working to recover pre-Christian religious expressions that center around a female deity with whom many women can more readily identify.

As the century draws to a close, we find ourselves in the midst of a society searching for meaning, searching for ways to make a difference, and still searching for a just world. The twentieth-century reformers have been a more divergent group than in previous centuries. They have faced a society that did not have a universal mythos to guide it. Twentieth-century religious reformers have had to struggle with the issue of how to relate to secular reform movements. And they have had to deal with failure. But through it all, a deep and abiding concern for justice, for love, and especially for other women links them to their mothers in reform.

Women are reformers by necessity and by conviction. Though various reforms have enjoyed varying degrees of success, it is women banding together to make the world better—free from oppression, fear, hatred, bigotry, and violence—that has made all the difference. Women have understood the source of their mandate for reform in different ways

Jennie Fowler Willing (1834–1916), a founder of the Women's Foreign Missionary Society and an early female local preacher in the Methodist Episcopal Church, was also an active social reformer for temperance and women's education. Her work naturally bridged social reform and institutional church leadership.

Anna Howard Shaw (1847–1915) was the first woman ordained in the Methodist Protestant Church, in 1880. Later president of the National American Woman's Suffrage Association, her vision of Christianity underlay her strong advocacy of women's rights.

Ida Scudder (1870–1960) founded the Christian Medical College and Hospital, Vellore, South India, first school of medicine for women in India, in 1918.

The Rev. Dr. Letty Russell, now professor of systematic theology at Yale Divinity School, is shown here in her office in the Presbyterian Church of the Ascension, East Harlem Protestant Parish, New York City, shortly after her ordination on September 19, 1958.

Dr. Georgia Harkness (1891–1974) was the first woman theologian to teach in a seminary in the United States, Garrett Biblical Institute, where she taught from 1940 until 1950. The only woman on the Dun Commission, appointed by the Federal Council of Churches in 1950 to consider the moral implications of obliteration bombing, she is shown here with Bishop Angus Dun, professors Paul Tillich, Reinhold Niebuhr, Robert Calhoun, John Bennett, and other ecumenical male church leaders on the commission.

Vida Scudder (1861–1954), active Episcopal laywoman and longtime teacher of English at Wellesley College, sought to reconcile differences between Christianity and socialism.

in American history, from the biblical God, from the Goddess of nature, or simply from inherent truths in human nature, but they have continually acted on these mandates to shape a society better suited to love and justice.

Documents

A WOMAN'S PLACE

Document 1. Lucretia Mott:
Why Shouldn't a Woman Be a Reformer?

Lucretia Mott (1793–1880), a minister in the Society of Friends, was a strong voice for reform in the nineteenth century. She worked, preached, and wrote for women's rights, abolition, peace, and reform of the church at large. She was a close friend of Susan B. Anthony and Elizabeth Cady Stanton. She delivered the following address in Philadelphia on December 17, 1849, as a response to a speech given by Richard Dana, in which he ridiculed the new demand of American women for civil and political rights and for a larger sphere of action.[7]

Why should not woman seek to be a reformer? If she is to shrink from being such an iconoclast as shall "break the image of man's lower worship," as so long held up to view; if she is to fear to exercise her reason, and her noblest powers, lest she should be thought to "attempt to act the man," and not "acknowledge his supremacy"; if she is to be satisfied with the narrow sphere assigned her by man, nor aspire to a higher, lest she should transcend the bounds of female delicacy, truly it is a mournful prospect for woman. We would admit all the difference, that our great and beneficent Creator has made, in the relation of man and women, nor would we seek to disturb this relation; but we deny that the present position of woman is her true sphere of usefulness, nor will she attain to this sphere, until the disabilities and disadvantages, religious, civil, and social, which impede her progress, are removed out of her way. These restrictions have enervated her mind and paralyzed her powers. While man assumes that the present is the original state designed for woman, that the existing "differences are not arbitrary nor the result of accident," but grounded in nature; she will not make the necessary effort to obtain her just rights, lest it should subject her to the kind of scorn and contemptuous manner in which she has been spoken of.

So far from her "ambition leading her to attempt to act the man," she needs all the encouragement she can receive, by the removal of obstacles from her path, in order that she may become the "true woman." As it is desirable that man should act a manly and generous part, not "mannish," so let woman be urged to exercise a dignified and womanly bearing, not womanish. Let her cultivate all the graces and proper accomplishments of her sex, but let not these degenerate into a kind of effeminacy, in which she is satisfied to be the mere plaything or toy of society, content with her outward adornings, and the flattery and fulsome adulation too often addressed to her. . . .

The question is often asked, "What does woman want, more than she enjoys? What is she seeking to obtain? Of what rights is she deprived? What privileges are withheld from her?" I answer, she asks nothing as favor, but as right; she wants to be acknowledged a moral, responsible being. She is seeking not to be governed by laws in the making of which she has no voice. She is deprived of almost every right in civil society, and is a cipher in the nation, except in the right of presenting a petition. In religious society her disabilities have greatly retarded her progress. Her exclusion from the pulpit or ministry, her duties marked out for her by her equal brother man, subject to creeds, rules, and disciplines made for her by him, is unworthy of her true dignity. . . .

Let woman then go on, not asking favors, but claiming as right, the removal of all hindrances to her elevation in the scale of being; let her receive encouragement for the proper cultivation of all her powers, so that she may enter profitably into the active business of life; employing her own hands in ministering to her necessities, strengthening her physical being by proper exercise and observance of the laws of health. Let her not be ambitious to display a fair hand and to promenade the fashionable streets of our city, but rather, coveting earnestly the best gifts, let her strive to occupy such walks in society as will befit her true dignity in all relations of life. No fear that she will then transcend the proper limits of female delicacy. True modesty will be as fully preserved in acting out those important vocations, as in the nursery or at the fireside ministering to man's self-indulgence.

Document 2. Mrs. J. T. Gracey: Evangelical Organizing

Many women found themselves creating women's organizations to work for reform. At times these were created of necessity, since women were barred from many reform societies. Other organizations felt the need to be independent of men's control. The following selection is by Mrs. J. T. Gracey, in her discussion of the history of women's missionary societies.[8]

If the Church in America is to be a power for the evangelization of the world, its latent energies must be developed, and its forces properly conserved. It is an encouraging fact that the value of organized efforts of women in Christian and philanthropic work is becoming more fully appreciated. Women constitute two thirds of the Church membership, and are, therefore, numerically, an element of strength; yet the additional number of workers that they furnish for the field is not the most important advantage. The great advantage is, that they bring an entirely new influence into the world of effort; a quiet, unseen, and pervading influence, the result of combined patience and strength, more potent even than what is gained by mere numbers and display.

Emerson says: "Civilization is simply the influence of good women." Righteous principles and pure motives of action planted in human hearts grow in power and give rise to moral reforms. The homes of the people are the real centers of the influences determinative of the character of the people. Woman's appropriate sphere of action is the home. As the spirit of practical philanthropy and religion thoroughly imbues the currents of her thought, she will be able more effectually to purify the sources of power and to send forth vitalizing influences that will reach, with elevating effect, all classes and conditions of society.

To meet successfully the momentous moral questions involving the destiny of the nation, philanthropic measures should be so planned as to utilize this hitherto latent force of Christian women. The value of woman's influences is in proportion as she labors in harmony with the laws of her being. Hence, to secure the best results of her labor, the plans of organization must be such as will enable her to enter the fields of effort in ways consistent with, and congenial to, her womanly nature and endowments.

The employment of women in mission work is one of the most hopeful indications of the speedy triumph of the Church of Christ. Since there is nothing in her recognized sphere of action nor in the delicacy of her nature to prevent, she may be welcomed to association in thought and effort with the other sex in the removal of human suffering, and in the introduction of a higher civilization. In the countries where the aid of women in benevolent work is rejected progress is well-nigh paralyzed; but in those where her intelligent co-operation furnishes the incentive to noble achievement, wonderful advancement has been made in every department of Christian effort.

REFORM AS AWAKENING

Document 3. Abigail Abbot Bailey:
Reform as Individual Empowerment
in the Eighteenth Century

For women throughout the centuries, reform has begun with a personal issue and that first step of claiming one's power and saying no. This selection from the memoirs of Abigail Abbot Bailey (1746–1815), a Congregationalist woman living in New Hampshire and Massachusetts, demonstrates how even in a limited sphere reform is born.[9] The memoirs show a development of consciousness of her and her children's oppression and abuse. The excerpt below is from the beginning phase of that awareness.

The black cloud, rising like a storm of hail, had rolled on, and had gathered over my head. I clearly saw that Mr. B. entertained the most vile intentions relative to his own daughter. Whatever difficulty attended the obtaining of legal proof, yet no remaining doubt existed in my mind, relative to the existence of his wickedness; and I had no doubt remaining of the violence, which he had used; and that hence arose his rage against her. It must have drawn tears of anguish from the eyes of the hardest mortals, to see the barbarous corrections, which he, from time to time, inflicted on this poor young creature; and for no just cause. Sometimes he corrected her with a rod; and sometimes with a beach stick, large enough for the driving of a team; and with such sternness and anger sparkling in his eyes, that his visage seemed to resemble an infernal; declaring, that if she attempted to run from him again, she should never want but one correction more; for he would whip her to death! This his conduct could be for no common disobedience; for she had ever been most obedient to him in all lawful commands. It seemed as though the poor girl must now be destroyed under his furious hand. She was abashed, and could look no one in the face.

None can describe the anguish of my heart on the beholding of such scenes. How pitiful must be the case of a poor young female, to be subjected to such barbarous treatment by her own father; so that she knew of no way of redress!

It may appear surprising that such wickedness was not checked by legal restraints. But great difficulties attend in such a case. While I was fully convinced of the wickedness, yet I knew not that I could make legal proof. I could not prevail upon this daughter to make known to me her troubles; or to testify against the author of them. Fear, shame, youthful inexperience, and the terrible peculiarities of her case, all conspired to close her mouth against affording me, or any one, proper information. My soul was moved with pity for her wretched case; and yet I cannot say I did not feel a degree of resentment, that she would not, as she ought, expose the wickedness of her father, that she might be relieved from him, and he brought to due punishment. But no doubt his intrigues, insinuations, commands, threats, and parental influence, led her to feel that it was in vain for her to seek redress. . . .

The next morning I took an opportunity with Mr. B. alone to have solemn conversation. My health being now restored, I thought it high time, and had determined, to adopt a new mode of treatment with Mr. B. I calmly introduced the subject, and told him, plainly and solemnly, all my views of his wicked conduct, in which he had long lived with his daughter. He flew into a passion, was high, and seemed to imagine, he could at once frighten me out of my object. But I was carried equally above fear, and above temper. Of this I soon convinced him, I let him know, that the business I now had taken in hand, was of too serious a nature, and too interesting, to be thus disposed of, or dismissed with a few angry words. I told him I should no longer be turned off in this manner, but should pursue my object with firmness, and with whatever wisdom and ability God might give me; and that God would plead my cause, and prosper my present undertaking, as he should see best. I reminded Mr. B. of my long and unusually distressing illness, how he had treated me in it; how wicked and cruel he had been to the wife of his youth; how unable I had been to check him in that awful wickedness, which I knew he had pursued; that all my inexpressible griefs and solemn entreaties had been by him trampled under foot.

I therefore had not known what to do better than to wait on God as I had done, to afford me strength and opportunity to introduce the means of his effectual control. This time I told him had arrived. And now, if God spared my life, (I told Mr. B.) he should find a new leaf turned over;—and that I would not suffer him to go on any longer as he had done. I would now soon adopt measures to put a stop to his abominable wickedness and cruelties. For this could and ought to be done. And if I did it not, I should be a partaker of his sins, and should aid in bringing down the curse of God upon our family.

Document 4. Mary Lyon and Mount Holyoke: Educating for Reform

Education was both a means to reform and an area of primary reform concern for women. Mary Lyon (1797–1849) was one of the first women to advance women's higher education. She founded the first institution of higher education for women in South Hadley, Massachusetts, in 1837. Mount Holyoke Female Seminary's prime purpose was to educate teachers and missionaries. The following document is a circular addressed to women, soliciting funds for the seminary. Written in 1836, it shows Mary Lyon's strong justification of the need for women's education.[10]

You would expect that I should feel deeply interested in the success of Mount Holyoke Female Seminary. Had I a thousand lives, I could sacrifice them all in suffering and hardship for its sake. Did I possess the greatest fortune, I could readily relinquish it all, and become poor, and more than poor, if its prosperity should demand it. Its grand object is to furnish the greatest possible number of female teachers of high literary qualifications, and of benevolent, self-denying zeal. The institution is to be only for an older class of young ladies, and every scholar is to board in the establishment. The general course of study, and the general character of the instruction, are to be like those at Ipswich. The institution is to be permanent, continuing onward in its operations from generation to generation. In the thousands of teachers which it will send forth, it will doubtless be an instrument of good, far beyond the present grasp of my feeble comprehension.

But this is not all. This experiment has an important bearing on the great subject of adopting suitable means for supplying our country with well-qualified female teachers, and it is testing the great question of duty on this subject. This constitutes its chief importance. It is like the signing of the Declaration of Independence; the battles were still to be fought, but the question of independence was then settled. It is like fitting out our first little band of missionaries. The great work of evangelizing a world was still before the American churches; but the grand question of duty, and the mode of meeting duty, were then settled, never again to be seriously doubted. Let this enterprise be carried through by the liberality of the Christian community, and it will no longer be doubted whether the work of supplying our country with well-qualified female teachers shall be allowed a standing among the benevolent operations of the day. The work will still be before us, but the principle on which it is to be accomplished will be settled. Another stone in the foundation of our great system of benevolent operations, which are destined, in the hand of God, to convert the world, will then be laid.

The work of bringing this institution into operation has been longer than was anticipated. But the progress of the enterprise in taking an acknowledged standing among the benevolent operations of the day has exceeded the expectations of its warmest friends. I doubt whether any benevolent object, not excepting even the missionary cause, has ever, within two years from its commencement, made a greater advance in gaining access to the understanding and hearts of the people. Many have rejoiced that so noble a design has been formed in the heart of

New England. Many hearts have been filled with hope, as they have beheld this enterprise go forward in obedience to the great command, "Love thy neighbor as thyself."

TO REFORM THE NATION

Document 5. Angelina Grimke: Abolition

Angelina and Sarah Grimke were strong advocates for the widening sphere of women in social reform. Born and raised in a South Carolina slaveholding family, Sarah (1792–1873) and Angelina (1805–1879) became convinced of the evils of slavery. Moving to Philadelphia and adopting Quakerism, abolition, and feminism, they became eloquent lecturers, despite heavy opposition. The following selection, written by Angelina in 1838, puts forth the case of the need for Northern women to be concerned about slavery.[11]

[In] a country where women are degraded and brutalized, and where their exposed persons bleed under the lash—where they are sold in the shambles of "negro brokers"—robbed of their hard earnings— torn from their husbands, and forcibly plundered of their virtue and their offspring, surely in *such* a country, it is very natural that *women* should wish to know "the reason *why*"—especially when these outrages of blood and nameless horror are practiced in violation of the principles of our national Bill of Rights and the preamble of our Constitution. We do not, then, and cannot concede the position, that because this is a *political subject* women ought to fold their hands in idleness, and close their eyes and ears to the "horrible things" that are practiced in our land. The denial of our duty to act is a bold denial of our right to act; and if we have no right to act, then may *we* well be termed "the white slaves of the North"—for, like our brethren in bonds, we must seal our lips in silence and despair. . . .

Out of the millions of slaves who have been stolen from Africa, a very great number must have been women who were torn from the arms of their fathers and husbands, brothers and children, and subjected to all the horrors of the middle passage and the still greater sufferings of slavery in a foreign land. Multitudes of these were cast upon our inhospitable shores; some of them now toil out a life of bondage, "one hour of which is fraught with more misery than ages of that" which our fathers rose in rebellion to oppose. But the great mass of female slaves in the southern States are the descendants of these hapless strangers; 1,000,000 of them now wear the iron yoke of slavery in this land of boasted liberty and law. They are our country women—*they are our sisters;* and to us, as women, they have a right to look for sympathy with their sorrows, and effort and prayer for their rescue. Upon those of us especially who have named the name of Christ, they have peculiar claims, and claims which *we must answer, or we shall incur a heavy load of guilt.* . . .

[Another] reason we would urge for the interference of northern women with the system of slavery is, that in consequence of the odium which the degradation of slavery has attached to *color* even in the free States, our *colored sisters* are dreadfully oppressed here. Our seminaries of learning are closed to them, they are almost entirely banished from our lecture rooms, and even in the house of God they are separated from their white brethren and sisters as though we were afraid to come in contact with a colored skin. . . .

Here, then, are some of the bitter fruits of that inveterate prejudice which the vast proportion of northern women are cherishing towards their colored sisters; and let us remember that every one of us who denies the sinfulness of this prejudice, . . . is awfully guilty in the sight of Him who is no respecter of persons. . . .

But our colored sisters are oppressed in other ways. As they walk the streets of our cities, they are continually liable to be insulted with the vulgar epithet of "nigger"; no matter how respectable or wealthy, they cannot visit the Zoological Institute of New York except in the capacity of nurses or servants—no matter how worthy, they cannot gain admittance into or receive assistance from any of the charities of this city. In Philadelphia, they are cast out of our widow's Asylum, and their children are refused admittance to the House of Refuge, the Orphan's House and the Infant School connected with the Alms-House, though into these are gathered the very offscouring of our population. These are only specimens of that soul-crushing influence from which the colored women of the north are daily suffering. Then, again, some of them have been robbed of their husbands and children by the heartless kidnapper, and others have themselves been dragged into slavery. If they attempt to travel, they are exposed to great indignities and great inconveniences. Instances have been known of their actually dying in consequence of the exposure to which they were subjected on board of our steamboats. No money could purchase the use of a berth for a delicate female because she had a colored skin. Prejudice, then, degrades and fetters the minds, persecutes and murders the bodies of our free colored sisters. Shall *we* be silent at such a time as this?. . .

Much may be done, too, by sympathizing with our oppressed colored sisters, who are suffering in our very midst. Extend to them the right hand of fellowship on the broad principles of humanity and Christianity, treat them as *equals,* visit them as *equals,* invite them to co-operate with you in Anti-Slavery and Temperance and Moral Reform Societies—in Maternal Associations and Prayer meetings and Reading Companies. . . .

Multitudes of instances will continually occur in which you will have the opportunity of *identifying yourselves with this injured class* of our fellow-beings: embrace these opportunities at all times and in all places, in the true nobility of our great Exemplar, who was ever found among the *poor and despised,* elevating and blessing them with his counsels and presence. In this way, and this alone, will you be enabled to subdue that deep-rooted prejudice which is doing the work of oppression in the free States to a most dreadful extent.

When this demon has been cast out of your own hearts, when *you* can recognize the colored women as a WOMAN—*then* will you be prepared to send out an appeal to our Southern sisters, entreating them to "go and do likewise."

Document 6. New York Female Moral Reform Society: Prostitution

The following document was drawn up at the organizational meeting of the New York Female Moral Reform Society on May 12, 1834. The society hoped not only to convert New York's prostitutes to Protestant Christianity but also to launch a women's crusade against sexual license in general and the double standard in particular. This crusade was to be part of God's work of reform and the bringing in of the new era.[12]

To the Ladies of the United States of every Religious Denomination:

BELOVED SISTERS:—Suffer a word of exhortation on a subject of vital interest to the entire sisterhood: we refer to the sin of LICEN-TIOUSNESS.

We need not inform you that this sin prevails to an alarming extent in our land. The fact is obvious to all. A moment's reflection will show you that it has woven itself into all the fibres of society, shaping its opinions, modifying its customs, and in one form or another spreading an atmosphere of corruption and death throughout the entire community. . . . So we believe; and so believing, we feel that it is time for *us,* in common with others, to take our stand on the side of virtue and God, and do what we can to turn back the tide of pollution that is sweeping over the land, and bearing its victims onward, by thousands, to the chambers of death.

And now, beloved sisters, we ask you to take your stand with us. The evil we know is great, and the public sentiment it has created for itself, and behind which it entrenches itself, is mighty. Nevertheless, we have confidence in the gospel; that it is mighty through God, to the pulling down of strongholds. And we believe that its efficacy will not fail in this case. The evil, great as it is, *can be reached,* and the public sentiment behind which it is entrenched, mighty as it is, CAN BE MET AND CHANGED. . . .

But this sin, we are persuaded, is one in respect to which it is emphatically true, that a radical reform can never be effected without the co-operation of woman. Here, if we mistake not, her influence may be most powerful and efficacious. She may wield a power that can be wielded by no one else. Ask you how?

The answer is—1st. Let her do what she can to disseminate light on the subject—by conversation—by the circulation of such papers and tracts as are fitted to be a discerner of the thoughts and intents of the heart, and, at the same time, to show the enormity and guilt, and fatal tendencies and results of this sin—though it be only the sin of the heart.

2d. Let her take the ground, so obviously in accordance with truth, that the libertine is no less guilty than his victim, and as such, shall be at once excluded from her society. This you will perceive by the annexed Constitution, is the ground that your sisters in New-York have taken. We ask you—we entreat you—to take the same. We point you to the whole sex, the entire sisterhood, and we say that demon in human shape, that fixed his lascivious eye upon your sister, and wrought her ruin, is the enemy of your sex. Exclude him then at once from all society with you—in self-defence—in defence of the sex, exclude him. He wants but the opportunity, and he will as soon make you his victim as that erring, fallen sister. Some of you, perhaps, are mothers. God has blessed you with a family of lovely children—daughters, pure, innocent, the joy of your heart, and objects of your purest, sweetest, strongest affections. But see, the demon has marked your first born as his victim. His wanton eye is already on her. Mothers, away with him—in defence of your beloved children, away with him, we entreat you, from your families, and from the society of your children. Teach them to shun him as they would a viper. He wants but the opportunity, and he will not hesitate to seize upon his victim, and thereby plunge a dagger to your heart. In self-defence—in defence of your families, and we may add, in defence of the whole community, away with such a one from all society and intercourse with you. This done, and the work of Moral Reform is done, and the virtue and peace of the community secured.

Beloved Sisters, we are persuaded that in this simple way, we may wield an influence on this subject that cannot be resisted. If we will but organize ourselves into associations on this principle, and have the moral courage thus to stand up for injured and outraged innocence, not heeding the reproach that may, for a little season, be heaped upon us, we verily believe, that in God, we shall triumph. God seems in a special manner to have committed this work to our hands; and without arrogance, it is not too much to say, that, if we will, we may, by this simple process, put such a brand of infamy upon the licentious man—we may gather upon him such a withering frown of virtuous indignation, as to save not only the victim, but the destroyer also, and thus put an effectual check to the tide of pollution that is now sweeping us away.

And now, sisters, what say you? Under God, the privilege and the responsibility of this holy and blessed work is yours. It is for you, in a special manner, to say what shall be done. Oh! then show, we do entreat you, that you have the virtue, the principle, the moral courage, to breast a corrupt and mighty public sentiment in defence of virtue and religion.

REFORM AS CHALLENGE

Document 7. Elizabeth Cady Stanton:
Christianity as Oppressor

Many women became aware through their reform work that the church was also in need of reform. One of the strongest critiques came from Elizabeth Cady Stanton (1815–1902). The following selection from the introduction of *The Woman's Bible* shows the indictment she leveled and the only possible solution.[13]

From the inauguration of the movement for woman's emancipation the Bible has been used to hold her in the "divinely ordained sphere," prescribed in the Old and New Testaments.

The canon and civil law; church and state; priests and legislators; all political parties and religious denominations have alike taught that woman was made after man, of man, and for man, an inferior being, subject to man. Creeds, codes, Scriptures and statutes, are all based on this idea. The fashions, forms, ceremonies and customs of society, church ordinances and discipline all grow out of this idea. . . .

The Bible teaches that woman brought sin and death into the world, that she precipitated the fall of the race, that she was arraigned before the judgment seat of Heaven, tried, condemned and sentenced. Marriage for her was to be a condition of bondage, maternity a period of suffering and anguish, and in silence and subjection, she was to play the role of a dependent on man's bounty for all her material wants, and for all the information she might desire on the vital questions of the hour, she was commanded to ask her husband at home. Here is the Bible position of woman briefly summed up. . . .

These familiar texts are quoted by clergymen in their pulpits, by statesmen in the halls of legislation, by lawyers in the courts, and are echoed by the press of all civilized nations, and accepted by woman herself as "The Word of God." So perverted is the religious element in her nature, that with faith and works she is the chief support of the church and clergy; the very powers that make her emancipation impossible. When, in the early part of the Nineteenth Century, women began to protest against their civil and political degradation, they were referred to the Bible for an answer. When they protested against their unequal position in the church, they were referred to the Bible for an answer.

This led to a general and critical study of the Scriptures. Some, having made a fetish of these books and believing them to be the veritable "Word of God," with liberal translations, interpretations, allegories and symbols, glossed over the most objectionable features of the various books and clung to them as divinely inspired. Others, seeing the family resemblance between the Mosaic code, the canon law, and the old English common law, came to the conclusion that all alike emanated from the same source; wholly human in their origin and inspired by the natural love of domination in the historians. Others, bewildered with their doubts and fears, came to no conclusion. While their clergymen told them, on the one hand, that they owed all the blessings and freedom they enjoyed to the Bible, on the other, they said it clearly marked out their circumscribed sphere of action: that the demands for political and civil rights were irreligious, dangerous to the stability of the home, the state and the church. Clerical appeals were circulated from time to time conjuring members of their churches to take no part in the anti-slavery or woman suffrage movements, as they were infidel in their tendencies, undermining the very foundations of society. No wonder the majority of women stood still, and with bowed heads, accepted the situation. . . .

How can woman's position be changed from that of a subordinate to an equal, without opposition, without the broadest discussion of all the questions involved in her present degradation? For so far-reaching and momentous a reform as her complete independence, an entire revolution in all existing institutions is inevitable.

Let us remember that all reforms are interdependent, and that whatever is done to establish one principle on a solid basis, strengthens all. Reformers who are always compromising, have not yet grasped the idea that truth is the only safe ground to stand upon. The object of an individual life is not to carry one fragmentary measure in human progress, but to utter the highest truth clearly seen in all directions, and thus to round out and perfect a well balanced character.

There are some who write us that our work is a useless expenditure of force over a book that has lost its hold on the human mind. Most intelligent women, they say, regard it simply as the history of a rude people in a barbarous age, and have no more reverence for the Scriptures than any other work. So long as tens of thousands of Bibles are printed every year, and circulated over the whole habitable globe, and the masses in all English-speaking nations revere it as the word of God, it is vain to belittle its influence. The sentimental feelings we all have for those things we were educated to believe sacred do not readily yield to pure reason. I distinctly remember the shudder that passed over me on seeing a mother take our family Bible to make a high seat for her child at table. It seemed such a desecration. I was tempted to protest against its use for such a purpose, and this, too, long after my reason had repudiated its divine authority.

To women still believing in the plenary inspiration of the Scriptures, we say give us by all means your exegesis in the light of the higher criticism learned men are now making, and illumine the Woman's Bible, with your inspiration. . . .

The only points in which I differ from all ecclesiastical teaching is that I do not believe that any man ever saw or talked with God, I do not believe that God inspired the Mosaic code, or told the historians what they say he did about woman, for all the religions on the face of the earth degrade her, and so long as woman accepts the position that they assign her, her emancipation is impossible. Whatever the Bible may be made to do in Hebrew or Greek, in plain English it does not exalt and dignify woman.

REFORM AS VISION

Document 8. Anna Howard Shaw:
Freedom and Rights for the Oppressed

In 1880 Anna Howard Shaw (1847–1915) became the first woman ordained to the ministry in the Methodist tradition. She served pastorates for seven years and obtained a medical degree during that period. She became convinced that suffrage was the key to women's advancement. She left the pastorate to lecture and organize for suffrage, temperance, and other moral reforms. She served as president of the National American Woman's Suffrage Association from 1904 until 1915. The following selection is taken from her sermon "The Heavenly Vision," which she preached at the International Council of Women in 1888.[14]

All down through the centuries God has been revealing in visions the great truths which have lifted the race, step by step, until to-day womanhood, in this sunset hour of the nineteenth century, is gathered here from the East and the West, the North and the South, women of every land, of every race, of all religious beliefs. But diverse and varied as are our races, diverse and varied as are our theories, diverse and varied as are our religious beliefs, yet we come together here with one harmonious purpose—that of lifting humanity into a higher, purer, truer life.

To one has come the vision of political freedom. She saw how the avarice and ambition of one class with power made them forget the rights of another. She saw how the unjust laws embittered both—those who made them and those upon whom the injustice rested. She recognized the great principles of universal equality, seeing that all alike must be free; that humanity everywhere must be lifted out of subjection into the free and full air of divine liberty.

To another was revealed the vision of social freedom. She saw that sin which crushed the lives of one class, rested lightly on the lives of the other. She saw its blighting effect on both, and she lifted up her voice and demanded that there be recognized no sex in sin. Another has come hither, who, gazing about her, saw men brutalized by the rum fiend, the very life of a nation threatened, and the power of the liquor traffic, with its hand on the helm of [the ship of] state, guiding her with sails full spread, straight upon the rocks to destruction. Then, looking away from earth, she beheld a vision of what the race and our nation might become with all its possibility of wealth, with its possibility of power, if freed from this, and forth upon her mission of deliverance she sped her way.

Another beheld a vision of what it is to be learned, to explore the great fields of knowledge the Infinite has spread out before the world. And this vision has driven her out from the seclusion of her own quiet life that she might give this great truth to womanhood everywhere. . . .

And so we come, each bearing her torch of living truth, casting over the world the light of the vision that dawned upon her own soul.

But there is still another vision which reaches above earth, beyond time—a vision which has dawned upon many that they are here not to do their own work, but the will of Him who sent them. And the woman who sees the still higher truth recognizes the great power to which she belongs and what her life may become when, in submission to that Master, she takes upon herself the nature of Him whom she serves. . . .

This, then, is God's lesson to you and to me.

He opens before our eyes the vision of a great truth, and for a moment, He permits our wondering gaze to rest upon it; then He bids us go forth. Jacob of old saw the vision of God's messengers ascending and descending, but none of them were standing still. . . .

No man or woman has ever sought to lead his fellows to a higher and better mode of life without learning the power of the world's ingratitude; and though at times popularity may follow in the wake of a reformer, yet the reformer knows popularity is not love. The world will support you when you have compelled it to do so by manifestations of power, but it will shrink from you as soon as power and greatness are no longer on your side. This is the penalty paid by good people who sacrifice themselves for others. They must live without sympathy; their feelings will be misunderstood; their efforts will be uncomprehended. Like Paul, they will be betrayed by friends; like Christ in the agony of Gethsemane, they must bear their struggle alone. . . .

This is the hardest lesson the reformer has to learn. When, with soul aglow with the light of a great truth, she, in obedience to the vision, turns to take it to the needy one, and instead of finding a world ready to rise up and receive her, she finds it wrapped in the swaddling clothes of error, eagerly seeking to win others to its conditions of slavery. She longs to make humanity free; she listens to their conflicting creeds, and yearns to save them from the misery they endure. She knows that there is no form of slavery more bitter or arrogant than error, that truth alone can make man free, and she longs to bring the heart of the world and the heart of truth together, that the truth may exercise its transforming power over the life of the world. The greatest test of the reformer's courage comes when, with a warm, earnest longing for humanity, she breaks for it the bread of truth and the world turns from this life-giving power and asks instead of bread a stone.

It is just here that so many of God's workmen fail, and themselves need to turn back to the vision as it appeared to them, and to gather fresh courage and new inspiration for the future. This, my sisters, we all must do if we would succeed. The reformer may be inconsistent, she may be stern or even impatient, but if the world feels that she is in earnest she can not fail. Let the truth which she desires to teach first take possession of herself. Every woman who to-day goes out into the world with a truth, who has not herself become possessed of that truth, had far better stay at home. . . .

Grand as is this vision which meets us here, it is but the dawning of a new day; and as the first beams of morning light give promise of the radiance which shall envelop the earth when the sun shall have arisen in all its splendor, so there comes to us a prophecy of that glorious day when the vision which we are now beholding, which is beaming in the soul of one, shall enter the hearts and transfigure the lives of all.

Document 9. Frances E. Willard: The New Woman

Frances E. Willard (1839–1898) was president of the Evanston (Illinois) College for Ladies between 1871 and 1874 but found her true vocation when she joined the temperance movement. She served the Woman's Christian Temperance Union as president from 1879 until her death. Her temperance work led her to the conviction of the need for women's suffrage and also to a far-reaching social critique that would lead her by the end of her life to socialism. In the following selection, Willard makes several predictions for the new century and the new woman.[15] She was writing an advice book for girls, and she hoped the book would serve as an influence for them and through them transform the society in which she lived. This was her vision of what the twentieth century could be, and, indeed, some of her visions have become reality.

No doubt my readers have asked ere this the inevitable question: "Why does that seem natural and fitting for a young woman to do and to aspire to now which would have been no less improper than impossible a hundred years ago?" Sweet friends, it is because *the ideal of woman's place in the world is changing in the average mind*. For as the artist's idea precedes his picture, so the ideal woman must be transformed before the actual one can be. In an age of brute force, the warrior galloping away to his adventures waved his mailed hand to the lady fair who was enclosed for safe keeping in a grim castle with moat and drawbridge. But to-day, when spirit force grows regnant, a woman can circumnavigate the globe alone, without danger of an uncivil word, much less of violence. . . . In brief, the barriers that have hedged women into one pathway and men into another, altogether different, are growing thin, as physical strength plays a less determining part in our life drama. . . .

What will the new ideal of woman *not* be? Well, for example, she will never be written down in the hotel register by her husband after this fashion: "John Smith and Wife." He would as soon as think of her writing, "Mrs. John Smith and Husband." Why does it not occur to any one to designate him thus? Simply because he is so much more than that. He is the leading force in the affairs of the Church; he helps decide who shall be pastor. (So will she.) He is, perhaps, the village physician, or merchant. (So she will be, perhaps—indeed, they are oftentimes in partnership, nowadays, and I have found their home a blessed one.) He is the village editor. (Very likely she will be his associate.) He is a voter. (She would be, beyond a peradventure.) For the same reason you will never read of her marriage that "the minister pronounced them MAN and *wife*," for that functionary would have been just as likely to pronounce them "husband and woman," a form of expression into which the regulation reporter will be likely to fall one of these days, it being, really, not one whit more idiotic than the time-worn phrase, "man and wife." The ideal woman of the future will never be designated as "the *Widow* Jones," because she will be so much more than that—"a provider" for her children, "a power" in the Church, "a felt force" in the State. . . .

The ideal woman will play Beatrice to man's Dante in the Inferno of his passions. She will give him the clew out of materialism's Labyrinth. She will be civilization's Una, taming the Lion of disease and misery. The State shall no longer go limping on one foot through the years, but shall march off the steps firm and equipoised. The keen eye and deft hand of the housekeeper shall help to make its every-day walks wholesome; the skill in detail, trustworthiness in finance, motherliness in sympathy, so long extolled in private life, shall exalt public station. Indeed, if I were asked the mission of the ideal woman, I would reply:

IT IS TO MAKE THE WHOLE WORLD HOMELIKE. . . . A true woman carries home with her everywhere. . . . But "home's not merely four square walls."

For the world is slowly making the immense discovery that not what woman *does,* but what she *is,* makes home a possible creation. It is the Lord's ark, and does not need steadying; it will survive the wreck of systems and the crash of theories, for the home is but the efflorescence of woman's nature under the nurture of Christ's Gospel. She came into the college and elevated it, into literature and hallowed it, into the business world and ennobled it. She will come into government and purify it, into politics and cleanse its Stygian pool, for woman will make homelike every place on this round earth. Any custom, or traffic, or party on which a woman cannot look with favor is irrevocably doomed. Its welcome of her presence and her power is to be the final test of its fitness to survive. . . .

FAITH, FEMINISM, AND THE FUTURE

Document 10. National Association of Colored Women: Racism and Rights

As a result of the democratic hopes raised by World War I and the polarization of the races at the end of the war evidenced by race riots, lynchings, and terror, women of both races felt the need to make efforts to bridge the race gap. In July 1919 the Women's Missionary Council Committee on Race Relations sent two white delegates, Mrs. Luke Johnson and Mrs. Haskins, as observers to a Tuskegee conference of the National Association of Colored Women. In a meeting after the public gathering, the Black women sought to enlist the aid of white club women in order to stop lynchings. The following selection is the statement prepared by the NACW women to be sent to white women's organizations.[16]

First of all, we wish to express our sincere gratification in the fact that race relations in the South have advanced to the place where the white women of the South are conscious of the part which colored women must play in any successful effort to adjust the unhappy conditions which have distressed the hearts of all lovers of right and justice, and dangerously threatened the common welfare and the safety of the Nation.

We are also keenly alive to the growing tendency to give a larger place to the influence of womanhood in the affairs of the Nation and to the increasing number of Southern white women whose vision includes the welfare of women of every race and condition, who desire to secure equal opportunities for development to all womanhood, and are determined to face the truth without flinching and to give themselves to creating an enlightened sentiment among their own people, and establishing a new and better foundation for relations between white and colored women in the South.

We have for a long time been painfully conscious of the many unjust and humiliating practices of which colored women in the South have been the victims. There is not one of us who has not at various times and places been called upon to face experiences which are common to the women of our race. We, therefore, take this opportunity to call to the attention of white women certain conditions which affect colored women in their relations with white people, and which, if corrected, will go far toward decreasing friction, removing distrust and suspicion, and creating a better atmosphere in which to adjust the difficulties which always accompany human contacts.

I. CONDITIONS IN DOMESTIC SERVICE
The most frequent and intimate contact of white and colored women is in domestic service. We, therefore, direct attention to—
1. Protection in white homes against
   a. Unnecessary and preventable physical hardship incurred by working hours
   b. Exposure to moral temptations
   c. Undesirable housing conditions
2. We recommend
   a. Definite regulation for hours and conditions of work
   b. Sanitary, attractive, and wholesome rooming facilities
   c. Closer attention to personal appearance
   d. Provision for and investigation of character of recreation

II. CHILD WELFARE . . .

III. CONDITIONS OF TRAVEL . . .

IV. EDUCATION . . .

V. LYNCHING
1. We deplore lynching for any crime whatever, no matter by whom committed.
2. We believe that any person who commits a crime should have punishment meted out to him, but not without thorough investigation and trial by the courts. We further believe that the present safety of the country depends upon a just and fair trial for all persons, white and colored alike.
3. Corrective measures
   a. We therefore urge such courage and foresight on the part of the officers of the law as will guarantee trials which will insure punishment of the guilty, and acquittal of the innocent.
   b. Further, we appeal to the white women
      i. To raise their voices in immediate protest when lynching or mob violence is threatened.
      ii. To encourage every effort to detect and punish the leaders and participants in mobs and riots.
      iii. To encourage the white pulpit and press in creating a sentiment among the law-abiding citizens and outspoken condemnation of these forms of lawlessness.

VI. SUFFRAGE
We believe that the ballot is the safe-guard of the Nation, and that every qualified citizen in the Nation should have the right to use it. We believe that if there is ever to be any justice before the law, the negro must have the right to exercise the franchise.

RECOMMENDATION
1. We ask therefore, that white women, for the protection of their homes as well as ours, sanction the ballot for all citizens.

VII. PRESS
In the great majority of cases the white press of the South gives undue prominence to crime and the criminal element among negroes to the neglect of the worthy and constructive efforts of law-abiding citizens. We feel that a large part of the friction and

misunderstanding between the races is due to unjust, inflamma-
tory, and misleading headlines in articles appearing in the daily
papers.

RECOMMENDATION

We earnestly urge that white women include in their local community program a united effort to correct this evil and to secure
greater attention to worthy efforts of Negro citizens.

In these articles, we are stating frankly and soberly what in our
judgment white women may do to correct the ills from which our race
has so long suffered, and of which we as a race are perhaps more conscious than ever.

We recall how in the recent days of our nation's peril so many of
us worked side by side for the safety of this land and the defense of the
flag which is ours as it is yours. In that spirit of unselfishness and sacrifice we offer ourselves to serve again with you in any and every way that
a courageous facing of duty may require as you undertake heroically this
self-appointed task. We deeply appreciate the difficulties that lie before
you, but as you undertake these things which are destined to bless us all,
we pledge you our faith and loyalty in consecration to God, home, and
country.

Document 11. Vida Dutton Scudder:
Christian Radicals and Revolutionary Forces

Vida Dutton Scudder (1861–1954) was a literary scholar, educator,
and Christian Socialist. She was active in the settlement house
movement and in the labor movement. She was a deeply committed
Anglo-Catholic Episcopalian and struggled to hold Christianity and
socialism together, as reflected in the following selection from her
autobiography.[17]

What then about the alliance of Christian radicals with secular revolutionary forces? Shall we form a United Front? Here is a burning
issue, and I am all for alliance. Advanced religious thought is now fairly
unanimous in denouncing the capitalistic order, and such denunciation
no longer interests me. Sometimes I think we religious folk move back-

ward; I hear us repeating the patter about patience we used fifty years ago. Yet fifty years count, even in perspective; I observe that the Lord Himself sometimes hastens the tempo, and I think the hour for Christian social action has struck. Am I then told that the Church should play a lone hand, retiring into the interior whence she may some day emerge bearing an adequate Christian sociology? Nay, I can not leave my house empty lest seven devils should come in; impartiality today is impossible, and I find mandates sufficiently clear in the Sermon on the Mount. Shall I refuse to co-operate because communism aims at mere material ends? This isn't true, as scrutiny of cultural activities in Russia makes plain; moreover, in the newer Marxism spiritual values return and freedom wins recognition once more. Thus, Christian thinking can never rest in regarding "God" as "the dialectic of history," but must always see in Him Alpha as well as Omega, the Source of the universe no less than a slowly manifest force, cumulative as the aeons pass. But we all agree that present economic conditions inhibit the spirit of man; why not join with those seeking for release, even if ends, the goals of communist effort, are to the Christian only provisional, and means? It will not help communism to further vision, to encounter a hostile or indifferent Church refusing to join in its terrific task of clearing the upward way.

I adhere then to the secular revolutionary movement in spite of frequent sharp sorrow over its methods, and I find, more particularly in recent communist thinking, elements vitally important to Christianity. Should I stay neutral in the class struggle, I should, as Gandhi among others points out, be allied with covert coercion far more pernicious than open violence. The problem reaches out beyond communist affiliation; it comes close in case of industrial conflicts every day. Pacifist organizations like the Fellowship of Reconciliation, and even the socialist party, are rent asunder by the issue; and solution is not easy. But I think Christian dialectic is slowly, painfully, working out a synthesis of personal non-resistance with adherence to militant groups.

Have I a constructive program? Yes. I put my faith in the movement toward political socialism, in the pressure exerted by organized labor, and in the growing development of Consumers' Co-operation. All three are essential; for my old facile reliance on government ownership grows feeble. No radical can look at Germany or Italy and derive comfort from the increased centering of social control in the political state; I look rather to the two voluntary and democratic agencies of the producers and the Consumers, working alike, consciously or not, toward the destruction of a classified society. The Labor Movement in America is itself divided and uncertain of its goal; but its mighty Messianic function I never deny. I think the Labor leaders who were friends of my youth would throw in their lot today with industrial unionism; I rejoice that "white collar workers" are driven more and more both by necessity and by conscience into union with labor; and in the class struggle, which exists, though in more complex forms than Marx foresaw, I am one with the workers in spirit.

But alas, I am no longer a worker myself, and toward the struggle of the producers I can be only a sympathetic observer; therefore just now I take particular interest in the movement of Consumers' Co-operation. I see it supplementing the Labor Movement and advancing with that movement toward the socialism of the future.

Document 12. Georgia Harkness: Peace

Georgia Harkness (1891–1974) was a theologian, an ethicist, and a committed churchwoman. She was involved in many reforms, including race relations, ecumenism, and pacifism, and was a staunch worker for women's rights. The following meditation reflects her understanding of how peace needs to be made and kept, and it expresses her condemnation of war, particularly the conflict in Vietnam.[18]

In 1681 King Charles II of England gave to the Quaker William Penn some 45,000 square miles of land in America in return for a debt owed to Penn's father. Penn asked for settlers to form a colony where there would be freedom of religion and government for the good of all, urging especially his fellow Quakers to join him. On arrival he bought land from the Indians and made a peace treaty with them in which both sides agreed that there should be no bloodshed between them "while rivers run, while moon and stars endure." The treaty held, and both the Indians and the settlers lived in peace and mutual security throughout the entire history of the colony.

Fantastic? So it may seem in view of today's clashes between opposing groups which so easily become war, and then more war until great numbers of persons on both sides are killed and all humanity is jeopardized. Many will say that Penn's way of dealing with the Indians, like the Quaker nonviolence of today, makes a pretty story but will not work amid the complexities of today's world. Yet within the twentieth century it worked with Gandhi to secure India's independence from what was the mightiest empire of the Western world. It might work again if given a chance, not with a supine surrender to evil forces but in a genuine spirit of reconciliation.

I went through the period of the First World War without any important deviation from conventional American thinking, justifying our intervention, thinking the Germans wholly the cause of the war, deploring its destruction, but believing there was no alternative. Like others I rejoiced with a frenzy of delight when we heard that the armistice had been signed. I was studying at Boston University at the time, and I shall never forget the enthusiasm with which we raced across the city to Fanueil Hall to celebrate the end of this and supposedly all wars. At that time a pacifist position that would oppose all war on grounds of Christian conscience did not occur to me.

It was not until the summer of 1924, when I went to Europe . . . that I began seriously to consider this position. We heard statesmen of many countries speak, making clear the broader causes of the recent war and showing that the blame could not all be laid on Germany. I became acquainted with some outstanding American pacifists, and their position made sense. As a result I joined the Fellowship of Reconciliation, of which I have remained a member to the present.

During the Korean War I offered to withdraw from the FOR, for I had come to believe that there were occasions when international police action under the United Nations might be justified. Its leaders advised me to continue, and I have done so, for I cannot in Christian conscience sanction the use of military force by one nation against another with all the horrible destructiveness which war entails. The Vietnam War is, I believe, a moral and social disaster for both the Vietnamese and the American people, and could not be otherwise under the conditions of modern warfare.

So that treaty of peace from long ago between William Penn and Chief Taminen is more than a curious tale. It reflects deep wisdom for our time and for every time of human conflict. Paul's dictum which reflects the mind of Jesus, "Do not be overcome by evil, but overcome evil with good," is not only right but realistic in the fullest sense. The sooner we begin to apply it, the better for our nation and for the world.

Document 13. Religious Coalition for Abortion Rights: The Right to Choose

Perhaps no other issue has continued to cause splits and heated discussion among twentieth-century women as has abortion. Religious women take polar opposite sides. One organization that has tried to bring reasoned discussion to the debate is the Religious Coalition for Abortion Rights. The following document is its statement of purpose.[19]

The Religious Coalition for Abortion Rights (RCAR) is comprised of 31 national religious organizations—Protestant, Jewish, and others. Our members hold in high regard the value of potential human life. We do not take the question of abortion lightly.

Because each faith group represented among us approaches the issue of abortion from the unique perspective of its own theology, members hold widely varying views on when abortion may be morally justified. It is precisely this diversity of belief which leads us to the conviction that the abortion decision must remain with the individual—to be made on the basis of conscience and personal religious principles— and free from governmental interference.

RCAR is deeply concerned about abortion. We believe that the religious community must provide leadership and guidance on family planning, contraception, abortion, genetic counseling, and other crucial moral issues. We believe that any woman facing a distressful pregnancy should be aware of all the resources available to her, and that she should be given compassionate caring support, whatever her decision. We are deeply disturbed about the number of teenage pregnancies in this country, and deplore the ignorance of teenagers about reproductive health care issues. We are strong advocates of educational programs which help develop responsible human sexuality and behavior.

We *do not* believe that the abortion issue will be solved through the legislative process. Experience has already shown that even when abortion is outlawed, women continue to seek them, whatever the risk. We dread a return to the time when illegal abortion forced women to place their health and even their lives on the line in the back alleys of our cities.

We oppose efforts by a vocal minority of anti-choice people to impose their narrow, absolutist views regarding abortion on the nation as a whole. We believe that the legislation they wish to enact would constitute a serious infringement on religious as well as reproductive freedom—the freedom of American citizens to make their private decisions privately, in accord with the teachings of their own faith.

Document 14. CLOUT, Christian Lesbians Out Together: Celebrating Identity

Reform deals with marginalization. Within women's movements, lesbians have been marginalized and indeed almost have disappeared. This is especially true in religious women's movements. As women discovered their need to work for their own rights through abolition and temperance, so lesbians are "coming out" of religious feminist work to claim their full participation and celebrate their own identity. The following document is the statement of commitment of CLOUT, Christian Lesbians Out Together, issued in 1991 as a way to empower lesbian Christian women and to challenge the churches to which they belong.[20]

We are initiating "Christian Lesbians Out Together" (CLOUT), an inter-cultural, multi-racial solidarity coalition of "out" lesbian Christians. Our primary purpose is to empower our lesbian Christian sisters and ourselves and to challenge the churches to which we belong.

We are committed not only to struggling against forces of sexism and misogyny and heterosexism and homophobia, but also against racism, anti-Semitism, anti-Arabism, U.S. imperialism, classism, ableism, clericalism and other structures of domination that foster oppression.

At this historical moment in the Protestant churches, when the oppression of lesbian clergy and seminarians is intensifying, we are committed especially to the empowerment of ordained lesbians and those who are being rejected for ordination because they are lesbian. We recognize the structural "privilege" of ordination. Those of us who are

Protestant clergy will try to use this privilege on behalf of justice and liberation for *all* lesbians—lay and ordained, Catholic and Protestant.

In initiating CLOUT, we state four primary aims:

1. To call upon lesbian Christians to come out of the closet, whenever and wherever possible, and to help empower and celebrate one another in taking this courageous step.

2. To embody a lesbian Christian praxis for justice-based theologies, ethics, liturgies, rituals, psychologies, recovery programs, and other spiritual resources. In so doing, we join with other feminists, womanists, mujeristas, and others committed to the healing and liberation of all creatures and the earth.

3. To explore new understandings of erotic power and sexuality, mutuality, commitment, faithfulness, and partnership that do not merely imitate or replicate sexist, heterosexist, or capitalist relationships of alienation and possession.

4. To network with Jewish lesbians, postchristian lesbians and other religious and secular groups of lesbians; with pro-feminist and pro-womanist gay men; and with pro-feminist/pro-womanist lesbian-affirming organizations within and beyond the churches—especially organizations of other marginalized women and men.

CHAPTER SEVEN

Women and Ordination

Barbara Brown Zikmund

Documents

HISTORICALLY, all branches of Christianity, as well as Judaism and Islam, excluded women from official or ordained ministry, although women have often exercised religious leadership on an informal basis. The question of the inclusion of women in ordained ministry in Christianity began to be raised in the nineteenth century, although it was not until the midtwentieth century that this began to reshape the polity of many Protestant churches.

Within mainstream established denominations, the efforts of women to become ordained took time. The journey began when laywomen within local congregations began to ask questions. Are women allowed to speak in church meetings? This was important because in the early nineteenth century there was a prohibition against women speaking in mixed groups or "promiscuous assemblies," as they were called. Are women allowed to vote? Are women able to serve on the governing boards or councils of a congregation? Can women represent a local congregation at regional, diocesan, or national meetings? In most mainstream denominations no progress was made toward the recognition of women clergy until women gained significant power and influence as laity.

Among Congregationalists, Baptists, and other denominations with congregational polity the battles over lay citizenship were fought long before the twentieth century. Once women were accepted as lay leaders, it was only a small step toward the authorization of women clergy. These denominations do not require wider approval before ordaining any candidate.

Denominations following presbyterial or episcopal polity moved much slower. With some of these denominations it was necessary to establish a widely accepted theological rationale justifying the election (or ordination) of women as lay leaders before the question of women clergy could be addressed. When it was agreed that there is no biblical or theological reason to keep women from lay leadership, arguments against women's ordination to clergy status ceased to be theological and became practical. Can a married woman do it? What is the relationship of ordained ministry to mission and educational work? What if local churches do not want women pastors? What if a woman becomes a bishop? Cautious church leaders hesitated to take any action if it was impractical. In some connectional systems, where clergy belong to a structure or professional organization beyond the local congregation, even ordination did not mean equality. Methodist women, for example, were ordained as "local pastors" long before they were granted full membership in annual conferences, the groups of congregations forming districts that oversee the placement of clergy.

From the early seventeenth century until the late eighteenth century churches showed no formal concern about the ordination of women. To be sure, women were actively engaged in church life, working out their salvation in many ways; women religious leaders, such as Anne Hutchinson in colonial Massachusetts, challenged the idea that a woman could not interpret Scripture; Quaker and Shaker women also exercised public religious leadership. But the formal question as to whether a woman could be ordained, called, or appointed to serve as clergy in the mainstream churches did not emerge.

Institutional concern about the ordination of women began shortly after the American revolution. As the colonies, now united, set about to write a constitution and to put their political houses in order, churches did the same. Many churches broke formal ties with English or continental ecclesiastical structures and established independent national structures. Practices that had gone unregulated during the colonial period were now ordered.

Key women religious leaders in American churches during the early national period provided hospitality or financial support for these newly independent churches. Women also functioned as itinerant evangelists, moving around the countryside "witnessing" and "sharing" their faith— even "planting" new churches. Women kept local congregations together following the untimely deaths of their pastor husbands. Women did what needed to be done or what seemed led by the Spirit, and nobody objected.

A good example of recognized but unauthorized female ministry is found in the life of Sarah Osborn. From the 1760s until her death in 1796, Sarah led many revivals near her home in Newport, Rhode Island (see document 4 of chapter 2).[1] Nancy Cram and Abigail Roberts in the Hudson River Valley are another case in point. In 1814, during one of the many frontier revivals that led to the formation of the small Christian denomination that later merged with the Congregationalists, Abigail Roberts was converted by a woman preacher named Nancy Cram. Nothing is known about Nancy Cram, but Abigail Roberts enjoyed an important unordained preaching ministry as a "female laborer," founding many churches until her death in 1841.[2]

QUAKERS, CONGREGATIONALISTS, AND UNIVERSALISTS

After 1800 the revivals of the Second Great Awakening highlighted the success of women's leadership. Among the Quakers, women became more visible. Although the Society of Friends had grave reservations about paid ministry and never formally ordained anyone to ministry, local Quaker meetings developed the custom of "recording ministers." When a member spoke up in meeting with some regularity and to the edification of the group, he or she might be "recorded" as a minister. Persons so designated were expected to give up local meeting obligations and become traveling evangelists. One of the most famous Quaker preachers was Lucretia Mott. Elizabeth Cady Stanton wrote that Lucretia Mott convinced her that she had the same right to think for herself about religion "that Luther, Calvin and John Knox had."[3]

The first woman formally ordained to the Christian ministry in an established denomination in America is generally thought to be Antoinette Brown. After receiving her theological education at Oberlin College, although the college refused to award her a theological degree, Brown was called to a small Congregational church in South Butler, New York, in 1853. She was twenty-eight years old, but she had already made a reputation for herself as a lecturer on temperance, slavery, and literary topics. Her ordination took place without a lot of controversy, because the free church polity of Congregationalism allows each congregation to ordain its own pastor. Brown was also helped by a progressive Wesleyan Methodist preacher, Luther Lee, who preached her ordination sermon (document 1). The Reverend Antoinette Brown served in South Butler only a few years, resigning due to ill health and doctrinal doubts. In 1856 she married Samuel C. Blackwell, brother of Elizabeth and Emily Blackwell, early women physicians. In her later years Antoinette Brown Blackwell authored many books in philosophy and science, supported the suffrage campaign, and returned to active ministry within the Unitarian fellowship.[4]

The first woman to be ordained by denominational action was also named Brown—Olympia Brown. She graduated from Antioch College, during the presidency of Horace Mann, in 1860. After pursuing theological studies at the Canton Theological School in Canton, New York, she was ordained to ministry in the Universalist denomination in June 1863. She served parishes in Weymouth, Massachusetts; Bridgeport, Connecticut; and Racine, Wisconsin.[5]

In spite of these developments, most people maintained traditional views of the sexes. Women, they believed, should be subject to men and know their place (document 2). By the end of the century denominations that call and ordain pastors without wider church authorization (Congregationalists, Universalists, Unitarians, Northern Baptists, Christians, and Disciples) had ordained a handful of women. Over the next seventy-five years every Christian and Jewish group in America confronted, even if they did not resolve, the question of women and ordination.

PRESBYTERIANS

Women's ordination in Presbyterian denominations was more difficult because Protestants in the Presbyterian/Reformed tradition practice two types of ordination. Clergy are "set apart" by prayer and laying of hands to a "ministry of Word and sacrament," and some lay leaders are "ordained" to a ministry of governance as "ruling elders." This practice is grounded in the sixteenth-century principle of the "priesthood of all believers."

Presbyterian attitudes toward the ordination of women were early shaped by controversies around frontier revivalism. In 1832 when the General Assembly was troubled by the unseemly involvement of women in public meetings, a pastoral letter was sent to the churches. It said, "Meetings of pious women by themselves, for conversation and prayer, whenever they can be conveniently held, we entirely approve. But, . . . to teach and exhort, or to lead in prayer, in public and promiscuous assembles, is clearly forbidden to women in the Holy Oracles."[6]

By the late nineteenth century, American Presbyterians felt growing pressures to change. Some congregations in the small populist Cumberland Presbyterian Church began electing and ordaining women as ruling elders in the 1880s and '90s. Not surprisingly, by November 1889 a woman named Louisa Woosley convinced the Nollin, Kentucky, presbytery of the Cumberland Presbyterian Church to ordain her to a ministry of Word and sacrament.[7]

Among mainstream Presbyterian bodies, however, the issue was far from settled. In the 1920s the Presbyterian Church in the USA (northern) looked more closely at women's place in the church. Receiving a report entitled the *Causes of Unrest Among the Women of the Church,* its 1930 General Assembly examined the questions: should women be ordained as ruling elders and ministers of Word and sacrament, should they be ordained only as ruling elders, or should women evangelists be licensed? The assembly voted to ordain women as ruling elders but not as clergy. From 1930 to 1955 several efforts were made to give women full ministerial rights (document 3). Not until 1955 did northern Presbyterians approve the ordination of women to the full ministry of Word and sacrament.[8]

The more conservative Presbyterian Church in the US (southern) avoided the issue even longer, defeating in 1955 an overture that merely approved women as ruling elders. It was not until 1964 that the southern Presbyterians finally approved the ordination of women as deacons, ruling elders, and ministers all at once. In spite of the vote, no one imagined that many women would want to or would be qualified to serve as pastors.[9]

METHODIST, HOLINESS, AND PENTECOSTAL CHURCHES

Methodism was even more complex. In the late nineteenth century mainstream Methodism remained split between northern and southern bodies and between groups committed to episcopal forms of government and those promoting congregational polity. By the turn of the century, Methodism had also splintered into a number of small Holiness denominations trying to recover Wesleyan theology. In 1880 two Methodist women, Anna Oliver and Anna Howard Shaw, who already held local licenses to preach in the Methodist Episcopal Church, North, came before the General Conference seeking ordination. Their request was denied, and the conference passed a new regulation forbidding the licensing of women. Anna Howard Shaw eventually joined the more liberal Methodist Protestant Church and was ordained.[10]

The struggle for full equality in ministry for Methodist women limped along for many years. In 1924 the Methodist Episcopal Church, North, approved the ordination of women as local preachers but refused to admit women to membership in the annual conference (document 4). In 1939 the union that created the Methodist Church out of the Methodist Episcopal Churches, North and South, and the Methodist Protestant Church struck a compromise around women's status. The southern Methodist Episcopal churches were forced to accept women as local preachers, the northern Methodist Episcopal churches retained ordination for women without conference membership, and the Methodist Protestants, who had previously ordained women *and* given them conference membership, were assured that women who held conference membership could keep it, but full status would no longer be available to women. Not until 1956, after voting down an amendment that would have limited conference membership to "unmarried women and widows," did the Methodist Church vote to give women full status in the "travelling ministry," or local conference membership.[11]

When the Methodist Church merged with the Evangelical and United Brethren Church in 1968 there were additional problems. The Evangelical and United Brethren Church (EUB) was an earlier merger of German Methodists who had worked out a compromise on women's ordination. Although the Evangelical Church and its predecessor bodies had never licensed or ordained women, the United Brethren had ordained women as far back as 1889. With the merger of these two churches in 1947, official policy denied ordination to women. In practice, however, women who had been ordained by the United Brethren continued to serve, and certain bishops proceeded to ordain more women. When the EUB Church united with the Methodist Church in 1968, all inconsistencies were cleared up and women were guaranteed full ecclesiastical standing in the new United Methodist Church.[12]

Among the Wesleyan/Holiness denominations that broke away from Methodism in the nineteenth century, the story is erratic. New denominations such as the Wesleyan Methodist Church, the Free Methodist Church, the Church of the Nazarene, the Church of God (Anderson, Indiana), and many other Holiness and Pentecostal denominations had no problem with the ordination of women. Following the logic of Phoebe Palmer, famous Holiness revivalist and writer, these Holiness churches argued, "Where church order is at variance with divine order, it is better to obey God than man." And if the Holy Spirit gave timid women "holy boldness," removing their "man fearing spirit" and empowering them to ministry, they should be ordained (document 5).[13]

Although these denominations ordained women in great numbers around the turn of the century, after 1920 the ranks of women pastors in Holiness churches steadily declined. Some people conjecture that as the focus of the Holiness movement shifted from traveling evangelistic ministers to local congregational ministry, women found fewer opportunities. Others blame the decline of women pastors on the influence of general social attitudes toward women. Still others point out that a "fundamentalist leavening" created an antiwoman mentality. Insisting upon a literal interpretation of the Scriptures, Fundamentalists declared that the Holiness churches were unduly influenced by the secular women's movement. Yet in the face of these forces Holiness writers consistently countered all literal approaches to Scripture intended to limit women's involvement in ministry. Benjamin T. Roberts, a founder of the Free Methodist Church, used Galatians 3:28 as the standard: "There is neither Jew nor Greek, slave nor free, male nor female, for you are all one in Christ Jesus." He wrote in 1891, "Make this the KEY TEXT upon this subject, and give to other passages such a construction as will make them agree with it, and all is harmony."[14]

The Pentecostal movement provided even more opportunities for women's leadership.[15] In fact, over 50 percent of all ordained women have consistently served in the Pentecostal, evangelical, and paramilitary denominations (for example, Salvation Army, Volunteers of America, and so forth). As late as 1977 only 17 percent of women clergy were found in the ten major Protestant denominations.[16]

LUTHERANS

The struggle for women's ordination in American churches was also affected by international developments, especially for the Lutheran, Episcopal, Roman Catholic, and Orthodox churches.

Lutherans were initially divided and isolated by the language and cultures of various immigrant groups. German Lutherans were different from Scandinavian Lutherans, and neither nineteenth-century immigrant group mixed well with Lutherans who had settled in America before the Revolutionary War. Until 1940 most Lutheran denominations were narrowly preoccupied with themselves, and Lutheran women related to the church in rather conventional ways (document 6).

After World War II, however, the assimilation of German immigrants into American society and the decisions of several progressive Lutheran Scandinavian state churches to ordain women pastors forced the issue of women's ordination upon American Lutherans. Furthermore, debates among biblical scholars and the growing participation of Lutherans in the ecumenical movement convinced many Lutherans that there were no biblical or theological barriers to women's ordination. In the late 1960s three major American Lutheran churches (the Lutheran Church in America, the American Lutheran Church, and the Lutheran Church–Missouri Synod) held an Inter-Lutheran Consultation on the Ordination of Women. When it was all over they agreed to disagree. Therefore, in 1970 the LCA and the ALC voted to ordain women, while the LC–MS reasserted its belief in the subordination of women in the church.[17]

In the late 1980s the Lutheran Church in America and the American Lutheran Church, along with a small progressive faction that had broken away from the Lutheran Church—Missouri Synod in 1977, merged to form a new unified Lutheran denomination. This new Evangelical Lutheran Church in America (ELCA) ordains both women and men. Lutheran ethnic habits, however, continue to make openness to the ministries of women uneven and ambiguous.

EPISCOPALIANS

The Protestant Episcopal Church in the United States also sees itself accountable globally, standing in communion with worldwide Anglicanism. Episcopalians define ordination and priestly orders within the framework of apostolic succession. Clergy form an unbroken connection (through ordination by a bishop) to the first apostles. For this reason any American Episcopal decision to ordain women is connected to Anglican churches in other parts of the world.

The issue of women's orders among Anglicans was raised formally in 1862 when the bishop of London "ordered" a deaconess by "laying on hands."[18] In the 1880s the Protestant Episcopal Church in the United

States began "setting apart" women as deaconesses. Over the years, however, it was unclear exactly how the ordering of deaconesses related to the priesthood. Therefore, in 1920 the Lambeth Conference, the every-decade meeting of Anglican bishops from all over the world, discussed the issue and agreed that the "ordination of a deaconess confers on her holy orders" (document 7). Unfortunately, in 1930 the Lambeth Confer-ence reversed that judgment and decided that deaconesses were not in holy orders.

In the 1930s the Church of England commissioned a study to exam-ine the ordination of women. Its report, issued in 1935, stated that there was no compelling theological reason for or against the ordination of women. Nevertheless, it argued that an all-male priesthood was still needed for the church of that day. Not all parts of the Anglican Church felt bound by that judgment. In 1944, citing special wartime needs, the bishop of Hong Kong ordained a Chinese woman named Li Tim-Oi.[19] Anglicans around the world protested, and although her ordination was never reversed, she ceased to function as a priest. In 1971 the bishop of Hong Kong ordained two additional women.

Meanwhile, American Episcopalians wrestled with the question of women's ordination. In 1964 the General Convention asserted that dea-conesses were "ordered" rather than "appointed"; and the following year Bishop James Pike recognized Phyllis Edwards as a deacon, based upon her ordination as a deaconess. The church continued to debate the issue (document 8). In 1972 the House of Bishops voted in favor of the princi-ple of women's ordination as priests. A year later the General Convention (made up of laity) rejected the principle. Fifty-six bishops issued a state-ment expressing distress at the convention's action.

On July 29, 1974, in Philadelphia, two retired and one resigned bishop, in the presence of a diocesan bishop who did not actually partic-ipate, proceeded to force the issue by "irregularly" ordaining eleven women deacons to the priesthood. The Episcopal Church debated how to deal with the bishops' "violation of collegiality" and how to respond to the ministries of the eleven women. Accusations, charges, censures, and petitions dominated the agenda of the church for two years. Finally, in September 1976 the General Convention approved the ordination of women to the priesthood and to the episcopate. It also agreed to recog-nize the irregular ordinations. Not until January 1, 1977, did a canon law authorizing the ordination of women to the priesthood in the Protestant Episcopal Church in the United States go into effect.

Feelings about women's ordination within the Episcopal Church continued to divide the church.[20] Women could be priests, but many people believed that the full status question for women within Anglicanism would not be resolved until a woman was elected and consecrated as a bishop. According to some Episcopalians, the consecration of a woman bishop would be an affront to Christian unity, reflecting insensitivity to Anglican diversity and to Anglican affinities with Roman Catholicism and Orthodoxy. Whether it was too soon, or long overdue, on September 24, 1988, the waiting came to an end when the Diocese of Massachusetts elected a woman as its suffragan bishop. On February 11, 1989, Barbara C. Harris, a fifty-eight-year-old Black woman priest, was consecrated as the first Anglican woman bishop in the world.[21] Five years later, in October 1993, Mary Adelia McLeod, the third American female to be elected an Episcopal bishop, was consecrated to serve as the head of the Diocese of Vermont.[22]

ROMAN CATHOLICS, ORTHODOX CHURCHES, AND THE ECUMENICAL MOVEMENT

The question of women and ordination in the Roman Catholic Church and in Orthodox churches in America is still not settled.

The Second Vatican Council, which opened in 1962, gave American Catholic women "new hope for their own expanded ministries in the church." Women in religious orders began a process of renewal that generated a growing feminist consciousness. Laywomen experienced new power within local parishes. By the 1970s both groups raised questions about women and ordination.[23]

In 1975 a Women's Ordination Conference in Detroit called for women's equality in ministry and the need for new models and images of church and priesthood. By October 1976 the Sacred Congregation for the Doctrine of Faith (a Vatican department) issued a statement to explain the traditional prohibition of women from the Roman Catholic priesthood. In summary, it said that the church can confer priestly ordination only on men because this norm, based on Christ's example, ". . . is considered to conform to God's plan for his church."[24]

Orthodox women have been the most silent on the question of women and ordination. Although pressed by the ecumenical movement to consider the question of women and the priesthood, the Orthodox community remains firm in its conviction that women are not called to the priesthood.[25]

Those arguing against the ordination of women in all denominations have regularly insisted that churches that ordain women jeopardize the hope for the organic reunion of various Christian denominations. The question remains a theological, practical, and ecumenical issue (document 9).[26]

THE HISTORICALLY BLACK DENOMINATIONS

Although Blacks are an important minority within many of the above churches, the story of Christian women and ordination is not complete without an examination of the situation of women in the predominantly Black denominations. Today over 85 percent of church-affiliated Black Christians in the United States belong to six major denominations: the African Methodist Episcopal Church, the African Methodist Episcopal Zion Church, the Christian Methodist Episcopal Church, the National Baptists, the Progressive Baptists, and the Church of God in Christ. The "call to ministry" for Black women in these denominations has its own rhythm.[27]

The Black Church in the African American experience is rooted in African religious life and Christian tradition. Because women held prominent roles in African religions, scholars believe that slave women served American plantation Blacks as healers, teachers, and preachers. Because African religious traditions were oral, and because it was against the law to teach slaves to read and write, Black women, as well as Black men who had gifts for storytelling and preaching, were highly respected. And finally, because the slave system split families, and because being a pastor in a Black congregation was one of the few positions where Black males could exercise power in a racist society, women experienced great ambivalence when they felt a call to preach.

A former slave woman named Elizabeth began preaching extensively in Maryland and Virginia in 1796. When the authorities detained her and asked if she was ordained, she answered, "Not by the commission of men's hands; if the Lord has ordained me, I need nothing better." They let her go.[28]

One of the most famous Black women preachers was Jarena Lee, who was born as a free Black in New Jersey. In 1809 she went to the pastor of the newly established Bethel African Methodist Episcopal Church in Philadelphia, the Reverend Richard Allen, and asked for a license to preach. He did not believe that women should preach. But Jarena Lee would not be stopped. She continued to preach and eventually married an AME clergyman. In 1816, shortly after the AME church organized as a denomination, she again asked the then Bishop Richard Allen to make her ministry legitimate. This time he was more supportive. Although church regulations did not allow female preachers, he permitted her to hold prayer meetings and to "exhort." She claimed to be "the first female preacher of the A.M.E. church," but it was never made official (document 10).[29]

Amanda Berry Smith was another AME woman preacher. She received a call to preach fifty years later in the Holiness revival of the 1860s and '70s. A gifted singer, evangelist, and missionary, Smith invited Christians to reach for "spiritual perfection" and to lead a more holy life.[30]

The first instance of a Black denomination officially ordaining a woman was in the AME Zion Church. In 1894 in Poughkeepsie, New York, Bishop James Walker Hood stated that at least one Methodist Episcopal Church guaranteed women "all rights in common with men" by ordaining a conference missionary, Julia A. Foote, to deacon's orders. The next year the Philadelphia and Baltimore Conference ordained Mary J. Small a deacon, and in 1898 she was ordained "elder" with full ministerial status and conference membership. Julia Foote achieved elder's orders in 1900.[31]

The situation in the AME Church and the Christian Methodist Episcopal Church was much more difficult. AME women were licensed without ordination in 1884 and finally granted full ordination in 1948. The CME church did not have any laywomen's organizations until after 1900 and refused to ordain women as clergy until 1954.[32]

Black Baptist women fared no better. Although one would have thought that the free church polity of Baptists might make the struggle easier, the important roles held by laywomen in Black Baptist churches actually made ordination for women preachers more difficult. Formal leadership "on the pulpit" was reserved for men, and women exercised complementary power from the pew. Although there was never any formal policy forbidding the ordination of women in any Black Baptist denomination, few congregations ordained women pastors. When it did happen, Black Baptist women were always "sponsored" by strong male pastors.

The Church of God in Christ, the largest Black Pentecostal denomination, developed more formal barriers. The *Official Manual* of the church argues on scriptural grounds that women cannot be ordained as elders, bishops, or pastors.[33] Women may preach in churches as evangelists or missionaries, but they cannot serve as pastors. Although a widow sometimes does take over a church after her husband's death, there is no official recognition of her leadership.

In spite of these difficulties within the more structured denominations, many Black women have exercised public religious leadership. Most of these women did not let the rules and regulations get in the way. If they felt the call to preach, they simply started their own independent Holiness or Pentecostal church. Although certain women have built up lasting congregations that attracted large numbers, most Black women pastors have been content to serve small independent storefront churches. Overall in American church history, in proportion to the population, there have probably been more Black women preachers and pastors than white women clergy.

JUDAISM

The situation of women in Judaism presents a varied picture. Although Reform Judaism, the oldest branch of American Judaism, is the least bound by traditional Jewish law, dealing with the issue of women rabbis was not easy. The question first arose among Reform Jews in the mid-nineteenth century although it was not acted upon. In the 1920s, when the daughter of a Hebrew Union College professor declared that she wanted to become a rabbi, the question was addressed more formally. It was not until the late 1960s, however, that Hebrew Union College allowed women to matriculate "for the purpose of entering the rabbinate." In 1972 Sally Priesand graduated to become the first woman rabbi in America.[34]

Reconstructionist Judaism, the youngest of the four movements within American Judaism, was founded on Mordecai Kaplan's egalitarian philosophy in the 1920s. Although it was aggressively "feminist" from its beginnings, when its Reconstructionist Rabbinical College opened in 1968 there were no women students. In its second year, Sandy Eisenberg (Sasso) entered, graduating to become the first woman rabbi in the Reconstructionist movement in 1974.[35]

Conservative Judaism is a product of the efforts of more traditional American Jews to integrate tradition with modernity. Conservative Jews blend the authority of the halachah (the body of religious laws binding on all good Jews) with contemporary mores and knowledge. Although Conservative Jews assert that the halachah has never been monolithic or immovable, the Conservative movement seeks to preserve a traditional "path" for authentic Jewish life. It acknowledges that certain command-ments for men are not binding on women, and it accepts the different obligations.[36]

For some women within the Conservative movement this inequality became increasingly troublesome. In 1972 a group of Conservative Jew-ish women issued a "Call for Change" at the annual Rabbinical Assembly convention. They asked for some relief from "the terrible choice between their identities as women and as Jews."[37]

For the next ten years the movement leaders and the faculty at the Jewish Theological Seminary debated the issues. Finally in 1983 the fac-ulty voted to admit women to rabbinical studies (document 11). The vic-tory, however, was a mixed blessing. In traditional Jewish law women are exempt from certain commandments binding upon men. Furthermore, because a rabbi is understood to serve as an intermediary to help others live by the law, tradition assumes that women cannot serve as prayer leaders or emissaries for male congregants. The final ruling upheld the traditional differences between men and women but stated that if some women chose voluntarily to assume religious obligations from which they had been exempted, it was possible for them to become rabbis. This logic, however, is not grounded in the equality of women with men. Rather it says that women are free to become like men. It continues to insist (to the consternation of some) that women are essentially defective, required to transcend their gender in order to become religious leaders.[38]

On the basis of this logic, nineteen women chose to assume all reli-gious obligations and were admitted into Jewish Theological Seminary for rabbinical studies in 1984. In May 1985, Amy Eilberg was ordained to become the first woman rabbi in Conservative Judaism (see document 7 of chapter 3).[39]

At present there are no Orthodox women rabbis. The increasing number of Orthodox Jewish women students of Talmud suggests that the challenge to women's exclusion from the rabbinate is rising as well (document 12). Although there is no formal ban against women rabbis, adjustments will need to be made in the law to enable them to carry out all rabbinical duties.[40]

AFTERWORD

During the past 150 years many Christian and Jewish groups have been challenged to ordain women leaders, and many of them are now doing so. The arguments for and against women's ordination show how the issue was engaged at several levels and why women, as well as men, resisted ordaining women. Everyone had biblical and theological reasons. Over time, however, the case against women clergy became more pragmatic. Women already had important responsibilities in the private sphere; women did not have the social stability needed for ministry; family responsibilities would suffer if women were ordained; men (and some women) would not tolerate women pastors; men needed employment in scarce job markets; the feminine mind was not up to the task of regular preaching; or it was not yet time for this dramatic change—although it would probably come to pass in the future.

Even with ordination many women still are denied full expression of their calling. This is because in many ecclesiastical structures, although formal regulations have changed, informal traditions presume that only men should serve as pastors, as teachers of Scripture, and as overseers of religious life and practice. Some observers suggest that only when ministry has become a "women's profession," devalued by the public sector, will women find full freedom as ordained leaders. If this happens it may be an opportunity rather than a loss. The ordination of women is already freeing religious communities from longstanding hierarchical assumptions, and it may provide the stimulus for important new patterns of leadership.

The Rev. M. Madeline Southard, founder of the American Association of Women Ministers and its journal, *The Woman's Pulpit,* begun in 1922.

Bishop Mary E. Jackson was a charter member of Mount Sinai Holy Churches. In 1969, at the age of eighty-eight, she became the fourth bishop to preside over the organization.

Bishop Marjorie Matthews surrounded by clergy at the United Methodist General Conference in 1984. Four years earlier she became the first woman to be elected to the episcopacy of any major denomination.

Bishop Leontyne Kelly, episcopal leader of the San Francisco Bay Area, was the second woman and the first Black woman to be ordained to the episcopacy of the United Methodist Church. This picture was taken at her consecration in 1984.

Rabbi Sally Priesand, of the Reformed Branch of American Judaism, graduated from seminary in 1971 to become the first woman rabbi in the United States. She is now pastor of the Monmouth Reform Temple in Tinton Falls, New Jersey.

Bishop Barbara Harris, a Black woman, during the service of her ordination to the episcopacy as the first female bishop of the Episcopal Church.

Documents

Document 1. The Reverend Luther Lee:
Women's Right to Preach the Gospel

Antoinette Brown became the first fully ordained woman in a recognized American denomination (Congregational) in 1853. After graduating from Oberlin College she took classes in Oberlin's graduate theological program, although the college refused to grant her a theological degree. Her popularity as a lecturer in the abolition and temperance movements led to her call to become the pastor of a small Congregational church in South Butler, New York.

At her ordination service, the Reverend Luther Lee, a well-known Wesleyan Methodist leader, preached. Excerpts from his sermon argue eloquently for the rights of women to preach the gospel.[41]

There were prophetesses or female prophets in the Primitive Church under the gospel. The fact that there would be, was foretold by the Prophet Joel. "And it shall come to pass afterward, that I will pour out my Spirit upon all flesh; and your sons and your daughters shall prophesy." Joel 2:28.

This text most clearly began to be fulfilled at the day of Pentecost, as we learn from Acts 2:17; where Peter declares the development of that day, to be what was foretold by the prophet. But how was the prediction, that daughters should prophesy, fulfilled on the day of Pentecost? The history of the subject answers this question. It is as follows:

In the first chapter, we are told who constituted the assembled Christians. "Then returned they unto Jerusalem from the mount called Olivet, which is from Jerusalem a sabbath-day's journey. And when they were come in, they went up into an upper room, where abode both Peter, and James, and John, and Andrew, Philip, and Thomas, Bartholomew, and Matthew, James the son of Alpheus, and Simon Zealotes, and Judas the brother of James. These all continued with one accord in prayer and supplication, with the women, and Mary the mother of Jesus, and with his brethren." Verses 12–14.

Here we have named the eleven apostles, then "the women," then Mary the mother of Jesus in particular, and lastly "his brethren." By his brethren is probably meant his near relatives. It is probable that there were a number of women in the company, as they are mentioned as forming one portion of the assembly. In the 15th verse we are told that the whole number present was about one hundred and twenty persons. In the fourth verse of chapter two, we are told that they were all filled with the Holy Ghost, and began to speak with other tongues.

Who were filled with the Holy Ghost, and began to speak with other tongues? Most clearly the hundred and twenty persons, consisting of the apostles, the women, and Mary the mother of Jesus, and his brethren. To deny this would be to falsify the plainest portion of the record. The record declares that there were about one hundred and twenty persons assembled together, that this number embraced the women, and that they were all filled with the Holy Ghost, and began to speak with other tongues. Thus did the Holy Ghost, in his first descent, crown females as well as males, with tongues of fire, to speak the wonderful works of God.

But the remarkable prophecy of Joel did not receive its entire fulfillment on the day of Pentecost, for about twenty-seven years afterwards we read, Acts 21:9, that Phillip of Cesarea, "had four daughters which did prophesy." As this fact is mentioned only incidentally and not as a new or strange thing, it appears probable that female prophets were not unusual in the Primitive Church.

This is the proper place to remark that prophesying is not to be understood in the restricted sense of foretelling. A prophet is not exclusively one who foretells, but who explains prophecies, and teaches; and to prophesy is to explain prophecies and to teach. In this sense every gospel minister is a prophet, and every prophet under the new dispensation is a gospel minister. Here then were four female gospel ministers, daughters of one man. When it is said, "Your sons and your daughters shall prophesy," the meaning is, your sons and your daughters shall become teachers, or gospel ministers.

The Greek word which we translate prophet, is *propheetuo,* and signifies "to foretell, to predict, to explain and apply prophecies." To explain and apply prophecies, was the peculiar work of the first ministers. The Greek word which we translate prophet, is *propheetees,* and signifies "a declarer, a foreteller, a priest, a teacher, and instructor." It was always the work of prophets to labor as religious teachers, and to explain and apply the predictions which had been previously uttered by others, and when we consider that there were whole schools of prophets, we may conclude that but few of the whole number were employed to foretell, and that their principal calling was to labor as religious teachers. That prophets were preachers or religious teachers, is perfectly clear from the use of the words, prophet and prophesy, by the apostles.

The church at Antioch sent Paul and Barnabas to Jerusalem for the settlement of the great question, whether Gentile converts were bound to keep the law of Moses concerning circumcision and other rites. The apostles and the church at Jerusalem, having considered the case, sent back a written answer, and sent also two messengers of their own company, Judas and Silas. "And Judas and Silas being prophets also themselves, exhorted the brethren with many words, and confirmed them." This proves beyond a doubt, that they exhorted, or preached in the common acceptation, by virtue of their prophetic office, and the conclusion is that to be a prophet, is to be a preacher, or public religious teacher. We read again, 1 Corinthians 19:3: "He that prophesieth, speaketh unto men to edification, and exhortation and comfort." Here the entire pulpit work of a gospel preacher is described as the act of prophesying, which renders it certain that prophets were preachers. Again, we read Revelation 2:20, "Nevertheless, I have a few things against thee, because thou sufferest that woman Jezebel, which calleth herself a prophetess to teach, and to seduce my servants to commit fornication, and to eat things offered to idols." This proves two points; first, that the doctrine must have prevailed that women might rightfully be prophets; and secondly, that being prophets, they taught the people. The complaint is not that she was a *woman,* but that she was a bad woman; not that she was a *prophetess,* but that she called herself one when she was not; not that she *taught,* but that she taught false and corrupting doctrine. It is clear that there would have been no false female teachers, had there been no true ones, and that a false female teacher could not have been sustained in the church, had the doctrine prevailed that the gospel forbade females to preach the gospel.

I have now proved that there were a class of females in the Primitive Church called prophetesses, that is, there were female prophets, and these prophets were preachers or public teachers of religion.

Document 2. C. Duren:
Woman's Place Separate Not Equal

Even though the Congregationalists pioneered in ordaining women, like most Americans they maintained traditional views of the sexes. Embracing Victorian values, they thought that women were eternally subject to men, in spite of "apparent exceptions." The following selection, written by C. Duren in 1868, describes "Woman's Place in Religious Meetings." It is a good example of a separate but equal argument that tried to appreciate women's gifts while denying women the full right to preach.[42]

Man is made the head of the woman. The place of woman, in the family and in society, is one of subjection to man. Man was first formed, and to have dominion of the earth. Woman was formed out of the man, and to be a "helpmeet for him" (Genesis 2:18), a help as over against him, corresponding to him, or the counterpart of him. The scriptural position of woman is one of subjection to man, both in the Jewish and Christian church. The Jewish religion raised the sex far above her rank among the Gentiles; the Christian religion has greatly elevated her. But Christianity has not changed her position in society. The Scriptures very definitely settle the place of woman, and give reasons for it; and we can plainly discern the propriety of the place assigned her. The divine word alone gives us satisfactory and fundamental truth on this point. It proves itself our guide in this, as well as in most matters both pertaining to this life and to the life to come. We find at the present time the "strong-minded" leaving the teachings of Scripture, and trying to reason out the duty and mission of woman; and they are quite confused by the acknowledged fact that she is the equal of man, and the unquestioned fact also that she is differently organized. The inspired word teaches us; and, in both the Jewish and Christian church of the Scriptures, we find her filling beautifully her proper sphere; and we find few, yet sufficient, regulations and admonitions in regard to her duties and work. She is the equal of man, and his help; in some qualities she is his inferior, in other qualities his superior. She is the counterpart of man; this word fitly expresses her place; so that together, and neither alone, they form one whole, one supplying, in many respects, what is wanting in the other. They are not equal, in the sense that they have both equal rule and authority, but equal in their respective spheres.

The Apostle insists that, as compared with man, she must be "in subjection," she must not "usurp authority over the man," she must "learn in silence," "be in silence." There is a seeming harshness, we should say in these days, indelicacy, uncourteousness, in these expressions. But this is according to the truth everywhere taught in Scripture. While the Apostle Paul thus decidedly expresses himself, he always shows his appreciation and honor of women. He associated them with him in his Christian labors. He makes affectionate remembrance of them as his "helpers in Christ." He sends numerous salutations to them in his epistles. He found a most useful place for them in the church. They have always performed with great earnestness and fidelity their duties as members of the church. Though their sphere is more private, they have accomplished at least as great and useful a work as the brethren. Yet the Apostle insists in this passage and elsewhere, that their place in the church is not as public teachers, nor in any way to act as assuming authority. . . .

Yet in ordinary social religious meetings, the instructions of the Apostle do not forbid her to take part. But they teach her to perform such a part, at such times, and in such circumstances, as become the subjection and modesty of her sex.

In meetings where both sexes are present, a responsibility and duty do not devolve upon women to participate in the services, as upon the men. But the teachings of Scripture do not debar her from taking part for the edification and interest of the meeting. So far as she can contribute to make it spiritual, social and enlivening, there is certainly an obligation resting upon her. Christianity has done much for woman, and it is fitting that she bear witness to its power, and speak of her love to the Saviour. It has cultivated her mental and moral powers, and given her rich inward experience, even superior to man's. She has unsurpassed social powers, a quickness of perception and sympathy, which eminently qualify her for the social, conference exercises of the prayer meeting.

She excels in pouring out her heart unto God in prayer, in conversation, in feeling, in nice discrimination, in spiritual experience. Shall she not use these qualities for the enlivening and edification of the social meeting? Shall she not join in the fellowship of Christians with each other and with God? This is not usurping the place of teaching which the Apostle forbids. Her words are certainly more animating and edifying than the stammering, hesitating words of many of the brethren. Men are engaged for the live-long day in the distractions and toils and worldliness of business. It is hard for them to leave these for the atmosphere of the prayer meeting. Woman is shielded from many of these withering and chilling influences. She preserves a more constant communion with God, and a more continual impression of truth. Shall not the social meeting receive the benefit of this? Is it not fitting that she appear there, not merely in silent worship, to help with her inward prayers and feelings, but as an active, living, speaking disciple? May she not communicate, as well as receive? As the Saviour first appeared to woman, after his resurrection, and as they ministered to him during his life, so the Saviour's most precious and intimate manifestations have been to woman. The social meeting is the becoming place for her to testify what the Saviour has done for her. . . .

Yet, while the Scriptures allow a place to woman in the services of the social meeting, and grace and experience beautifully prepare her for that place, let the teachings of the Apostle not be forgotten. Let her not be assuming. Let modesty, the nice sense of female propriety, govern her conduct, and her mode of using her gifts. Let her not undertake the unseemly part to teach, to dictate, to control. Her place is in the social meetings, and not in the promiscuous gathering, or large assembly; in private and not in public worship. . . .

Document 3. The *New York Times:*
Pros and Cons on Women in Ministry

In 1947 the Presbyterian Church in the USA voted to ordain women clergy and sent the action to the presbyteries for approval. As the New York Presbytery prepared to vote, the following article appeared in the *New York Times,* outlining the arguments on both sides of the issue.[43]

. . . Let me first present the main reasons advanced against women in the ordained ministry.

The first is a matter of women's emotional balance, which many feel is not as stable as men's. They believe that the record of women in public life, especially in politics, sustains this judgment. The word "glob-aloney," coming at a time when it did, was an emotional blurb that had its natural emotional reaction in the life of the woman who uttered it.

Now the pulpit has lived through a century of over-emotionalism, say the folks who feel that today restrained and accurate teaching is desperately needed. The world sits on a powder keg, and not sparks but sober and judicial advice is needed. This they feel, by and large, and with exceptions, men can better deliver.

At the Presbytery meeting I joked about how a woman pastor might come home from church with a couple of elders to dinner. Who else, under the economic status of an average minister (not yet like the teachers under the wing of AFL), could or would be there to greet them at the parsonage door but a beruffled husband, hot and anxious from his vigil over the kitchen range, stamping his delicate number twelve shoe when he got the good parson aside because the post-service meeting had taken longer than the roast lamb to get done?

This may be an exaggeration, like the musical moment before the sermon for the preacher to powder her nose, but what about the young married pastor and her children? Must the church be closed for three months for a number of years while the pastor gets her own little flock? Or will the vows of celibacy be ordered as in the Church of Rome? Even birth control has not been developed enough to synchronize births with the summer vacation.

Others think that there is a feminine overbalance in the average congregation now. They feel that women pastors would so feminize the church that men would frequent it in even smaller numbers. Women will listen to men "tell them off" for their sins, but men will not seriously do the same for women. A man who has been taken over the coals on Saturday night or Sunday morning in his own house by the little lady will not lightly enter a church to hear another woman continue the rebuke. For that matter, say these folks, neither will a woman sit and let another woman preach to her for half an hour with no chance for rebuttal.

Again, the inability of women to keep confidences is advanced by those who think that even a pastor, be she of the feminine sex, would flit from home to home like a busy bee with "the dirt" instead of pollen and what would germinate in no time might not be rosemary for remembrance but poison ivy for the congregation.

Of course, the most conclusive argument for those who believe each admonition of the Holy Writ is timeless in its application, are such passages as I Timothy, ii, 11–12, "Let the women learn in silence with all subjection. But I suffer not a woman to teach nor to usurp authority over the man."

Those who favor women being admitted to the regular ordained ministry have very different ideas. They take the negative arguments and pull them to pieces. Women, they say, have in a short time of greater freedom taken their place by men in fields where emotional balance and discretion are prime considerations. They practice as famous physicians, they work as famous scientists, they sit as judges, are Congressional Representatives and will soon get their full political rights to occupy the nation's highest office. It is an insult to her whole species to say a woman cannot keep a confidence as well as a man, say both men and women of the affirmative.

Of course, there are physical difficulties in connection with motherhood, but these are gradually being overcome as in the case of school teachers.

As for the female overbalance in churches it might be that a few attractive personalities with goodness and eloquence plus personal charm would attract many more men than now attend. Perhaps that is just the reason for any real imbalance in the sex proportion of attendance. Who can say that every male preacher does not exert any personal magnetism he possesses? And, in fact, some overplay this appeal shamefully, as some women might do also.

There is a strong point made by those who say that God combines the virtues of both mother and father. It might be that a woman could better depict the former. Just as in the home the balance of family influence is disturbed by removal of either mother or father, the church may be lacking that balanced ministry. Perhaps, say those who believe this, the heavy hand of punishment would be modified in the preaching, by the wooing and winning side of God's love, as the mother's patient understanding in the home sometimes tempers the father's stern unyielding discipline.

As for the scriptural admonitions against women speaking in churches, we must distinguish between timeless truth and local admonition. Again and again Jesus brought the commands of Moses up to date.

Women kept veiled and silent in many other places than the synagogues in the time of Paul, but today they are vocal in all these other spots such as the forum, the market place and the theatre. "Time makes ancient good uncouth." Why not admit them to the pulpit also?

To these protagonists there is one practical reason advanced for ordained women pastors. Many if not the majority of women are home all day. Male pastors are not too welcome or in place visiting these mothers and housewives in the daytime. Their husbands, away at business, at times resent it. But women ministers and pastors could do so and get close to the problems besetting the housewife, counseling her with the knowledge and understanding of a woman's point of view. How fine, too, her tender touch in sickness or in emergencies where a man, no matter how well trained in theology and good intent, would be fumbling and awkward.

I have tried to express the opinions of both sides as judicially as possible. I cannot keep a gleam of humor out of my eye when I speak for the negative. I feel that women get what they want, given time, and will get the privilege of the pulpit and the pastorate in the Presbyterian Church as they got the vote in the affairs of the nation.

Of course, the same arguments hold in the case of the Negroes from the South and immigrants from the underprivileged sections of the world. We deny them equal rights because they do not prove they have the requirements that can and will only come to them by the possession and use of those rights.

The vote in the New York Presbytery will not be so close, I predict, as it will in the whole country, allowing for the backward sections. Women may not win this year, but win they will, and God bless them. But also, God keep too many of them from taking up this new field all at once. Letting folks learn new things, even in a democracy, is a necessary nuisance. It's like the baldish head I am just beginning to acquire. It's not a pleasant process and some think not a nice thing to have put on us, but I'll fight to keep it.

Document 4. *The Woman's Pulpit:*
Reflections on the Status
of Methodist Women Preachers

In 1919 the American Association of Women Preachers (later IAWM, International Association of Women Ministers) was founded to give support to women from many mainstream denominations who felt the call to preach and desired to be ordained ministers. Organized by an evangelical Methodist woman pastor from Kansas named Madeline Southard, this association published a small journal entitled *The Woman's Pulpit.* Reports and reflections on the ecclesiastical status of women fill its pages. During the thirty-two years that elapsed between the ordination of Methodist Episcopal women as local preachers and the vote that gave them full membership in annual conferences, many articles in *The Woman's Pulpit* discussed women and ordination.[44]

How the Opposition Helped at the 1924 General Conference.

A group of the strongest men signed a substitute for complete equality and gave arguments that I wish we had space to quote. The other side seemed to become fearful that the substitute might carry, and closed with a strong plea on the ground that it would imperil unification with the M. E. South Church. That carried great weight, and the report was adopted. One curious thing was that not one single voice in that whole assembly, in the hours of debate, was raised against ordination. Some of the people who fought it so four years ago, stood for it this time. By our keeping the whole attention centered upon what was not granted, and so opposing the report, our opponents themselves did all the talking for ordination. Some did not know just what they had done when it was over, they felt they had defeated us. In reality it is a great victory, incomplete as it is.

Madeline Southard

How the Double Standard Works
When Women Are Not Members of Annual Conference

To have this background, to see how every step woman has taken in the church has been against stubborn resistance, is necessary if we would consider the matter of admitting women to membership in the Annual

Conferences. For the same arguments are now advanced against all the others. But before considering them let us see what conference membership means. For it has been said that with license and ordination granted, woman has about as much opportunity as she would have as a member of Conference.

In answer to this we simply say, ask any young man who is entering the Methodist ministry if he intends sometime to become a member of a Conference. He will certainly answer yes. Ask him why. If he knows his church at all, he will tell you that unless he becomes a member of a Conference he will go through life as a supply pastor, and that no young man of the right sort would dream of going through life as a "supply" unless terribly hampered by hopeless limitations.

But this state that Methodism desires her keen alive young men to reject with scorn, this it is that she offers to her keen, alive young women, saying to them: "See how generous I have become to you. I am willing that you should go and preach in any of my difficult fields that can not or will not support a man as pastor. I am willing that you shall build them up for me. I have always held that you were delicate and needed protection, therefore I will send you to circuits where there are no modern conveniences, where there are long trips to make to distant outpoints, where the income is small and uncertain, and the community indifferent or torn by church quarrels. If you will work hard and build this up for me so that it will be a desirable charge for some man, a member of my Conference, I will say many lovely words about your consecration, your feminine humility—and I will send you to another difficult point to do the same thing over again. Of course you will not have money for books and magazines and contact with the big movements of the day, but it is very wrong and worldly to desire these things. I teach my sons to desire them, they run a neck-to-neck race for them, but to you my daughters I give the high privilege of living a meek and humble life."

How the Arguments Are Never Theological

You have heard arguments against the admission of women to the annual conferences. Seldom is it argued on Biblical grounds in our denomination today for the sound scholarship of our leaders and the fact of women's ordination would preclude such arguments. The so called "practical grounds" are the basis of the arguments usually advanced.

That practical problems would be incurred, in the admission of women to the annual conferences, no one can deny. The great Methodist church with her genius for organization can meet every such problem and solve it. In fact at the present time, she has the disciplinary provisions in the articles on location and supernumerary relations to handle any special problems which might arise.

How Parenthood Should Not Cause Problems

Parenthood does not deter either men or women from being good ministers. In fact, parenthood is an asset, for family problems of the parish are better understood by those who have children of their own. There is no place in the world where children can be better nurtured intellectually and spiritually than in a parsonage and the problems involved in bringing children into the world and caring for them can be met by the parents if common sense, consecration, and prayer are brought to bear on each situation.

The conference need not worry about the fate of the husband of a woman minister. If both husband and wife are thoroughly Christian, even though their vocations may differ, they will work out their problems in harmony and good faith with no loss to their family relations or to the annual conference.

How the Spiritual Integrity of the Church Is Threatened by This Inequality.

The Church makes bold, glorious, and fearless pronouncements on temperance, ecumenical relationships, need for ministers, rural problems, education, missions, church union, international situations, racial injustice, nationalism, the emancipation of labor, and other causes, proclaiming in these pronouncements that "We judge practices by the Christian gospel." In spite of the pleas of the underprivileged the same Church ignores the liberating gospel which declares that "in Christ Jesus there is neither male nor female," by keeping the doors of the annual conferences barred to qualified women. Such a church needs an awakening, a repentance and works meet for repentance.

This prevailing condition threatens the spiritual integrity of the church, for how can a church preach justice and deny it to some of her own members, and remain utterly sincere? It is not surprising that more and more of our most brilliant women are turning to secular organizations for places of leadership, since they cannot find them in the church. This entails the loss of talent and ability that should be used directly for Christ and the church.

How can a church preach against class legislation and continue to legislate against sex without losing spiritual power?

Document 5. Phoebe Palmer: "A Supposition" on the Promises of the Father

The most famous woman leader in the Holiness revival, which flourished in the midnineteenth century, was Phoebe Palmer. After her marriage in 1827 to Walter C. Palmer, the couple traveled widely and spoke extensively in church meetings. Following the logic that women can receive the gifts of the spirit as readily as men, Palmer built an eloquent case that women must be allowed to accept the promises of God, which have been withheld for centuries. In her 1859 book, *Promise of the Father: or, A Neglected Specialty of the Last Days,* she invites women to claim their power and chides men (particularly clergy) for keeping women down.[45]

Suppose one of the brethren who had received the baptism of fire on the day of Pentecost, now numbered among those who were scattered every where preaching the word, had met a female disciple who had also received the same endowment of power. He finds her proclaiming Jesus to an astonished company of male and female listeners. And now imagine he interferes and withstands her testimony by questioning whether women have a right to testify of Christ before a mixed assembly. Would not such an interference look worse than unmanly? And were her testimony, through this interference, restrained, or rendered less effectual, would it not, in the eye of the Head of the Church, involve guilt? Yet we do not say but a person may err after the same similitude and be sincere, on the same principle that Saul was sincere when he withstood the proclamation of the gospel, and made such cruel havoc of the church. He verily thought he was doing God service. But when his mind was enlightened to see that, in persecuting these men and women, he was withstanding God, and rejecting the divinely-ordained instrumentalities by which the world was to be saved, he could no longer have been sincere unless he had taken every possible pains to make his refusal of error as far reaching as had been his wrong. And how the heart of that beloved disciple of the Saviour would have been grieved, and her hands weakened, by one whom she would have a right to look to for aid against the common enemy, and for sympathy in her work!

A large proportion of the most intelligent, courageous, and self-sacrificing disciples of Christ are females. "Many women followed the saviour" when on earth; and, compared with the fewness of male disciples, many women follow him still. Were the women who followed the incarnate Saviour earnest, intelligently pious, and intrepid, willing to sacrifice that which cost them something, in ministering to him of their substance? In like manner, there are many women in the present day, earnest, intelligent, intrepid, and self-sacrificing, who, were they permitted or encouraged to open their lips in the assemblies of the pious in prayer, or speaking as the Spirit gives utterance, might be instrumental in winning many an erring one to Christ. We say, were they permitted and encouraged; yes, encouragement may now be needful. So long has this endowment of power been withheld from use by the dissuasive sentiments of the pulpit, press, and church officials, that it will need the combined aid of these to give the public mind a proper direction, and undo a wrong introduced by the man of sin centuries ago.

But more especially do we look to the ministry for the correction of this wrong. Few, perhaps, have really intended to do wrong; but little do they know the embarrassment to which they have subjected a large portion of the church of Christ by their unscriptural position in relation to this matter. The Lord our God is one Lord. The same indwelling spirit of might which fell upon Mary and the other women on the glorious day that ushered in the present dispensation still falls upon God's daughters. Not a few of the daughters of the Lord Almighty have, in obedience to the command of the Saviour, tarried at Jerusalem; and, the endowment from on high having fallen upon them, the same impelling power which constrained Mary and the other women to speak as the Spirit gave utterance impels them to testify of Christ.

"The testimony of Jesus is the spirit of prophecy." And how do these divinely-baptized disciples stand ready to obey these impelling influences? Answer, ye thousands of Heaven-touched lips, whose testimonies have so long been repressed in the assemblies of the pious! Yes, answer, ye thousands of female disciples, of every Christian land, whose pent-up voices have so long, under the pressure of these man-made restraints, been uttered in groanings before God.

Document 6. The *Lutheran Quarterly:* "Shall Women Preach?"

Most of the printed arguments against women preaching were written by male clergy. However, at the turn of the century, the *Lutheran Quarterly* published an interesting series of articles in which a woman reinforced the biblical arguments presented by a man. Professor Neve presented a careful exegetical case that Paul's prohibitions were binding on all Christians for all times. Margaret R. Seebach agreed that women should not preach because of the practical obstacles and innate differences between men and women.[46]

Are there reasons of practical expediency which justify the position of our Church in not accepting women as preachers? Do the education of women and their altered social standing make it unjust to deny them this privilege? There has been much discussion of this question during the last few years, when the papers have been full of notices of pulpits "supplied in the pastor's absence by his wife." An able and spirited plea has come before our own Church in the form of a story from the pen of one who would be herself richly qualified for such service. Meantime our Lutheran women are doing all but preaching, and often, in connection with their missionary work, addressing audiences larger than many a pastor has before him on Sunday. In these we glory, and even apply to them the words of the conservative Paul in saying "Help those women!" Why, then do we withhold from them the crowning privilege? Why not educate and ordain them as pastors?

Some may reply that it is on account of prejudice, which must be overcome gradually by individual successes. The woman who supplies her husband's pulpit steps imperceptibly, they may say, into work for which she is fitted and opens a door to her sisters. Of all the proposed methods, this seems to us the worst. It is not entering into the fold by the door but climbing up another way. If an unordained layman of one sex may do this, why not of the other? Yet who would want to see the significance of ordination and the value of ministerial education thus set aside, and our pulpits supplied by anyone who knows enough to talk for thirty minutes on religious subjects? When we define the place of a woman in the Church let us never forget that she is a *layman*—pastor's wife or not. It is no more proper and lawful for her to occupy a pulpit on the Sabbath day as a preacher and spiritual guide than to solemnize marriage or baptism. This is said with no intention to exalt the priest-hood of the ordained. The universal priesthood of believers is so great and real an honor that no one need envy the ordained minister as nearer to God or more blest by Him. We have self-government in this country, and every citizen can feel himself the equal of a king. Yet all are not magistrates, and it goes ill when those who are not attempt to take the law into their own hands.

Whatever, then, any other laymen may do in the Church, let us grant, if we will, to women. Let them teach in the schools of the Church, let them pray in prayer meetings, let them conduct mid-week services where it is customary for laymen to do these things. But keep the Sabbath ministrations for those who have received training for this very thing, and whose life-work it is.

Then why not educate women for this work? is the next question we have to meet. The answer is manifold, but it all amounts to this: Because it would involve, on the part of women, the celibacy of the clergy. Without going into details, it is just as impossible for a woman to combine home duties with the work of a pastor and preacher as with any other business or profession. Were it possible for her to leave her household in the hands of others so as to give her time for a work which is supposed to occupy the whole time of a man who adopts it, she would lose in moral influence by such indifference to home and children. Even if she had no one but her husband to consider, his own profession would be an obstacle. Should she receive a call from another charge, would he be expected to leave his medical practice, his store, his factory, and follow her? Or if he were a preacher, would it frequently happen that they could get adjoining charges? Evidently, marriage would mean, for a woman, retirement from the active ministry.

Some one objects that there are many unmarried women who could do this work. It must be remembered, however, that in order to gain the best results, education for such a sphere should begin at an age considerably earlier than that at which most women can be considered confirmed spinsters. Would it not be necessary, especially in the case of beneficiaries, to exact from those who entered on such a course a promise not to marry for an almost prohibitive number of years? The Deaconess is not a case in point. Her training is not so protracted nor so costly, nor is her specialty useless after marriage, as much of the technical theological training would be to a woman.

But even if we can conceive of a moral, healthful, helpful woman permanently without family ties or the desire for them, there is another and a fundamental reason why women should not be taught and ordained as preachers. The quality of a woman's mind is different from that of a man. This does not mean necessarily that it is inferior. It simply means that things do not appeal to her from the same side, do not appear to her in the same light as to man. We are not to be startled any more by the saying that reason is the province of the masculine mind, intuition of the feminine. Yet this means that a woman ordinarily cannot convince a man of a thing by argument. In logical presentation of truth, she is usually a failure. Thus arises a serious question: Can a woman's preaching win and hold men in the Church? And when we consider that the great lack of the Church in all ages has been such a virile and logical interpretation of truth as will appeal to *men,* and hold their allegiance, this question assumes large proportions. The Church *has* the women—has always had them; she needs the men!

Personally, it seems to us that even a limited participation in public speech is a dangerous intoxicant for a woman who has any taste at all for it. A woman can sell her mental and spiritual powers in just as meretricious a desire for admiration and influence as her bodily graces. The aesthetic sense, ever the serpent tempter of woman, would too often gain the ascendancy, and we should have lectures on philosophy, art, literature, but not sermons. The mere topics of most of the reported "sermons by a woman" are significant examples of this. Woman in public life is too new to be trusted with this most subtle of temptations. Her intentions are good, but she does not realize what a powerful stimulant success of this kind would prove to spiritual dilettantism. Then the balance would swing to the opposite extreme, and we should have women preaching reactionary dogmas to an extent that would amount to intolerance. Logic would save a man from this, while feeling would drive a woman into it. The very sensationalism of doing a thing so new would be a positive spiritual injury to a sensitive mind. As long as we see in the newspapers such startling headlines as "A Woman Preacher," "Filled Her Husband's Pulpit," and the like, let us stand by St. Paul. The time is not ripe.

Document 7. Elizabeth Wilson: Anglicans Debate the Advantages of Ordaining Women

When Charles E. Raven, a progressive writer in the Church of England, wrote a small book in the 1920s arguing for the ordination of women, it was reprinted in America with an introduction by an American woman. In that introduction, Elizabeth Wilson lists the gains the church might anticipate if it authorized women priests.[47]

The fear has long been expressed that much would be lost by the removal of the prohibitions against ordaining women and calling them to pastorates. The fear is now being expressed that something is being lost by not removing these prohibitions. Speaking in terms of gain instead of loss, what is it reasonable to suppose might be the gain to the cause of Christ and His Righteousness in the United States if Canon Raven's premises should be agreed to and his conclusions acted upon?

Would it not be this: First, a return to the practice of Jesus Christ and the early Church in welcoming women to the fellowship of the Gospel and in using their ministry in *accordance with the social customs of the day.* Second, recruits for the ranks of preachers from among the young women who have been classmates in colleges and theological seminaries of the young men candidates who have been presenting themselves in less than sufficient numbers—a dearth which we hear constantly lamented. Third, the employment of women's inherent gifts, not competing with the ministry of men but supplementing it. Canon Raven's comment on the English war workers, "They brought with them what few men possess: the personal touch, the sense of personal values, which we with our concern for problems and abstract principles so easily lose," is only half of the case. The other half is that women with their resourcefulness may work out new forms of preaching, new avenues through which the soul may find God, just as the English situation led to the introduction of the Pilgrims. Fourth, a general increase of interest in religion and in religious education among women and girls, as it is recognized that the churches allow and expect women to take a full share in their leadership: at present the disabilities attaching to women's work react unfavourably upon the whole attitude of women towards the study and service of Christianity. Fifth, the adoption of a more Christlike outlook upon personal, social, and political problems on the part of the churches as these, by taking women into full partnership in their councils, assume a more human because less purely masculine character. The absence of women's distinctive contribution weakens and to some extent distorts the witness of the Church on many prominent moral and spiritual issues. Those who have had full experience of it will realize most easily the advantages that equal cooperation between men and women might give. Women may sew together the new wine skins which will hold fresh revelations of the truth as it is in Christ Jesus and of His power to resolve the perplexities of thinking, praying Christians today. But such mental processes are now too often inhibited.

Document 8. Committee to Study the Proper Place of Women in the Ministry of the Church: Episcopalians Examine the Issue of Marriage

When the Committee to Study the Proper Place of Women in the Ministry of the Church reported to the Episcopal House of Bishops in 1966, it argued that there was no reason not to ordain women. Moving beyond the usual theological arguments it addressed the practical question of marriage and ordination.[48]

Marriage Versus Ministry: There is alleged the impossibility or impracticality of combining the vocation of a clergyman with domestic responsibilities, with marriage, as well as the bearing and care of children. Would it be possible for a wife and mother of a family to bring to the priesthood the required degree of commitment, concentration, and availability?

First, it must be said that many women choose careers and never marry, others combine marriage and careers. The Church recognizes that the latter is an entirely legitimate vocation, both in the secular world and in the Church itself.

Secondly, the question of married women is partly answered by the fact that married men are permitted to serve as bishops, priests and deacons in the Anglican Communion. Such permission implies an acknowledgment of the strong claims that the wife and family of a married clergyman rightfully have upon his time, his money, and the conduct of his vocation. All would grant that a clergyman has a duty, as well as a right, to take into account his wife's health, or his children's education, in considering a call, in negotiating about his salary, in determining his standard of living and the amount of money he will give away.

While other, and perhaps more serious, problems might exist for a woman who wished to combine ordination with marriage, the Commission is by no means convinced that such a combination would not prove practical in many instances. Even such demanding professions as teaching and medicine are finding ways of using skilled and trained married women with children, both on a part-time and a full-time basis. Many intelligent women find that they are better wives and mothers by combining an outside calling with the care of a family. Many also can look forward to years of full-time professional work after their children are grown.

The Commission would ask whether the leadership of the Church does not possess resourcefulness and imagination similar to that displayed by other institutions in using married women, if not often as ministers in charge of parishes, yet as assistants, or for the specialized types of ministry that are sure to develop much more rapidly in the future. It is thought unlikely that any great number of women would seek ordination, considering the very real difficulties involved. But difficulty is not impossibility, and at the least there need be no fear that women will "take over" the Church.

Document 9. World Council of Churches: Women's Ordination as an Ecumenical Issue

In 1948 a Committee on the Life and Work of Women in the Church of the World Council of Churches (WCC) conducted a survey to examine all facets of women's role in Christian churches. It simply listed the common arguments for and against women's ordination. Fifteen years later, the WCC Commission on Faith and Order held a consultation on the ordination of women, arguing that regardless of differences the question had serious ecumenical ramifications. Excerpts from these two reports summarize the ecumenical debate.[49]

1948 Report

The Enquiry has noted that the full ordination of women to the ministry is indeed a controversial subject. Perhaps no subject related to women in the Church stands in such great need of full, ecumenical study as this one, not because of the great number of women who at this moment are seeking ordination, but because in certain groups throughout the world there is great interest and concern with the principles involved, and because it raises questions related to the unity of the churches.

A few of the reasons set forth against the ordination of women are:

1. The nature and God-given functions of women preclude their being called to this high office.

2. Specific injunctions such as "let a woman learn in silence with all submissiveness. I permit no woman to teach or have authority over man, she is to keep silent."

3. The authority and tradition of the Church have not included the possibility of women serving as clergy.

4. The fact that certain churches consider this a closed issue would make the reunion of the churches more difficult—perhaps impossible.

5. There would be resistance in parishes to having a woman clergyman. In part, this might be because of sex prejudice, and in part because churches of the Reformation have put a high value on the Christian parsonage and the contribution of the pastor's wife. In this connection it would be presumed that most women coming forward for the Ministry would be single women.

6. There would be especially difficult problems for a woman clergyman to face in case she married and had family and home responsibilities.

7. If women should be admitted to the full ministry, it might deter men from answering the call to it.

A few of the viewpoints of those favouring the ordination of women are as follows:

1. Women are now satisfactorily thus serving in some Communions.

2. The problems which they face in the Ministry have been met and largely overcome in other spheres of work.

3. The full ministry of women is required by the Christian doctrine of human nature.

4. "In Christ there is neither male nor female; for ye are all one in Christ Jesus."

5. Under the stress of danger and trouble the Church has been thankful to use them to the full.

6. In the present godlessness and indifference to religion throughout the world, the Church needs the joint service and leadership of men and women.

7. In some of the Younger Churches where women missionaries have been relatively free from traditional restrictions, there is a desire for women to serve the Church in the fullest way.

Two observations perhaps may be allowed concerning the foregoing. First, that important as the subject of "women clergy" is, in its need for further exploration, it represents only one phase of the life and contribution of women in the Church and should not be allowed to overshadow the whole. Second, that further study should be freed from fear, pride, resentment and prejudice, relying on the promised assistance of the Holy Spirit to lead the Church into all truth.

1964 Report

Many churches welcome women to the ordained ministry and have found the policy advantageous. Others, having adopted this policy, face serious internal tensions. In others, the policy is under discussion and provokes heated debate. The matter frequently becomes acute in negotiations for church unity. And even apart from formal negotiations, it affects the mutual relations of churches which ordain women to those which do not. It would be wrong, therefore, to view this issue as a result of feminist demands or agitation by a few enthusiasts. It concerns the total understanding of the ministry of the church and therefore has deep theological significance.

The range of the discussion and the urgency of the problem is something new in Christian history; it has been occasioned by social and cultural movements, although the solution of the problem requires theological decision. Social and cultural movements have their proper place as a challenge to translate Christian doctrine into possible new forms of church life and church order. It is true that the danger must be avoided of accommodating Christian truth to the current ideology, but we must also say that God may use secular movements for showing his will to us.

In our day there has been a rediscovery of two theological factors particularly relevant to our present study: a new insight into the nature of the wholeness of the body of Christ and a better understanding of the meaning of the partnership of men and women in God's design.

a) It is a basic tenet of the New Testament that the whole body is called to witness to the name of Christ; all members—men and women—have therefore their appropriate ministry to which they are called by him. This basic Christian truth was for many centuries overlaid. It has been rediscovered in our own day by all parts of Christendom.

b) It is an essential element of the Christian message that men and women are created in the image of God and are therefore of equal dignity and worth before him. The developments in our time have shown us that this truth has not always been sufficiently understood and emphasized. All the churches are confronted with the necessity of finding a new expression for this basic truth.

It is in this context that the question of the ordination of women is raised. Even the churches which oppose such ordination will realize that these new theological emphases have a relevance for them. The question involves many controversial points of exegesis, of dogmatic formulation and of ecclesiastical life.

Document 10. Jarena Lee: Black Women Wrestle with the "Call to Preach the Gospel"

Often called the first woman preacher of the First African Methodist Episcopal Church, Jarena Lee was never ordained. Born in

New Jersey in 1783, she later felt a call to preach the gospel within emerging Black Methodism. Although at first the Reverend Richard Allen drew the line at female preaching, he later supported her work. She traveled widely and kept a detailed record of her ministry, which was finally published. The following selection gives her description of her call.[50]

Between four and five years after my sanctification, on a certain time, an impressive silence fell upon me, and I stood as if some one was about to speak to me, yet I had no such thought in my heart.—But to my utter surprise there seemed to sound a voice which I thought I distinctly heard, and most certainly understand, which said to me, "Go preach the Gospel!" I immediately replied aloud, "No one will believe me." Again I listened, and again the same voice seemed to say—"Preach the Gospel; I will put words in your mouth, and will turn your enemies to become your friends."

At first I supposed that Satan had spoken to me, for I had read that he could transform himself into an angel of light for the purpose of deception. Immediately I went into a secret place, and called upon the Lord to know if he had called me to preach, and whether I was deceived or not; when there appeared to my view the form and figure of a pulpit, with a Bible lying thereon, the back of which was presented to me as plainly as if it had been a literal fact.

In consequence of this, my mind became so exercised, that during the night following, I took a text and preached in my sleep. I thought there stood before me a great multitude, while I expounded to them the things of religion. So violent were my exertions and so loud were my exclamations, that I awoke from the sound of my own voice, which also awoke the family of the house where I resided. Two days after I went to see the preacher in charge of the African Society, who was the Rev. Richard Allen, the same before named in these pages, to tell him that I felt it my duty to preach the gospel. But as I drew near the street in which his house was, which was in the city of Philadelphia, my courage began to fail me; so terrible did the cross appear, it seemed that I should not be able to bear it. Previous to my setting out to go to see him, so agitated was my mind, that my appetite for my daily food failed me entirely. Several times on my way there, I turned back again; but as often

I felt my strength again renewed, and I soon found that the nearer I approached to the house of the minister, the less was my fear. Accordingly, as soon as I came to the door, my fears subsided, the cross was removed, all things appeared pleasant—I was tranquil.

I now told him, that the Lord had revealed it to me, that I must preach the gospel. He replied, by asking, in what sphere I wished to move in? I said, among the Methodists. He then replied, that a Mrs. Cook, a Methodist lady, had also some time before requested the same privilege; who, it was believed, had done much good in the way of exhortation, and holding prayer meetings; and who had been permitted to do so by the verbal license of the preacher in charge at the time. But as to women preaching, he said that our Discipline knew nothing at all about it—that it did not call for women preachers. This I was glad to hear, because it removed the fear of the cross—but no sooner did this feeling cross my mind, than I found that a love of souls had in a measure departed from me; that holy energy which burned within me, as a fire, began to be smothered. This I soon perceived.

O how careful ought we to be, lest through our by-laws of church government and discipline, we bring into disrepute even the word of life. For as unseemly as it may appear now-a-days for a woman to preach, it should be remembered that nothing is impossible with God. And why should it be thought impossible, heterodox, or improper for a woman to preach? seeing the Saviour died for the woman as well as for the man.

If the man may preach, because the Saviour died for him, why not the woman? seeing he died for her also. Is he not a whole Saviour, instead of a half one? as those who hold it wrong for a woman to preach, would seem to make it appear.

Did not Mary *first* preach the risen Saviour, and is not the doctrine of the resurrection the very climax of Christianity—hangs not all our hope on this, argued by St. Paul? Then did not Mary, a woman, preach the gospel? for she preached the resurrection of the crucified Son of God.

But some will say that Mary did not expound the Scripture, therefore, she did not preach, in the proper sense of the term. To this I reply, it may be that the term *preach* in those primitive times, did not mean exactly what it is now *made* to mean; perhaps it was a great deal more simple then than it is now—if it were not, the unlearned fishermen could not have preached the gospel at all, as they had no learning.

To this it may be replied, by those who are determined not to believe that it is right for a woman to preach, that the disciples, though they were fishermen and ignorant of letters too, were inspired so to do. To which I would reply, that though they were inspired, yet that inspiration did not save them from showing their ignorance of letters, and of man's wisdom; this the multitude soon found out, by listening to the remarks of the envious Jewish priests. If then, to preach the gospel, by the gift of heaven, comes by inspiration solely, is God straitened: must he take the man exclusively? May he not, did he not, and can he not inspire a female to preach the simple story of the birth, life, death, and resurrection of our Lord, and accompany it too with power to the sinner's heart. As for me, I am fully persuaded that the Lord called me to labor according to what I have received, in his vineyard. If he has not, how could he consistently bear testimony in favor of my poor labors, in awakening and converting sinners?

In my wanderings up and down among men, preaching according to my ability, I have frequently found families who told me that they had not for several years been to a meeting, and yet, while listening to hear what God would say by his poor female instrument, have believed with trembling—tears falling down their cheeks, the signs of contrition and repentance towards God. I firmly believe that I have sown seed, in the name of the Lord, which shall appear with its increase at the great day of accounts, when Christ shall come to make up his jewels.

Document 11. Joel Roth: The Ordination of Women as Conservative Jewish Rabbis

Conservative Judaism seeks to integrate tradition with modernity. In the 1970s, after the Reform and Reconstructionist movements had decided to ordain women, women within the Conservative movement challenged the faculty at the Jewish Theological Seminary (in New York) to rule on the issue. In 1983 Joel Roth made a persuasive case, and the faculty voted to admit women to rabbinical studies.[51]

Women who wish to observe *mitzvot* [the law binding on Jewish males] should be given every encouragement to do so, since there is sufficient legal precedent for allowing them to do so. At present, regrettably, such women are subjected to the most virulent type of vilification by two very different groups. Observant men have looked so askance at women who have adopted the observance of *mitzvot* from which they are exempt, that they give the impression that their behavior must be forbidden. The very people to whom such women turn for assurance that their behavior falls within legal parameters, for that is a great concern of many of them, give the opposite impression by merely tolerating their behavior, even if they do not actively attempt to discourage it.

These women, too, are often castigated by women who accept their traditional exemption from *mitzvot*. They are told either that they are trying to be like men or that they are allowing men to dictate what women should be. To the best of my knowledge and observation, these women are motivated, by and large, by purely religious motives. That does not imply that they were not at all affected by the spirit that animates the various women's or feminist movements.

Women must be allowed to increase their patterns of religious observance without hindrance from men or other women. Indeed, since their observance of *mitzvot* is permissible, there is no reason why they should not be encouraged in their quest, if that is the path they have chosen.

To be sure, it must be made absolutely clear to all women who adopt the observance of *mitzvot* that there is often more involved than observance alone. That is particularly true either where a *minyan* [quorum required for prayers] is needed or where the issue of agency is involved. They must understand that only obligated individuals constitute a quorum and only one who is obligated can serve as the agent for others. Just because a woman comes to services, or dons *tallit* [prayer shawl] and *tefillin* [phylacteries], or receives an *aliyah* [a call to bless the Torah] does not mean she has the right to be counted toward a *minyan* or to act as agent in behalf of one who is obligated to perform a *mitzvah*.

Women may be counted in a *minyan* [quorum] or serve as *shatz* [cantor] only when they have accepted upon themselves the voluntary obligation to pray as required by the law, and at the times required by law, and only when they recognize and affirm that failure to comply with the obligation is sin. Then they may be counted in the quorum and serve as the agents for others. This is the position which I would recommend to the Faculty for adoption. . . .

One of my most revered teachers has recommended to me in private discussion that women should be encouraged to adopt the observance of *mitzvot* and that the question of ordination be put off for a generation, until such behavior by women becomes common. I must respectfully disagree with that recommendation. I have already stated my view that only women who have accepted the obligation to observe all the *mitzvot* should be considered candidates for ordination. If this position is affirmed, then the Committee on Admissions would seek evidence that the women who apply have complied with that requirement. In that case, the earliest group of women applicants would undoubtedly be those whose observance of *mitzvot* already reflects voluntary acceptance of all of the *mitzvot*. They will be the women who have had the fortitude to be trailblazers on previously unmarked paths. I cannot see why the forerunners should be denied the right which their very behavior will have bequeathed to those who follow them.

Document 12. Blu Greenberg: "Orthodox Women Rabbis?"

Orthodox Jews assume that the law makes it impossible for women to function as rabbis. As the numbers of female students of Talmud increase, a leading Orthodox Jewish woman predicts that the flexibility of Jewish law over the centuries will enable it to adapt to support the ordination of Orthodox women rabbis.[52]

. . . A close look at the convention of ordination (*smicha*) reveals that it is not a conferral of holy status nor a magical laying on of hands to transmit authority. Nor does the process uniquely empower a rabbi to perform special sacramental functions that a knowledgeable layperson cannot.

Ordination is the confirmation of an individual's mastery of texts (largely from the Talmud and codes); familiarity with precedents; and ability to reason analogically and apply precedents to contemporary questions. Conferring the title "rabbi" is a guarantee to the community that this person has been judged fit by a collective of rabbis or by a single great scholar to give guidance on matters of *issur v'heter,* the forbidden and the permitted, primarily as it concerns the laws of *kashrut* [dietary restrictions], *Shabbat* [sabbath] and family purity. The *smicha* process assumes but does not even test for personal piety, good character or a spiritual bent. The formal criteria are almost wholly intellectual.

Why, then, have some Orthodox rabbis asserted that *smicha* for women is not permitted? *Halachic* [legal] decision making, particularly when a new issue is at hand, is a creative process, part the word of God at Sinai, part rabbinic tradition, part human interpretation. Selective choice of precedents is a powerful shaper of the outcome. Today, some *poskim* (rabbinic decisors) pin their judgments on rabbinic interpretation of the verse, "And you shall surely place upon yourselves a King" (Deuteronomy 17:15). In *Sifre,* the Rabbis [of Talmudic times] comment, "A king but not a queen," thereby legitimating for the ages men, but not women, in positions of authority. Other contemporary Torah scholars raise the standard of "honor of the community," which can broadly be interpreted as that which offends the faithful.

Other rabbis say that while there may be no *halachic* objections to ordination, its linkage to other issues creates obstacles. Rabbis function as witnesses in the *beit din,* a Jewish court of law where women's testimony is inadmissible. Other complex linkages are to *mechitzah,* the separation of men and women and to *minyan,* the quorum of 10 men required for communal prayer that excludes women because they have a lesser *halachic* obligation. As the discussion proceeds, some rabbis will surely raise the issue of *kolisha,* the prohibition against men hearing the voice of a woman under certain circumstances.

Witness, *minyan, mechitzah, kolisha*—these objections cannot be lightly dismissed. Given the weight of authority vested in contemporary rabbinic decisions, it seems almost pointless to press the issue forward. And yet, Orthodox views are not monolithic. *Halachah* is not static. It contains internal mechanisms of repair; it holds sparks of dynamism and creativity; it is and always has been responsive to special-interest groups (if women can be called such) and cases of special pleading; all of which explains why *halachah* has served the Jewish people so well, for so long.

Some highly respected Yeshiva University–ordained, modern Orthodox rabbis see no *halachic* barriers to women's ordination. These minority views carry great significance, as this is a community where religious authority is decentralized. . . .

Orthodox women should be ordained because it would constitute a recognition of their new intellectual accomplishments and spiritual attainments; because it would encourage greater Torah study; because it offers wider female models of religious life; because women's input into *p'sak* (interpretation of Jewish texts), absent for 2,000 years, is sorely needed; because it will speed the process of reevaluating traditional definitions that support hierarchy; because some Jews might find it easier to bring *halachic* questions concerning family and sexuality to a woman rabbi. And because of the justice of it all.

Nevertheless, many problems remain, not only connected to *halachah* but to communal unity and mainstream attitudes. That is why I do not foresee that Orthodox women will serve initially—or perhaps not for a long while—as pulpit rabbis of traditional congregations. Nor do I believe it must necessarily be part of the agenda, though I know that some feminists would fault me for taking that stance. But a respect for community sensibilities, an appreciation of incremental steps, a desire for internal unity and a realism about *shul* [synagogue] politics propel me along this path.

CHAPTER EIGHT

Gender in Utopian and Communal Societies

Rosemary Radford Ruether

Documents

THE ANDROGYNOUS GOD
AND THE NEW HUMANITY

1. The Shaker Bible: Androgynous Deity and the Dual Order of Christ
2. A Rappite Hymn: To Sophia, the Harmonists' Goddess
3. Rebecca Jackson: A Black Evangelist Empowered by the Mother God
4. The Rebirth of the Goddess in Women's Spirituality

ALTERNATIVES TO THE TRADITIONAL FAMILY

5. Ephrata Cloister: The Order of the Rose of Sharon
6. Oneida: Complex Marriage and Family Planning
7. The Mormons: Joseph Smith Commands Emma Smith's Assent to Polygyny

FEMALE FOUNDERS AND LEADERS

8. Jemima Wilkinson: Public Universal Friend
9. Frances Wright: The Vision of Equality at Nashoba
10. Barbara Heinemann Landmann: Amana Inspirationist *Werkzeuge*

GENDER EQUALITY AND WOMEN'S WORK ROLES

11. The Women's Commonwealth: Autoemancipation
12. The Farm: Spiritual Midwifery
13. Twin Oaks: Labor Credits and Gender Equality

THE idea of America as a new land with an open future early attracted people holding utopian and millenarian visions of Christ reigning on earth in justice, prosperity, and peace. In the colonial period, European heirs of the Radical Reformation formed communal societies as the true church and the new redeemed humanity. They migrated to America to find the space to live these visions and prepare themselves for the coming millennium. In the late seventeenth to early eighteenth centuries followers of Jean de Labadie, Jacob Zimmerman, and Conrad Biessel planted the monastic colonies of Bohemia Manor on the Chesapeake Bay of Maryland, Woman in the Wilderness in Coxsackie, Pennsylvania, and Ephrata in Pennsylvania.[1]

Another pietist group, the Moravian Brethren, descended from fourteenth-century Hussites, were reorganized in the 1720s by Count von Zinzendorf in Saxony. A missionary rather than monastic group, the Moravians planted many colonies in the eighteenth-century American colonies, beginning with Bethlehem, Pennsylvania, in 1741.[2]

A second wave of German separatist pietist immigration began with the Harmony Society, followers of George Rapp, who moved to Pennsylvania in 1803, followed by the Zoarites in Ohio in 1817 and the Amana Inspirationists in Iowa in 1842. They organized prosperous colonies that lasted to the end of the century. A third wave was the Hutterites, founded in 1528, who came to the Dakotas in the 1870s to avoid new persecutions. Many moved to Canada when the U.S. government refused to recognize their pacifist principles in World War I. Today the Hutterites are the largest and most enduring communal society in North America, with over three hundred colonies.[3]

The Quakers or Society of Friends, founded by George Fox and Margaret Fell in the 1650s, carried a millenarian impulse and a vision of women's restored equality in Christ that allowed female participation in ministry. Quakers have been the source of various communal offspring, the most important being the Shakers, whose foundress, Ann Lee, was seen as the female representative of Christ. Lee led her followers to America in 1774, where they planted nineteen major communities over the next sixty years, some still existing today. An American-born female Messiah of Quaker background was Jemima Wilkinson, who conducted preaching tours from 1774 to 1788 and then gathered three hundred followers of her Society of Universal Friends into a colony in Seneca Lake, New York, that lasted until her death in 1819.[4]

The 1820s to 1860s saw waves of utopian socialist movements that arose in England and France and then came to the United States. Robert Owen, a successful industrial reformer in Scotland, founded New Harmony in Indiana in 1825 in a former Rappite colony to try out his vision of an egalitarian moral order through economic cooperation and rational education. Feminist reformer Frances Wright sought to apply Owen's vision to the emancipation of slaves in her colony, Nashoba, in Tennessee.[5]

New England Unitarianism and Universalism were deeply influenced by the communal enthusiasm. Transcendentalists founded Brook Farm and Fruitlands near Boston in 1841 and 1843. In same period Universalists, under Adin Ballou, put their vision of Christian communalism to the test in the colony of Hopedale, at Milford, Massachusetts.[6]

In the 1840s the writings of French utopian socialist Charles Fourier were translated into English and inspired several of these communities to try to model themselves after his theories. Fourier's system of "attractive labor" sought to combine individualism and collectivism in communities where each person could do the work to which she or he was attracted. The North American Phalanx, founded in 1843 near Albany, New York, was one such Fourierite experiment. Another French socialist, Etienne Cabet, wrote a utopian novel, *Le Voyage a Icarie,* in 1840 and then led a group of several hundred followers to Texas in 1848. The French Icarians subdivided and moved to several successive colonies over the next decades, one group finding its way to California in 1881. Although opposing organized church leadership, these nineteenth-century forms of utopian socialism still evidenced a legacy of religious millennialism, expecting a coming age of perfection on earth.[7]

The 1830s was a time of heightened apocalyptic expectation in America. One adventist preacher, William Miller, fixed the date for the Second Coming in 1843. When this event failed to materialize, many Millerites dispersed, but some reorganized themselves as the Seventh Day Adventist Church, led by the ecstatic revelations of Ellen Harmon White. Another wave of apocalyptic expectation in the 1880s fed into movements such as the Jehovah's Witnesses.

Another American religious movement that arose from the revivalist and millenarian expectations was the Church of Latter Day Saints or Mormons. Their founder, Joseph Smith, claimed to have discovered a revealed Scripture in 1830. The movement developed communal features as it moved West and adopted polygyny in 1842. The 1840s also saw the rise of the Oneida Perfectionists, led by John Humphrey Noyes, that sought to anticipate redeemed humanity through a love communism that included shared sexuality.[8]

The three decades after the Civil War saw new communal groups arising from the perfectionist vision.[9] One of these was the Sanctificationist Women's Commonwealth of Belton, Texas, led by Martha McWhirter. Beginning as a Methodist women's prayer meeting, the Sanctificationists eventually separated from their husbands and pooled their economic skills for self-support. Growing increasingly prosperous, they bought a hotel and several farms. In 1899 they moved to Washington, D.C., and a farm in Maryland, where they continued into the 1930s.[10] Spiritualism, a strong movement in the 1860s, also inspired several communal societies, such as the Brotherhood of the New Life, led by Thomas Lake Harris.[11] Christian Science, founded by Mary Baker Eddy in the 1870s, drew on the spiritualist impulse and introduced mainstream Americans to mental healing. Spiritualism and fascination with Eastern religions fueled the English theosophist movement of the 1870s. In 1896 Katherine Tingley emerged as the leader of the break-away Theosophical Society in America. Tingley built a large complex of buildings for educational and communal life in Point Loma, California, to model theosophy as a new cosmic consciousness and way of life.[12]

The economic crises of post–Civil War industrialization, as well as new waves of immigration, created the environment for many new socialist communities in the 1880s. Secular socialism was matched by Christian communities springing from the Social Gospel. The Salvation Army, which came to the United States in 1898, experimented with several back-to-the-land communities for the poor in this era, such as Amity Colony in Holly, Colorado.

The first decades of the twentieth century also saw the rise of communal societies. The Depression era saw new communal developments from both the Catholic Worker movement and Black urban movements, such as the cooperative run by Father Divine in Harlem, New York City, and other large Eastern cities. The communal impulse was partly taken over in this era by the New Deal state, which sponsored greenbelt cities (planned suburban communities) and homesteading settlements. In 1942 Baptist minister Clarence Jordan united Depression-era communalism and growing criticism of racism to found Koinonia Farm in Georgia.[13]

Jews also took part in this era of communal experiments. Both in the 1880s and in the 1930s Jews from Russia founded kibbutzim in the United States, parallel to those being developed in Israel.[14] Today the fastest growing form of Judaism in America is seen in the semicommunal Hasidim, who live a strict Orthodoxy in their own enclaves in urban areas such as Brooklyn.[15]

The 1960s saw an explosion of new communal experiments across a wide spectrum of ideological and religious impulses. When the 1923 ban on Asian immigration was lifted in 1965, a wave of Asian gurus arrived in the United States, ranging from more traditional Buddhist, Sufi, and Hindu teachers to those of new Asian-inspired religions, such as the Unification Church and the Hare Krishna Society. Buddhism traditionally promoted celibate communal life in monasteries for its devotees, and a core group of many of the Asian or Asian-inspired religious groups live communally.[16]

A mixture of Pentecostalism, millennialism, and ministry to street people inspired a number of communal movements, such as the Way International, which sprang from the radio ministry of Victor Paul Wierwille, and the Children of God, founded by Pentecostal missionary David Berg. Evidence that the leaders of several such groups engaged in economic and sexual exploitation of members who were separated from families and society sparked growing alarm in wider society over brainwashing by "cults." The leaders of two such groups, Jim Jones, who began the People's Temple in 1966, and David Koresh, founder of the Branch Davidians, led their followers to mass suicide when challenged by government intervention.[17]

Other Christians, inspired by liberation theology, feminism, concern for racism, and opposition to war, developed new social gospel movements with communal aspects. One such group is the Sojourner community, which moved to Washington, D.C., in 1975, where it lives among the Black poor and also publishes *Sojourner* magazine as the voice of radical evangelicals.[18]

Many communal experiments of the 1960s arose from a combination of Asian spirituality and various healing therapies, dubbed "New Age" spirituality. Feminism also inspired new efforts to envision sexually egalitarian societies, while the concern for ecological devastation caused many such communities to adopt a lifestyle and culture intended to restore connections with the earth. The Farm, a San Francisco hippie movement that moved to Tennessee in 1971, and Twin Oaks in Louisa, Virginia, are examples of New Age communities. Womanshare and Owl Farm in Oregon, begun in 1974 and 1976, reflect a lesbian separatist perspective. Owl Farm is one of a network of women-only rural communities in Oregon, Wisconsin, Minnesota, and New Mexico that have arisen since the 1970s based on land held collectively by and for women.[19]

Despite great diversity in ideological inspiration, all these utopian groups share some kind of vision about the perfectibility of humanity through reorganized social relations. Those with a religious or spiritual orientation interconnect social with personal transformation. In this chapter I will discuss and document four aspects of this transformed self and society found in utopian movements: (1) androgynous God-language and the new humanity; (2) alternatives to the family; (3) female founders and leaders; and (4) gender-based division of labor and equality.

THE ANDROGYNOUS GOD
AND THE NEW HUMANITY

Many utopian movements linking social with spiritual transformation saw God as dual or androgynous. These ideas were drawn particularly from mystics Jacob Boehme (1575–1624) and Emmanuel Swedenborg (1688–1772),[20] and they shaped a complex of ideas shared by many millennialist, spiritualist, and theosophical utopians. God and the spiritual powers governing the universe were seen as composed of complementary principles, male and female. The original human was androgynous, uniting these male and female principles, but through sin this unity was lost. Spiritual transformation will restore the original spiritual wholeness.

The Shakers believed that God is both Father and Mother. This duality in God is reflected in the dual nature of humanity, male and female.
Christ also must appear in both male and female form in order to reveal
the full nature of God. For the Shakers, Mother Ann Lee was this female
Christ, the revelation of divine Wisdom, the Mother-nature of God. Lee
taught that sexual reproduction is sinful, manifesting the fallen nature of
present humanity, while the redeemed men and women of the Millennial
Church are to be celibate to express their transcendence of fallen sinfulness and their recovery of their original spiritual unity (document 1).

The Rappite Harmonists, led by George Rapp, shared a similar view
of God's dual nature and human fall and restoration. They also adopted
celibacy and cultivated a fervent devotion to the Divine Sophia, the feminine, virginal aspect of God (document 2). Many spiritualists also saw
God as androgynous and believed that sexual relations would cease as
humans became increasingly spiritualized.[21] Rebecca Jackson, a Black
evangelist, has recorded the empowering effect of this revelation of God
as Mother for Black women seeking liberation from social and religious
oppression. Jackson joined the Watervliet Shakers in 1844 and in 1851
founded a Black Shaker community in Philadelphia (document 3).

Mary Baker Eddy rewrote the Lord's Prayer as "Our Father-Mother
God," popularizing for many Americans this concept of divine androgyny. American popular preaching in the late nineteenth century
increasingly abandoned the angry, judgmental God of Puritanism for an
emphasis on God as loving and merciful, even though the name *Father*
was retained.[22]

Some radical feminists of the late nineteenth and early twentieth
centuries, such as Matilda Joslyn Gage, believed the original form of
human society was matriarchal, linked to the worship of God as female.
Judaism's exclusively male image of God to her represented a patriarchal
revolution overthrowing the original power of women and substituting a
concept of God as a warlike, angry dominating male for the original
understanding of God as sacred mother.[23] Charlotte Perkins Gilman, in
her book *His Religion and Hers* differentiated between a female understanding of religion linked with birth and growth and a redeemed society
within history and the male concept of religion based on war, hunting,
death, and life after death.[24]

These critical theories about God-language, gender, and society have been revived and developed in the feminist spirituality that has grown since the late 1960s. Some seek the basis for transformation of God imagery within Christianity; others believe that Christianity, rooted in the sacralization of patriarchal power, cannot be reformed and must be abandoned. Women and men seeking wholeness must recover the religion of the Goddess that was repressed by the patriarchal revolution thousands of years ago.[25]

When ecological concerns unite with feminist spirituality, Goddess religion becomes connected with the recovery of a healing relation between humans and the plants, animals, and earth. Goddess spiritual groups have promoted large gatherings in the country to experience healing, earth-based rituals.[26] Several feminist utopian groups have been promoters of such women's gatherings and see themselves as creating a new consciousness and holistic humanity through communing with the Goddess as the power of life and renewal of life within nature (document 4).

ALTERNATIVES TO THE TRADITIONAL FAMILY

Sexuality, marriage, and family were hotly debated issues in many utopian movements. The concept of a private nuclear family was often in tension with the vision of community as having "all things in common." Many mystical, millennialist, and spiritualist utopians were celibate, like the monastic colonies of Bohemia Manor, Woman in the Wilderness, and the Shakers. Ephrata had male and female celibate orders and a third order of married members (document 5). Others, such as the Rappite Harmonists, Zoarites, Amana Inspirationists, Belton Sanctificationists, the Brothers of the New Life led by Thomas Lake Harris, and some Christian Scientists included married members but saw celibacy as a direction of spiritual growth into a higher state of perfection.

John Humphrey Noyes took the millennialist quest for spiritual perfection in a different direction. He believed that the New Testament vision of a redeemed state in which "all shall be one" meant communal sharing of both goods and sexuality. He instituted a system of "complex marriage" in which all adult males and females could have sexual access to one another. Sexual liaisons were ordered through the governing structure of the community. Noyes himself monopolized sexual access and reproduction and initiated pubescent girls into sexuality. Noyes also promoted birth control, eugenics, and women's rights to sexual pleasure, teaching that the amative function of sex should be separated from the reproductive so that no woman would have to bear an unwanted child (document 6).

Mormon founder Joseph Smith saw himself as restoring the patriarchal order of the Hebrew Bible, including plural wives (document 7). Polygyny was originally a privilege of the male leaders, who were allowed the largest number of wives. Mormonism is hostile to birth control, teaching that women should have as many children as possible to clothe souls in heaven with bodies.

The Moravian Brethren emphasized the exclusive marriage tie and the partnership of married couples in missionary work. But they assigned eligible women to husbands through a system of marriage lot and then married the couples in a mass ceremony, a practice seen as submission to the will of God.[27] Contemporary sectarian groups, such as the Unification Church, also practice mass marriage in which the names of the partners are drawn by lot.

Socialist utopians often saw the permanent marriage tie as oppressive, subordinating the woman or man to a loveless bond. They agitated for the right to divorce and believed that the communal economic system would allow women to marry for love rather than being forced to trade their sexuality for economic support. Frances Wright and Robert Dale Owen were notorious for linking "free love" to Owenite egalitarianism, particularly in the interracial Nashoba community. Josiah Warren, formerly at New Harmony, founded a colony, Modern Times, on Long Island, using anarchist principles that rejected all community regulation of marriage.[28]

The Christian socialist community of Hopedale, in Milford, Massachusetts, responded to the "scandals" at Modern Times by emphasizing the strictly monogamous character of marriage and expelling any who deviated from this pattern.[29] Pietist societies, such as the Hutterites, also have demanded strictly monogamous patriarchal marriage. Rejecting birth control, the Hutterites maintain their identity through strong religious cohesion, shared property, and large families.

Some utopian communities have been characterized by sexually exploitive relations with women by a leader claiming total power over others, based on privileged access to God. This occurred in Cyrus Spragg's New Jerusalem, Illinois[30] (and some might argue in Noyes's role in Oneida and in Mormon polygyny). This pattern has recurred in authoritarian religious groups in recent years, such as David Berg's Children of God, Jim Jones's People's Temple, and David Koresh's Branch Davidians.

Some communal movements of the 1960s championed a contemporary version of free love, either by free exchange of sexual partners in "serial monogamy" or group sexual sharing by mutual consent. The Farm originally promoted married groups of four or more. Some lesbian feminists have demanded that female bonding be accepted as one pattern in a plurality of sexual relations; others have created separatist communities.[31]

Child raising has also been a major concern for utopian groups. Communal childcare has generally been provided by communities, either to supplement family parenting and to free the mother for other work roles, or else to remove the children from their parents in order to create the "new child" through an education shaped by the vision of the community. Socialist, spiritualist, theosophical, and New Age communities have typically created schools and new forms of education that become part of their outreach to the larger society.

FEMALE FOUNDERS AND LEADERS

Some utopian movements were founded or led by women. Others, particularly socialists, made sweeping claims to liberate women as equals to men in all things. Yet even with a woman founder or prophet, few utopian movements really empowered women as equals in power and authority. In the eighteenth and nineteenth centuries women were generally excluded from ordained ministry in churches (see chapter 7 on ordination) and could not vote or hold property (laws that were being challenged by the end of the century).

The Christian tradition did recognize a special role for the woman as prophetess, where she was seen as a passive vehicle for God working through her. Mystical millennialist movements with an androgynous view of God often believed that there must be a revelation of God in female form to complete human redemption. Female charismatic figures built on these views of woman as prophetess and bearer of the divine feminine.

Mother Ann Lee of the Shakers was seen as revealer of Divine Wisdom and the completion of the disclosure of Christ. She was both founder and charismatic preacher, holding unique authority in her lifetime. After her death in 1784, the leadership was passed to Joseph Meacham, who converted to Shakerism after having been a New Light Baptist revival leader. Meacham set up the organizational structure of the Shakers to reflect the dual male and female lines of God and revelation through a dual ordering of community. This duality did not assume gender equality but rather reflected a scheme of complementarity of masculine and feminine qualities, which made women auxiliaries of men in a separate female sphere.

Shaker communities were organized into strictly segregated male and female sections. There were parallel male and female leaders, elders and elderesses for spiritual leadership, and deacons and deaconesses for temporal affairs. Meacham appointed Lucy Wright as the first elderess. But women oversaw only the female sphere. Men controlled financial affairs and external relations of the community. Only toward the end of the nineteenth century, when women greatly outnumbered men, did Shaker women begin to insist on equal control of financial decisions. Some Shaker women in this era, particularly Anna White (1831–1910), Shaker historian and peace activist, began to interpret the Shaker religious vision and system as feminist.[32]

Several other women founders of religious movements made claims of direct revelatory experience that gave them unique authority. Jemima Wilkinson (1752–1819) said that she had risen from the dead and was animated by the Spirit of Christ, which descended into her body. She had been delegated to preach the final chance of repentance to humanity before the last judgment. There could be no successor to her role, although she did rely on several close women friends for leadership (document 8).

Mary Baker Eddy claimed to be imparting a new revelation in her *Science and Health*. She created a strong system of government in which she held unique authority as "Leader." Although women were empowered in Christian Science as "Practitioners" to pray with and heal the sick, Eddy preferred to gather around herself men subservient to her authority as financial officers, and she repelled other women who challenged her charismatic role. In a similar way Katherine Tingley claimed to be both a religious authority and active organizer of her theosophical establishment but preferred to surround herself with men who accepted her role.[33]

Frances Wright's founding constitution for her colony of Nashoba embodied strong principles of gender equality (document 9). But the slaves she sought to emancipate were totally subordinate and were treated much as they were on other plantations. While struggling for her own emancipation, Wright was oblivious to the marginalized role of other women, such as her sister Camilla, left to do the "wifely" duties while she lectured.[34]

Other prophetesses of the era, such as Barbara Heinemann, the vehicle of the Holy Spirit for the Amana Inspirationists, and Helen White, recipient of revelations that guided the Seventh Day Adventists, held unique roles that did not empower other women.[35] Amana women were subservient and marginalized from men as sexually dangerous, and they played no role in decision making (document 10). The Adventists also kept the regular leadership in male hands. The one foundress who empowered other women was Sanctificationist Martha McWhirter. Her movement helped other women to leave abusive husbands and created a sisterhood of shared spiritual power and authority, but it did so only by separating the women from their husbands.

Communal movements of the twentieth century reveal a similar ambivalence. Even women founders were not necessarily feminist. Dorothy Day rejected birth control, forcing her daughter, Tamara, to produce a large family that she could not support.[36] Evangelical male founders have insisted on returning women to traditional sexual and work roles, while New Age men tend to see women's liberation primarily as women's sexual availability. Only in a few communal groups with conscious feminist principles and strong female leadership, such as Twin Oaks, has there been an approximation of female equality in leadership. Feminism is most strongly represented in lesbian groups where men are excluded.

GENDER EQUALITY AND WOMEN'S WORK ROLES

The mixed record of utopian communities on the status of women is also evident in their division of labor. German pietist groups, such as Rappites and Zoarites, assumed the traditional division of labor where women did the cooking, cleaning, sewing, and female handicrafts, although both groups did give women the vote. The last leader of the Rappite community of Economy, Pennsylvania, was a woman, Suzie Duss. Among Shakers the traditional division of labor between female "indoor" work and male "outdoor" work was reinforced by a theology and anthropology built on complementarity. Only in the late twentieth century did women begin to become economic producers for the outside world, setting up stores to market their "fancy work" (ornamental sewing and handicrafts).[37]

Among the Oneida Perfectionists men also dominated in income-producing work and made the financial decisions. Women did the housework, laundry, and sewing for both men and women and also worked in printing and the silkspool factory. Boys continued their education to the college level, while girls left school at twelve to be incorporated into women's work and sex roles. Women did wear a bloomer outfit rather than skirts to allow them greater freedom of activity, and they were occasionally allowed to drive teams of horses or to work in the machine shop. Mothers had their children taken from them at the age of one to be raised in a separate nursery and school by male and female teachers. Many women experienced this as disempowering, an agonizing repression of their maternal affections.[38]

The Owenites advocated total equality between men and women, particularly under the influence of feminists Anna Wheeler and Frances Wright.[39] But Robert Owen himself was a patriarchal personality who assumed that the cooking, cleaning, sewing, and childcare would be done by women, not only for their own husbands and children but for all men in the community, many of whom were single. Women's equality was expressed by assuming that women would also do teaching, agricultural labor, and other productive work. The result was that middle-class women found themselves doing a double workday without the servants they were accustomed to in their homes. Owenite and other socialist communities were plagued by unhappy wives who had not chosen to join such communities and were treated as appendages to their husbands, without decision-making power or authority over their children and burdened by longer hours of more arduous labor than in the private family.[40]

A comparison of the Owenite experience with that of the Sanctificationist Women's Commonwealth at Belton, Texas, shows that the issue of women's oppression lies not just in doing particular kinds of work, such as cooking, sewing, and cleaning, but rather in the lack of economic control over the fruits of their labor. The Belton women built a prosperous society, reducing their work to four hours a day and enjoying ample time for cultural activities by collectivizing and marketing the fruits of women's traditional skills (document 11).

The contemporary commune, The Farm, presents a mixture of reversion to traditional male and female division of labor and gender role complementarity, together with efforts to modify male aggression and to idealize female mothering. Promiscuity is forbidden and abortion is discouraged, and high status is given to the midwives who assist the women in natural childbirth (document 12).

Twin Oaks is the contemporary communal society that seems to have most successfully equalized work roles. It began as a Skinnerite experiment, using behaviorist incentives for work. Twin Oaks has worked out a system of labor credits in which every member must do forty-seven hours of work a week but receives equal labor credit for all types of work, from car repair to childcare or backrubs. There is an organized effort to train and integrate women in traditional male work and vice versa (document 13).

Utopian movements are a Janus-faced phenomenon, looking for a new world of freedom and justice and yet also restoring self-sufficient agrarian, handicraft economies of the preindustrial world. They have often betrayed their promises to women, claiming liberation while practicing male domination. Few have sustained themselves beyond the founding generation, and they have had little impact on the larger society. But they continue to attract pioneering men and women deeply alienated from the dominant society and seeking a visionary alternative. In a time of growing economic and ecological crisis of the late twentieth century, one can expect this attraction to continue and to take new forms today.

Frances Wright (1795–1852), feminist and abolitionist, founded a racially integrated community near Memphis, where slaves she purchased at auctions could earn their freedom through work.

Katherine Tingley (1847–1929), leading theosophist and founder of the Pt. Loma Theosophical Community in Pt. Loma, California.

Anna White (1831–1910), eldress of the Shaker Community of Mount Lebanon, New York, was a leading historian and theoretician of the Shaker Community. She also gained prominence in the international peace movement.

Katherine Tingley, seated among the officers of the Theosophical Peace
Committee at the Temple of Peace, Pt. Loma, California.

Ina Gaskin and other Farm women
share the community aura with an
infant in 1970.

Women of the Oneida Perfectionist
Community in the nineteenth century
adopted short hairstyles to enhance
their freedom.

Documents

THE ANDROGYNOUS GOD
AND THE NEW HUMANITY

Document 1. The Shaker Bible:
Androgynous Deity and the Dual Order of Christ

The Shaker Bible, *Testimony of Christ's Second Appearing* (second edition published in 1810), held a comprehensive understanding of divine androgyny. The Shakers took the Genesis text that God created the human, male and female "in their image" to mean that God is both male and female. The plural form in the Genesis text was believed to reflect the discourse between the Father and Mother in Deity.[41]

THE ORDER OF DEITY, MALE AND FEMALE, IN WHOSE IMAGE MAN WAS CREATED. All who profess the Christian name, mutually believe in *one God,* the eternal *Father,* the Creator of heaven and earth; the original Father of spirits, of angels, and of men. They also believe in the first begotten *Son* of God in man; the Saviour of the world; the Redeemer of men. By the Son, the *true* being and *true character* of the Father, was first revealed: and, the existence of the Son, while it proved the existence of the *Eternal Father,* proved also the existence of the *Eternal Mother.*

Neither argument, nor illustration, would seem necessary to prove this! For, without both a *father* and *mother,* there can be neither son nor daughter; either natural or spiritual, visible or invisible! The visible order of *male* and *female,* by which all animated creation exists, proves the existence of the order, in the invisible world, from which our existence is primarily derived.

For "God said, *Let us make man in our image, after our likeness.*" "So God created man; *male and female* created he them, in his own image, and after his own likeness." To whom did God say, "Let US make man in OUR image?" Was it to the Son the Father spoke, as the divines (so called) have long taught, and still teach? How then came man to be created male and female? *father* and *son* are not male and female; but *father* and *mother* are male and female, as likewise are *son* and *daughter.* It was in this order that man was created. It was the order that existed in Deity, and superior spiritual intelligences before him, even *"before the world was;"* and in the image and after the likeness of which he was made, and placed as a probationer on the earth.

But it was not the Son with whom the Father spoke or counselled; or with any other being, angel or spirit, save only with the Eternal *Mother;* even *Divine Wisdom;* the Mother of all celestial beings! It was the *Eternal Two* who thus counselled together, and said, *"Let* US *make man in our image, after our likeness."* This is the same Eternal Mother who was with the Father, whom the *"Lord possessed in the beginning of his way, before his works of old; even from everlasting, before ever the earth was."*

And this was, and is, the voice of the Eternal Mother, through the inspiration of her holy spirit: "When the Lord prepared the heavens, I was there: When he appointed the foundations of the earth, then I was by him as one brought up with him; and I was daily his delight, rejoicing always before him. Now, therefore, hearken unto me, my children; for blessed are they that keep my ways."

Thus we may see the true order and origin of our existence, descending through proper mediations, not only in the state of innocent nature, but in the state of grace; proceeding from an Eternal *Parentage;* the Eternal Two, as distinctly Two, as *Power* and *Wisdom* are Two; and as the *Father* and *Mother* are two; yet immutably, unchangeably, *One Spirit:* One in *Essence* and in *substance,* One in *love* and in *design;* and so of the whole *spiritual* relationship in the new creation and household of God, *Father* and *Mother, Son* and *Daughter, Brother* and *Sister, Parents* and *Children;* of which the order in the natural creation is a similitude.

Document 2. A Rappite Hymn:
To Sophia, the Harmonists' Goddess

The Harmony Society, founded by George Rapp in 1803, took from Jacob Boehme a mystical idea that the original Adam was androgynous and the redeemed human could recover this original androgyny, transcending the Fall into sin and sex. Fervent devotion to Sophia, the virginal feminine aspect of the divine, lifts the devotee above carnal to spiritual, ecstatic union.[42]

O, Sophia, when thy loving hands carefully have guided my path
Through the thorny rose-bush, let my shadow soar;
You, the Harmonists' goddess, play now your golden strings;
Bind with loving golden chains those who follow you
to the designated goal.
Tell me, where do I find one like you,
Sophia, whom all revere,
Whom shall I entreat to show me, you, you angel?
You must be a goddess of radiant beauty
Who receives all who see her.
Sophia, from your glances rapture flows into my heart
When a friendly love delights my soul;
O the pure instincts your charm arouses in me;
This flame feeds the blessed heavenly love.
You surmise in silence all wild passion,
And uncover what is hidden within us;
For my endeavors rob me of all rest;
Beloved, would you desert me if I am unwise?
Beloved, let me experience the gentleness and faith;
If we were united, with your sweet caress
many an anxious hour would flee,
My wounds would be healed,
Pure fire would be drawn to love.
Let no Delilah sneak into my heart, and rob me of my strength!
Let me be constant and true,
Let nothing ever weaken me
through its false brilliance.
O heal what was wounded, cut what is unclean!
Give me, noble Virgin, a virgin-heart;
Give me a hero's spirit for my sufferings;
Let brightly burn in me the light of truth.
Sophia, I cannot let go, my heart burns with sweet fire;
My heart desires to hold you, and wants to let go all the mire
Until my spirit rests with you;
Nothing but you I want to love,
My heart is refreshed with increasing fiery-zest;
Call me yours, then I am free.

Document 3. Rebecca Jackson:
A Black Evangelist Empowered by the Mother God

Rebecca Jackson (1795–1891) was an evangelist preaching to independent Black Methodist Churches before the Civil War, often experiencing hostility from male preachers. She joined the Shakers in the 1840s with her close friend, Rebecca Perot, and drew particular inspiration from visions of the Mother nature of God. She founded a Black Shaker community in Philadelphia in 1851. Her diary of her visionary experiences covers the period of her life between 1830 and 1864.[43]

At night we went to meeting and while they were worshiping God, I saw the head and wings of their blessed Mother in the center of the ceiling over their heads. She appeared in a glorious color. Her face was round like a full moon, with the glory of the sun reflecting from her head, formed itself into a round circle with a glorious crown. And her face in the midst. And she was beautiful to look upon. Her wings were gold. She being in the center, she extended her golden wings across the room over the children, with her face toward me and said, "These are all mine," though she spoke not a word. And what a Mother's look she gave me. And at that look, my soul was filled with love and a motion was in my body, like one moving in the waves of the sea. I was happy. And I felt to embrace all her children in the arms of my soul. I understood by one of the discerners that there was sixteen angels in the room that night. I only saw our Blessed Mother, and that was as much as I was able to bear. . . .

Oh, how I love thee, my Mother! I did not know that I had a Mother. She was with me, though I knew it not, but now I know Her and She said I should do a work in this city, which is to make known the Mother of the New Creation of God. Because Thou art the Mother of all the children of Eve that ever can be saved, as Christ is the Father of all the regenerated children of Adam. And none can come to God in the new birth but through Christ the Father, and through Christ the Mother. . . . And I then understood the Mother I saw in the Deity, in 1834 or 1835, when the ministers shut their church doors against me and gave orders to their members not to suffer me to come in their doors, if they did they should be turned out of church, and the drunken man opened his house and said, "I don't belong to church. Let the woman come and hold her meeting in my house." And then it was that I had the first light on a Mother in the Deity. And then I could also see how often I had been led, comforted, and counseled in time of trial by a tender Mother and knowed it not.

Document 4. The Rebirth of the Goddess in Women's Spirituality

The *Pilgrim Warrior Songbook* is a compendium of songs used in women's spirituality groups seeing themselves as reclaiming the sacred in nature through ritual, music, dance, and meditation. The songbook is used in Pilgrim Warrior Training, an intense retreat experience of women in communion with nature. It reflects the spirituality adopted by many feminist communitarian groups. Sandra Boston de Sylvia founded Pilgrim Warrior Training in 1985.[44]

> Goddess of life, please speak through me
> Though your world is bloodied and torn.
> There'll be a full moon rising on the ruins of our dreams
> If your life force is not soon reborn.
> In ages gone by we were fed by the moon,
> And our strong hearts filled the world with love.
> We had power and laughter, and music in the sky,
> Dancing in your pale light from above.
> But they came with their one god the Father, and the son,
> And they shamed our priestesses with thorns
> And we bled and we're bleeding and our power is drained,
> Lost in the crashing of their swords.
> And now in this time, we gather again,
> And our open hearts fill the world with truth,
> With a vision of power that makes each other whole,
> Circling and spiralling the Earth.
> Goddess of life, you speak through me,
> Though our world is bloodied and torn.

There is a full moon rising on the birthing of our dreams
As your life force is this night reborn.

ALTERNATIVES
TO THE TRADITIONAL FAMILY

Document 5. Ephrata Cloister:
The Order of the Rose of Sharon

The female order of Ephrata Cloister lived by a written rule that identified the sisters as "the Rose, or the acceptable flower for Sharon's Spiritual betrothal with their celestial Bridegroom." Both their ascetic regime of life and their piety of spiritual marriage with Christ link these German Baptist sisters with classical Catholic sisterhoods. Ephrata Cloister existed from 1732 until 1770, and the rule for the sisters' order is dated 1745.[45]

What shall we say more of the quiet and justly in God enamoured souls, how they arrange their lives and conduct, so as to please only and alone their King of Heaven, whose kingdom is not of this world. Therefore our life and conduct cannot agree or conform to the world, whether it be eating and drinking,—sleeping or waking,—in clothing or other requisite things pertaining to the natural life. Thus we have taken it into hand to deny and refute such engagements, and have schooled ourselves to be moderate in our eat and drink, and subsist upon little, and that with scant preparation, not according to the usual desire of nature, but merely reflecting upon the necessity of human frailty, so that the spirit may the more readily accomplish its divine task. . . .

As we have first renounced all vanities of the world, our future conduct will be guided according to the discipline of the body. We will begin by contracting to the utmost our eating and drink, sleep and waking. So that our whole life and conduct be that of a suffering and dying pilgrim upon earth, for which reason we have divorced ourselves from the ways and customs of this world, and daily and hourly learn the manner and laws of our crucified Jesus, who instructs us in all things and taught us abnegation of self, and to take up the cross and follow him. . . .

What then further concerns our intercourse with and toward one another, is this: It is to be striven in all seriousness and diligence, that our life be modest, quiet, tranquil and retired, so that each becomes an example for the other, and exemplifies the secret course of life and communion with God. All levity and needless gossip with one another, or light laughter, is not to be thought of, nor shall it occur in this spiritual society. Therefore it is unnecessary to make much of this rule, as it is not considered and much less likely to occur. It is further to be said of the mood of the hearts and souls who have sacrificed their whole life unto God, and live for him in the silent contemplation of their heart, and walk in his ways.

Document 6. Oneida:
Complex Marriage and Family Planning

This extract from John Humphrey Noyes's pamphlet, *Male Continence,* describes how his discovery of this method of birth control arose from his concern with his wife's repeated pregnancies. Noyes linked birth control, eugenics, and women's right to voluntary motherhood and to sexual pleasure with equality between the sexes. These theories were the basis of complex marriage at Oneida, a community that Noyes founded in 1848.[46]

If amativeness is the first and noblest of the social affections and if the propagative part of the sexual relation was originally secondary, and became paramount by the subversion of order in the fall [as had previously been shown], we are bound to raise the amative office of the sexual organs into a distinct and paramount function.

Our theory, separating the amative from the propagative, not only relieves us of involuntary and undesirable procreation, but opens the way for *scientific* propagation. We are not opposed to the increase of population. We believe that the order to "multiply" attached to the race in its original integrity, and that propagation, rightly conducted and kept within such limits as life can fairly afford, is a blessing second only to sexual love. But we are opposed to involuntary procreation. A very large proportion of all children born under the present system are begotten contrary to the wishes of both parents, and lie nine months in their mother's womb under their mother's curse or a feeling little better than a curse. Such children cannot be well organized. We are opposed to *excessive,* and of course oppressive procreation, which is almost universal. We are opposed to random procreation, which is unavoidable in the marriage system. But we are in favor of intelligent well-ordered procreation. . . . We believe that good sense and benevolence will *very soon* sanction and enforce the rule that women shall bear children only when they choose. They have the principal burdens of breeding to bear, and they rather than men should have their choice of time and circumstances, at least till science takes charge of the business.

The separation of the amative from the propagative, places amative sexual intercourse on the same footing with other ordinary forms of social interchange. So long as the amative and propagative are confounded, sexual intercourse carries with it physical consequences which necessarily take it out of the category of mere social acts; . . . it is not to be wondered at that women, to a considerable extent, look upon ordinary sexual intercourse with more dread than pleasure, regarding it as a stab at their life, rather than a joyful act of fellowship.

But separate the amative from the propagative—let the act of fellowship stand by itself—and sexual intercourse becomes a purely social affair, the same in kind with other modes of kindly communion, differing only by its superior intensity and beauty. Thus the most popular, if not the most serious objection, to communistic love is removed. The difficulty so often urged, of knowing to whom children belong in complex-marriage, will have no place in a Community trained to keep the amative distinct from the propagative. . . . In a society trained to these principles, as propagation will become a science, so amative intercourse will have place among the "fine arts." Indeed, it will take rank above music, painting, sculpture, etc.; for it combines the charms and benefits of them all. There is as much room for cultivation of taste and skill in this department as in any.

The practice which we propose will give new speed to the advance of civilization and refinement. The self-control, retention of life, and ascent out of sensualism, which must result from making freedom of love a bounty on the chastening of physical indulgence, will raise the race to new vigor and beauty, moral and physical. And the refining effects of sexual love (which are recognized more or less in the world) will be increased a thousand-fold, when sexual intercourse becomes an honored method of innocent and useful communion, and each is married to all.

Document 7. The Mormons: Joseph Smith Commands Emma Smith's Assent to Polygyny

In 1843 Joseph Smith (1805–1844) had built a Mormon kingdom of sixteen thousand in Nauvoo, Illinois, over which he ruled as spiritual, economic, political, and military leader. Smith claimed divine revelation in reinstituting Old Testament polygyny, commanding his reluctant wife, Emma Smith, to accept the new teaching. As fear of Smith's power grew, he and his brother Hyrum were seized and lynched by a mob on June 27, 1844. The main body of Mormons, led by Brigham Young, maintained the practice of polygyny and migrated to Utah. Emma Smith and her son Joseph II remained behind, leading the Reorganized Church of Latter Day Saints, which rejected polygyny.[47]

Revelation on the Eternity of the Marriage Covenant including Plurality of Wives. Given through the Seer, in Nauvoo, Hancock County, Illinois, July 12, 1843

1. Verily, thus saith the Lord unto you, my servant Joseph, that inasmuch as you have inquired of my hand, to know and understand wherein I, the Lord, justified my servants Abraham, Isaac and Jacob; as also Moses, David and Solomon, my servants as touching the principle and doctrine of their having many wives and concubines: . . .

34. God commanded Abraham, and Sarah gave Hagar to Abraham to wife. And why did she do it? Because this was the law, and from Hagar sprang many people. This, therefore, was fulfilling, among other things, the promises.

35. Was Abraham, therefore, under condemnation? Verily, I say unto you, Nay; for I, the Lord, commanded it. . . .

40. I am the Lord thy God, and I gave unto thee, my servant Joseph, an appointment, and restore all things; ask what ye will, and it shall be given unto you according to my word: . . .

51. Verily, I say unto you, a commandment I give unto mine handmaid, Emma Smith, your wife, whom I have given unto you, that she stay herself, and partake not of that which I commanded you to offer unto her; for I did it, saith the Lord, to prove you all, as I did Abraham; and that I might require an offering at your hand, by covenant and sacrifice;

52. And let mine handmaid, Emma Smith, receive all those that have been given unto my servant Joseph, and who are virtuous and pure before me; and those who are not pure, and have said they were pure, shall be destroyed, I saith the Lord God;

53. For I am the Lord thy God, and ye shall obey my voice; and I give unto my servant Joseph, that he shall be made ruler over many things, for he hath been faithful over a few things, and from henceforth I will strengthen him.

54. And I command mine handmaid, Emma Smith, to abide and cleave unto my servant Joseph, and to none else. But if she will not abide this commandment, then shall my servant Joseph do all things for her, even as he hath said; and I will bless him and multiply him, and give unto him a hundredfold in this world, of fathers and mothers, brothers and sisters, houses and lands, wives and children, and crowns of eternal lives in the eternal worlds.

56. And again, verily I say, let mine handmaid forgive my servant Joseph his trespasses; and then shall she be forgiven her trespasses, wherein she has trespassed against me; and I, the Lord thy God, will bless her, and multiply her, and make her heart to rejoice. . . .

FEMALE FOUNDERS AND LEADERS

Document 8. Jemima Wilkinson: Public Universal Friend

Jemima Wilkinson grew up in a Quaker family in Pennsylvania and was converted in a New Light Baptist Revival in 1774. Calling herself the Public Universal Friend, she began a preaching career in 1776 after a death and resurrection experience in which she claimed that the Spirit of Christ had descended upon her. An account of this experience in her own handwriting was found in her Bible at her death.[48]

On the fourth Day of the 10th Month, on the Seventh Day of the weak, at night, a certain young-woman, known by the name of Jemima Wilkinson was seiz'd with this mortal disease. And on the 2d. Day of her illness, was render'd almost incapable of helping herself. And the fever continuing to increase until fifth Day of the Weak about midnight, She appear'd to meet the Shock of Death; which [illegible] the Soul.

The heavens were open'd And She saw too Archangels decending from the east, with golden crowns upon there heads, clothed in long white Robes, down to the feet; Bringing a sealed Pardon from the living God; and putting their trumpets to their mouth, proclaimed saying, Room, Room, Room, in the many Mansions of eternal glory for Thee and for everyone, that there is one more call for, that the eleventh hour is not yet past with them, and the day of grace is not yet over with them. For every one that will come, may come, and partake of the waters of life freely, which is offered to Sinners without money, and without price.

And the Angels said, The time is at hand, when God will lift up his hand, a second time, to recover the remnant of his People, whos day is not yet over; and the Angels said, The Spirit of Life from God, had descended to earth, to warn a lost and guilty, perishing dying World, to flee from the wrath which is to come; and to give an Invitation to the lost Sheep of the house of Israel to come home; and was waiting to assume the Body which God had prepared, for the Spirit to dwell in. . . . And then taking her leave of the family between the hour of nine & ten in the morning dropt the dying flesh & yielded up the Ghost. And according to the declaration of the Angels,—the Spirit took full possession of the Body it now animates.

Ruth Prichard, a follower of Jemima Wilkinson, described her own conversion and the early days of the preaching career of the Universal Friend.[49]

I was sincerely a Seeker; and did not mean to mock the Sacred Name. . . . While I was thus a lost Enquirer, and as I was then must never have seen the Smiling Face of Jesus; Lo! The Universal Friend was to pass thro' Wallingford where I kept school: And I with some more went on First Day, (hearing the Friend was to Preach at such a House) about 7 Miles to hear. And blessed be the day I went; O! Blessed be the

Lord for giving me this great Day of visitation: And I do testify unto Thee, my dear Friend it was the Voice that spake as never Man Spake. It is that which if obey'd will bring Light Life & Love unto the Soul; That peace that the world can neither give nor take away. And there is nothing below the Sun shall tempt me back, the Lord helping me.

The Friend of Sinners began to serve In the year 1777 When this Nation was still in arms and America had embroiled her hands in human blood. There appeared the Messenger of Peace going from City to City and from Village to Village proclaiming the News of Salvation to all that would Repent and believe the Gospel. The Friend was not staid by guards of armed men. She went through to visit the poor condemned prisoners in their Chains. Naked swords shook over the Friend's head, she was not in terror because of the mighty Power of the Lord. No storms or severity of weather could hinder the Friend's journey to speak unto Souls like the unwearied Sun, Determ'd its faithful race to run, spreading heavenly benediction far abroad that wandering sinners might return to God. And Traveling far & wide to spread the glad tidings & news of Salvation to a lost and perishing & dying World who have all gone astray like Lost Sheep;—The Lord has lifted up his Hand To the Gentiles and set his Hand the Second Time to recover the remnant of the lost Sheep of the House of Israel. He that hath ears to hear, let him hear.

Document 9. Frances Wright:
The Vision of Equality at Nashoba

Frances Wright (1795–1852), radical feminist, abolitionist, and socialist, founded Nashoba in 1825 in Tennessee as an abolitionist community in which Negro slaves would earn their freedom. Her plans for this community, enunciated in the *New Harmony Gazette,* also embodied her dreams of a society freed from any subordination of women to men. Lack of practical management led to its demise, and in 1830 Wright conveyed the remaining emancipated slaves to Haiti.[50]

Political liberty may be said to exist in the United States of America. . . . *Moral liberty exists no where.* By political liberty we may understand the liberty of speech and of action without incurring the violence of authority or the penalties of law. By moral liberty may we not understand the *free exercise of the liberty of speech and of action,* without incurring the intolerance of popular prejudice and ignorant public opinion? . . . It is much to have the fetters broken from our limbs, but yet better is it to have them broken from the mind. It is much to have *declared* men free and equal, but it shall be more when they are rendered so; when means shall be sought and found, and employed to develope all the intellectual and physical powers of all human beings, with regard to sex or condition, class, race, nation or color; and when men shall learn to view each other as members of one great family, with equal claims to enjoyment and equal capacities for labor and instruction, admitting always the sole differences arising out of the varieties exhibited in individual organization. . . .

The Institution of Nashoba being thus founded on the broad basis of human liberty and equality, every provision made by the legal act of the founder, as well as the subsequent regulations of the trustees are shaped in accordance with it. . . . It is declared in the deed of the founder, that no individual can be received as member, but after a noviciate of six months, and then only by a *unanimous* vote of the resident proprietors. It is also provided that the admission of a husband shall not involve that of a wife, nor the admission of a wife that of a husband, nor the admission of either or both of the parents that of the children *above the age of fourteen.* . . . The marriage law existing without the pale of the Institution, is of no force within that pale. No woman can forfeit her individual rights or independent existence, and no man assert over her any rights or power whatsoever, beyond what he may exercise over her free and voluntary affections; nor may any woman assert claims to the society or peculiar protection of any individual of the other sex, beyond what mutual inclination dictates and sanctions, while to every individual member of either sex is secured the protection and friendly aid of all. . . .

The tyranny usurped by the matrimonial law over the most sacred of the human affections, can perhaps only be equalled by that of the unjust public opinion, which so frequently stamps with infamy, or condemns to martyrdom the best-grounded and most generous attachments, which ever did honor to the human heart, simply because unlegalized by human ceremonies, equally idle and offensive in the

form and mischievous in the tendency. . . . Let us look to the victims—
not of pleasure, not of love, nor yet of their own depravity, but of those
ignorant laws, ignorant prejudices, ignorant codes of morals, which
condemn one portion of the female sex to vicious excess, another to as
vicious restraint, and all to defenceless helplessness and slavery, and generally the whole of the male sex to' debasing licentiousness, if not to
loathsome brutality. . . . Let us teach the young mind to reason, and the
young heart to feel, and instead of shrouding our bodies, wants, desires,
senses, affections and faculties in mystery, let us court enquiry, and show
that acquaintance with our own nature can alone guide as to judicious
practice, and that in the consequence of human actions, exists the only
true test of their virtue or their vice.

Document 10. Barbara Heinemann Landmann:
Amana Inspirationist *Werkzeuge*

Barbara Heinemann Landmann was regarded as a *Werkzeuge*
or incarnate vehicle of the Holy Spirit through whom the Amana
Inspirationists, a German pietist sect who settled in Iowa, obtained
direct guidance from God. Despite this female leadership role, the
community held repressive views of women, as is evidenced by this
account written by Charles Nordhoff, who visited them in 1874.[51]
Celibacy, although not enforced, was encouraged as a higher spiritual
state, and women were seen as dangerous sexual temptresses.

The sex, I believe, is not highly esteemed by these people, who
think it dangerous to the Christian's peace of mind. One of their most
esteemed writers advises men to "fly from intercourse with women, as a
very highly dangerous magnet and magical fire." Their women work
hard and dress soberly; all ornaments are forbidden. To wear the hair
loose is prohibited. Great care is used to keep the sexes apart. In their
evening and other meetings, women not only sit apart from men, but
they leave the room before the men break ranks. Boys are allowed to
play only with boys, and girls with girls. There are no places or occasions for evening amusements, where the sexes might meet. On Sunday
afternoons the boys are permitted to walk in the fields; and so are the
girls, but these must go in another direction. "Perhaps they meet in the

course of the walk," said a member to me, "but it is not allowed." At meals and in their labors they are also separated. With all this care to hide the charms of the young women, to make them, as far as dress can do so, look old and ugly, and to keep the young men away from them, love, courtship, and marriage go on at Amana as elsewhere in the world. The young man "falls in love," and finds ways to make his passion known to its object; he no doubt enjoys all the delights of courtship, intensified by the difficulties which his prudent brethren put in his way; and he marries the object of his affect, in spite of her black hood and her sad-colored little shawl, whenever he has reached the age of twenty-four. . . .

In every village four or five of the older and more experienced elders meet each morning to advise together on business. This council acts, as I understand, upon reports of those younger elders who are foremen and have charge of different affairs. These in turn meet for a few minutes every evening, and arrange for the next day's work. Women are never members of these councils, nor do they hold, as far as I could discover, any temporal or spiritual authority, with the single exception of their present spiritual head, who is a woman of eighty years. . . .

They regard the utterances, while in the trance state, of their spiritual head as given from God; and believe—as is asserted in the Catechism—that evils and wrongs in the congregation will be thus revealed by the influence, or, as they say, the inspiration or breath of God; that in important affairs they will thus receive the divine direction; and that it is their duty to obey the commands thus delivered to them.

There were "inspired instruments" before Christian Metz. Indeed, the present "instrument," Barbara Landmann, was accepted before him, but by reason of her marriage fell from grace for a while. . . . The words of "inspiration" are usually delivered in the public meetings, and at funerals and other solemn occasions. They have always been carefully written down by persons specially appointed to that office; . . .

The "inspired" words are not always addressed to the general congregation, but often to individual members; and their feelings are not spared. Thus in one case Barbara Landmann, being "inspired," turned upon a sister with the words, "But you wretched creature, follow the true counsel of obedience"; and to another: "And you, contrary spirit, how much pain do you give to our hearts. You will fall into everlasting pain, torture, and unrest if you do not break your will and repent, so that you may be accepted and forgiven by those you have offended, and who have done so much for you."

The warnings, prophecies, reproofs, and admonitions, thus delivered by the "inspired instrument," are all, as I have said, carefully written down, and in convenient time printed in yearly volumes, entitled "Year-Books of the True Inspiration Congregations: Witnesses of the Spirit of God, which happened and were spoken in the Meetings of the Society, through the Instruments, Brother Christian Metz and Sister B. Landmann," with the year in which they were delivered. . . .

The celebration of the Lord's Supper is their greatest religious event. It is held only when the "inspired instrument" directs it, which may not happen once in two years; and it is thought so solemn and important an occasion that a full account of it is sometimes printed in a book. . . . The present inspired instrument being very aged, I asked whether another was ready to take her place. They said No, no one had yet appeared; but they had no doubt God would call some one to the necessary office. They were willing to trust him, and gave themselves no trouble about it.

GENDER EQUALITY
AND WOMEN'S WORK ROLES

Document 11. The Women's Commonwealth:
Autoemancipation

The Sanctificationists originated from a Methodist women's prayer meeting started in 1866 by Martha McWhirter, who led the group to separate from the local church and then from their husbands' households, forming by 1876 an economically self-supporting community that became increasingly prosperous. In 1898 the women moved to Washington, D.C., where they bought a large house and also a farm in Maryland, renaming themselves the Women's Commonwealth. The following account was written by George Garrison, who spent two weeks with the community in 1892.[52]

The original leader of the Sanctificationists, and their present head, is Mrs. Martha McWhirter. . . . Her convictions were most effectively set forth in a ladies' weekly prayer meeting which was held from house to house in the town for some years succeeding her "sanctification." This finally merged into a meeting of her followers alone. . . . From this time Mrs. McWhirter and her followers were more and more out of harmony with the churches. They developed and dwelt upon their peculiar views in regard to sanctification, and declined to be any longer subject to pastoral control or advice. . . .

The communistic practices of the Sanctificationists had a definite beginning near the end of 1879. Previous to this time Mrs. McWhirter had refused to accept money from her husband for household expenses, and had managed to provide it herself by selling milk and butter from four or five cows which she kept. This refusal seems to have originated in the circumstance that he threatened to withhold what she required unless she would account for him for its use. Others of the Sisters followed her example. At the time which has been mentioned they had a meeting upon one occasion and discussed the propriety of living in common, dwelling mainly upon the question as to whether their faith required it. While the discussion was in progress one of the Sisters, who had been supporting herself by teaching school, and had saved, in this way, twenty dollars, took the money and laid it down in the presence of all, saying that there was what she had. This money was the beginning of a common fund. Mrs. McWhirter was treasurer, and the fund grew by the addition, at irregular intervals, of such amounts as the Sisters had been respectively able to lay by. It was paid in mostly at the meetings held each week, and averaged at first perhaps fifteen dollars weekly. The money was saved in various ways, among them being the sale of milk and butter and of rag carpets, for the weaving of which they bought a loom out of the common fund and contributed material and labor. . . .

Pretty soon a use was found for this fund. One of the Sisters had lost her home as well as her husband by a divorce, and she had to be provided for. A room was rented for her from Mr. McWhirter, and the rent was paid from the fund. After a time he gave his wife the rent that should be collected subsequently, and she declined to collect it, thereby causing this drain to cease. During all this time any one of the Sisters who had anything about her house she could spare would give it to any other one that stood in need of it.

In August, 1882, some of the Sisters overheard the complaint of a lady living in the town that she could get no one to wash for her family. They sent to her for clothes, and washed them at Mr. McWhirter's house. The story went abroad, and they were soon asked to do work of the same nature for others. They consented, and the business grew until, without any soliciting on their part, they were unable to meet the demand for their services. At length it became the source of quite a considerable income to them. The washing was done in the old-fashioned way, without the help of any machinery. It passed from house to house among the Sisters until it came to one of them whose husband had most decided objections to its being done upon his place; so when they gathered there, at an appointed time, for that purpose, he drove them away with sticks and stones. In doing this he struck his wife and unintentionally no doubt, cut a quite severe gash in her head. That evening the Sisters gathered at the house again, where those of them most prominent in the affair were arrested on the charge of assault. They were tried, and four were fined twenty dollars and costs each, making the total about one-hundred dollars. This was paid out of the common fund.

The Sister at whose home the trouble occurred went back there no more after the trial, but lived with one or another of the rest until the next spring, when it was thought best to provide her with a house. Accordingly, a lot belonging to Mr. McWhirter was selected for its location, the material was purchased out of the common fund, and the work was done by the Sisters themselves, with the help of the young sons of two of them, and with about two days' assistance from a regular house-builder. The building was nearly completed before Mr. McWhirter knew of it. As soon as he learned what was going on, he expostulated earnestly with his wife, but did not interfere with the occupation of the house by the Sister for whom it was intended. Mrs. McWhirter claimed that as she had brought a large portion of the McWhirter estate into the family herself, she was exercising a moral, if not a legal, right to take possession of a part of it. . . .

From the summer of 1883 the Sisters began to make money fast. Just after that time the receipts from the sale of milk and butter were sometimes five or six dollars per day, from that of wood eight or ten dollars per day, and from the laundry work as much as two hundred dollars per month. . . . The community now owns property worth at cash value fifty thousand dollars, nearly all of which has been purchased with the surplus of the common fund. . . . The net income of the community is about eight hundred dollars per month. Most of this is from the hotel, a considerably smaller portion being from the rents of store houses and dwellings. The laundry, as it is now managed, brings in no money, but simply reduces the general expense account. The management of the hotel, together with that of the farm, of which only a part is rented, is very systematic. Usually two of the women and four of the children are kept at the farm, which is about two miles from the hotel. During the winter the weaving of rag carpets is carried on at the former. . . . There is a change all round, including the farm, every month, and the cooks are now changed every two weeks. The average day's work is only about four hours, and, when that is done, each is free to amuse herself as she chooses. . . .

The Sisters spend their leisure in various ways, such as reading, practising on the piano, painting, etc. No uniform is worn by the Sanctificationists, nor have they ever adopted one, though it has been their custom to dress plainly. There seems to be a tendency among them now to allow themselves a little more latitude in this respect. Formerly they wore sun-bonnets without exception, but now they wear hats a great deal.

While the Sisters do not visit, and while they are usually to be found only where their work is, they have not despised to travel and see something of the world. In the summer of 1880, the whole band visited New York, making quite an excursion of it. . . . It is the desire of the Sisters to make their community as complete within itself and as independent of the world as practicable. To this end they keep up a school for the smaller children, which is taught by one of themselves. It is kept up most of the time, but has not been very regular in its hours since the hotel was occupied. Only the younger members of the community are taught, and the instruction is not very extensive including only the elementary branches up to geography, grammar and arithmetic. The community has also its own dentist, in the person of one of the Sisters. She has learned the art mostly from books, with some instruction from dental surgeons who practice in Belton and the neighboring town of Temple. She does all the work for the band, extracting teeth, filling them, and putting in new sets whenever necessary. An office has been properly equipped for her, and she has done a considerable amount of work for the boarders at the hotel and the people of the town. . . .

As to the present faith of the Sanctificationists, it is worth while perhaps to say but little. They claim to be "living the Bible," but, of course, the life is according to their own interpretation of the book. They do not hesitate to work on Sunday when it is either necessary or convenient. They no longer have formal worship of any kind. In this, they have changed greatly from what they were at first. They then had regular and frequent devotional exercises. At present the nearest approach to such exercises is to be found in their discussion among themselves of their religious experience, which they try to interpret so that it will serve to guide them. They frequently obtain this guidance from dreams; but Mrs. McWhirter claims that they get their greatest help from a delicate sense which belongs to the entire community rather than to any individual member, and which enables them to detect any mistake they have made or false step they have taken, by causing an unpleasant reaction to be felt by the whole body.

There seems to be at work in this community no disorganizing force due to dissatisfaction arising from equality of service. No one appears to toil unwillingly, or to think that the others do less than their respective shares. The whole matter is summed up by Mrs. McWhirter in the statement that it is the work of God, under whose protection the Sisters live, and by whom a way will always be opened for them. The people of Belton sum it up by saying that Mrs. McWhirter is the centre and the soul of the organization, that its prolonged existence and success are due to her really extraordinary powers and to her strange influence over her followers, and that when she is gone there will be the end of it.

Document 12. The Farm: Spiritual Midwifery

The Farm originated in the popular New Age lectures of Stephen Gaskin in Haight-Ashbury, San Francisco, in the late 1960s. After a five-month tour of the United States, Gaskin and two hundred fifty followers founded The Farm, a rural commune in Tennessee. The Farm is characterized by a strong emphasis on "natural" living that encourages mutual sexual pleasure and childbearing. Ina May, Gaskin's wife, has been the leader in developing a special role of women as midwives who guide women through childbirth as a peak experience of unity with the cosmos.[53]

Every birth is Holy. I think that a midwife must be religious, because the energy she is dealing with is Holy. She needs to know that other people's energy is sacred. Spiritual midwifery recognizes that each and every birth is the birth of a child of God. The midwife's job is to do her best to bring both the mother and the child through their passage alive and well and to see that the sacrament of birth is kept Holy. The Vow of the Midwife has to be that she will put out one hundred percent of her energy to the mother and to the child that she is delivering until she is certain that they have safely made the passage. This means that she must put the welfare of the mother and child first, before that of herself and her own family, if she has to make a choice of that kind. A spiritual midwife has an obligation to put out the same love to all children in her care, regardless of size, shape, color, or parentage. We are all One. *The kid in front of you is just the same as your kid. We are all One.* By religious, I mean that compassion must be a way of life for her. Her religion has to come forth in her practice, in the way she makes her day-to-day, her moment-to-moment decisions. It cannot be just theory. Truly caring for people cannot be a part-time job.

During a birthing there may be fantastic physical changes that you can't call anything but miraculous. This daily acquaintance with mira-cles—not in the sense that it would be devalued by its commonness, but that its sacredness be recognized—this familiarity with miracles has to be part of the tools of the midwife's trade. Great changes can be brought about with the passing of a few words between people or by the mid-wife's touching the woman or the baby in such a way that great physical changes happen.

For this touch to carry the power that it must, the midwife must keep herself in a state of grace. She has to take spiritual vows just the same as a yogi or a monk or a nun takes inner vows that deal with how they carry out every aspect of their life. So must a midwife do this if she is to have touch that has any potency. A person who lives by a code that is congruent with life in compassion and truth actually keys in and agrees with the millions-of-years-old biological process of childbirth.

If the midwife finds habits in herself where she does not always behave as if we are all One, she must change these habits and replace them with better ones. A midwife must constantly put out effort to stay compassionate, open and clear in vision, for love and compassion and spiritual vision are the most important tools of her trade. She must know that she has free will and that she can change if she needs to. This is the spiritual discipline that she must maintain in order to be fit to do her work, just as an Olympian athlete must keep her or his physical and mental discipline to stay in top condition.

To one who understands the true body of *shakti,* or the female principle, it is obvious that she is very well-designed by God to be self-regulating. We are the perfect flower of eons of experiment—every single person alive has a perfectly unbroken line of ancestors who were able to have babies naturally, back for several millions of years. We are the hand-selected best at it. The spiritual midwife, therefore, is never without the real tools of her trade: she uses the millennia-old, God-given insights and intuition as her tools—in addition to, but often in place of, the hospital's technology, drugs, and equipment.

One of the midwife's most valuable tools is the same intimate knowledge of the subtle physiology of the human body that is the province of yoga. The spiritual midwife brings about states of consciousness in women that allow physical energy transformations of great power, great beauty and great utility.

Document 13. Twin Oaks:
Labor Credits and Gender Equality

Twin Oaks, founded in 1967 in rural Virginia, espouses no single ideology. The community sponsors both men's and women's gatherings, which have a component of spiritual communion with nature, and observes seasonal celebrations of the winter and summer solstices and spring and fall equinoxes.[54] Committed to gender equality, the people of Twin Oaks work by a labor credit system designed to overcome gendered division of labor. This excerpt is taken from an essay by Batya Weinbaum, a socialist feminist who lived and worked at Twin Oaks in the early 1980s.[55]

At Twin Oaks, the community, initially not socialist or feminist in intent, is both, in function and in fact. The labor credit system I will describe . . . is run to meet people's needs, not for ego enhancement and profit, and so many of the structural requirements for the liberation of women are met. The community operates a hammock industry from which income is derived, and a farm on which some foods are grown, animals raised, and animal products processed. Twin Oaks also organizes consumption for each of its seventy members. Thus, it serves as a collective production and consumption unit, requiring little circulation of money to purchase goods and services for household and individual purposes. Because of the collective living, there is also a reduction in amounts spent on stoves, kitchen equipment, furniture, or decoration.

Every individual of age works the quota hours—forty-seven a week—and, in exchange, can live, eat, and receive an $11 monthly allowance. Forty-seven hours might sound steep, but on the outside, income-producing labor, in addition to commuting and organizing personal services (going to the bank, shopping, cleaning, cultural stimulation, etc.) takes at least sixty hours a week per individual. Eleven dollars a month is low, but necessary outlay is less: for example, yoga classes on the grounds by members are free, and one needn't pay for car upkeep or subways. And you don't need a clothes budget as you can get what you need to wear in the centralized, free thrift store known as Commie Clothes.

All labor for the quota is valued equally, although this wasn't always the case. In the beginning, if the work was desirable, it was given one credit; if it was undesirable, more credits were assigned to give people the incentive to do it. For example, you could get paid more credits for cleaning toilets than construction work, which many wanted to do. This system was dropped as being too complicated to figure, and now an hour of laundry earns credit equal to an hour of auto repair or community planning.

Thus, domestic work disappears for the individual "homemaker" as she joins the community living-situation and no longer carries the double burden of work for the employer and work for the house. . . . Additionally, since work in production does not depend on unseen labor servicing the home, and income-pooling is not facilitating capital accumulation by means of division of labor by sex and age, the basis is laid for breaking down much of the "standard" social divisions. Men can and do work in child care, laundry, and kitchen: women can and do work in auto mechanics, planning, and construction. A woman doesn't have to become a "superwoman," handling the running of a home while she aims for a promotion at the office. Neither male nor female is at a particular disadvantage as both must work forty-seven hours a week and neither has individual or total home responsibilities. Also there are no full-time jobs: someone working ten hours a week in the auto shop can also work twenty hours a week as kitchen manager. As a result, doing work out of one's traditional sex role does not have to be threatening and undermining to the society or to the individual.

Of course, affirmative action is still necessary to get women into non-traditional jobs. This does not dissipate the energies of the few feminist women there. The economic argument, that it takes more time to train women than to operate with peers, is still heard, yet it is encouraging that those who run the shop make an effort to rectify the situation. They teach auto mechanics to girls and encourage women to sign up for six-week car-maintenance shifts on a rotation basis. All this can occur because there is no structural economic basis supporting psychological prejudice, intimidation, and conditioning. . . .

The institution of motherhood has been reevaluated and the traditional experience of childhood along with it. This is the third way labor-crediting is subversive. Decisions are made at the community level about how many births can be handled each year. In the history of the community, this began as an economic issue since pregnancy is considered work and the labor-credit system grants pregnancy hours. The pregnant woman is also able to earn labor credits throughout her pregnancy, and her absence from "normal" labor-credit work is not extensive because, if she is not feeling well, she can produce a product in bed, sew for Commie Clothes, or have a planning meeting scheduled in her small-group living situation so that she can attend without much exertion. The separation between work and home being obliterated, a woman doesn't require a long leave-of-absence and she can be reintegrated into work quite easily. . . .

Besides areas in which there is massive subversive potential, there are important process issues: first, dominance of female values, or values that have been associated with women rather than with men in the dominant culture. For example, nurturance rather than intimidation is the norm in the learning-experience. . . . Trying to break out of the sex role and acquire non-traditional skills is considered the norm rather than an oddity in the environment. . . .

A final step in the process of challenging patriarchy is what I want to call the "economic efficiency breakdown." There are those who think that affirmative action and task rotation are not economically efficient and that investing labor time in teaching women construction detracts from reaching other investment goals. But the counter-argument is also heard: the goal is to improve the standard of living, which might be different from improving the material wealth of the community. If it can be argued that breaking down sex-role socialization improves the quality of living, that androgyny is better than rigid sex-role socialization, then gains for women might be made. But to argue that a less repressive, freer environment leads to greater efficiency in the long run would be an even bolder statement. . . . Certainly, living at TO is . . . an attempt to structure a more humane society which inadvertently drops many of the oppressive structures based on the division of labor and the women's "double duty" unseen domestic and consumption work.

CHAPTER NINE

Seeing Red
American Indian Women Speaking About Their Religious and Political Perspectives

Inés Maria Talamantez

Documents

Deep within
I am wild in my sorrow
I am a woman

        a working woman
        a good Apache woman
        a gathering woman
        a Red World woman
        a brown Chicana woman
        a mother woman
        a loving woman
        a blue woman
        a eucalyptus woman
        a soft woman
        a loud woman
        a resisting woman
        a trouble making woman
        a hunting woman
        a moving woman
        a quiet woman
        a dancing woman
        a singing woman
        a pollen woman
        a spirit woman
        a desert woman
        a mountain woman
        an ocean woman
        a White World woman
        a trail making woman
        a changing woman

Look around you
Look around you

        What do you see
        What do you see
        What will you do
        What will you do

When will we walk together
When will we walk together[1]

WITH the dawn breaking in the east over the Sacramento Mountains of New Mexico, the barrenness of the white gypsum sand dunes glimmers to the west. The early desert sun of the Tularosa Valley is already hot. I was born less than one hundred miles south from where I am now standing, and I am remembering what the women of this place have taught me. It is their stories that have helped me explore who I am today. They have given me the sense of self and place. Learning our stories as we move through our lives, collecting and gathering until we fill our baskets to the brim (or our files to overflowing, and we move on to entering our ideas on computer disks), we are reminded of the minds and imaginations of our ancestors and how they acquired the knowledge necessary to survive the struggle throughout the centuries.

Central to these teachings from Native American traditions are the elaborate explanations about the beginning of the cosmos and the role of female deities who were present at the time of creation. The role of many Native American women today is still influenced by the teachings passed on to us by those that went before us and their concern for the generations to follow. Acknowledging the perseverance of indigenous women for social justice and religious freedom is as necessary for Native American women as for American feminists. In a world where distorted images of native women's spirituality abound, spiritually impoverished American women often appropriate those aspects of our lives that fill their needs. Our struggle continues.

Those who write without knowing the truth provide glib, shallow accounts of what they consider to be "other," and the perspective they take places them beyond accountability to those on whose lives they draw for spiritual nourishment. Neither are they native women, nor do they want to be connected to their own female ancestors. They are detached from knowledge of their own past and seek meaning in the lives of others who are in no position to object. This is offensive and constitutes a form of intellectual imperialism. The belief that the traditions of others may be appropriated to serve the needs of self is a peculiarly Western notion that relies on a belief that knowledge is disembodied rather than embedded in relationships, intimately tied to place, and entails responsibilities to others and a commitment and discipline in learning.

Feminist explorations of the distinctive knowledge that women's distinctive experiences generate provide a helpful perspective on the struggle of native women to be heard and to see their traditions respected and their truths acknowledged. Diane Bell, Australian feminist, has argued that women's experience of subordination predisposes them to a reflexive stance on their lives and those of others.[2] Within this schema, Native American women may speak in a specially true and insightful voice. Of course, men as well may write of their experiences, which reflect their truths and their lives, but their narratives do not always represent the clearest expositions of what it means to be a gendered, colonized subject.

This work is not just a research project; it is part of my life. I am connected to these women and their truths. We are taught in our cultures that as young girls we are moving through the world with others, that we are moving in relationships with others, including the lives of the flora and the fauna. We are told to respect the lives and movements of others. The invisible forces at work in the natural world are revealed through the wondrous world created in the sacred narratives, the stories that provide the frame of reference through which we are instructed about our heritage as women of Native America. It is this aesthetic, created in the minds of our ancestors, that has given us a different way of looking at and thinking about time and place. The cycles of growth in the natural world or the movement of the sun, for example, explicate time as cyclical rather than linear, as represented on my digital wristwatch, on which of course I also depend.

The natural cycles of growth are closely watched, as is decay. Complex rituals embedded in our ceremonial structures provide a perspective into the world of the supernatural. The sacred is reflected in everyone and in everything, in our minds and worlds, in the moving bodies of dancers and in the voices of singers. However, we face profound political and sociocultural challenges in keeping our cultures alive through creative and religious introspection and work and not letting the devastating forces of change overwhelm us. Yet we know through understanding our ceremonies that transformation brings change. It is, however, the knowledge gained through ritual transformation that then gives us the responsibility to apply the lessons learned to our lives and the lives of those around us. It is here that we understand both the values and the social systems under which all individuals in diverse cultural locations must operate in order to maintain balance within their societies.

The indigenous framework within which many of us work reveals the systems of relatedness, obligation, and respect that govern the lives of many native women. There is a driving purpose behind our work; we know what we are expected to do. There are political commitments to social justice, concerns for what constitutes activism in our present day, complex issues of identity and naming ourselves. The political survival issues of the day—land claims, freedom of religion, environmental racism, lack of appropriate health, education, and employment, for example—engage us as persons who labor under the twin oppressions of being woman and native. This narrative of inquiry requires deep reflection. It is an exploration in both humility and authority. Insight is gained through analysis, interpretation, and critique.

In practice today our lives are shaped by the complex intertwining of several controlling regimes that discriminate against us in a variety of ways. Native American women living on reservations are subject to the will of tribal governments, which are under the control of the Bureau of Indian Affairs, an arm of the Department of the Interior. The concerns of women are not a priority for the bureaucrats or the elected officials, any more than they are in the dominant society. For urban Indian women, who are not registered in federal government records—that is, have no number indicating that they are enrolled and are therefore "legitimate Indians" according to the government—social services and benefits are difficult or almost impossible to obtain. For example, those who do make it through the school system and plan to attend a junior college or university are denied access to scholarships unless they can prove that they are Indian. No one else in this country has to prove their ethnicity; why do we?

Health care issues are also viewed in this way. If you are enrolled, you qualify for federal Indian Health programs, but if you are not enrolled, you are just another minority woman seeking health care. In reforming the health care system, the particular needs of those of us who are women and native need to be addressed. We are American women. We are indigenous women. We share many of the health concerns of other American women, but we have been disproportionately exposed to some additional health risks. In seeking to heal our bodies, we look to religion, land, and medicine in ways that the present health care system finds difficult to accommodate. As Meredith Begay (document 1) tells us, medicine, health, ceremony are all intertwined, and her work as a cross-cultural communicator shows one path forward.

Churches are also guilty. Many Christian churches, especially in areas largely populated by Indians, still require that their parishioners give up participating in their own religious traditions if they wish to be Christians. This discrimination has been met in a variety of ways. Some native women continue to resist completely all forms of Christianity and practice their own native ways, which beautifully blend culture and spirituality in one complete worldview. Other women continue to follow their cultural ways and have found a method that allows them to be Indians from a specific culture but yet accept and embrace Christian dogma. And of course some Indian women have accepted Christianity completely and have opted for assimilation into the dominant American culture.

The struggle for religious freedom and a land-based pedagogy require that we reconfigure the roles of native women and their distinctive features. We are looking at tangled historical processes and systems that integrate cultural, political, and ecological dimensions. We need a new schemata, one that frees us from the constraints of a Western patriarchal paradigm of control, one that takes us beyond victim status and blame. We need a framework that enables us to understand our own cultures as well as allows us to teach about them. We must not forget, however, that we are working within institutions that have continued to exert control over the very substance of our research, the publication of our work—institutions that have the power to determine what counts as scholarship. It will take reflection and a willingness to scrutinize the power of church and state before native and non-native, men and women can share in a meaningful way. It will be a long time before we can be equal partners in a dialogue. We women are at a historical juncture where as workers, mothers, scholars, healers, poets, we have the necessary tools to move forward. Our fight for religious freedom is a fight for life and for land. If you are fighting for social justice, you are fighting for our freedom. If you are raising children, you are fighting for our freedom. If you are writing as a woman, you are fighting for our freedom.

VOICES OF WISDOM

Having articulated the underlying philosophy, albeit in the abstract, and alluded to the complexity of the context within which we give expression to our beliefs, let me now ground this discussion in the specific writings of Native American scholars. Indian societies, long before the coming of

Europeans to America, were in the process of significant and dynamic development in the areas of religious practice, economic production, and artistic and material achievements. These were hardly simple, savage, or "primitive" peoples. Alfonso Ortiz from San Juan Pueblo and professor of anthropology at the University of Albuquerque, remembers that in New Mexico

> long ago, when first informing their worlds with meaning, the San Juan people took their three-tiered social order and projected it outwards and upwards to encompass the whole of their physical world as well by imbuing that world with a three-tiered spiritual meaning, one both reflecting and reinforcing their social order. The fit among their ideas of order in society, in the physical world, and in the spiritual realm is ingenious, for these three orders interlock and render order into everything within the Tewa world.[3]

In Keres Pueblo, in New Mexico, Paula Gunn Allen (Laguna/Sioux, and professor of English at UCLA), tells us that Sun Woman, who was present at and participated in the creation of the universe, left to go to the east and it is said that she will return in times to come. At Laguna, Gunn tells us, people believe that she has already returned in the form of the atomic/hydrogen "suns," which were put together in her original lands. These are the lands that provided the uranium that was mined to create the atomic devastations.[4]

Vickie Downey, writing of her home pueblo, Tesuque, tells us about keeping alive the religious traditions of the Southwest Pueblos in spite of Spanish priests and soldiers:

> About our religion, yes, we've kept that alive even with exploitation that came in and tried to wipe out our religion. We've maintained that. Among the pueblos there's a church in each pueblo. With the Spanish they brought the priests along with the soldiers. Together they tried to exterminate our communities, our villages, our spirit. But we've maintained our way to this time. It's been a struggle, but we've maintained it. A lot of other Indian reservations, they've also maintained it.[5]

The settlers who came even later to this land felt the need to exploit it even further for its natural resources in the name of what they believed to be civilization. Their attitudes were very different from those of the diverse tribal societies they encountered. The sharp contrast in ideals and values that affected the way the newcomers viewed the religious practices of these societies is still felt today. The settlers feared nature and wilderness; they were, after all, from another land and ecosystem. Perhaps the settlers were haunted by memories of former times and the fear of going back to the earlier uncivilized states that had existed in Europe if they were not successful in mastering this new, strange land and its peoples.

The way these colonists acted toward this land had less to do with the natural world than with their ideals of individualism and independence and their desperate need for a new beginning in a new world. In shaping their own adjustment to this new environment, they inherited much from the Native American societies they encountered but were more concerned with conquering than understanding. Their belief that God had given them this natural world to exploit allowed them to rationalize their behaviors in the name of European manifest destiny, civilization, and Christianity. Everywhere, in every direction, the consequence was the laying waste of souls and natural resources.

Many Dene (Navajo) women today are dealing with these issues in an ongoing struggle for religious freedoms and social justice. To be a Dene woman requires living in and practicing the Dene way of life. The power manifested by Changing Woman, a female deity in the myth of the Blessingway ceremonial complex, is a power that Dene women call upon in their struggles today, especially their struggle for a land base, for they continue to be forced to relocate from what they consider to be their spiritual homeland. According to a Dene woman traditionalist and friend involved in this political, religious struggle, to be moved away from her place means to be living out of balance and harmony. The ideas set forth in the concepts of Blessingway provide the sanctions for Dene peoples' roles in human life and require participation in ceremonial life in a specific land base.[6]

In the *Kinááldá,* the girls' initiation ceremony, Dene girls are instructed to live their lives modeled after Changing Woman. Women's beliefs about the attributes of Changing Woman and the nature of her interconnectedness to all living entities is of great significance and clarifies for the initiates what their roles and responsibilities will be as Dene women. Female sponsors for the initiates derive their power from a codified body of ceremonial knowledge and personal experience. The ceremony itself requires of the women sponsors that they be responsible for ritually guiding the initiates from childhood through the doors of adolescence into womanhood. This is a tremendous task that requires rigorous, dedicated religious commitment if the ceremony is to be effective. Initiated women will sometimes gain prestige in the community by learning from their own sponsors how to carry on the *Kinááldá* ceremony. This of course takes years of apprenticeship if it is to be done correctly. The important fact here is that initiated women often become the carriers of the Dene female tradition. Dene woman, who are also known to perform the ceremonial roles of Hand Tremblers, praying over a patient's body with trembling hands as they search for answers, or of Diagnosticians, locating the source of an illness and then referring the patient to the appropriate ceremonies, are usually not free to pursue these demanding roles until after menopause.[7]

The struggle to pursue one's religion has many faces. For example, Flora Jones, a Wintu religious leader, like Pilulaw Khus, the Chumash elder (document 3), is concerned with desecration by the federal government and commercial interests of lands considered sacred and central to the continuity of their ceremonial life and practices. Flora has complained she has not been able to collect essential medicines in the forests of northern California.[8] Pilulaw has fought oil companies whose development would desecrate Chumash ceremonial areas. When there are oil spills, she is the first out there to clean up the beaches and to assist the endangered animals. Knowledge of a sustainable environment, revealed in the languages in which the myths are told and in the concept of Mother Earth and the interconnectedness of all living things, is central to what it means to be indigenous to a place.

The tensions between the spiritual forces at work in Native America and the ideas of forced religious conversion, along with new introduced technologies, has had a tremendous impact on the lives of native women. In the sphere of religion, men were moved into positions of power over religious women leaders. Too often missionization meant the disempowerment of women. This is made explicit in *Jesuit Relations,* the journals of the Jesuit missionaries of the seventeenth century, which advocates placing men in religious leadership roles and counsels against dealing with women in positions of religious or political power.[9] Despite the pervasive power of these agents of change, the resistance of native women persists. Though often graciously stepping aside from former leadership roles, they continue in many places to be respected for their religious knowledge and women's wisdom.

The women of the Iroquois Longhouse, for example, have not permitted patriarchal distortion of the natural world or newly introduced technologies and commodities, such as fast food, disposable diapers, and television, to diffuse their powerful cultural positions as clan mothers and keepers of the Longhouse ceremonial complex. They are responsible for choosing the chiefs of the clan, who can govern only if they are in agreement with the rest of the clan members. The final decisions are made by the careful consideration of the clan mothers, who are concerned for the well-being of all the people, especially the young children.[10] This, of course, is a very different perspective on Indian women from one that blends many traditions into the stereotype of the Indian woman as subservient. It is important that we remember that women had many and varied tasks, ceremonies, and social roles, in different places, at different times, and in different nations. Yet when we look to the historic record and ethnographic accounts, women are often invisible.

One notable exception is Ella Cara Deloria's (Yankton Sioux) novel *Waterlily*. Writing of the dramatic changes taking place in her society in the late nineteenth century, she paints a moving portrait of the elaborate rite *hunka,* or "child beloved," a ceremony for children who are selected for a place of honor in Teton society. Through this rite the girl Waterlily is taught the knowledge necessary for understanding the principles of daily life and why ritual practices are important for both men and women.[11]

In the American Southwest, interreligious dialogue in churches and at conferences has ignored the religious life of Native American women and our relationships with other indigenous women of the borderlands. Historically Chicana and Mexican women south of the border have been denied access to knowledge of their indigenous heritage in a manner similar to that of their sisters in the north. Church and state have combined in powerful ways to divide and conquer, yet the religious and medical practices of these women today demonstrate a rich complex blend of ideas, commitments, and identities. Coatlicue (an Aztec female deity), Guadalupe (a melding of an Aztec deity and sixteenth-century Spanish Catholicism), Curanderas (Mexican folk healers), Parteras (midwives), and more recently Mexican and Chicana Espiritualistas (document 5) stand as testimony to the strength and creativeness of women of the borderlands. Today, Chicana and indigenous women, in dialogue with our elders, are finding a place for ourselves as we redefine the history of our religious experience. *Mujeres Activas en Letras y Cambio Social* is an important forum for exploring these matters.[12] Rigoberta Menchu, Quiche woman of Guatemala, has so brilliantly named our struggle as the spirituality of the Western hemisphere.[13]

My own identity incorporates the richness of my Apache, Mexican Indian, and Chicana heritage. It was that background and my female kin that guided me along a path of even deeper reflection and understanding of the diverse roles of women. When I draw on the tradition of the Sun Clan at the Mescalero Apache Reservation in New Mexico, I make the linkages among myself, my research, and my political activism as a woman. In elaborate detail the Sun Clan creation myth, when told in Apache, relates that from the very beginning of time, the earth existed and was in a process of continual change, which was seen and continues to be seen as the manifestation of the cyclical powers of nature.

In the ceremony *'Isánáklésh Gotal,* which marks the transition from girlhood to womanhood, the symbols used to influence the young girls vary in their function, but their overall purpose is to convince the adolescent that she will undergo good and positive changes if she participates fully in the ceremony. However, it is up to the girl herself to decide if she wishes to undertake this responsibility. At this young age girls are thought of as soft and moldable, suggesting that they are still capable of being conditioned and influenced by female kin. It is easier to convince some girls to participate than others. Some need to be awakened to their female identity, while others need to be calmed down and taught to be more feminine. Within the ritual design of the ceremony two concepts are at work: one is awakening the initiate to the world around her and to her abilities, and the other is to carefully calm down the unrestrained nature of adolescence. Both concepts are nurtured and encouraged in the young girl's everyday activities (document 4).

Preparation for the ceremony begins early in the life of a young girl. She is slowly and carefully made ready, then suddenly uprooted from her special privileged childhood in a family where female kin watch over her from the time of her birth. Menarche signals a physiological marker that the young girl immediately recognizes. Suddenly her life changes. Her first menstruation is usually celebrated by family and kin. At this time she is sung over to emphasize the importance of this intimate celebration, the gift of 'Isánáklésh to a young changing woman. Nearly all girls had this ritual in prereservation times. Today a girl may look forward to a feast around the age of eleven or twelve years, at which time many members of her community will gather to honor her in the eight-day ceremony of 'Isánáklésh Gotal.

The first time that I observed this ceremony was when, at the age of nine, I was taken by my mother and aunt to Mescalero to attend the feast of a relative. The image of the girl dancing in the tipi at night stayed with me and became the impetus for my present research.[14] Although I was born in Las Cruces in Doña Ana county, New Mexico, I grew up in Barrio Logan neighborhood in San Diego. My first paying job was at El Porvenir, a tortilla factory that is still there today. As I listened to the older women talk about the realities of their lives, and they provided me with what I now know was an insightful critique of what they were experiencing. Our Lady of Guadalupe Catholic Church was the religious center for most of us. With both humility and religious authority the women created beautiful personal home altars when they felt the need for a more intimate form of prayer and reverence. Many of these altars honored the Virgin de Guadalupe, the principal religious figure in all of her different manifestations.

It was in the Barrio Logan years later that I first heard about Sarita Macias. Her Templo Espiritualista was across the street from the Chicano Cultural Center. Mexican and Chicana/o espiritualismo, as practiced today, encompasses a complexity of religious and cultural elements. It uses pre-Columbian medicinal traditions, sixteenth-century Spanish Catholicism, and messianic and shamanistic ritual beliefs and practices. The practice of espiritualismo involves trance, soul voyaging, and visionary traits, such as videncia (spiritual sight). For believers its teachings are legitimized by a divine charter that originates with an Ultimate Reality and other major Spirits who regularly speak through the spirit mediums (guias). The guias are, for the most part, women who act as spiritual guides, healers, and counselors. They have visionary experiences that become a source of power, according them respect and credibility in their congregations and the community at large.

Espiritualismo was first introduced into Mexico in the 1860s as a blend of native beliefs, Mexican folk Catholicism, and apocalyptic expectations that responded to the conflicts of church and state taking

Pilulaw Khus, Chumash Elder, spiritual adviser, and active environmentalist, Santa Barbara, California.

Inés Hernández-Ávila, Native American/Chicana scholar and poet, at the University of California, Davis.

Guia Sarita Macias, spiritual leader of El Templo de Poder y Sabiduria, Templo Espiritual Trinitario, Mariano, San Diego, California.

Female initiation, Mescalero Apache Reservation, New Mexico.

Meredith Begay, Apache medicine woman.

place in Mexico at that time. An exseminarian, Rogue Rojas, heralded the coming of the "Era de Elias," a messianic reign on earth that would bring salvation to the oppressed, called "espiritualistias Israelites." Rojas named his church "La Iglesia Mexicana Patriarcal Elias." Contemporary Mexican *espiritualismo* derives from this movement. My introduction to *espiritualismo* by Sarita in San Diego eventually led to my initiation by a *guia* in Mexico City. I did not myself seek to become a practitioner so much as to study the process of initiation, one that has deep ties to my Apache and Chicana heritages. Over time Sarita became a source of strength, and it was her guidance that saw me through my doctoral examinations and dissertation (document 5).

I don't presume to speak for the women whose voices I document in this essay. Yet I feel that their voices are also my voice, and I am in the process of understanding how to write the history that they speak about and how to describe their religious perspectives. I focus here on the voices of contemporary indigenous women. Too often we look to the old texts and feel comforted by the wisdom of those women who have now passed on. Yet there are indigenous women across this land whose religious and political perspectives can enrich us all today. The Chicano and American Indian Movement of the sixties produced writers who gave voice to our struggles and helped me to begin to find my own voice. Examining the warp and woof of a history whose tightly woven threads are not easily unraveled, I remember what a Dene weaver at the Hubbell Trading Post, Ganado, Arizona, once said to me as she sat before her loom. "Weaving," she said, "is about understanding power."

Documents

Document 1. Meredith Begay:
An Apache Medicine Woman

Meredith Begay is a contemporary medicine woman, spiritual adviser, and teacher of the traditions of the Mescalero Apache Reservation in New Mexico. The following is an interview on the role of medicine in Apache culture, recorded June 1994 on a trip to collect Indian Banana for an Apache female initiation ceremony.

Inés: Meredith, you're a Medicine Woman and very much respected by your people here at the Mescalero Reservation, and you're also trying to teach people beyond Mescalero. I am interested in talking with you to find out how you deal with it. A lot of people think of Medicine Women as something from the past, except for New Agers who keep inventing Medicine Women. So I would like to know what it is you do, why you do it and what your concerns are in terms of the present Apache Traditions and some of the political issues you face in being a Medicine Woman today.

Meredith: Medicine is Traditional Indian medicine. The focal point of it is healing. To be healed, the person has to live a healthy, good life. What I feel I am doing is just being an instrument to help heal. This is what I am doing for my people to help the young children. To help them understand that there is medicine and that there is Apache religion and that all of these cohese in order to be an Apache, a proud Indian. That's what it is. I don't profess to be the greatest medicine person. I don't profess to say that I know all medicines, *no.* I know my area; I know how far I can go with my medicines. And if somebody needs further medicine with a more stronger power I refer that person. A lot of times I have helped other people heal. I have talked to them, or sometimes they ask for herbs, so I give them herbs, but I use them holistically. I don't just give it to them in a tea form and say here, drink this—no, I don't do that. I use it holistically.

And I always stress that I am just a little person in this world trying to help my Indian people wherever they are, to help them understand that there is still good in traditional medicine and that medicine is all around us, the pharmacy is all around us, and it doesn't cost anything; it's free. It's for the people to get healed and live right. These are the things that I stress, and especially for the children I try to stress that they know their medicine, know that they have a heritage—something to be proud of and especially the Apache child. I always do this. I give them a lot of insight and teach them how to harvest medicine, when to get it, how to preserve it, and how to use it when they need it. This is what I do. But in order to become a medicine person you have to have lived the life on a reservation with Indian people. You have to know the intricacies of equalness between earth, plant, trees, rock, clouds. All of nature you have to know, have equalness with it and understand it, even the tiniest little insect. You have to understand that.

It is said that when a little black ant gets sacred pollen that has dropped to the ground, and the little ant is under you, and it gets pollen on it, it feels good. It's happy because it was blessed, and that's the way you have to be with Mother Nature. You don't over use it, and you don't under use. You equalize everything. That's the way you live. And a lot of these people that are now coming into medicine, it's not going to take one day or one night or one year to learn. It's going to take about 10, 15 years before they really understand and get to the focal point of what medicine is. You cannot practice Indian medicine at all in the United States unless you have been brought up into a particular life way. You have to have a background, people in your background, people that know how to heal, that tell you the story of the medicine, the way that it was applied, how it was used. You don't learn those things in just a matter of four days or five days. You learn it over a period of time, and then when you perform for other people, it will show.

A lot of it is fake today. You can tell the fake medicine from the real. A lot of people will copy you. Coyote copied a lot of people but he always came out at the short end of the stick. You have to do it with dignity, with faith, and if you don't have that you are not performing right. Anybody can copy a sweat; anybody can copy a ceremony or dance; anybody can copy these things, but if they don't have the essence, it's no use; it's no good; it's a waste of time; it's a waste of money; it's just a lot of hogwash—because the end result is what you look at after you've performed something. The end results show the truth. If it was good, the person will feel good when they come out of it. If it was just an act, the person will still feel the same as when they went into the healing, dance or ceremony. That's how it is, and medicine is not to be played with because since you're an instrument or something to that effect—you're an instrument for the Supreme Being—you have to do within your own realm what you can do.

Like I said, if you can't do anymore than what you've done, if you've helped the person as much as you can, you refer them to the next medicine person that has a little more power or maybe a different approach. Usually your true medicine people are poor—they don't have much. They don't have much in ways of physical things, maybe they don't have a big house and cars—things like that—they are poor people. Their spirit is very, very big. They are strong, they are giving, they are kind.

But a person that goes into medicine for money, then that person is in it for me, I and myself—nobody else matters. Their attitude is, I don't care. I'm just copying so I get the money. That's their whole idea. It's not like that. A true medicine person doesn't do that, doesn't put these things ahead. A true medicine person puts the sick person or whomever needs help ahead of me, I and myself. They put it ahead, they want to help. They give all that they can give, and the end result, like I said, is what comes out after the person is either healed or half healed or is on its way to healing. So this is why there could be a lot of people out there saying I'm a medicine person, but within their own life they are going to come to a crossroads.

Document 2. Inés Hernández-Ávila: Land Base and Native American Religious Traditions

Inés Hernández-Ávila is a Native American/Chicana poet and scholar at the University of California at Davis. In the following document she presents a challenging understanding of the indigenous vision of the natural world. The excerpt is drawn from an address given at the 1993 annual meeting of the American Academy of Religion.[15]

Last June, I was present at a gathering, a "conversation," at Bucknell University that was called "Land and the Human Presence," which was attended by about forty people, seventeen of whom were Native Americans. One of the Native American elders present was Leon Shenandoah, Chief of Chiefs of the Six Nations people, the Iroquois Confederacy. One part of his message each time he spoke had to do with what happens when someone takes another person's life. The first time he spoke of this, I took his message very personally, because one of my relatives had just died violently (and possibly not accidentally), and I felt that his statements were helping me to make sense of the death. He and I spoke of these matters afterwards. The second time he repeated this portion of his message to us, I was struck by another level of its meaning.

What Chief Shenandoah said was this: When someone takes another person's life, that person cheats the Creator. He cheats the Creator because the Creator has his own plans for the person. If someone's life is taken, the one who dies has free passage to the beyond. All that the one who died left behind, all the errors, comes on to the one who took the life.

As I emerged from my initial interpretation, I realized that there are many ways to take another person's life aside from physically killing them. You take another person's life when you deny or distort their voice and appropriate their traditions for personal benefit without permission, or as a means to control them. You take another person's life when you use your institutional privilege to practice intellectual hegemony over them, or when you pretend that their discoveries and understandings are your own or valid only when you claim them.

In this regard it strikes me as rather appropriate that the popular environmental movement as we know it has been carried out formally and initially by white people, given what we know of the historical trajectory of many of their ancestors with respect to degradation of the earth. It seems to me that the concepts of "landscape," "wilderness," "nature" all represent Western ideological perceptions, intellectualizations of the land, of the earth, and it occurs to me that when European Americans (in particular) intellectualize (and sometimes romanticize) in such a way, they are perhaps exhibiting a nostalgia for their own land bases, and for their severed relationship with these land bases. It is my understanding that native people in this hemisphere regard the earth not only as a mother, but as a loving grandmother and strict teacher. As I have said in another essay,

> The distinct land base (in the sense of relationship, not ownership) of a people informs and nourishes their culture and in a precisely detailed manner directs the movement and meaning of their ceremonies.
> Through careful observation and the development of a respectful and intimate relationship with their land bases, . . . indigenous population[s] learn(ed) from their teachers how to live in harmony with their environment and how to sustain themselves through the changing seasons.[16]

This relationship, which was nurtured in a profoundly reverent and conscious manner, was founded, I believe, on an understanding that the earth, indeed, the cosmos, was/is itself a complex, exact and intentional manifestation of the Creative Spirit. This understanding is one of the fundamental assumptions of indigenous belief systems. It is an assumption that speaks to the depth of the sacred relationships between indigenous peoples and their particular land bases, to their awareness of the interrelatedness of all life within the universe, and to their conceptualizations of identity, family, community, spirituality, and pedagogy.

The late Mayan scholar Domingo Martinez Paredez wrote that one of the names in Maya for the Supreme Being was Hunab Ku, which means El Unico Dador de Movimiento y Medida, or The Only Giver of Movement and Measure. In other words, "God," or the Creative Spirit (called by many names) was/is, as Chicano poet Jose Flores Peregrino said years ago "Ciencia con conciencia" ["Science with conscience"]. Or I would say, Sacred Science, due to the sacralized dynamics of inquiry, observation, and experiment upon which native "science" was based. These dynamics give shape to a cultural discipline that reflects the reciprocal relationship that exists between "we, the People, the Human Beings," and the entire cosmos. This discipline, which emanates from the Creative Spirit, is the creative pedagogy that informs native perceptions of the "natural world." In fact, the history (and even "prehistory" in Western terms) of mutual trust, intimacy of matter (or body) and spirit, constancy, loving attention, and respect between native peoples and their land bases here in this hemisphere, which are apparent in the understandings they came to have of their environment, speaks not only to their longevity on this land but perhaps represents the key to Native American conceptualizations of sovereignty.[17]

"What are the implications of an appreciation that human differences—of gender, race, class, and culture—shape people's perceptions and experiences of the natural world?" I think of how an appreciation of the differences in a sacralized and animated "natural world" might shape people's perceptions and experiences of the human world. I think also of how it is possible that it is humans who must be reinvented, especially humans who consider themselves to be civilized. "Civilized" to me means dominated, domesticated, tame, brought into order, brought into line, molded, indoctrinated in the art of appearance, the art of facade, trained to think in a "civilized" manner (read Western European). Perhaps it is a mark of "civility" that this dynamic is played out in the patriarchal manner in which the earth is treated. It has been my own observation that in this contemporary society the overall practice towards the earth has been to tame her, control her, manipulate her, degrade her, profane her, strip her, rape her, plunder her and deny her voice. There is, for me, a correspondence between the way the earth is perceived and treated and the way women, children, and any other "feminized" groups are perceived and treated, always by "civilizing forces."

Mexican feminist scholar Maria Antonieta Rascon reminds us that what Catholicism forced upon native people of Azteca descent was a male trinity in place of Ometeotl, in place of the Dual Duality that is the Supreme Being, MotherFather, FatherMother.[18] More pointedly, I would say that Christianity and Catholicism separated the mother(earth) from the deity and so separated the woman from the teacher. In separating the woman (as earth) from the teacher, we began to be separated from the Earth and from all of our animal, plant, water, and sky relations as well. The creative spirit has been perverted, commodified, and appropriated by those who can afford it or take it by entitlement. The logic of capitalist accumulation and consumption which antagonizes the earth contributes to the degradation of the creative spirit just as much as do institutionalized religions which abhor the flesh, perpetuate notions of sin, and dislocate humans from the earth. From many oral traditions I have heard elders say that the earth is a strict grandmother capable of love in abundance, and capable of discipline of the most rigorous kind. I have listened to them speak about human beings needing to know the humility that nurtures itself in respect. The earth purifies herself, either harmoniously or by blows; she does what she has to, as we saw with floods that recently hit the Midwest.

I would like to end by telling two stories. In 1987, I went to Cuba for two weeks as a participant in the 18th Contingent of the Venceremos Brigade. One of the days that we were given to visit different sites, I chose to go to the Santeria Museum. One part of the museum consisted of replicas of home altars as they had been cared for during the time when this religious expression was practiced more. On some of the altars I was surprised to see plaster of Paris statues of Plains style Indians which had been painted by hand. I was stunned to learn of the curator's response when people asked him why the statues were there. He said, "Oh, we always pay our respects to the original peoples of these lands and we always ask their permission to be here." Upon my return I immediately rushed to tell a Paiute elder who is dear to me of the news; he simply nodded his head in affirmation.

Last spring at Easter time my husband and I had the good fortune to be able to attend the Yaqui Easter *pahko* ceremonies in Arizona. On Easter Sunday we were at Barrio Libre where we were privileged to see Luis Maseo Cienfuegos as he was the Deer. As the procession began to get organized, we were invited to have responsibility; my husband was asked to carry one of the poles of the canopy that shaded the sacred image, and I was asked to carry one end of an arch of paper flowers under which the entire procession passed even as we walked. From my vantage point, I could see the Deer leading us; I could see his head clearly as he gestured to us and showed us the way, opening the paths for us. Even though I was raised Roman Catholic on my dad's side, my Nimipu mom has effectively (and effortlessly) subverted the rigidity of that training all my life, and I have certainly rejected the patriarchal foundations of Catholicism. I was still moved in a way I had not expected, however, when I saw the Deer lead us up to the altar and I understood what he had done, this emissary from seyewailo, this saila maso, little brother deer. He led his pueblo to pay respects to the imported religion, the Catholic religion; he led us respectfully to the altar; he took that responsibility on himself for the people.

In both of these stories there are lessons and examples. How many peoples besides the santeros have paid their respects to the spirits of this land and asked their permission to be here? How many religious traditions which in many ways have been embraced by native peoples of this hemisphere have in turn paid their respects to the traditions of indigenous peoples? Vine Deloria, Jr., says, in his "Afterword" to the volume *America in 1492,*

> From an Indian point of view, the general theme by which to
> understand the history of the hemisphere would be the degree to which
> the whites [I would add all immigrants] have responded to the rhythms
> of the land—the degree to which they have become indigenous.[19]

For me, this "becoming indigenous" does not have to do with the New Age movement, or with the appropriation, commodification, and consumption of native traditions.[20] It does have to do with the paying of respects (I am quite conscious of the English term "to pay" in this phrase), or the offering of respect in concrete gestures of solidarity with the contemporary struggles for sovereignty of indigenous peoples as well as in the validation of indigenous belief systems. These recognitions have been a long time coming.

Document 3. Pilulaw Khus: Chumash Culture

Pilulaw Khus is a highly respected Chumash elder who lives in Santa Barbara, California. In the following account she analyzes Chumash culture from daily life in Chumash villages before missionization until recent struggles for recovery of the sacred site of Point Conception. She also discusses her own role within that culture.[21]

Mother Earth, Hutash, is very important to us. It is hard to understand. I'm not saying that any other nation or area of the world is less. I just know that within our nation, there is an incredible amount of power. There are amazingly powerful sacred places within the Chumash nation, and that is one of my primary jobs, that's the direction I've been given. The assignment I've been given is to protect the sacred places and to do the ceremonies. Point Conception, commonly known as Western Gate, is a very powerful place for our people, and not just our people; it also includes the stories of other native people.

When the Europeans came here, first there were the Spaniards, the military, and the priests. Secondly came the Mexican government and then the U.S. government. With each invasion our people suffered more. Within one generation, the population of our people was reduced by half: our systems were pretty much out the window. There was a well-thought-out and specific plan of genocide. Take a minute and think about it, that in one generation people were watching their world being destroyed. Their families were being pulled apart. If we went into a mission together there—because we were very spiritual people of course we were interested in this new spirituality the people were bringing—we weren't allowed to leave. We became slave labor. And, later, when our people did leave, the military was sent out to bring us back. Frequently we were killed in those raids. Think about the holocaust coming down on us, in one generation. We'd been going along for thousands and thousands and thousands of years, doing things for the most part in the same way.

When a baby was conceived that baby was beginning to be taught about people and about the baby's place within the group and the environment, and as soon as the baby was born, there would be ceremonies and there would be certain things to take care of that baby, to introduce that baby not just to the parents, but to all the people, to the environment and to the universe. And that baby would know its place, and it worked well.

The idea of changing by assimilating, by contact with others, it didn't work that much for us. We were a very integrated group. We were very satisfied with how it operated. We lived in a paradise, and so we had no real need to change a whole lot. We're still that way. We're what people might call clannish. We're not real interested in having people bringing their ways of doing things and doing it on our land. If you think about that consistency and that persistence coming through time, in that way, and that all of a sudden, something hits and everything is wiped out in one generation, that is devastation, that is holocaust. The death rate soared during that time and the birth rate dropped during that time, and that makes perfect sense to me. Who would want to bring a baby into the world when that world was no longer your own any more? Who would want to live in that kind of situation?

When the U.S. government came in, they said okay, we want to make a treaty with you tribes, and they were really determined to take over all our land. In that treaty, the one thing we held onto (we said they could take everything if they would leave us one thing) and that was Point Conception, because it was so important. The Western Gate, that's where our spirits go through, pierce that veil and go into the next reality. And it's very important that it be left open so that we can go through.

In 1975/76, companies called Western Light and Natural Gas and Pacific Gas and Electric decided they were going to put a facility there, a big plant, and we didn't know anything about the treaties. The reason we didn't know anything was that when it got back to Washington, D.C., the politicians in California here prevailed on the officials back in D.C. to put our treaty under a seal of secrecy. This was done with about

eighteen treaties here in California. So people treated in good faith with
the representative of the government and believed that this was going
to give some protection to the Western Gate, and the seal of secrecy
allowed them to do what they want to and not live up to the conditions
of the treaty. These treaties have only recently surfaced. Ours was found
when we were on the occupation out there at Point Conception.

When these companies decided to put that facility out there, I had
already been married, had children, divorced, and been in and out of
the area. At about this time I was pulled back to Santa Barbara and
started to work on an educational project, and then this occupation
came up, and that was pretty much when I began to work in a more
public open way. I went out in the occupation because we couldn't
allow the plant to be put there. It would interfere with the spirits from
this reality. We did everything the way you're supposed to do. We had
lawyers, people from the Environmental Defense Center. . . . We did
everything, tried every legal way, but the court said this may be good for
your spirituality, but the greater good is for the natural gas plant to be
put there. This was crazy, not just from a spiritual point of view, but
from an environmental point of view, because a lot of earthquake faults
are there and seas are very rough, and they were going to be loading and
off-loading these volatile fuels out there, in what they called the grave-
yard of ships.

So we were very innocent and naive. We said we'd go and occupy
because we can't allow this to be put out there. So we were innocent, all
of us, and we packed up our backpacks and sleeping bags and we went
out there and we set up a sweat lodge and we sweated, and we prayed
and we sat out there. We thought now they'll see we're really serious
and they'll go away. But no, we ended up being out there for close to a
year on that occupation, and that was an incredibly important period of
time. There were people who came here to support us from all the different nations and from Alaska, Canada, Mexico, and over and over and
over again, when I talked to people, they said we know of this place,
that's why we've come to help you, because it's our story. We had a phe-
nomenal amount of help out there. That was one the Native people
won. They did not put their plant out there. We won that one, and it's
still clean out there. Our spirits can still travel back and forth out there.

That's the way I got started on the protection of sites and battling
in that way, for that particular place and that particular purpose. I feel

very strongly about any place where our people were, whether it's just an ordinary village or a sacred site. Remember that at ordinary village sites people have been living there for thousands of years, and as people lived there, that place became more and more sacred. Why? Because they were birthing there, they were dying, they were doing ceremonies there, and they were going into spirits there. Their bodies were being returned to the embrace of our mother, and each time these kinds of things occur, a place becomes increasingly sacred. . . . I tell my children, when I die I want to go like an Indian into the mother, because she gave me my life and sustained me all my life, and it is only right that I return to her and that the life cycles can continue. Somebody is returned to the earth in that way. They go into the earth. There is a change that begins to happen in that soil, and the longer the burial stays in the earth, the more that change occurs. That person's essence permeates throughout the soil, so even the grasses, trees, flowers are all that person coming into all of that, and beyond to even the birds and animals that are there and feed are being benefited by the essence of that person.

We can't stop the ceremonies. I've received my bundle in a ceremony. I was given the opportunity to walk away from it, because once accepted I have responsibility that goes with that. I was told there would be times when no one would come, when I'd do it by myself and that's the way it is. It doesn't matter if anyone else is there, I have a responsibility to earth, to ancestors, to spirits, the universe, the people, to earth, to myself.

The way I've been taught, if someone comes here, they need to be taught. I say to non-Native, you're welcome to come here and sit by the fire. All people are connected to the earth and recognize what people are doing, the destruction. Come and be part of this, but at some point you need to give up and leave my fire and find your own ancestors, become strong and knowledgeable in your own way.

Document 4. The Presence of 'Isánáklésh and Apache Female Initiation

The following account by Inés Talamantez examines the Apache belief in the female deity, 'Isánáklésh, and the initiation ceremony for a young girl at puberty, 'Isánáklésh Gotal.[22] The songs and music of the ceremony are in collaboration with Ann Dhu McLucas.

The Presence of 'Isánáklésh

In southern New Mexico, east of the great White Sands, stands Dzil gais'ani, or Sierra Blanca. This 12,000-foot sacred mountain is the home of 'Isánáklésh, who has been revered as a powerful female deity since oldest Apache memory. At the time of creation, after the world was made safe for people, Apaches gathered together in small bands to receive knowledge and to learn the traditions. 'Isánáklésh then spoke and proclaimed her special ceremony:

> We will have a feast for the young girls when they have their first flow. Many songs will be sung for them, so that they will grow strong and live a long life.

This eight-day ceremony, called 'Isánáklésh Gotal, is celebrated in recognition of the significance of a young Apache girl's first menses. According to Apache myth, the ceremony was founded by 'Isánáklésh as a means through which the girl might temporarily experience herself as 'Isánáklésh and be honored as such by the people. The first four days of the ceremony are marked with elaborate ritual detail and festive social activities. The ceremony's songs, sacred narratives, and images combine to leave a powerful imprint of 'Isánáklésh both on the girl herself and on attending relatives, friends, and family members. Throughout the final four days the girl secludes herself to reflect on her ritual experiences.

The name given to this ceremony, 'Isánáklésh Gotal, literally means "Ceremonial Sing for 'Isánáklésh." The Apache term *gotal,* "ceremonial sing," suggests not only a festive celebration but also a raising of supernatural power to accomplish the many moments of transformation that the young girl experiences. Not only is the girl temporarily transformed during this rite of passage; she is also permanently transformed into a mature Apache woman by the end of the ritual.

This transformation into womanhood is accomplished by ceremonially awakening the initiate to the world around her. For some girls, the ceremony is said to calm their adolescent imbalances. The Mescalero conceive of "fixing" the young initiate, ridding her of her baby ways and helping her through the door of adolescence, for at this young age the girls are said to be soft and moldable, capable of being conditioned and influenced by their female kin and others around them. Timid girls may need to be awakened to their female identities; others may need to be taught to settle down and be more sensible and feminine.

Initiates are well aware that they have undergone special teachings during the ceremony. Analysis of the ceremonial procedures and their religious implications helps us to understand the transformative aspects of the ceremony. There is no single moment at which the transformation of the girl to 'Isánáklésh, or to woman, occurs. It is the fusion of all the ceremony's elements, especially the songs sung over the eight-day period, that produces the desired goals. During the ceremony, great attention is paid to the ritual details, and the meanings of the symbols are carefully explained to the girls. As the Singer and sponsor explain these teachings to the initiate, the girl begins to understand important elements of Apache culture that from now on she will be charged to maintain. After her ceremony, she will be a keeper of Apache traditions and the pattern of everyday living in which they will continue to endure. Thus she is not only taught and protected by this ceremony; like 'Isánáklésh, who gave it, she will also ideally teach and work to protect her tribe.

Sometimes it is not easy to convince young girls to participate in 'Isánáklésh Gotal. Many are intimidated by the prospect of becoming such a center of attention. Thus the mothers and grandmothers of the tribe's young girls try to prepare them psychologically and spiritually for the ceremony long before the girls reach their menarche. The women try to convince the girls that they will change in a positive way if they participate fully—and that the ceremony will bring them a good and healthy life. Older women will often encourage prepubescent girls to observe the ceremonies of other initiates closely so they will know what to expect. I have heard mothers or other female kin say to a girl, "Go up toward the front of the Big Tipi where you can see and hear everything better."

The family begins preparations for the ceremony several years in advance of their daughter's menarche. They begin collecting the necessary ritual objects, including sacred pollen, which can only be gathered during the season when cattails are ripe. It is no less important to gather relatives' support, because the ceremony will be a tremendous burden on family resources. When the proud day of the girl's first menstruation arrives, her family may celebrate with a small private dinner. In the ideal, a male Singer and a woman sponsor are secured in the proper ritual manner: four gifts must be given, and the proper words must be exchanged.

Throughout the year following menarche, the girl's women kin and female sponsor then teach her the proper Apache ways. These include the use of medicinal herbs and healing skills. The women also prepare her deerskin dress, like 'Isánáklésh's dress, with elaborate symbolic beadwork; attached to the ends of the fringes are the tiny metal cones that now replace deer hoofs, which will gently jingle when she walks or dances. If the girl is to have a private ceremony or "feast," as it is called today, her family and kin will usually host it at a carefully selected site well away from congested areas. The girl also has the option to join the several girls honored at the annual public Feast; in this case, her ritual will occur on the ceremonial grounds of the Mescalero tribal headquarters on whatever weekend falls closest to the Fourth of July. In either case, friends and family gather, supplies are stored, temporary tipis and cooking arbors are assembled; and preparations are made to feed all who come to the first four days of the ceremony.

Prior to dawn on the first day of the ceremony, the girl is placed in her own private tipi and carefully attended by female kin and her sponsor. The sponsor blesses the initiate with pollen and ritually bathes and dresses her for the ceremony. She reminds the girl of how good it feels to be cared for, so that the girl will learn to care for others. The girl's hair is washed with *Ishee,* yucca suds; she is fitted with leggings and moccasins; she is ritually fed traditional Apache foods. She is given a special reed, or *uka,* through which she will sip water, since water is not allowed to touch her lips for fear that this will bring floods; she also receives a scratching stick, or *tsibeeichii,* for she is not to scratch with her fingernails.

Meanwhile, outside on the ceremonial grounds, the Singers and the girl's male kin begin to construct the sacred tipi. This will be the central structure where most of the rites take place. It is called the ceremonial home of 'Isánáklésh or the Big Tipi. According to Apache sacred songs, only when this tipi's four main poles are properly erected can 'Isánáklésh reside there. Then the power of the songs will go out from the tipi to carry the ceremony's benefit out to all of the people on earth. To raise these poles, first four rocks are used to mark the sacred place that was touched by the first rays of the sun. Then the four poles are sung into place. A song is sung for each pole as it is placed into the earth and tied to the others at the top of the structure. Thus the Apache sacred number four is established musically as well as visually. Ideally, the first songs should be sung approximately at dawn, as the sun rises to the east, where the opening of the tipi must face. This way both song and sunrise mark the beginning of sacred time. Since the voice of the Singer can only carry so far in an outdoor setting, the songs also serve to mark off a sacred space for the circle of participants, who must move close enough to hear as well as to see.

The sacred tipi is now completed and readied for 'Isánáklésh, who has been symbolically approaching from the east with the early dawn light. The tipi's upper portion is wrapped with a clean white canvas cloth, and its lower portion is filled in with branches. The eastward opening is built out to the sides, as wings, in order to let the sun's light inside. After the tipi is in place, the initiate in her ritual garment appears with her sponsor and family. She is freshly bathed and dressed and carries a blanket and white deerskin to be unfolded and placed in front of the tipi. The initiate, now taking on the role of 'Isánáklésh, then blesses with pollen members of the tribe who come forward, and the people in turn bless the initiate. An essential component of this rite is the *tadadine,* the cattail pollen, which is the pollen that 'Isánáklésh used in the creation story. The girl motions in the Apache way to the four directions and then applies the yellow life-giving substance over the bridge of the person's nose, moving from the right to the left side; she may also apply it to other parts of the person's body. This blessing assures the people of a good long life. Hence, to remind the girl of her role as healer, the sponsor, Meredith Begay, now tells her:

> When you become 'Isánáklésh in the ceremony, you will have her power to heal because it is 'Isánáklésh who handed this knowledge to us. There is a sacred story about this. Since you will be 'Isánáklésh, you will be asked to heal and bless people who come to see you. You must always remember how you felt during your ceremony, when you were the living 'Isánáklésh, then, later in life, you can call on her for help whenever you face problems; you will remember how you felt when you were her, when you became her.

The initiate's young, soft body is next "molded," that is, massaged and aligned by her sponsor to insure the transformation of the girl to 'Isánáklésh as well as for continuing health and strength and a long, productive life. The Singer then draws four naturally paced footprints on the deerskin with pollen. While a sacred basket is put in place to the east of the tipi, the initiate steps on the pollen prints and is then gently "pushed off" to run around the basket and return to the tipi. This sequence symbolizes walking on the pollen path, again to bring the initiate a long, healthy life. The initiate runs around the basket four times, as four verses of the ritual song are sung. Before each run, the ceremonial basket is moved a little closer to the tipi. Meanwhile, the girl's female sponsor makes the "ritual marker" during the song, a long high-pitched sound, to draw the attention of the supernatural. For, as she runs, the initiate meets the approaching 'Isánáklésh and escorts her back to the Apache people.

After the first morning's rituals, the initiate ideally appears in public only during the next four nights. During the day, she may not have any ordinary social contact; only relatives, close friends, and those who wish to be blessed or healed may visit her in her private tipi.

When dusk arrives on the first night of the ceremony, male dancers appear to bless the young initiate, the tipi, and the central ceremonial fire. These dancers have been ritually transformed into *hastchin,* supernaturals, who live inside the mountains near Mescalero.

At about 10 P.M., the initiate, her sponsor, and the Singer appear at the sacred Tipi. The Singer leads the girl into the home of 'Isánáklésh by extending an eagle feather, which he holds in his right hand. The girl takes hold of the other end of the feather and follows as he takes four steps into the tipi; each step is accompanied by the verse of a song that refers to the tipi as the home of 'Isánáklésh. Inside, facing the fire at the center of the tipi, the initiate and her sponsor sit on deerhides and blankets. The Singer prays and then kneels in front of the girl with his back to the fire and prays as he blesses the initiate.

As other songs are sung in groups of four, the initiate dances back and forth across a deerhide, looking always just above the fire or at the Singer's rattle, as the ritual rules prescribe. Accompanied by the light, regular pulse of the Singer's deerhoof rattles, each song and dance lasts for about four to six minutes. Between songs, the girl rests for three to four minutes; sometimes the Singer and sponsor will talk, but usually they are silent. As each group of four songs ends, a short formula is sung to mark its conclusion. Then the Singer lights hand-rolled cigarettes of ritual tobacco, and a longer break is taken, during which the initiate is sometimes offered water through her drinking tube. During nights two and three, the same pattern occurs, with no morning or daytime activity. Only the content of the songs varies with each nightly performance as the initiate moves through the ceremony.

A closer look shows that this seemingly endless repetition is a tightly structured and deliberate ritual form. The repetition establishes a stable place, quite literally when combined with the dancing, which is restricted to the area of a small deerhide. In the matrix of this stability, thoughts are free to wander. The young 'Isánáklésh appears to be in a trancelike state as she dances more vigorously each night. The Singer tells her to think in images about the tribe—to visualize troubles and illness and to send them over the mountain and away from the tribe. She is to set her mind and spirit in motion, even as her physical space is confined.

Similarly, the repetition also alters the sense of time. All necessary elements for a good life are said to be present in the ceremony; all the important symbols of Apache culture and of the world of women are contained in the songs that are sung each night. By calling on these symbols with the songs' powerful words, participants evoke images that are sometimes literally seen in the sacred space. The mind can travel between these two images. When similar tunes are used it is as if no time has elapsed between one set of songs and the next—or between the present ceremony and the first ceremony ever sung. 'Isánáklésh is *there;* and her healing power is present, as it was during the first moments of the world's creation.

The ceremony lasts almost until dawn on the fourth day. Songs are counted by wooden markers that are driven into the ground around the fire. Many of these songs, both words and tunes, are repeated from the previous evenings. Then, on the fifth and final morning of the ceremony's public segment, the ceremonial circle is completed by actions that reverse the pattern of the first morning. The initiate, the sponsor, and the Singer assemble in the tipi just as dawn is about to break. 'Isánáklésh has again been freshly bathed. The sacred basket is beside them, holding pollen, the girl's eagle feather, tobacco, a gramma grass brush, several kinds of clay, and galena, a shiny black lead ore found in the mountains of Mescalero. Using the clays, pollen, and galena, the Singer paints an image of the sun on the palm of his hand. As he sings, he holds his hand up to the sun, so that the galena glitters as the early sun's rays hit it. When the song is finished, the Singer turns and touches his sun-painted hand to her shoulders and chest. Then he touches each side of her head and rubs the sun-image into her head.

Singing another song, the Singer paints her with white earth clay, covering all the exposed skin on her arms and legs, as well as the lower half of her face. As this is happening, other participants remove the cloth and branches covering the sacred tipi, so that only the four main poles remain. Within this skeleton structure, the ritual blessing and healing of the tribe again take place. Taking red clay from a basket beside him, the Singer blesses members of the community (and anyone else seeking blessing) by marking them with the clay, taking special care for young children, the elderly, and the sick.

The next and final ritual sequence occurs very quickly. 'Isánáklésh is led out of the tipi to the same tune and eagle feather that led her in; she walks on pollen footsteps, which are again painted on the deerskin. The sacred basket is once again placed to the east of the tipi, at the same distance from the tipi as it had been during the final run of the ceremony's first morning. Once again 'Isánáklésh takes the four ceremonial pollen footsteps and runs off, accompanied by the four verses of her running song. This time, after each run, the basket is moved further to the east. On the last run, she runs to the basket—now very far to the east. She picks up her eagle feather and runs to the east, then turns around and begins to rub the white clay from her face while returning to her private tipi, where she will stay during the next four days. During the past four days she has symbolically left behind her childlike youth and has been ritually transformed into 'Isánáklésh. Now 'Isánáklésh has herself departed into the east. After the next four days of quiet reflection, the initiate will emerge from her tipi as an adult Apache woman.

As the girl performs her last run, the Singer chants as the rope that tied together the tipi poles is loosened and undone. Now the tipi's last four poles fall to the ground with a great crash. During all of this excitement, the Singer has continued to sing, accompanied by his rattle. However, the crowd, which knows the traditions of this ceremony, has by now moved toward the cooking arbor. Here pickup trucks have driven in, loaded with candy, fruit, and household goods. These are thrown to the crowd as gifts from the family sponsoring the feast. The effect of the final run, the dismantling of the sacred tipi, and the give-away with all of its accompanying excitement are meant to decisively break the sense of sacred space and time.

Document 5. *Espiritualista* Initiation in Southern California and Mexico

In the following account Inés Talamantez recounts her introduction to *espiritualismo* in Barrio Logan in San Diego, California, which led to her eventual initiation by a *guia* in Mexico City. The two *guias* who provided information for this analysis are Sarita Macias from El Templo Amor Poder y Sabiduria in San Diego and Manuela Cegudo, "la Guia de Guias" at El Templo del Mediodia in Mexico City. Both were interviewed in their respective *templos,* offices, and homes, where they talked of their training, professional methods as healers, and attitudes toward their calling. These *guias* belong to the movement of Mexican *Espiritualismo* that emerged from the teachings of Rogue Rojas, founder of La Iglesia Patriarcal Elias.[23]

The approach for recruiting initiates to *espiritualismo* and the steps taken in the process of shaping and performing the initiatory ritual known as La Marca tells us how the female practitioners, or *guias,* manipulate provocative symbolic images to transform and move the initiates from one religious and social status to another.

The initiation follows a three-part pattern common to rites of passage: (1) the preliminal phase of *separation* from the initiate's community and everyday activities; (2) the liminal phase of transition, in which the initiate is ritually marked with consecrated oils and holy water; and (3) the postliminal phase or *incorporation* back into society with a new social and religious status.[24]

According to Guia Macias the following teachings are still practiced today at all the *templos:*

Desarrollo, or the practice of spiritual development that leads to "La Marca," defines the nature of the initiate's task in life. It is a gift of spiritual inheritance that is validated at the time of the ritual initiation. It focuses on the development of the initiate's powers in what are called the *siete virtudes y etapas graduadas* (seven virtues and graduated stages):

1. *Recibir el ser espiritual:* to take a name provided by her protector
2. *Ungeamiento:* anointing by the help of the Holy Spirit
3. *Dar consejo curación:* modes of spiritual and psychological counseling
4. *Curar con medicina:* healing with herbs and homeopathic techniques
5. *Tomar el Rayo:* receive the sacred touch (*toque espiritual*) in preparation for trance—women receive this from Mary and men from *el Padre Elias*
6. *Radiación del maestro:* ecstasy or trance
7. *Alta luz:* pure spiritual communication with the Ultimate Reality, the Eternal Father, Jehovah; this refers to enlightenment and communication between spirits

According to Guia Cegudo in Mexico City, only those who attain the highest spiritual development of *alta luz* become *guias,* and they are sanctioned by the major *templo* of *espiritualismo,* Templo del Mediodia in Mexico City, to open and operate *templos* or *recintos.* At their *templos,* these authorized *guias* implement the teachings and initiate others through the process of "La Marca."

"La Marca" is an invisible sign that "marks" or bestows upon initiates their task in life; it serves as a confirmation that the initiate has completed the necessary stages of spiritual development. La Marca opens the initiate's understanding of the "third eye," which contains the knowledge and teachings of God. The *guia* knows through her *videncia* (vision) if the initiate is ready to be marked. La Marca thus becomes a public recognition of one's spiritual ability, which is further recognized by a special certificate. A practicing *guia* usually displays in her *templo* the certificate verifying she has received La Marca.

In La Marca, the initiate receives the Holy Spirit (*recibir el ser espiritual*) and is given a spirit guide by the *guia* in trance. It introduces the initiate into the world of mediumship through trance, *curaciones unidas* (healing with the help of other *guias*), and *ungeamiento espiritual y físico* (spiritual and physical cleansing with holy water only). The process occurs as follows. *Guias* who operate on a highly developed spiritual plane go into trance and lend their consciousness so that the spirit may work through them. This *toque espiritual,* or sacred touch, is known as the word or breath of God which represents all truth. While in trance the *guia,* with the help of her own spirit guide, speaks and counsels the initiate, answering whatever questions she may have. The *guia* gives advice and sometimes provides a spiritual guide if the person is considered to be appropriately prepared.

During the ritual, a person appointed as *la pluma de oro* (golden pen) records the message coming through the medium. Later the transcription is used to decode the *carga* (task in life). This *carga* ritually marks the person who must then seek to analyze and understand the message. Sometimes no message comes through. In this situation, the person is rejected and informed that no spirit has come forth. This is interpreted as meaning that something in that person's life is out of harmony or that she may lack spiritual preparation.

Guia Sarita in San Diego explained to me that the spiritual "calling" may come to the *guia* through personal crisis at a young and impressionable age. Sarita, for example, was ill as a child and was cured by a *curandera* (Mexican folk healer). At the time, she did not believe in the healer's powers and rejected *curanderismo* as nonsense. Later, as an adult, she became ill with chest pains and a heart murmur. Rejecting the idea that she needed an operation, she instead went to a *templo espiritualista* and through a psychic operation was healed. Informed that the procedure was entirely spiritual, she was eventually transformed into a believer of *espiritualismo.*

Sarita apprenticed herself to the healer Petra Castro in Tijuana, Baja California, for three years and then moved to Mexico City, where she studied for the next eight years with Guia Cegudo at Templo del Mediodia. At the end of this time, she was instructed by the directors of the Templo to go to San Diego to set up the first *templo* in California in Barrio Logan to provide for Mexicans and Chicana/os a place of refuge.

As a *guia espiritualista,* Sarita serves two sets of clients: those who need to have health or spiritual problems met, and those members of the community at large who are in need of a communication network and support system. Her clients are usually, but not exclusively, Mexicans or Chicana/os. Sarita performs *limpias* (cleansings) using the burning of incense over a charcoal fire and various plants such as sage, pepper tree branches, and geraniums in an effort to remove malevolent spirits. Her clients are mostly women, including white women who sometimes are believers in holistic healing or other alternative healing systems.

For physical ailments, Sarita uses *curaciones* (healings), healing with massage, manipulation, kneading, rubbing, rotating and aligning the body, and spiritual operations and injections. The latter are healing maneuvers in which she uses her thumb and forefinger to function as a syringe and needle. She also employs *bálsamo de curación* (holy water), oil, garlic, chile, lemon or eggs, as well as a variety of herbs in her healing. In addition, she prays while in trance to her spirit guide and other divinities to work through her for the healing of her clients.

On Sundays she holds *catedras* (doctrinal teachings) from ten in the morning until noon in her *templo* in San Diego. Usually twenty to thirty people are present. When they enter, they take the *bálsamo de curación* (holy water) and rub it between their hands, wiping the water over their heads and down the sides of their bodies, after making the sign of the cross. At the front of the *templo,* a tiny altar symbolically represents the major canons of *espiritualismo:* seven steps (which correspond to the above-mentioned *siete virtudes y etapas graduadas*) leading to a triangle above the altar with an *ojo de dios* (God's eye) in the center and rays of divinity shining down. The altar is covered with burning candles, ritual objects, and freshly cut flowers, the aroma of which permeates the air.

The "Pedro" or pillar of the church and the "Guardian" assist Sarita by leading the congregation in several songs or hymns. After the singing, Sarita, who is now in trance, delivers the *catedra* or *mensaje de Cristo* (the word of Christ). Then the chosen *vidente* (visionary) who is selected by Sarita for the day stands with eyes closed, lifts her palms, and begins to channel the message of the spirit. When she finishes telling what she envisioned, five or six participants from the congregation, including Sarita, describe the spiritual visions that they received with their eyes closed during the channeling. These revelations often use the iconography of the *templo:* the altar, the *ojo de dios* (the God's eye) over the seven steps, and the symbols of the *templo* banner. Then, more hymns are sung and everyone gathers for social interaction before leaving the *templo.*

In her *templo,* Amor Poder Sabiduria (love, power, knowledge) in the Barrio Logan in San Diego, at Sarita's invitation, I participated in a *catedra*. Listening to her words while she was in trance possession, words of charismatic force yet tender kindness, I was fascinated by the meta-phorical aspects of her speech and beautiful incantations. For Sarita, spirits are essential; she works very hard to contact her spirit guide through powerful language. In her role of medium, under the posses-sion of her spirit guide, *patas de águila gris* (Gray Eagle Foot), she has attained status in her community as well as in other cities where she heals and advises.

A woman of keen awareness and personal warmth, Sarita always welcomed me to her *templo* with an *abrazo* (warm hug) and told me ini-tially that she knew I would be coming to see her. She claimed to know what my role in life was, and she, of course, knew exactly how far I had come in my spiritual development simply by laying her hands on my head. This information she acquired by seeing and interpreting my aura, gently pulling down my lower eyelids, and gazing intently into my eyes. She was already in the process of pulling me into her flock.

Sarita claimed that I was in a bad way and that I seemed to be undergoing stress. I was in the last days of completing work on my dis-sertation. Indeed, I had very red eyes. After a sage smoke, cleansing (*limpia*) and prayer sessions using candles and holy water, she invited me to come to the next *catedra* on the following Sunday so I could witness her at work.

I returned many times to Sarita's *templo*. She soon sensed my inter-est in her work and often enlisted me to help her. I frequently inter-viewed patients about their primary reasons for coming to a *templo;* sometimes I served as translator for non–Spanish speaking patients, escorted them into Sarita's presence, and prepared the articles she used in her healing. An incident related to translating was especially memo-rable. One day an African American man arrived at the *templo* seeking a cure for his terminal illness. Since he did not speak Spanish and Sarita does not speak English, she turned to me and said, "*Hermana, ayúdame con el hermano*" (Sister, help me with our brother). I agreed, and she then went into trance for the healing and I was confronted with the task of translating the message from the spirit world. Such participation in-creased my interest in *espiritualismo*. It was Sarita who initially insisted that in order for me to understand I should prepare myself for initiation into *espiritualismo*. As I resisted, she reminded me, "If you want to truly understand, the best way is to experience it." I was reminded of African American sociologist Bennetta Jules Rosetta's initiation into the African Apostolic Church under similar circumstances. The next thing I knew she was insisting that I go to the Templo del Mediodia in Mexico City to meet the *guia* there to determine if I was eligible for La Marca. Since this experience with Sarita, I have often observed how *guias* actively recruit and give special consideration to those in teaching, medical, or counseling professions in order to further legitimize their positions in the community.

In my case La Marca required two months of preparation and daily concentration on meditation and body purification to try to raise my spiritual awareness. I was told to fast one or two days a week, to take sweat baths, and to put a glass of water covered with a white cloth at the head of my bed every night. This water would draw away any negative force around me and help me spiritually. In the morning, I was instructed to pour the water down the drain.

Finally, after two months of *consejo* (spiritual counseling) and meditative training, I was ready, according to the *guia* Manuela, to leave this state of preparation and enter the state of transition as described by Van Gennep. Dressed in a white dress with the emblem of Templo del Mediodia in red letters enclosed by a triangle, I was escorted up to the altar to undergo La Marca.

After a warm welcome before the congregation of about 1,200 people, I was introduced as "*la Hermanita Piel Roja* (Red-Skin Sister) from California." They sang hymns as Manuela went into possession trance. I was instructed by a *materia* to come forward and kneel before the *guia,* who was by now in trance. The *materias* are those women from the congregation who are carefully selected by the *guia* because of their higher state of spiritual development. They are groomed through a special training process to become *guias.* As part of their special training, they assist the *guia.* The material being of the guia serves as the instrument of the spirit.

Kneeling before Manuela, I was given the name of the tribe of Abraham as the tribe to which I would belong from then on. Then she delivered the message from the spirit world to me. The message contained what I was given as an *herencia espiritual* (spiritual heritage); that is *videncia* (vision), *enseñanza* (teaching), and *curación* (healing). To not develop these gifts, I was told, would produce dire consequences.

Manuela then laid her hands on my head, shoulders, and chest; she wiped my hands with holy water and touched my body with a flower, all in an act of purification. I was then prayed over and advised to incorporate my *carga* into my everyday life. I was asked to return to my seat walking backwards. As I did so, I noticed that the *materias* occupied the first ten pews, acting as a protective barrier for the *guia* who was in trance.

After this, other *videntes* (visionaries) in the congregation revealed what they had experienced while the *guia* was in possession trance seeking my message from the spirit world. Five people related their experiences. All of them claimed to see me in the role of teacher or healer. A final hymn was sung and the ceremony was over. The congregation moved to the back of the *templo*. I was soon surrounded by people who wanted to meet me and welcome me for coming such a long distance to be with them. Many asked questions about Apache culture and language because they had Apache spirit guides.

The entire possession trance and ceremony was taped, and I was told to return in two weeks for a transcription of the text and an interpretation of its content. The person who has this task at Templo del Mediodia is the participant, usually a male, who takes the role of *Pedro* (Peter), the foundation of the *templo*. Several weeks later, after the reading and analysis of the text, I received a personal copy of La Marca with the seal of the *templo* as well as a new status—that of *marcada* (spiritually marked). I now had a new responsibility: to carry out the message of my *marca* and my *carga* as uncovered by the ritual of La Marca.

CHAPTER TEN

Growing Pluralism, New Dialogue
Women in American Religions

Rosemary Radford Ruether

Documents

1. Elisabeth Schüssler Fiorenza: Feminist Hermeneutics for Women-Church
2. Toinette Eugene: Womanist Theology
3. Ada María Isasi-Díaz and Yolanda Tarango: *Mujerista* Theology
4. Judith Plaskow: Jewish Feminist Theology
5. Riffat Hassan: Muslim Feminist Hermeneutics
6. Rita Gross: Buddhist Feminism
7. Starhawk: Wiccan Thealogy

RELIGION in the United States has become increasingly pluralistic in the last decade of the twentieth century. From being the historically dominant form of religion in the United States, Protestant churches in 1993 account for about 35 percent of Americans, and other forms of Christianity another 25.5 percent. Jews are about 2.4 percent. While many of the other 37 percent of Americans (some 93 million people) are nominally Christian, perhaps as many as 20 million of these belong to other religions.[1] They are Muslims, Hindus, Buddhists, Sikhs, Zoroastrians, Bahais, or members of New Age spiritualities, such as the Covenant of the Goddess. The 1993 World's Parliament of Religions reported that, in the greater Chicago area, there are more Muslims than Jews, more Thai Buddhists than Episcopalians. In this area alone there are seventeen Hindu temples.

American interest in Eastern religions goes back to New England transcendentalists who read newly translated texts from the Hindu mystics. Spiritualists, Swedenborgians, and theosophists also popularized "esoteric" Eastern wisdom from 1840 through the 1880s. But the first major presence of intellectual spokesmen for Asian and Muslim religions took place at the World's Parliament of Religions in Chicago in 1893. Swami Vivekananda presented Hindu neo-Vedanta thought, Soyen Shaku that of Zen Buddhism, and American convert Muhammad Alexander Russell Webb spoke for Islam.[2]

The result of the World's Parliament was the founding of a number of Zen Buddhist and Hindu Vedanta centers aimed at Western searchers, and the first courses in comparative religions were established in American colleges and universities. The 1960s brought a new wave of teachers of various schools of Asian spirituality—Buddhist, Hindu, and Sufi— that appealed to the new quest for spiritual experience among Americans, while at the same time waves of immigration brought Asians, Africans, and Arabs who founded temples, ashrams, mosques, and Buddhist churches that served the religious needs of their people.[3]

In the 1990s Islam became one of the fastest growing American religions, with as many as five million adherents in this country. Some Muslims were present in America among slaves or slave traders in the colonial period, but their presence was soon obliterated. The first wave of Muslim immigrants were Lebanese and Syrians of the 1890 to 1920 era. Then, in the 1920s, African Americans began to turn to an indigenous form of Islam as a way of separating from a white racism identified with dominant American Christianity. In the 1970s Black Muslims increasingly integrated into Orthodox Islam and dissolved separate sectarian organizations. Today over 30 percent of American Muslims are African American.

From the 1950s to the present a new wave of immigration from the Middle East, Africa, and South Asia has brought millions of new Muslims to North America. Many Muslim young men came to study and ended by settling here, some marrying American-born women who converted to Islam.[4]

The 1993 World's Parliament of Religions, held in Chicago on the centenary of the earlier parliament, became a showcase for the new religions in America, especially since mainstream Christianity was much underrepresented. Hindus, Buddhists, Muslims, Jains, Sikhs, Bahais, Theosophists, as well as Native Americans and New Age groups were prominently represented. Two feminist neopagan groups, the Covenant of the Goddess and the Fellowship of Isis, were among the sponsors of the parliament. Some Eastern Orthodox Christians withdrew because of the presence of neopagans, and some Jews left because of the presence of Louis Farrakhan, militant leader of the Nation of Islam.

Although males were the majority of the presenters, the parliament demonstrated a strong awareness of women's issues in religion. Many women presented papers covering the whole range of religious traditions. At least fifty of the main presentations, panels, and workshops addressed women's issues. There were presentations on Jewish women, women in Jainism, in Islam, in Vedanta, in Buddhism, in Zoroastrianism, in Taoism, and in Native American religion. No fewer than nine presentations came from the various Wiccan or Goddess groups. Many panels addressed women's issues in spirituality or social justice from a comparative religious perspective. There was a keen concern throughout the conference for environmentalism and its relation both to religion and to women.[5]

In 1993 feminist issues in religion had somewhat arrived in mainstream American churches and theological seminaries. Most Christian seminaries included at least one woman professor teaching women's issues in theological studies. In more liberal seminaries a quarter to a third of the faculty were women, equipped to do more specialized courses on women in Bible, theology, church history, ethics, pastoral psychology, and worship. Between 20 and 60 percent of seminary students were women.[6] At the same time, there continued to be backlash movements in both Catholicism and Protestantism, seeking to discredit feminist theology and liturgy as heretical or even "pagan."[7]

In the twenty-five years since the late sixties, feminist religious scholars have produced a notable and ever-growing bibliography of both general and specialized studies in the whole range of theological disciplines. A bibliographic guide to Christian feminist theological literature in English published in 1991 filled 200 pages and was quickly outdated by new books and articles.[8]

FEMINIST HERMENEUTICS AND THEOLOGY

In the early nineties, feminist hermeneutics of the New Testament continues to be led by the magisterial Elisabeth Schüssler Fiorenza at Harvard University Divinity School. Schüssler Fiorenza's hermeneutical principles both demand a dismantling of claims to scriptural authority by patriarchal readings of the text and also call for creative discovery of women's experience as normative for the gospel, both in the early church and today.[9] Women-church, the discipleship of equals of women and men, is the context from which the liberating potential of the text must be discerned (document 1).

Schüssler Fiorenza's work is joined by that of a host of other feminist biblical exegetes: Phyllis Bird and Phyllis Trible, Cheryl Exum, Mieke Bal, and Katherine Sakenfeld[10] among Christians, and Drorah Setel, Tikva Frymer-Kensky, Carol Meyers, Esther Fuchs, Marcia Falk, Ross Kraemer, and Savina Teubal among Jewish scholars of Hebrew Scripture and early Judaism.[11] Christian feminist scholars of New Testament and early Christianity include Deirdre Good, Elizabeth Tetlow, Winsome Munro, Jane Schaberg, Elaine Pagels, Pheme Perkins, Sharon Ringe, Sandra Schneiders, Luise Schottroff, Mary Ann Tolbert, Mary Rose D'Angelo, Antoinette Wire, Bernadette Brooten, and Karen Torjesen.[12]

Feminist theology in a Christian context is well established with major books by Letty Russell, Carter Heyward, Anne Carr, Rebecca Chopp, Sallie McFague, Rita Brock, Rosemary Ruether, Elizabeth Johnson, Sharon Welch, and others.[13] Now coming of age is a second generation of feminist theologians who have already read the works of these writers in their graduate studies. New groups of feminist writers are developing in the African American, Hispanic, and Asian American communities, as well as among lesbians, challenging the lack of attention to racism and ethnic diversity, and to homophobia, in established Christian feminism.

WOMANIST, MUJERISTA, AND ASIAN THEOLOGIES

African American women theologians and ethicists have claimed the name *womanist* to distinguish their work done from the context of their historical and cultural experience. The powerful work of novelists such as Toni Morrison and Alice Walker has become the normative texts for womanist exegesis. Renita Weems has defined the womanist stance toward use of the Bible, while Jacquelyn Grant delineates the difference between white woman's Christ and black woman's Jesus. Katie Cannon reclaims the life and writings of foremother Zora Neale Hurston and Emilie Townes that of Ida B. Wells-Barnett as sources for womanist ethics. Delores Williams has taken the figure of Hagar as the prototype for womanist theology, while Toinette Eugene connects womanist ethics and theology to pastoral care of Black families (document 2).[14]

Hispanic American women, such as Ada María Isasi-Díaz and Yolanda Tarango, claimed the name *mujerista* to distinguish their context as Latina women doing theology and ethics in Anglo North America.[15] *Mujerista* theologians seek to distinguish the Hispanic women's voice in North America from those of Latin American liberation theologians and North American Hispanic males who ignore the experience of Hispanic women. They also celebrate the diversity in Hispanic women's communities, especially the Cubans, the Chicanas, and the Puerto Ricans, who, in the North American context, become lumped together by the dominant Anglo world. By locating their reflections in the context of popular urban and rural Hispanic women, *mujerista* theologians also seek to bridge the class gap between educated women and Hispanic women's popular culture (document 3).

Asian American women in the 1990s can draw on a growing body of Asian Christian feminist theology that has been pioneered by inter-Asian feminist journals such as *In God's Image*.[16] Korean feminist theologian Chung Hyun Kyung gained a high profile for the emerging Asian Christian feminist voice with her plenary address to the 1991 World Council of Churches meeting in Canberra, Australia.[17] Chung and other Asian feminists were educated in North America, but they maintain their ties to their home countries, moving back and forth between Asia and major theological schools in the United States. A distinctive feminist voice from American-born Asian Christian women is beginning to emerge.

American society in the last decades of the twentieth century, including both Christian churches and other religious bodies, is deeply divided by questions of sexual orientation. Although tensions between "straight" feminists and lesbians continue in religious as well as secular movements, generally the two groups have been able to come together in denouncing heterosexism as one of the expressions of sexist oppression in patriarchal societies and religions. Lesbian writers such as Mary Hunt, Carter Heyward, Tess Tessier, Bernadette Brooten, Joanne Brown, Sheila Briggs, and Emily Culpepper, among others, are defining a lesbian perspective on biblical, theological, historical, and ethical discourse.[18]

JEWISH FEMINIST THEOLOGY

Although Jewish women have long been leaders in American secular feminism, feminist critique and reconstruction of religious Judaism has gained momentum in the last third of the twentieth century. Women students in rabbinical colleges and increasing numbers of women rabbis can draw upon Jewish feminist biblical exegesis and reconstruction of women's history in Judaism. We have already noted the rise of Jewish women biblical scholars. These have begun to take their places as teachers in the theological schools of the Reformed and Reconstructionist traditions.

Although some issues, such as male God-language, are shared by Christian and Jewish religious feminists, other issues are distinct. Jewish women do not have to deal with the linking of original sin to Eve as women's representative, since original sin is not a part of Jewish anthropology. On the other hand, ceremonies such as circumcision and bar mitzvah privilege the Jewish male as the normative Jew, and rabbinical laws exclude women from the time-bound commandments of prayer. Jewish feminists work to create inclusive language, ceremonies, and religious observance.[19]

Some Jewish religious feminists find it necessary to develop distinctive women's *minyanim,* to explore worship from a Jewish women's context, just as Christian women are creating women-church. Judith Plaskow has taken the lead in insisting that it is not enough to work piecemeal on practices; it is necessary to confront the androcentric theological worldview that lies behind these practices (document 4).[20]

MUSLIM FEMINIST HERMENEUTICS

Although both Christian and Jewish religious feminists still face right-wing critics who seek to disallow their questions, women of these traditions seem relatively secure, at least in the liberal wings of their communities and theological schools, compared to the embattled feminists in Islam. Feminism is not a new issue for women of the Muslim world. Arab feminists, particularly from Egypt, Lebanon, and Palestine, claim a history going back into the 1920s of writing critical literature and struggling for legal and social reform of their societies. But these movements came from secular women allied with secularizing movements in Arab nations.[21]

The 1960s to 1990s have seen increasing militancy from Muslim Fundamentalists challenging the trends of secularization and seeking to reestablish the *Sharia* (Muslim law) as the norm of a good and godly society. Muslim Fundamentalist movements, perhaps even more than Fundamentalist Judaism or Christianity, take the reestablishment of women's traditional roles in the patriarchal family as normative. Although Muslims in America live as a minority in a secular, pluralistic society, where there is no likelihood of such traditions becoming the law of the land, nevertheless they are affected by these pressures within their subcultures.

Although Muslim Fundamentalism demands a return to traditional patterns of life for both men and women, circumscribing women's lives through dress codes, subordination to male authority, and segregated domesticity have been its major emphases. Independent women with careers are looked on with suspicion by the Muslim community. The Muslim woman who tries to live between the larger American culture and the Muslim subculture is in a double bind, made a visible "alien" by her distinctive garb on the job, while regarded as a "loose" woman by her community without such garb. The Black Muslim woman becomes doubly set apart, both from the African American Christian and the white communities, defined by her dress as a hostile apostate from both societies.[22]

Yet Muslim women, like conservative Christian women, are keenly aware of the failed promises of a "modern" male society, which allows women some equality in education and employment and then abandons them to female-headed households to be both sole parent and breadwinner. Conservatives promote readopting traditional roles for women by promising that this will also draw men to greater responsibility as husbands and fathers.[23]

Muslim feminists challenge the Fundamentalist interpretation of Islam. In so doing, they confront deep and volatile conflicts. On the one hand, they face a religion that has resisted historical-critical study of its Scripture and tradition. Thus they must make the case that the Qur'an does not mandate female subordination without questioning the authority of this text itself. On the other hand, they must reconcile female equality with family values that link male responsibility to female submission. In the interface between her personal life story and her work as a feminist Qur'anic exegete, Riffat Hassan demonstrates the difficulties of this role as a Muslim feminist (document 5).[24]

FEMINIST BUDDHISM

Buddhist feminism in the United States has been developed mostly among American-born women, many of whom were feminists and social activists in the sixties. They turned away from Christian or Jewish traditions that they found alienating or else came from secularized families that promoted education and achievement but lacked spiritual nurture. As these women experienced disappointment in personal relationships and burnout in social struggles whose goals appeared ever more difficult to achieve, they sought forms of meditation and spirituality that could provide a calm, sustaining center in the midst of chaos.

Buddhism was attractive to such women because it offered disciplines of meditation that had been honed over two thousand five hundred years, but there was no ultimate male God to which the seeker was asked to submit. Rather, the center of its spirituality was the close observance of reality itself, the reality of one's inner states in the flux of coming to be and passing away. By detaching oneself from anxiety and desires, one came to experience a sustaining peacefulness and unity with all things beyond the ephemeral ego and its unsatiable drives.

Intuitively these women saw Buddhism as deeply compatible with feminism, for it taught one to trust one's experience before all else. It also called for the dismantling of faith in an illusionary cultural world that deceived one about the true nature of reality. However, these American women soon became aware of disturbing sexist practices and ideologies in the forms of Buddhism that had been shaped in Asian patriarchal cultures.

Not only were women generally excluded from institutional and spiritual leadership, but male monastic leaders were celibates who drew their support from the laity and showed little sensitivity to those with family concerns, much less to women who might be single parents of children. Traditional concepts of incarnation inferiorized women by making one's present incarnation as a female the expression of bad karma, caused by a failed previous existence. Like the Christian myth of Eve's culpability for the fall, whereby women must atone for original sin through submission, this concept in Buddhism (derived from Hinduism) made women's very existence punitive.

As American women began to study the history of the development of the various Buddhist traditions, other contradictions appeared. The Buddha originally did not want to admit women as nuns and was persuaded to do so by his aunt, but only on condition that the nuns be strictly subservient to the monks. It was even said that Buddhism would have lasted a thousand years, rather than falling into crisis in five hundred years, if women had not been admitted as monastics. In some lineages female monasticism had died out. American women began to meet Buddhist nuns—some Asians, others European converts—working to reestablish a monastic lineage that had disappeared, struggling against male monastics who denied them training and ordination.[25]

Yet as these American women delved into the heart of Buddhist practice and its supporting theory, they felt all the more strongly that the authentic original meaning of Buddhism implied a dismantling of all social hierarchies, including gender hierarchy. This promise had failed to be fulfilled because Buddhism was shaped by patriarchal cultures in

India, China, and Japan. Yet the American context allowed for a fresh start for Buddhism stripped of these Asian cultural patterns, reshaped by an egalitarian feminist perspective.

The quest for a democratic feminist Buddhism was given both a rough jolt and a new impetus in 1983 when it was revealed that several of the major male Zen spiritual leaders were guilty of prolonged sexual abuse of female followers. The monastic discipline of total submission to one's guru had kept many of these women victims silent or even forced them to rationalize such behavior. At several conferences on women in Buddhism this silence was broken as women shared the pain of these experiences with one another. The result was that many women left centers run by men and developed their own groups for study and practice or to study with women.

Increasingly, female spiritual teachers began to appear, and a new mode of relations between teacher and student has begun to be shaped. More traditional centers are also starting to recognize women's leadership and to acknowledge women's concerns. The patterns of practice and organization of the centers are being adapted to needs of women who have to catch some time for meditation before or after work and who might need day care for their children during their time of practice. Forms of prayer and visualization that respond to women's experience are being developed. A feminist Buddhism adapted to the American environment is being created.[26]

Rita Gross is one of those women who made this journey to a feminist Buddhism. Growing up in a conservative Wisconsin Lutheran farm family, Rita was alienated from Christianity as a teenager when her church excommunicated her for singing in the choir of another Lutheran church of a different synod. Her religious search carried her into comparative religion, and for a while she was a practicing Jew.

The personal crisis of the death of a lover impelled her to seek a sustaining spirituality in the midst of mortality, and she found Buddhism responded to that need. Although Rita credits Buddhism with tempering her feminist anger, she also claims a prophetic voice from the Jewish and Christian traditions. Buddhist inner peacefulness and biblical protest meld in her work of developing a Buddhism freed of patriarchal trappings, freed to be a vehicle of liberation from both social dominance and the anxieties of finitude (document 6).

FEMINIST SPIRITUAL QUESTERS

While some American women were turning to Buddhism in their quest for a liberating spirituality, others felt women should reject all religious traditions shaped by patriarchal cultures, religions created to sanctify male domination. Mary Daly was one of these spiritual leaders whose study and experience convinced her that women must break with all religions and cultures historically created and led by males. Growing up a Roman Catholic, Daly was steeped in the traditional Catholic theology of the period and obtained her doctorates in Thomistic philosophy at the University of Fribourg. Daly returned to the United States in 1966 to teach at the Jesuit-run Boston College.

Although Daly still teaches at Boston College, her spiritual quest has led her to a more and more radical repudiation not only of Christianity but of all male world cultures. In Daly's view, women delude themselves if they believe they can reform such cultures, for these cultures have as their primary purpose the entrapment of women and the cannibalizing of female power. In their insidious grasp women become "fembots," drained of their own energy and made tools of a necrophilic male control over the very sources of life. Women must strip away the many layers of male delusionary myth, enshrined in the patterns of language itself, and leap into the liberating realm of female life power hidden and made invisible by the false appearances of male society and culture. Daly's successive books have sought to direct women to this journey of liberation and to create a new language to shatter the death-dealing hold of male culture on women's consciousness.[27] Daly does not shape alternative communities for female spiritual practice but remains at the crossroads of disaffiliation with all patriarchal culture, pointing to a promised land beyond it.

Other feminist spiritual questers feel they have found the authentic spirituality of a matricentric world before and beyond patriarchy in the revival of ancient Goddess religion. They use the term *Thealogy* (*Thea* means "Goddess") for their reflection on the Goddess. Carol Christ finds in the religion of the ancient Goddess the thread that can lead women (and men, if they wish) back to a spirituality of female power, gender equality, and harmony with nature. Trained in religion and literature at Yale Divinity School in the 1960s, Christ broke with Christianity and finally with male academic life to move to Greece, where she conducts study tours of the ancient centers of Goddess worship, such as Crete.[28]

Goddess spirituality as it developed in the United States in the 1970s is not simply a critical theory; first of all it is a practice, a way of life. That way of life is manifest in gatherings of small groups of thirteen (covens, a term that comes from the Latin *conventus* or assembly), where the sacred circle is cast and the assembly communes with the Goddess immanent in all things through the cycles of the renewal of the earth and the cosmos: the winter and summer solstices, the spring and fall equinoxes. Other key festivals in the yearly cycle are Candlemas, dedicated to Brigid, the Irish Goddess of fire and inspiration; Beltane or May Day, the time of renewal of earth's fertility; Lugnasad on August first, the harvest festival; and Samhain (Halloween), the Witch's New Year.[29]

Wiccans or Goddess worshipers also create more personal rituals geared to daily life: birthdays, self-blessings, puberty rites, and attracting a lover; rituals for conception, menstruation, and menopause; croning, or the celebration of wisdom in women's old age; attracting money or a job; exorcism of negative experience and dispelling the malignant power of enemies; overcoming loneliness; healing a broken heart; and making friends with one's inner child. Some rituals are appropriate for group celebrations, and others can be practiced alone with one's personal altar.[30]

Among the leading priestesses of feminist witchcraft are Z Budapest, a Hungarian immigrant who is a hereditary witch, having learned her craft from her mother. Budapest practices a separatist Dianic witchcraft for women alone. Another major theoretician and organizer of feminist witchcraft is Starhawk, who is Jewish in background and since 1982 has taught in the Creation Spirituality program of Matthew Fox in Oakland, California. Starhawk is ecumenical in outlook, seeking to help Christians and Jews find roots in their own traditions of Goddess spirituality. Her groups are open to both men and women. She is an ecofeminist and peace activist, linking feminist spirituality with overcoming war and destruction of the earth (document 7).[31]

Native American women have also been involved in the quest for a feminist spirituality within their own indigenous traditions. For many Native American feminists the original traditions of native peoples of the Americas were matricentric and pacific. Warrior traditions arose as these people faced invaders. The Euramerican conquest of the Americas has

Among the leading Jewish, Roman Catholic, and Buddhist American feminist theologians today are Judith Plaskow, professor of religious studies at Manhattan College, New York City; Rita Gross, professor of religious studies, University of Wisconsin, Eau Claire; and Elisabeth Schüssler Fiorenza, Stendahl professor of New Testament studies, Harvard Divinity School, Cambridge, Massachusetts.

Riffat Hassan, the leading Islamic exponent of feminist Qur'anic exegesis in the United States, was born in Pakistan and teaches religious studies at the University of Louisville.

Starhawk is one of the leading developers of Wiccan spirituality. To neopagan women, *wicca* (witch) means a wise woman with deep mystical powers to reshape reality.

Toinette Eugene, a Roman Catholic and associate professor of Christian ethics at Garrett-Evangelical Theological Seminary, Evanston, Illinois, is a leading creator of African American womanist theology and ethics.

Yolanda Tarango, a Chicana and Roman Catholic nun, is a member of the Sisters of Charity of the Incarnate Word, founder of a shelter for the homeless and children in San Antonio, and former coordinator of Las Hermanas, a national organization of Hispanic women.

been both physically and culturally genocidal, seeking both to remove native peoples from their lands and to destroy their distinct cultures. For Native American feminist Paula Gunn Allen, this history of genocide has been at heart gynocidal, an effort to exterminate a female-centered culture and replace it with a patriarchal one.[32]

Native peoples find they must not only recover their own spiritual traditions, but also sift through the centuries of patriarchalization that have distorted Native Americans' own understanding of their cultures. This prolonged assault on native cultures by white America has left native peoples pathologically demoralized, often expressing that demoralization in violence against themselves: alcoholism, fights between men, and battering of women. Feminism is often resisted by native people as both a threat to this precarious power of Native American males in a culture that despises them and another imposition of an alien ideology.

Paula Gunn Allen and other Native American feminists see their quest, not as an imitation of white feminism, but as the reclaiming of the spiritual and social balance of their own original cultures. Reclaiming the matricentric way of life will not only rebalance gender relations but also provide native peoples with a sustaining power of survival, liberated from the internalized self-destruction that lacks a life-giving future.

Native Americans seeking the recovery of their own spirituality often feel angry at white New Agers who "cannibalize" bits and pieces of native tradition, making no deep effort to undergo initiation into those traditions or to come to real understanding or commitment to the struggle of native peoples for survival. Native American women who appear at gatherings of women-church or New Age spirituality shock white feminists, who imagine themselves very friendly to native spirituality. Native women present hard, confrontational criticism of what they see as a new expression of white cultural genocide of native peoples.[33] For those who listen, however, this criticism is a call to go beyond a consumerist spiritual trip and become serious about transforming consciousness, calling society to face those people who in America have been the prime victims of European colonialization.

Feminist theology, thealogy, and spirituality in the last decade of the twentieth century present an expanding picture of increasing diversity, of contextualization in the many religious paths of human history. This diversity, however, is also accompanied by a difficult but ongoing dialogue among feminist seekers following these many ways. These women and men sense that the many paths must be part of a converging whole, a union of transformed global cultures of inner well-being and social and ecological balance freed from all forms of domination.

Documents

Document 1. Elisabeth Schüssler Fiorenza:
Feminist Hermeneutics for Women-Church

Elisabeth Schüssler Fiorenza is the leading creator of New Testament feminist hermeneutics. German-born and Roman Catholic, Schüssler Fiorenza has taught in the United States since 1970 and presently is Stendahl professor of New Testament studies at the Harvard University Divinity School in Cambridge, Massachusetts.[34]

The expression the *ekklesia [the democratic assembly] of women* or *women-church* is a theological political term. It asserts both that women are church and always have been church and that neither patriarchal society nor church are what they claim to be: *ekklesia*—the democratic congress of all citizens who have the power of self-determination. Hence as the movement of self-identified women and women's struggle identified men in society and church, the *ekklesia* of wo/men is the hermeneutical center of feminist biblical interpretation. It is part of the wider women's movement in democratic societies and biblical religions that conceives of itself not just as a women's rights but as a women's liberation movement. Its practice and vision is women's religious self-determination, theological authority and spiritual power for liberation from patriarchal alienation, marginalization and oppression.

Patriarchy as the basic analytic concept for feminist analysis allows us to conceptualize not only sexism but also racism and property-class relationships as basic structures of women's oppression. In a patriarchal society or religion, all women are bound into a system of male privilege and domination, but impoverished Third World women constitute the bottom of the oppressive patriarchal pyramid. Patriarchy cannot be top-pled except when the women who form the bottom of the patriarchal pyramid, triply oppressed women, become liberated.

The more we identify as women and thereby overcome our patri-archal self-alienation, the more we will realize that the separation be-tween white and black women, middle-class and poor women, native American and European women, Jewish and Christian women, Protes-tant and Catholic women, lesbian and heterosexual women, nun-women and lay-women is, in the words of Adrienne Rich, "a separation from ourselves." Conversely, option for the most oppressed woman is an option for our women selves. Such an option allows us "to find God in ourselves"[35] and to "love Her fiercely."[36]

The patriarchal dehumanization and victimization of multiply oppressed women exhibits the full death-dealing powers of patriarchy, while their struggle for liberation and courage to survive is the fullest experience of God's grace in our midst. A feminist critical theology of liberation must therefore be particular and concrete. It must theologi-cally explore women's particular experiences of marginalization, vic-timization, and oppression. At the same time it has to articulate our individual and historical experiences of liberation.

Feminist biblical interpretation must therefore challenge the scrip-tural authority of patriarchal texts and explore how the Bible is used as a weapon against women in our struggles for liberation. It also must explore whether and how the Bible can become a resource in this strug-gle. A feminist biblical interpretation is thus first of all a political task. It remains mandatory because the Bible and its authority has been and is again today used as a weapon against women struggling for liberation.

. . . A feminist critical theology of liberation develops a multidi-mensional model of biblical interpretation in order to assist women in their struggle for liberation. Such a model must be a feminist-critical and a historical-specific model. It must not only show how individual biblical texts and writings functioned in their historical-political settings but also pay increased attention to the intersection and interplay of bib-lical texts with contemporary politics and socialization.

Key elements in such a model, as far as I can see, are the following: (1) suspicion rather than acceptance of biblical authority, (2) critical evaluation and/or hermeneutics of proclamation, (3) remembrance and historical reconstruction, and (4) interpretation through celebration and ritual.

First, . . . a feminist critical hermeneutics of suspicion places a warning label on all biblical texts: *Caution! Could be dangerous to your health and survival.* Not only is scripture interpreted by a long line of men and proclaimed in patriarchal churches, it is also authored by men, written in androcentric language, reflective of religious male experience, selected and transmitted by male religious leadership. Without question, the Bible is a male book.

The first and never-ending task of a hermeneutics of suspicion, therefore, is to elaborate as much as possible the patriarchal, destructive aspects and oppressive elements in the Bible. Such an interpretation must uncover not only sexist biblical language but also the oppressive language of racism, anti-Judaism, exploitation, colonialism, and militarism. An interpretation of suspicion must name the language of hate by its true name and not mystify it or explain it away.

Second: If the *ekklesia* of women has the authority "to choose and to reject" biblical texts, we have to develop a theological interpretive principle for feminist critical evaluation rather than an interpretive principle and method of correlation. Such an interpretation must sort through particular biblical texts and test out in a process of critical analysis and evaluation how much their content and function perpetrates and legitimates patriarchal structures, not only in their original historical contexts but also in our contemporary situation. Conversely, all biblical texts must be tested as to their feminist liberating content and function in their historical and contemporary contexts. Such a feminist hermeneutics of critical evaluation has to articulate criteria and principles for evaluating particular texts, biblical books, traditions, or interpretations. Such criteria or principles must be derived from a systematic exploration of women's experience of oppression and liberation. We have therefore to develop a hermeneutics of proclamation that undercuts the authority claims of patriarchal scriptural texts.

Third: Such a hermeneutics of proclamation must be balanced by a hermeneutics of remembrance, which recovers *all* biblical traditions and texts through a feminist historical reconstruction. Feminist meaning is not only derived from the egalitarian-feminist surplus of androcentric texts but is also to be found in and through androcentric texts

and patriarchal history. Rather than abandon the memory of our foresisters' sufferings, visions, and hopes in our patriarchal biblical past,
such a hermeneutics reclaims their sufferings, struggles, and victories
through the subversive power of the "remembered" past. Rather than
relinquish patriarchal biblical traditions, a hermeneutics of remembrance seeks to develop a feminist critical method and historical model
for moving beyond the androcentric text to the history of women in
biblical religion.

An interpretation through remembrance must articulate theoretical
models that can place women not on the periphery but at the center of
biblical community and history.

Therefore a feminist hermeneutics of remembrance can reclaim
early Christian history as our own history and religious vision. Women-
church has a long history and tradition, which can claim the discipleship
of equals as its scriptural roots. In sum, a feminist hermeneutics of remembrance has to keep alive the memory of patriarchal biblical oppression as well as the memory of the struggles and victories of biblical
women who acted in the power of the Spirit.

Fourth: Interpretation through remembrance and historical reconstruction must be supplemented by a hermeneutics of creative ritualiza-
tion. Such an interpretation allows women-church to enter the biblical
story with the help of historical imagination, artistic recreation, and
liturgical celebration. A method of creative actualization seeks to retell
biblical stories from a feminist perspective, to reformulate biblical visions
and injunctions in the perspective of the discipleship of equals, and to
create narrative amplifications of the feminist remnants that have survived in biblical texts.

We rediscover in story and poetry, in drama and dance, in song and
liturgy our biblical foresisters' sufferings and victories. In ever-new
images and symbols, feminist liturgies seek to rename the God of the
Bible and the biblical vision. We sing litanies of praise to our foresisters
and pray laments of mourning for the wasted lives of our foremothers.
Only by reclaiming our religious imagination and our ritual powers of
naming can women-church dream new dreams and see new visions.

In conclusion, what leads us to perceive biblical texts as providing
resources in the struggle for liberation from patriarchal oppression, as
well as models for the transformation of the patriarchal church, is not
some special canon of texts that can claim divine authority. Rather, it is

the experience of women themselves in their struggles for liberation. I have therefore suggested that we understand the Bible as a structuring prototype of women-church rather than as a definite archetype; as an open-ended paradigm that sets experiences in motion and invites trans- formations. Such an understanding of the Bible as formative prototype allows us to explore models and traditions of liberating praxis as well as of patriarchal repression. It allows us to reclaim the whole Bible not as normative but as an experiential enabling authority, as the legacy and heritage of women-church. Such a notion of the Bible not as a mythic archetype but as a historical prototype provides women-church with a sense of its own ongoing history as well as Christian identity. It is able to acknowledge the dynamic process of biblical resources, challenges, and new visions under the changing conditions of the church's cultural- historical situations.

In and through structural and creative transformation, the Bible can become holy scripture for women-church. Insofar as the interpre- tive model proposed here does not identify biblical revelation with androcentric texts and patriarchal structures, it maintains that such reve- lation and inspiration is found among the discipleship community of equals in the past and the present. Insofar as the model proposed here locates revelation not in biblical texts but in the experience of women struggling for liberation from patriarchy, it requires that a feminist critical hermeneutics of liberation read and actualize the Bible in the context of believing communities of women, in the context of women-church.

Document 2. Toinette Eugene: Womanist Theology

Toinette Eugene, one of the leading creators of African American women's or womanist theology, defines this movement. A Roman Catholic, Eugene is presently professor of ethics at Garrett-Evangelical Theological Seminary in Evanston, Illinois.[37]

In the preface to her collection of womanist prose entitled *In Search of Our Mothers' Gardens*, Alice Walker defines a "womanist" as a black feminist or feminist of color who, among other things, is willful, serious, loving, and "committed to survival and wholeness of entire people, male and female." Walker's literary use of this folk expression common in African American communities has become the foundational source for identifying womanist theology. This concept has generated attention from theologians and ethicists because its inherent claims seem to resonate in the plurality of life and faith experiences of black women that are clearly in contradistinction to white feminist cultural, social, and theological perspectives.

At issue in the appropriation of the term "womanist" as a descriptive genre for theology is the power of self-definition or self-naming. Womanist theology is a signification for a theology that permits African American women to define themselves, to embrace and consciously affirm their cultural and religious traditions, and their own embodiment. Thus, womanist theology directly taps into the roots of the historical liberation capability of black women, according to the derivation of Walker's definition.

Informed by biblical, theological, and economic bases, womanist theology searches in particular for the voices, actions, opinions, struggles, and faith of African American women in order to shape a distinctive perspective that takes seriously their experiences and traditions in response to the liberating activity of God. Womanist theology, as a disciplined commentary about the nature of God, intimates a critical posture toward sexism, misogyny, and the objectification and abuse of black women, both within African American communities and within the dominant patriarchal culture. Womanist theology agrees with black theology in its critique of white racism and the need for black unity, and it agrees with feminist theology in its criticism of sexism and the need for the unity of women. Womanist theology moves beyond both by providing its own critique of racism in feminist theology and of sexism in black theology. It also emphasizes the dimension of class analysis since historically most African American women have been poor or are negatively affected by the unequal distribution of capital and gainful employment as a direct consequence of the economic system operative in the United States. Consequently womanist theology must be based on a tridimensional analysis of racism, sexism, and classism.

Furthermore, womanist theology is a particular consequence of the black nationalism inherent in black theology that focuses on womanist concerns. However, materials that convey black women's traditions—narratives, novels, and prayers—only recently have become a primary resource for black theology.

In addition to the social and ecclesial experiences and activities of African American women as points of departure for womanist theology, a distinctive use of the Bible and the role and significance of Jesus uniquely characterize the womanist tradition. On the one hand those in power have most consistently and effectively used the Bible to restrict and censure the behavior of African American women. On the other hand, the Bible has significantly captured the imagination of African American women because extensive portions of it speak to the deepest aspirations of oppressed people for freedom, dignity, justice, and vindication.

Womanist theology relies on the Bible as a principal resource because of its vision and promise of a world where the humanity of everyone will be fully valued. Womanist theology engages in a liberationist hermeneutical interpretation of the Bible in spite of numerous voices from within and without the Christian tradition that have tried to equivocate on the biblical vision and promises made to oppressed and marginal persons and communities.

The prominence given to Christology by womanist theology discloses a perspective that is congruent with and flows from its liberationist interpretation of biblical revelation. For womanist theology, the humanity, the wholeness of Christ, is paramount, not the maleness of the historical person, Jesus.

This particularly "egalitarian" Christology evokes a womanist commitment to struggle not only with oppressive symptoms that are abundantly extant for African American women within church and society, but also with the causes of pervasive inequality and disenfranchisement. This egalitarian womanist revision yields deeper theological and christological questions related to images and symbolism. Such a Christology challenges womanist theology to forge a distinctively different genre as required by the particular constraints and circumstances in which it finds a locus.

Document 3. Ada María Isasi-Díaz and Yolanda Tarango: *Mujerista* Theology

Hispanic women have coined the term *mujerista* ("womanist" in Spanish) theology for their contextualization of theological reflection. Ada María Isasi-Díaz, a Cuban by birth and professor of theology at

Drew University, and Yolanda Tarango, a Chicana, member of the
Sisters of Charity of the Incarnate Word, founder of Visitation House in
San Antonio, Texas (a shelter for the homeless and children), and former
coordinator of Las Hermanas (a national organization of Hispanic
women), are leaders of this movement.[38]

For the last twenty years, there has been a growing number of Hispanic women or latinas (there is no consensus at present as to which of
these two terms to use) in the U.S.A. who have struggled against the
sexism in their own culture as well as in the dominant one. Recently,
they have felt the need to name themselves, conscious that a name not
only is a means of identification but also provides the conceptual framework, the point of reference, the mental constructs that are used in
understanding and relating to persons, ideas and movements. Thus, Hispanic women who place the analysis of and struggle against sexism at
the center of their liberation movement have started to use the term
mujerista. From the beginning the description of the term *mujerista* has
had a strong religious component due to the centrality of the sacred to
Hispanic/latino culture. A *mujerista* is a Hispanic woman who struggles
to liberate herself not as an individual but as a member of a community.
She is one who builds bridges among latinos instead of falling into sec-
tarianism and using divisive tactics. A *mujerista* understands that her task
is to gather the hopes and expectations of the people about justice and
peace and to work for a radical change of oppressive structures. A
mujerista is called to gestate new women and new men—Hispanics who
are willing to work for the common good, knowing that such work
requires the denunciation of destructive self-abnegation. A *mujerista* is a
latina who makes a preferential option for herself and her Hispanic sisters, understanding that the struggle for liberation has to take into consideration how racism/ethnic prejudice, economic oppression and
sexism work together, how they reinforce each other.

Mujerista theology is a praxis—critical, reflective action based on
and dealing with questions of ultimate meaning. This praxis is a reflective action based on analysis of a historical reality done through the lens
of an option for and a commitment to the liberation of latinas. A clear
understanding of the use of the word *praxis* is very important.

Praxis is not reflection that follows action or is "at the service of
action."[39] Both action and reflection become inseparable moments in

praxis. Praxis "combines reflection with action to create the human world of ideas, symbols, language, science, religion, art, and production." To bring reflection to bear upon action—that is praxis.

Truth is relevant at the level of action, "not in the realm of ideas." Therefore, like other liberation theologies, *mujerista* theology is concerned not with orthodoxy but with orthopraxis. . . .

Because *mujerista* theology is praxis, it demands three very clear and concrete commitments: to *do* theology; to do theology from a *specific* perspective; to do theology from a specific perspective *as a communal process.*

To *do* theology is to free theology from the exclusive hold of academia; it is also a matter of denouncing the false dichotomy between thought and action so prevalent in Western culture. To do theology is to recognize that the source of theology is human existence, its questions and concerns as well as its beliefs. To do theology is to validate and uphold the lived experience of the oppressed, since the dominant cultures and countries not only deny its validity, but even question its very existence.

To do theology from a *specific perspective* requires a clear identification of the day-to-day life of those engaged in doing this theology, their needs and their struggles. Because of this, it is presumptuous to speak of "theology" as if there were only one and as if theology were an objective science.

Mujerista theology as a praxis has as its base and lens an option, a commitment. It does not try to be objective but rather to state clearly its subjectivity at the levels of analysis and strategy. Because of this, the particularities out of which *mujerista* theology emerges become important:

1. Due to the sexism and ethnic prejudice they suffer, Hispanic women face a most perilous situation. Classism, especially the economics of classism, is part of the oppression of the majority of latinas.

2. There is a lack of recognition by Hispanic men of Hispanic women and their oppression.

3. Latinas have come to understand that they have a very important contribution to make. The particularity of their oppression has led

them to understand that the solution to their oppression has to be liberation and not equality.

Out of these particularities arise the questions of ultimate meaning with which *mujerista* theology is preoccupied: questions of survival. Survival has to do with more than barely living. Survival has to do with the struggle *to be* fully. To survive, one has to have "the power to decide about one's history and one's vocation or historical mission."

The specificity of mujerista theology has cultural-historical reality as its *locus theologicus*. This immediately places the theological task in contact with three very different cultures and histories: the Amerindian, the African, and the Spanish.

A *mestizaje* has resulted from the mixture of these three races, cultures, and histories. The Hispanic understandings of the divine, the human, the meaning of life—these understandings emerge from this *mestizaje*. The theological task of any and every latina cannot ignore this three-pronged *mestizaje*. Though the Hispanic cultural-historical reality is often ignored in theology, the present and active popular religiosity of the latino community requires that theology give equal consideration to all three cultural strata out of which this *mestizaje* emerges. Up to now almost exclusive attention has been given to the Catholicism brought by the Spaniards. But in popular religiosity the religious, cosmological, theological, and anthropological understandings that the Amerindians and the Africans brought to America are just as operative.

Mujerista theology is a *communal process*. There are three main reasons for this. First, the source of *mujerista* theology is the lived experience, experience that has to include both personal and communal aspects.

Second, the theological process is an intrinsic part of the liberation task because it is one of the ways in which the community becomes the agent of its own history. Liberation is a personal process that takes place within a community and through a community.

Third, one of the most pervasive themes in Hispanic culture is the community. *La comunidad* is the immediate reality within which latinos find their personal identities and function. In concrete terms, the sense of community revolves around the *familia* (family) and the *barrio, barriada* (neighborhood). Certain aspects of the *iglesia* (church) also provide an important focus for the development and maintenance of the sense of community among Hispanics. Social functions, such as fairs and other fundraising activities, as well as procession, novenas, and other religious functions that are a part of popular religiosity, are the aspects of church that relate to the sense of community.

The importance of *mujerista* theology lies in its being an intrinsic element in the process of creating a Hispanic women's culture and an articulation of a new reality being birthed right now. In the U.S.A. the cultures of different latino groups come together, and new cultural patterns begin to emerge according to the reality Hispanic women face. The main reason this is happening now is that the need for economic and cultural survival has led latinas to begin to understand themselves as one, to find similarities among themselves and capitalize on them; to see differences not as dangerous and divisive, but as an enriching factor.

Mujerista theology has been born. As a process and a praxis, it is always being birthed by Hispanic women who struggle for liberation and for whom *la vida es la lucha* (life is the struggle). But *mujerista* theology also does the birthing—it births hope and a vision of the future in which all peoples will be free because latinas are free.

Document 4. Judith Plaskow:
Jewish Feminist Theology

Insisting that the "right question is theological," Judith Plaskow defines the key issues for the shaping of a Jewish feminist theology. Plaskow is professor of religious studies at Manhattan College in New York City.[40]

The Jewish women's movement of the past decade has been and remains a civil-rights movement rather than a movement for "women's liberation."[41] It has been a movement concerned with the images and status of women in Jewish religious and communal life, and with halakhic and institutional change. It has been less concerned with analysis of the origins and bases of women's oppression that render change necessary. It has focused on getting women a piece of the Jewish pie; it has not wanted to bake a new one!

Of the issues that present themselves for our attention, *halakhah* has been at the center of feminist agitation for religious change. . . . But . . . it is specific *halakhot* that have been questioned and not the fundamental presuppositions of the legal system. The fact that women are not counted in a *minyan,* that we are not called to the Torah, that we are silent in the marriage ceremony and shackled when it comes to divorce—these disabilities have been recognized, deplored, and in non-Orthodox Judaism, somewhat alleviated. The *implications* of such laws, their essentially nonarbitrary character, has received less attention, however. Underlying specific *halakhot,* and *outlasting their amelioration or rejection,* is an assumption of women's Otherness far more basic than the laws in which it finds expression. If women are not part of the congregation, if we stand passively under the *huppah,* if, even in the Reform movement, we have become rabbis only in the last ten years, this is because men—and not women with them—define Jewish humanity. Men are the actors in religious and communal life because they are the normative Jews. Women are "other than" the norm; we are less than fully human.[42]. . .

Our legal disabilities are a *symptom* of a pattern of projection that lies deep in Jewish thinking. They express and reflect a fundamental stance toward women that must be confronted, addressed and rooted out at its core. While it is Jewish to hope that changes in *halakhah* might bring about changes in underlying attitudes, it is folly to think that justice for women can be achieved simply through halakhic mechanisms when women's plight is not primarily a product of *halakhah.*

. . . The Otherness of women is also given dramatic expression in our language about God. Here, we confront a great scandal: the God who supposedly transcends sexuality, who is presumably one and whole, is known to us through language that is highly selective and partial. The images we use to describe God, the qualities we attribute to God, draw on male pronouns and male experience and convey a sense of power and authority that is clearly male in character.

The female images that exist in the Bible and (particularly the mystical) tradition form an underground stream that reminds us of the inadequacy of our imagery without, however, transforming its overwhelmingly male nature. The hand that takes us out of Egypt is a male hand—both in the Bible and in our contemporary imaginations. . . . The maleness of God is not arbitrary—nor is it simply a matter of pronouns. It leads us to the central question, the question of the Otherness of women, just as the Otherness of women leads to the maleness of

God. . . . If God is male, and we are in God's image, how can maleness *not* be the norm of Jewish humanity? If maleness is normative, how can women not be Other? And if women are Other, how can we not speak of God in language drawn from the male norm?. . .

Women's greater access to Jewish learning, our increased leadership in synagogue ritual only bring to the surface deep contradictions between equality for women and the tradition's fundamental symbols and images for God. While the active presence of women in congregations should bespeak our full membership in the Jewish community, the language of the service conveys a different message. It impugns the humanity of women and ignores our experience, rendering that experience invisible, even in the face of our presence. But since language is not a halakhic issue, we cannot change this situation through halakhic repair. It is not "simply" that *halakhah* presupposes the Otherness of women but that this Otherness reflects and is reflected in our speech about God. The equality of women in the Jewish community requires the radical transformation of our religious language in the form of recognition of the feminine aspects of God.

Here we encounter a problem; for it is impossible to mention the subject of female language without the specter of paganism being raised. . . .

It might seem we are now distant enough from paganism to understand the historical context of suppression of the Goddess without feeling the need to refight this struggle. But if Ba'al is impotent and voiceless, an object of purely theoretical condemnation, the Goddess still evokes resistance which is vehement and deeply felt. Albeit through the lens of our monotheistic tradition, she seems to speak to us as powerfully as ever. Yet this is itself a strong argument for the incorporation of female language into the tradition. It is precisely because she is not distant that the Goddess must be recognized as a part of God. For the God who does not include her is an idol made in man's image, a God over against a female Other—not the Creator, source of maleness and femaleness, not the relativizer of all gods and goddesses who nonetheless includes them as part of God's self. Acknowledging the many aspects of the Goddess among the names of God becomes a measure of our ability to incorporate the feminine and women into a monotheistic religious framework. At the same time, naming women's experience as part of the nature of the deity brings the suppressed experience of women into the Jewish fold.

This brings us to our last issue, one that is closely related to the other two. . . . The Jewish tradition is not the product of the entire Jewish people, but of Jewish men alone. Of course women have lived Jewish history and carried its burdens, shaped our experience to history and history to ourselves. But ours is not the history passed down and recorded; the texts committed to memory or the documents studied; the arguments fought, refought, and finely honed. Women have not contributed to the formation of the written tradition, and thus tradition does not reflect the specific realities of women's lives.

This fact, which marks so great a loss to tradition and to women, is cause and reflection both of the Otherness of women and the maleness of God. Women are not educated as creators of tradition because we are Other, but of course we remain Other when we are seen through the filter of male experience without ever speaking for ourselves. The maleness of God calls for the silence of women as shapers of the holy, but our silence in turn enforces our Otherness and a communal sense of the "rightness" of the male image of God. There is a "fit" in other words, a tragic coherence between the role of women in the community, and its symbolism, law, and teaching. The Otherness of women is part of the fabric of Jewish life. . . .

Clearly, the implications of Jewish feminism, while they include halakhic restructuring, reach beyond *halakhah* to transform the bases of Jewish life. Feminism demands a new understanding of Torah, God, and Israel: an understanding of Torah that begins with acknowledgment of the profound injustice of Torah itself. The assumption of the lesser humanity of women has poisoned the content and structure of the law, undergirding women's legal disabilities and our subordination in the broader tradition. This assumption is not amenable to piecemeal change. It must be utterly eradicated by the withdrawal of projection from women—the discovery that the negative traits attributed to women are also in the men who attribute them, while the positive qualities reserved for men are also in women. Feminism demands a new understanding of God that reflects and supports the redefinition of Jewish humanity. The long-suppressed femaleness of God, acknowledged in the mystical tradition, but even here shaped and articulated by men, must be recovered and reexplored and reintegrated into the Godhead. Last, feminism assumes that these changes will be possible only when we come to a new understanding of the community of Israel which includes the whole of Israel and which therefore allows women to speak and name our experience for ourselves.

Document 5. Riffat Hassan: Muslim Feminist Hermeneutics

Riffat Hassan is the leading exponent of feminist Qur'anic exegesis in the United States. Born in Pakistan, Hassan is professor of religious studies at the University of Louisville, Kentucky.[43]

I have been asking questions such as "What is the Islamic view of women?" and "What does it mean to be a Muslim woman?" for a long time. I was born female to a Muslim family living in Lahore, a Muslim city in a Muslim country, Pakistan. Not until 1974, however, did I begin my serious study of women's issues in Islam and—I am still shocked to reflect—this happened almost by accident.

I was, at that time, faculty adviser to the Muslim Students' Association chapter at Oklahoma State University in Stillwater. (I had acquired this "honor" solely because there was no Muslim man on the faculty, and it was mandatory for each chapter to have a faculty adviser.) Their annual seminar included an address by the faculty adviser, so I was asked—albeit not with overwhelming enthusiasm—if I would read a paper on women in Islam. I knew that speakers were not generally assigned subjects and that I had been asked to speak on women in Islam because, in the opinion of the group, it would have been totally inappropriate to expect a Muslim woman, even one who taught them Islamic studies, to be competent to speak on any other subject pertaining to Islam. I resented what the assigning of the subject meant.

Still, I accepted the invitation for two reasons. First, I knew that being invited to address an all-male, largely Arab-Muslim group that prided itself on its patriarchalism was itself a breakthrough. Second, I was so tired of hearing Muslim men pontificate on the position or status or role of women in Islam, I thought that it might be worthwhile to present a woman's viewpoint. I began my research on the subject more out of a sense of duty than out of any deep awareness that I had embarked on perhaps the most important journey of my life.

I do not know exactly at what time my "academic" study of women in Islam became a passionate quest for truth and justice on behalf of Muslim women—perhaps it was when I realized that impact on my own life of the so-called Islamic ideas and attitudes regarding women. What began as a scholarly exercise became simultaneously an Odyssean venture in self-understanding. But "enlightenment" does not always lead to "endless bliss." The more I saw the justice and compassion of God reflected in the Qur'anic teachings regarding women, the more anguished and angry I became at seeing the injustice and inhumanity to which Muslim women, in general, are subjected in actual life. I began to feel that it was my duty—as a part of the microscopic minority of educated Muslim women—to do as much consciousness-raising regarding the situation of Muslim women as I could.

The Need for Women's Theology in Islam

Despite the fact that women such as Khadijah and 'A'ishah (wives of the Prophet Muhammad) and Rabi'a al-Basri (the outstanding woman Sufi) figure significantly in early Islam, the Islamic tradition has, by and large, remained rigidly patriarchal until the present time, prohibiting the growth of scholarship among women particularly in the realm of religious thought. Thus the sources on which the Islamic tradition is based, mainly the Qur'an, the Hadith literature (oral traditions attributed to the Prophet), and Fiqh (jurisprudence), have been interpreted only by Muslim men, who have arrogated to themselves the task of defining the ontological, theological, sociological, and eschatological status of Muslim women.

Unless and until the theological foundations of misogynistic and androcentric tendencies in the Islamic tradition are demolished, Muslim women will continue to be brutalized and discriminated against, despite statistical improvements relating to female education, employment, or social and political rights. No matter how many socio-political rights are granted to women, as long as they are conditioned to accept the myths used by theologians or religious hierarchs to shackle their bodies, hearts, minds, and souls, they will never become fully developed or whole human beings.

The Qur'an describes human creation in thirty or so passages which are found in various chapters. Generally speaking, it refers to the creation of humanity (and nature) in two ways: as an evolutionary process where diverse stages or phases are mentioned sometimes together and sometimes separately, and as an accomplished fact or in its totality. In the passages in which human creation is described "concretely" or "analytically," we find that no mention is made of the separate or distinct creation of either man or woman. In those passages in which reference is made to Allah's creation of human beings as sexually differentiated mates, no priority or superiority is accorded to either man or woman.

In summary, the Qur'an evenhandedly uses both feminine and masculine terms and imagery to describe the creation of humanity from a single source. That Allah's original creation was undifferentiated humanity, and neither man nor woman (who appeared simultaneously at a subsequent time), is implicit in a number of Qur'anic passages.

Hawwa' in the Hadith Literature

If the Qur'an makes no distinction between the creation of man and woman, as it clearly does not, why do Muslims believe that Hawwa' (Eve) was created from the rib of Adam? Although the Genesis 2 account of woman's creation is accepted by virtually all Muslims, it is difficult to believe that it entered the Islamic tradition directly for very few Muslims ever read the Bible. It is much more likely that it became a part of Muslim heritage through its assimilation in Hadith literature, which has been in many ways the lens through which the Qur'an has been seen since the early centuries of Islam.

That the story of Eve's creation from Adam's rib had become part of the Hadith literature is evident from the following *hadith* [oral tradition] cited by Jane Smith and Yvonne Haddad in their article, "Eve: Islamic Image of Woman": "When God sent Iblis out of the Garden and placed Adam in it, he dwelt in it alone and had no one to socialize with. God sent sleep on him then He took a rib from his left side and placed flesh in its place and created Hawwa' from it. When he awoke he found a woman seated near his head. He asked her, 'Who are you?' She answered, 'Woman.' He said, 'Why were you created?' She said, 'That you might find rest in me.' The angels said, 'What is her name?' and he said, 'Hawwa.' They said, 'Why was she called Hawwa'?' He said, 'Because she was created from a living thing.'"

This *hadith* clashes sharply with the Qur'anic accounts of human creation, while it has an obvious correspondence to Genesis 2:18–33 and Genesis 3:20.

Some changes, however, are to be noted in the story of woman's creation as retold in the above *hadith*. It mentions the left rib as the source of woman's creation. In Arab culture great significance is attached to right and left, the former being associated with everything auspicious and the latter with the opposite. In Genesis woman is named Eve after the Fall but in the above *hadith* she is called Hawwa' from the time of her creation. In Genesis woman is named Eve because "she is the mother of all who live" (thus a primary source of life), but above she is named Hawwa' because she was created from a living thing (hence a derivative creature). These variations are not to be ignored. Biblical and other materials are seldom incorporated without alteration into *ahadith* [plural form of *hadith*]. The above example illustrates how, with respect to woman, Arab biases were added to the adopted text.

The theology of woman implicit in the *ahadith* is based upon generalizations about her ontology, biology, and psychology that are contrary to the letter and spirit of the Qur'an. These *ahadith* ought to be rejected on the basis of their content alone.

In regard to the issue of woman's creation as more important, philosophically and theologically, than any other. If man and woman have been created equal by God, who is believed to be the ultimate arbiter of value, then they cannot become unequal, essentially, at a subsequent time. Hence their obvious inequality in the patriarchal world is in contravention of God's plan. On the other hand, if man and woman have been created unequal by God, then they cannot become equal, essentially, at a subsequent time. Hence any attempt to equalize them is contrary to God's intent.

Given the importance of this issue, it is imperative for Muslim women's-rights activists to know that the egalitarian accounts of human creation given in the Qur'an have been displaced by the contents of *ahadith,* even though this cannot happen in theory. The only way that Muslim daughters of Hawwa' can end the history of their subjection at the hands of the sons of Adam is by returning to the point of origin and challenging the authenticity of the *ahadith* that make women derivative and secondary in creation, but primary in guilt, sinfulness, and mental and moral deficiency. They must challenge the later sources that regard them not as ends in themselves but as instruments created for the convenience and comfort of men.

Document 6. Rita Gross: Buddhist Feminism

Rita Gross is one of many American women converts who have been developing a distinctly American feminist Buddhism. Gross is professor of religious studies at the University of Wisconsin at Eau Claire.[44]

Buddhism and feminism can be brought into relationship with each other through a definition of feminism in Buddhist terms, which I often use when trying to present feminism to Buddhists. According to this definition, feminism involves "the radical practice of the co-humanity of women and men."

To see feminism as a "practice" is not usual in feminist circles because the language is so very Buddhist. Buddhism is at root a "practice," a spiritual discipline; various meditation techniques are the heart of the tradition, and its method for achieving its goals of calm, insight, and liberation. Feminists, more used to the Western predominance of theory over practice, are prone to talk of "feminist theory," but feminism really involves a fundamental reorientation of mind and heart that cannot bear fruit if it is merely theoretical. To be effective, feminism needs to become an ongoing practice of changing one's language, one's expectations, one's ideas of normalcy, which happens as soon as things "click," as soon as one "wakes up," using Buddhist language, to feminism's fundamental and outrageous truth of the *co-humanity* of woman and men. . . . Some women involved in both Buddhism and feminism simply say "Buddhism *is* feminism!" by which they express intuitively the conviction that when Buddhism is true to itself, it manifests the same vision as does feminism. . . .

At least four profound similarities between the fundamental orientations of Buddhism and of feminism strengthen the claim that Buddhism is feminism.

First, contrary to most of the Western philosophical and theological heritage, both Buddhism and feminism begin with experience, stress experiential understanding enormously, and move from experience to theory, which becomes the expression of experience. Both share the approach that conventional views and dogmas are worthless if experience does not actually bear out theory. In other words, in a conflict between one's experience of one's world and what one has been taught by others about the world, both feminism and Buddhism agree that one cannot deny or repress experience.

Allegiance to experience before theory leads to a second important similarity between Buddhism and feminism, the will and the courage to go against the grain at any cost, and to hold to insights of truth, no matter how bizarre they seem from a conventional point of view. In its core teachings about the lack of external salvation (nontheism), about the nonexistence of a permanent abiding self (nonego), and about the pervasiveness and richness of suffering, Buddhism goes against the grain of what religions generally promise. Yet Buddhists continue to see these unpopular religious insights as the only way to attain liberation "beyond hope and fear." . . .

Thirdly, both perspectives use their willingness to hold to experience over convention and theory and their tenacious courage to explore how mental constructs operate to block or enhance liberation. For Buddhism, this exploration has involved the study of conventional ego, its painful habitual tendencies, and the underlying freedom of the basic egoless state. For feminism, this exploration involves looking into ways in which the social conditioning that produces gender stereotypes and conventional gender roles trap both women and men in half-humanity, encouraging mutual incompetence and threatening to destroy the planet. In sum, both Buddhism and feminism explore how habitual ego patterns block basic well-being.

Finally, both perspectives speak of liberation as the point of human existence, the aim toward which all existence strains. . . . Feminism, like Buddhism and like all other visions of the human spirit, looks beyond the immediate and compelling entrapments of easy solutions and conventional perspectives to the radical freedom of transcending those entrapments. . . .

Though it is compelling and accurate to speak of Buddhism *as* feminism, that statement is not the complete story. Potential mutual transformation between Buddhism and feminism provides an equally significant resource for Buddhist feminism. When mutual transformation, rather than similarity, is focused upon, the emphasis changes from how compatible the two perspectives are to what they might learn from each other. . . .

Mutual transformation is usually thought to result when two partners from different spiritual perspectives interact with each other. In the case of the dialogue and mutual transformation between Buddhism and feminism, the process is usually an internal dialogue within a person seriously committed to both perspectives. That this is an internal dialogue does not make the process less real or less transformative. . . . In my case, feminism was more deeply transformed initially by Buddhist practice than vice versa and this transformation was an ungrounding and profound experience. I continue to believe that Buddhism can make a significant critique of feminism as usually constituted and that Buddhist thought and practice could have a great deal to contribute to feminists.

. . . Buddhist practice has a great deal to offer in helping feminists deal with the anger that can be so enervating, while allowing them to retain the sharp critical brilliance contained in the anger. Buddhist meditation practices can also do wonders to soften the ideological hardness that often makes feminists ineffective spokespersons in their own behalf. Buddhist teachings on suffering help feminists remember that basic human sufferings and existential anxieties are not patriarchy's fault and will not be eliminated in postpatriarchal social conditions. Finally, Buddhist spirituality with its long-tested spiritual disciplines, can do much to undercut the tendencies towards trippiness and spiritual materialism that often plague feminist spirituality movements.

At this point, however, my main topic is transformation from the other direction, from feminism into Buddhism. This is a feminist history, analysis, and reconstruction of Buddhism, not an assessment of "Feminism from the Perspective of Buddhist Practice."[45] What transformation from feminism to Buddhism involves is, in my view, best summed up by saying that I am taking permission, as a Buddhist, to use the prophetic voice. . . . Feminism, especially the Christian and post-Christian feminist thought with which I am most familiar can, with great cogency, be seen as in direct continuity with biblical prophecy, in its true meaning of social criticism, protest against misuse of power, vision for a social order more nearly expressing justice and equity, and, most importantly, willingness actively to seek that more just and equitable order through whatever means are appropriate and necessary.

This prophetic voice is the missing element that has allowed Buddhists to tolerate with ease the combination of lofty and extremely refined teachings about compassion, including some theoretical understanding of gender equity, with often extremely repressive social regimes, not only regarding gender, but also regarding politics and economics. Herein lies the major problem for Buddhism. It is not that Buddhism lacks a social ethic, as is sometimes claimed, for Buddhism has an extremely sophisticated set of guidelines for moral interactions. But Buddhists have generally not been willing to engage in social action to see the realization of that ethic in realms of politics, economics, or social organization. . . .

"Compassion" is a word that comes easily and naturally in Buddhist discussion of social ethics. The word "righteousness" does not. Compassion for those caught in the ocean of *samsara,* suffering all the indignities inherent in such existence, is a prime motivation for and justification of the Buddhist lifestyle. Living the eightfold path of Buddhist individual and social morality involves nonharming and working for the benefit of all sentient beings on all levels. The method, however, has been individual and somewhat passive, especially when compared with ringing calls for and acts on behalf of overall justice and righteousness common to those who use the prophetic voice. In taking permission to use the prophetic voice as a Buddhist feminist, I am seeking to empower compassion, as understood so well in Buddhist social ethics, by direct infusion of concern for righteousness, for the actual manifestation in Buddhist societies of Buddhism's compassionate vision.

I most certainly am not content to accept the status quo of gender arrangements in most of the Buddhist world. In fact, if I had to be a Buddhist woman under the conditions that exist in most parts of the Buddhist world, Buddhism would not be my religion of choice. Only an auspicious coincidence of Buddhism and feminism, central to my vision, permits the internal dialogue. That internal dialogue has resulted in mutual transformation. The prophetic voice, derived from earlier trainings in Western modalities of the spirit, is coming through loudly and clearly in my Buddhist discussions of women. Furthermore, the permission to use that prophetic voice in Buddhist discourse is perhaps the greatest, most necessary, and most useful resource for a Buddhist feminism.

At the same time, mutual transformation comes through from the other side, for Buddhist meditation training and the Buddhist emphasis on gentleness will modulate the prophetic voice, which can sometimes be strident in expressing its truth and insights. Perhaps we can envision a marriage of compassion and righteousness in social ethics, a gentle and active approach to such issues as gender inequity, privilege, and hierarchy.

Document 7. Starhawk: Wiccan Thealogy

Wicca (witch) is understood by neopagan women to mean a "wise woman" with deep mystical powers to reshape reality. Starhawk, born Miriam Simos, is one of the leading developers of Wiccan spirituality. A peace activist, she works with the Reclaiming collective in San Francisco, where she offers workshops and leads public rituals. She also teaches in the Creation Spirituality program at Holy Names College in Oakland, California.[46]

Witchcraft is a religion, perhaps the oldest religion extant in the West. Its origins go back before Christianity, Judaism, Islam—before Buddhism and Hinduism, as well, and it is very different from all the so-called great religions. The Old Religion, as we call it, is closer in spirit to Native American traditions or to the shamanism of the Arctic. It is not based on dogma or a set of beliefs, nor on scriptures or a sacred book revealed by a great man. Witchcraft takes its teachings from nature, and reads inspiration in the movements of the sun, moon, and stars, the flight of birds, the slow growth of trees, and the cycles of the seasons. . . .

Witchcraft has always been a religion of poetry, not theology. The myths, legends, and teachings are recognized as metaphors for "That-Which-Cannot-Be-Told," the absolute reality our limited minds can never completely know. The mysteries of the absolute can never be explained—only felt or intuited. Symbols and ritual acts are used to trigger altered states of awareness, in which insights that go beyond words are revealed. When we speak of "the secrets that cannot be told," we do not mean merely that rules prevent us from speaking freely. We mean that the inner knowledge literally *cannot* be expressed in words. It can only be conveyed by experience, and no one can legislate what insight another person may draw from any given experience. . . .

The primary symbol for "That-Which-Cannot-Be-Told" is the Goddess. The Goddess has infinite aspects and thousands of names— She is the reality behind many metaphors. She *is* reality, the manifest deity, omnipresent in all of life, in each of us. The Goddess is not separate from the world—She *is* the world, and all things in it: moon, sun, earth, star, stone, seed, flowing river, wind, wave, leaf and branch, bud and blossom, fang and claw, woman and man. In Witchcraft, flesh and spirit are one.

As we have seen, Goddess religion is unimaginably old, but contemporary Witchcraft could just as accurately be called the New Religion. The Craft, today, is undergoing more than a revival, it is experiencing a renaissance, a re-creation. Women are spurring this renewal, and actively reawakening the Goddess, the image of "the legitimacy and beneficence of female power."[47]

Since the decline of the Goddess religions, women have lacked religious models and spiritual systems that speak to female needs and experience. Male images of divinity characterize both Western and Eastern religions. Regardless of how abstract the underlying concept of God may be, the symbols, avatars, preachers, prophets, gurus, and Buddhas are overwhelmingly male. Women are not encouraged to explore their own strengths and realizations; they are taught to submit to male authority, to identify masculine perceptions as their spiritual ideals, to deny their bodies and sexuality, to fit their insights into a male mold. The symbolism of the Goddess is not a parallel structure to the symbolism of God the Father. The Goddess does not rule the world; She *is* the world. Manifest in each of us, She can be known internally by every individual, in all her magnificent diversity. She does not legitimize the rule of either sex by the other and lends no authority to rulers of temporal hierarchies. In Witchcraft, each of us must reveal our own truth. Deity is seen in our own forms, whether female or male, because the Goddess has her male aspect. Sexuality is a sacrament. Religion is a matter of relinking, with the divine within and with her outer manifestations in all of the human and natural world. . . .

The importance of the Goddess symbol for women cannot be overstressed. The image of the Goddess inspires women to see ourselves as divine, our bodies as sacred, the changing phases of our lives as holy, our aggression as healthy, our anger as purifying, and our power to nurture and create, but also to limit and destroy when necessary, as the very force that sustains all life. Through the Goddess, we can discover our strength, enlighten our minds, own our bodies, and celebrate our emotions. We can move beyond narrow, constricting roles and become whole.

The Goddess is also important for men. The oppression of men in Father God–ruled patriarchy is perhaps less obvious but no less tragic than that of women. Men are encouraged to identify with a model no human being can successfully emulate: to be minirulers of narrow universes. They are internally split, into a "spiritual" self that is supposed to conquer their baser animal and emotional natures. They are at war with themselves: in the West, to "conquer" sin; in the East, to "conquer" desire or ego. Few escape from these wars undamaged. . . .

Our relationship to the earth and the other species that share it has also been conditioned by our religious models. The image of God as outside of nature has given us a rationale for our own destruction of the natural order, and justified our plunder of the earth's resources. We have attempted to "conquer" nature as we have tried to conquer sin. Only as the results of pollution and ecological destruction become severe enough to threaten even urban humanity's adaptability have we come to recognize the importance of ecological balance and the interdependence of all life. The model of the Goddess, who is immanent in nature, fosters respect for the sacredness of all living things. Witchcraft can be seen as a religion of ecology. Its goal is harmony with nature, so that life may not just survive, but thrive. . . .

Love for life in all its forms is the basic ethic of Witchcraft. Witches are bound to honor and respect all living things, and to serve the life force. While the Craft recognizes that life feeds on life and that we must kill in order to survive, life is never taken needlessly, never squandered or wasted. Serving the life force means working to preserve the diversity of natural life, to prevent the poisoning of the environment and the destruction of species. . . .

In Witchcraft, however, what happens in the world is vitally important. The Goddess is immanent, but she needs human help to realize her fullest beauty. The harmonious balance of plant/animal/human/divine awareness is not automatic; it must constantly be renewed, and this is the true function of Craft rituals. Inner work, spiritual work, is most effective when it proceeds hand in hand with outer work. Meditation on the balance of nature might be considered as a spiritual act in Witchcraft, but not as much as would cleaning up garbage left at a campsite or marching to protest an unsafe nuclear plant. . . .

Witchcraft strongly imbues the view that all things are interdependent and interrelated and therefore mutually responsible. An act that harms anyone harms us all. . . .

Life is valued in Witchcraft, and it is approached with an attitude of joy and wonder, as well as a sense of humor. Life is seen as the gift of the Goddess. If suffering exists, it is not our task to reconcile ourselves to it, but to work for change.

Magic, the art of sensing and shaping the subtle, unseen forces that flow through the world, of awakening deeper levels of consciousness beyond the rational, is an element common to all traditions of Witchcraft. Craft rituals are magical rites: they stimulate an awareness of the hidden side of reality, and awaken long-forgotten powers of the human mind. . . .

Witchcraft is not a religion of masses—of any sort. Its structure is cellular, based on covens, small groups of up to thirteen members that allow for both communal sharing and individual independence. "Solitaries," Witches who prefer to worship alone, are the exception. Covens are autonomous, free to use whatever rituals, chants and invocations they prefer. There is no set prayer of liturgy. . . .

Each ritual begins with the creation of a sacred space, the "casting of a circle," which establishes a temple in the heart of the forest or the center of a covener's living room. Goddess and God are then invoked or awakened within each participant and are considered to be physically present within the circle and the bodies of the worshippers. Power, the subtle force that shapes reality, is raised through chanting or dancing and may be directed through a symbol or visualization. With the raising of the cone of power comes ecstasy, which may then lead to a trance state in which visions are seen and insights gained. Food and drink are shared, and coveners "earth the power" and relax, enjoying a time of socializing. At the end, the powers invoked are dismissed, the circle is opened, and a formal return to ordinary consciousness is made. . . .

Mother Goddess is reawakening, and we can begin to recover our primal birthright, the sheer, intoxicating joy of being alive. We can open new eyes and see that there is nothing to be saved *from,* no struggle of life *against* the universe, no God outside the world to be feared and obeyed; only the Goddess, the Mother, the turning spiral that whirls us in and out of existence, whose winking eye is the pulse of being—birth, death, rebirth—whose laughter bubbles and courses through all things and who is found only through love: love of trees, of stones, of sky and clouds, of scented blossoms and thundering waves; of all that runs and flies and swims and crawls on her face; through love of ourselves; life-dissolving world-creating orgasmic love of each other; each of us unique and natural as a snowflake, each of us our own star, her Child, her lover, her beloved, her Self.

NOTES

Introduction

1. Sydney E. Ahlstrom, *A Religious History of the American People,* 2 vols. (Princeton: Yale Univ. Press, 1972), 1:29, 30.

Chapter 1. Catholic Women in North America

1. Jay P. Dolan, *The American Catholic Experience: A History from Colonial Times to the Present* (Garden City, NY: Doubleday, 1985), 127–57; see also *Harvard Encyclopedia of American Ethnic Groups,* ed. Stephen Thernstrom (Cambridge: Harvard Univ. Press, 1980), s.v. "Arabs," "Central and South Americans," "Cubans," "Czechs," "Filipinos," "Germans," "Haitians," "Hungarians," "Indochinese," "Irish," "Italians," "Lithuanians," "Mexicans," "Poles," "Portuguese," "Puerto Ricans," "Slovaks," "Spanish," and "Ukrainians."
2. The 1993 *World Almanac* lists the U.S. resident population as 248.7 million (1990 census) and Catholics as 58.5 million for the fifty states. But the Catholic Almanac of 1993 lists the Catholic population as 55.3 million for the fifty states and 58.3 million when the U.S.-held territories are counted (1991). The *World Almanac* lists 22.4 million Hispanics resident in the fifty states, 80 percent of which are calculated as being baptized Roman Catholics. This would make the Catholic Hispanic population resident in the fifty states 18 million, and 21 million when the territories are added. See the *World Almanac and Book of Facts, 1993,* ed. Mark S. Hoffmann (New York: World Almanac, 1993), 387–88, 718; and *The Catholic Almanac, 1993,* ed. Felician A. Foy (Huntington, IN: Our Sunday Visitor Publishing Division, 1993), 431, 488.

3. Asuncion Lavrin, "Women and Religion in Spanish America," in *Women and Religion in America,* vol. 2, *The Colonial and Revolutionary Periods,* ed. Rosemary R. Ruether and Rosemary S. Keller (San Francisco: Harper & Row, 1983), 42–78.

4. For example, Marie de Jars Gournay, *Égalité des hommes et des femmes* (1622), and Poulain de la Barre, *De l'égalité des deux sexes* (1873).

5. See Christine Allen, "Women in Colonial America," in *Women and Religion in America,* 2:79–131.

6. Henry C. Semple, ed., *The Ursulines in New Orleans: A Record of Two Centuries, 1729–1925* (New York: Kennedy, 1925).

7. Dolan, *American Catholic Experience,* 83; also Julia C. Spruill, *Women's Life and Work in the Southern Colonies* (Chapel Hill: Univ. of North Carolina Press, 1938), 231–41.

8. Dolan, *American Catholic Experience,* 83; also James J. Kenneally, *The History of American Catholic Women* (New York: Crossroad, 1990), 3–4.

9. William Hand Browne, ed., *The Archives of Maryland* (Baltimore: Maryland Historical Society, 1883–1952), 1:215, 225, 226, 238–39, 297, 316; 3:120, 123, 187, 386; 4:552 (124 entries); also Julia C. Spruill, "Mistress Brent, Spinster," *Maryland Historical Magazine* (December 1934), 259–69.

10. Browne, ed., *Archives of Maryland,* 30:334–35.

11. Mary Ewens, *The Role of the Nun in Nineteenth Century America* (Salem, NH: Ayer, 1984), 35–64, 86, 252; also her "Women in the Convent," in *American Catholic Women: A Historical Exploration,* ed. Karen Kennelly (New York: Macmillan, 1989), 18.

12. Mary J. Oates, "Organized Volunteerism: The Catholic Sisters of Massachusetts, 1870–1940," in *Women in American Religion,* ed. Janet Wilson James (Philadelphia: Univ. of Pennsylvania Press, 1980), 143–45.

13. Annabelle M. Melville, *Elizabeth Bayley Seton, 1774–1821* (New York: Scribners, 1951).

14. Ewens, *Role of the Nun,* 49–56.

15. Florence Wolff, *A History Sampler: Sisters of Loretto, 1812–1986* (Nerinx, KY: Sisters of Loretto, 1986), 7–23.

16. Sister Mary Helena Finck, *The Congregation of the Sisters of Charity of the Incarnate Word of San Antonio, Texas* (Washington, DC: Catholic

Univ. of America, 1925), 57–60. Other travel and adventure accounts of nuns are: Sister Monica Taggart, "Diary of the Journey of the Sisters of St. Joseph to Tucson, Arizona, 1870," *St. Louis Catholic Historical Review* 2 (April–July 1920); Sister Lilliana Owens, "Pioneer Days of the Lorettines in Missouri, 1823–41," *American Catholic Historical Society of the Philadelphia Record* 70 (December 1959): 67–87; Sister Evangeline Thomas, *Footprints on the Frontier* (Westminster, MD: Newman Press, 1948).

17. Ewens, "Women in the Convent," 22.

18. Ewens, *Role of the Nun,* 51–55.

19. See Mary Ewens, "The Leadership of Nuns in Immigrant Catholicism," in *Women and Religion in America,* vol. 1, *The Nineteenth Century,* ed. Rosemary S. Keller and Rosemary R. Ruether (San Francisco: Harper & Row, 1981), 104, 132–37.

20. Ewens, *Role of the Nun,* 27, 66–67.

21. Ewens, *Role of the Nun,* 201–51, and Ewens, "Leadership of Nuns," 102, 137–41.

22. Ewens, "Women in the Convent," 32–33.

23. Oates, "Organized Volunteerism," 160; also Dolan, *American Catholic Experience,* 289–90.

24. Ewens, *Role of the Nun,* 267–73.

25. Ewens, *Role of the Nun,* 68, for slaveholding among nuns. Catholic canonical tradition, like mainline Protestantism, followed a long-established Christian view that condoned slavery. For the Catholic tradition, see John Francis Maxwell, *Slavery and the Catholic Church* (London: Anti-Slavery Society, 1975).

26. See Michael Francis Rouse, *Negro Education under Catholic Auspices* (Baltimore: Johns Hopkins Univ. Press, 1935), 83; also Ewens, *The Role of the Nun,* 153.

27. "Black Nuns as Educators," *Journal of Negro Education* 51, no. 3 (1982): 238–53; also Sister Mary Francis Borgia, S.S.F., *Violets in the King's Garden: A History of the Holy Family of New Orleans* (New Orleans: Sisters of the Holy Family, 1976), and Sister Audrey Marie Detiege, *Henriette Delille, Free Woman of Color* (New Orleans: Sisters of the Holy Family, 1976); M. Bonaface Adams, "The Gift of Religious Leadership: Henriette Delille and the Foundation of the Holy Family Sisters," in *Cross, Crozier and Crucible: A Volume Celebrating*

the *Bicentennial of a Catholic Diocese in Louisiana,* ed. Glen R. Conrad (New Orleans: Roman Catholic Archdiocese, 1993), 360–74.

28. Consuela Marie Duffy, *Katherine Drexel: A Biography* (Cornwall Heights, PA: Mother Katherine Drexel Guild, 1965); also Patrice Lynch, "Mother Drexel's Rural Schools," in *Cross, Crozier and Crucible,* 262–74.

29. Kenneally, *History of American Catholic Women,* 89–112; also Mary J. Oates, "Catholic Lay Women in the Labor Force, 1850–1950," in *American Catholic Women,* ed. Kennelly, 81–125.

30. Debra Campbell, "Reformers and Activists," in *American Catholic Women,* ed. Kennelly, 152–53; also Dolan, *American Catholic Experience,* 362. Alice Timmons Toomey, in her article counteracting Katherine Conway (see document 8), stated that tens of thousands of Catholic women were in the Woman's Christian Temperance Union because of lack of opportunities for work in Catholic temperance organizations: *Catholic World* 57 (August 1893): 675.

31. Dolan, *American Catholic Experience,* 327–40.

32. Kenneally, *History of American Catholic Women,* 114–20; also his *Women and American Trade Unions* (St. Albans, VT: Eden Press, 1978); see also Hasia Diner, *Erin's Daughters in America: Irish Immigrant Women in the Nineteenth Century* (Baltimore: Johns Hopkins Press, 1983).

33. Kenneally, *History of American Catholic Women,* 121–26. The archives and back issues of the newspaper *Glos Polek,* of the Polish Women's Alliance, are located in their national headquarters in Park Ridge, IL.

34. Kenneally, *History of American Catholic Women,* 131–44.

35. James Kenneally, "A Question of Equality," in *American Catholic Women,* ed. Karen Kennelly, 140–49.

36. Major biographies of Dorothy Day are William D. Miller, *Dorothy Day: A Biography* (San Francisco: Harper & Row, 1982), and Mel Piehl, *Breaking Bread* (Philadelphia: Temple Univ. Press, 1982).

37. Dolan, *American Catholic Experience,* 365–69.

38. The archives of Friendship House are in the Chicago Historical Society; see also Elizabeth Sharum, *A Strange Fire Burning: A History of the Friendship House Movement* (Ph.D. diss., Texas Tech University, 1977).

39. Interview with Janet Kalven, Grailville, Ohio, May 31, 1993; also her "Women Breaking Boundaries: The Grail and Feminism," *Journal of Feminist Studies in Religion* 5, no. 1 (Spring 1989): 119–42. See also *The Grail in the Eighties,* ed. Joan Dilworth (Amstelveen, The Netherlands: The Grail, 1982).

40. Interview with Patty Crowley in her home, Chicago, Illinois, June 17, 1993; also see John Kotre, *Simple Gifts: The Lives of Pat and Patty Crowley* (Kansas City, MO: Andrews and McMeel, 1979), and Rose M. Lucey, *Roots and Wings: Dreamers and Doers of the Christian Family Movement* (San Jose, CA: Resource Publications, 1987).

41. See Sister M. Patrice Noterman, S.C.C., *An Interpretive History of the Sister Formation Movement, 1954–1964* (Ph.D. diss., Loyola University, Chicago, 1988).

42. Cyprian Davis, *The History of Black Catholics in the United States* (New York: Crossroad, 1990), 98–115.

43. Helen Kelly, "The Hollywood Nuns" (unpublished manuscript), and Anita M. Gaspary, "The California IHM Story" (unpublished manuscript), available from the Immaculate Heart College Center, Los Angeles.

44. *New York Times,* October 7, 1984; reprinted in *Conscience* (September/October 1984), 9.

45. Mary E. Hunt and Frances Kissling, "The *New York Times* Ad: A Case Study in Religious Feminism," *Conscience* (Spring/Summer 1993), 16–23.

46. Madonna Kolbenschlag, *Between God and Caesar* (New York: Paulist Press, 1985), and *Authority, Conflict and Community* (Kansas City, MO: Sheed and Ward, 1986).

47. I was a member of the dialogue with the Bishops' Committee on Women, representing the Women's Ordination Conference, from 1979 to 1981 and so write from personal experience.

48. "Why the Pastoral Was Defeated," *The National Catholic Reporter* 29, no. 6 (December 4, 1992): 2–5.

49. See Helen Hitchcock, *The Politics of Prayer: Feminist Language and the Worship of God* (San Francisco: Ignatius Press, 1992).

50. See Rosemary Ruether, *Women-Church: Theory and Practice of Women's Liturgical Communities* (San Francisco: Harper & Row, 1985).

51. Mary Jo Weaver, *New Catholic Women: A Contemporary Challenge to Traditional Religious Authority* (San Francisco: Harper & Row, 1985); also see Anne Brotherton, *The Voice of the Turtledove: New Catholic Women in Europe* (New York: Paulist Press, 1992).

52. *The Letters of Marie Madeleine Hachard, 1727–1728,* trans. Myldred Masson Costa (New Orleans: Laborde, 1974), 43–45, 59, 60.

53. Browne, ed., *Archives of Maryland,* 1:215, 238–39.

54. Blandina Segale, *At the End of the Santa Fe Trail* (Milwaukee: Bruce Publishing, 1948), 59–62, 75.

55. *Journals and Letters of Mother Theodore Guerin,* ed. Mary Theodosia Mug (St. Mary of the Woods, IN: Providence Press, 1937), 193–94.

56. "Bishop England's Institute of the Sisters of Mercy," *American Ecclesiastical Review* 20, no. 2 (May 1899): 456–58.

57. *The Autobiography of Mother Jones* (Chicago: Charles H. Kerr, 1990), 89–93.

58. John Mitchell, president of the United Mine Workers, with whom Jones had many disagreements.

59. Katherine E. Conway, "Woman Has No Vocation to Public Life," in "The Woman Question Among Catholics: A Round Table Conference," *Catholic World* 57 (August 1893): 681–84.

60. Mrs. Francis Slattery, "The Catholic Woman in Modern Times," *The Catholic Mind* 28 (March 22, 1930): 124–31.

61. Robert Ellsberg, ed., *By Little and by Little: The Selected Writings of Dorothy Day* (New York: Alfred Knopf, 1983), 261–66.

62. Janet Kalven, "Woman and Post-War Reconstruction," *The Catholic Mind* 43 (February 1945): 78–82.

63. Kotre, *Simple Gifts,* 98–99.

64. Sister M. Madeleva Wolff, *My First Seventy Years* (New York: Macmillan, 1959), 110–13.

65. "Stepping Stones: Conclusion," *Focus on Women,* packet of the Leadership Conference of Women Religious, 38.

66. Yolanda Tarango and Tim Matovina, "Las Hermanas" (unpublished manuscript, 1991), 2–3, 8, 18–19. See also Yolanda Tarango and Ada María Isasi-Díaz, *Hispanic Women, Prophetic Voice in the Church* (San Francisco: Harper & Row, 1988).

67. Rosalie Muschal-Reinhardt, "The Assembly Speaks: Women Called to Ordination," in *Women and Catholic Priesthood: An Expanded*

Vision: Proceedings of the Detroit Ordination Conference, ed. Anne Marie Gardiner (New York: Paulist Press, 1976), 187.

68. Catholics Speak Out, "Reject the Pastoral on Women's Concerns," *National Catholic Reporter,* November 20, 1992, 13.

69. Mary E. Hunt, "Women-Church: An Introductory Overview," in *Women-Church Source Book,* ed. Diann L. Neu and Mary E. Hunt (Silver Spring, MD: WATER, 1993), 2, 3, 4, 5.

Chapter 2. The Organization of Protestant Laywomen in Institutional Churches

1. Helen Barrett Montgomery, *Western Women in Eastern Lands: Fifty Years of Woman's Work in Foreign Missions* (New York: Macmillan, 1910), 269; all of chap. 6. Some material included in this essay and document section is found in Rosemary Radford Ruether and Rosemary Skinner Keller, eds., *Women and Religion in America: A Documentary History,* 3 vols. (New York: Harper & Row, 1981, 1983, 1986).

2. Montgomery, *Western Women,* 268.

3. See David D. Hall, *The Antinomian Controversy, 1636–1638: A Documentary History* (Middletown, CT: Wesleyan Univ. Press, 1968); Lyle Koehler, "The Case of the American Jezebels: Anne Hutchinson and Female Agitation during the Years of Antinomian Turmoil, 1636–1640," *William and Mary Quarterly,* ser. 3, vol. 31 (January 1974): 55–78; Ben Barker-Benfield, "Anne Hutchinson and the Puritan Attitude Toward Women," *Feminist Studies* 1 (Fall 1972): 65–96; Carol Karlson, *The Devil in the Shape of a Woman* (New York: Vintage Books, 1989), 176.

4. In addition to document 2 and its source, see the Rev. Newman Smyth, D.D., ed., "Mrs. Eaton's Trial (in 1644); as it Appears upon the Records of the First Church of New Haven," *Papers of the New Haven Colony Historical Society* (New Haven, n.d.), 134, 135. This very old source is located in the Special Collections, Newberry Research Library, Chicago.

5. Smyth, ed., "Mrs. Eaton's Trial," 134, 135.

6. Smyth, ed., "Mrs. Eaton's Trial," 134, 135.

7. See Alice Matthews, "The Religious Experience of Southern Women," *Women and Religion in America,* ed. Ruether and Keller, 1:193–232.

8. In addition to the source for document 3, see Isabel Ross, *Margaret Fell: Mother of Quakerism* (London: Longmans, Green, 1949). For early sources related to early Quaker women, see Mabel Brailsford, *Quaker Women 1650–1690* (London: Duckworth, 1915), 268, 269; William Sewel, *The History of the Rise, Increase and Progress of the Christian People Called Quakers* (London: James Phillips, 1799); George Bishop, *New England Judged by the Spirit of the Lord,* 2 parts (London, 1661, 1667).

9. In addition to the source for document 4, see William McLoughlin, *New England Dissent, 1630–1833: The Baptists and the Separation of the Church and State* (Cambridge: Harvard Univ. Press, 1971), 102, 181, 182, 248; Sarah Osborn's *Nature, Certainty and Evidence of True Christianity, In a Letter from a Gentlewoman in New-England, To Another her Dear Friend, in great Darkness, Doubt and Concern of a Religious Nature* (Boston, 1755).

10. In addition to the source for document 5, see Edward T. James, Janet James, and Paul Boyer, eds., *Notable American Women* (Cambridge, MA: Belknap Press, 1971), 2:174, 175.

11. For civil religion, see Robert Bellah's classic article, "Civil Religion in America," first published in *Daedalus* 96 (Winter 1967): 1–21; Bellah, "The Revolution and the Civil Religion," in *Religion and the American Revolution,* ed. Jerald C. Brauer (Philadelphia: Fortress Press, 1976), 55–73; Henry May, *The Enlightenment in America* (New York: Oxford Univ. Press, 1976); Russell E. Richey and Donald G. Jones, eds., *American Civil Religion* (New York: Harper & Row, 1974). Related to women's role in the American Revolution and early republic, see Mary Beth Norton, *Liberty's Daughters: The Revolutionary Experience of American Women, 1750–1800* (Boston: Little, Brown, 1980), 167, 168, 195; Linda Kerber, *Women of the Republic: Intellect and Ideology in Revolutionary America* (Chapel Hill: Univ. of North Carolina Press, 1980); Nancy Cott, *The Bonds of Womanhood: "Woman's Sphere" in New England, 1780–1835* (New Haven: Yale Univ. Press, 1977).

12. Abigail Adams to John Adams, July 30, 1777, in *Adams Family Correspondence,* ed. L. H. Butterfield (Cambridge: Harvard Univ. Press, 1963, 1973), 3:195, 196 n. 2; D. Hamilton Hurd, *History of Essex County, Mass.* (Philadelphia: J. W. Lewis, 1888), 1:704; Edwin Stone, *History of Beverly, from its Settlement in 1630 to 1842* (Boston:

J. Munroe, 1843), 83, 84; Norton, *Liberty's Daughters,* 156, 160, 161.

13. Cott, *Bonds of Womanhood,* 132, 133.

14. Anne Firor Scott, *Natural Allies: Women's Associations in American History* (Urbana: Univ. of Illinois Press, 1991), 13; 193 n. 11.

15. Scott, *Natural Allies,* 13–20.

16. See Rosemary Keller, "Lay Women in the Protestant Tradition," in *Women and Religion in America,* ed. Ruether and Keller, 1:242–52.

17. R. Pierce Beaver, *All Loves Excelling* (Grand Rapids: Eerdmans, 1968), 85.

18. Lois A. Boyd and R. Douglas Brackenridge, *Presbyterian Women in America: Two Centuries of a Quest for Status* (Westport, CT: Greenwood Press, 1983), and Elizabeth Howell Verdesi, *In but Still Out: Women in the Church* (Philadelphia: Westminster Press, 1976), are excellent in conveying the story and significance of the title within the Presbyterian denomination itself.

19. Beaver, *All Loves Excelling,* chap. 4.

20. Barbara Brown Zikmund, "Women's Organizations: Centers of Denominational Loyalty and Expressions of Christian Unity," in *Beyond Establishment: Protestant Identity in a Post-Protestant Age,* ed. Jackson W. Carroll and Wade Clark Roof (Louisville: Westminster/John Knox Press, 1993), identifies the first five of these, 118–26.

21. Zikmund, "Women's Organizations," 130; "Come and Rejoice: Centennial Celebration of the World Day of Prayer, 1887–1987" (New York: Riverside Church, 1986).

22. See document 15 and its source. The collaborative leadership of Montgomery and Peabody is considered in Keller, "Patterns of Laywomen's Leadership in Twentieth-Century Protestantism," in *Women and Religion in America,* ed. Ruether and Keller, 3:267–69.

23. Anna Kugler, *Guntur Mission Hospital* (Philadelphia: United Lutheran Church in America, 1928), 273–76; Margaret Seeback, "Indian Goddess: Anne S. Kugler, M.D.," in *Answering Distant Calls,* ed. Mable H. Erdman (New York: Association Press, 1942), 130–35.

24. Keller, "Lay Women in the Protestant Tradition," in *Women and Religion in America,* ed. Ruether and Keller, 1:246, 248, 277–81.

25. Zikmund, "Women's Organizations," 120–24.

26. Priscilla Stuckey-Kauffman, "Women's Mission Structures and the American Board," chap. 5 in *Hidden Histories in the United Church of Christ,* ed. Barbara Brown Zikmund, 2 vols. (New York: United Church Press, 1984, 1987), 2:99.

27. Thomas Hutchinson, *History of the Colony and Province of Massachusetts Bay* (Boston, 1767), appendix 11.

28. Charles J. Hoadley, ed., *Records of the Colony and Plantation of New Haven, from 1630–1649* (Hartford: Case, Tiffany, 1857), 242–45, 253, 257.

29. Edited by Milton Speizmann and Jane Kronick, *Signs* 1 (Autumn 1975): 135–45.

30. Excerpts are from Mary Beth Norton, ed., "'My Resting Reaping Times': Sarah Osborn's Defense of Her 'Unfeminine' Activities, 1767," *Signs* 2 (1976): 522–29.

31. Abel Stevens, *The Women of Methodism* (New York: Carlton and Porter, 1866), 235–40, 243–46.

32. Broadside, "An Address to New England: Written by a Daughter of Liberty" (Boston, 1774), Newberry Library, Chicago.

33. The Reverend Absalom Peters, "Serious Impressions on the Minds of Sinners Vary According to the Variation of the Prayers of Saints," *The Home Missionary, and American Pastor's Journal* 1, no. 5 (September 1, 1828): 87, 88.

34. Ashbel Green, "The Christian Duty of Christian Women, A Discourse, Delivered in the Church of Princeton, New Jersey, August 23d, 1825, before the Princeton Female Society, for the Support of a Female School in India," *The Christian Advocate* 4 (1826): 1–14.

35. Charles G. Finney, *Lectures on Revivals of Religion,* rev. ed. (Oberlin, OH: E. J. Goodrich, 1868), 27–29, 109, 111.

36. Lucy Williams, "Our Mission," *The Woman's Evangel* 1, no. 4 (April 1882): 54, 55.

37. Editorial, *The Woman's Evangel* 1, no. 1 (January 1882): 1, 2.

38. "Suggestions for the Formation of Auxiliaries," *The Missionary Helper* 1, no. 4 (July 1878): 82, 83.

39. Sarah E. Tanner, "The Mite Society and Its Convention," *The AME Church Review* 13, no. 3 (January 1896): 378–82.

40. Lucy Rider Meyer, *The Message and Deaconess Advocate* 11, no. 12 (December 1895): 8; *The Message and Deaconess Advocate* 11, no. 11 (November 1895): 3, 4.

41. Montgomery, excerpts from "Problems and Policies," chap. 6 in *Western Women in Eastern Lands.*

42. Abby Gunn Baker, *The Watchman Examiner* (November 30, 1922), 1526, 1527.

43. Kugler, *Guntur Mission Hospital,* 126, 127.

44. "The Churchwoman," *Christian Century,* March 19, 1930, 300–303.

45. Hannah Bonsey Suthers, "Religion and the Feminine Mystique," *Christian Century,* July 21, 1965, 911–14.

46. "Ministries with Women and Ministries with Children and Youth: A Gift for the Whole Church," policy statement of the Women's Division (Cincinnati: General Board of Global Ministries, United Methodist Church, 1993), 2, 6, 7, 19.

47. "Equity, Opportunity, a Continuing Challenge," GCOSROW Report to General Conference 1992, *The Flyer* 12, no. 4 (Winter/ Spring 1992): 1, 2.

Chapter 3. Women and Religious Practice in American Judaism

1. General accounts of Jewish immigration to America include Irving Howe, *The World of Our Fathers* (New York: Simon and Schuster, 1976), and Moses Rischin, *The Promised City: New York's Jews, 1870–1914* (Cambridge: Harvard Univ. Press, 1962). On Jewish women see: Charlotte Baum, Paula Hyman, and Sonya Michel, *The Jewish Woman in America* (New York: New American Library, 1977); Anita Libman Lebeson, *Recall to Life* (New York: Thomas Yoseloff, 1970); Rudolf Glanz, *The Jewish Woman in America: Two Female Immigrant Generations, 1820–1929* (New York: KTAV, 1976); and Jacob R. Marcus, *The American Jewish Woman* (New York: KTAV, 1981).

2. *American Jewish Year Book* (New York: American Jewish Committee, 1992).

3. For examples of techinot translated into English for the use of American women, see M. J. Raphall, ed., *Devotional Exercises for the Daughters of Israel* (New York: L. Joachimssen, 1852), and Abraham E. Hirschowitz, ed., *Religious Duties of the Daughters of Israel* (New York: A. E. Hirschowitz, 1902). See also Chava Weissler, "The Traditional Piety of Ashkenazic Women," in *Jewish Spirituality,* vol. 2,

From the Sixteenth-Century Revival to the Present, ed. Arthur Green (New York: Crossroad, 1987), 245–75.

4. James G. Heller, *Isaac M. Wise: His Life, Work and Thought* (New York: United Association of Hebrew Congregations, 1965), 568–72.

5. Morris A. Gutstein, *A Priceless Heritage: The Epic Growth of Nineteenth-Century Chicago Jewry* (New York: Bloch Publishing, 1953), 306.

6. Isaac Leeser, ed., *The Occident* 2 (1844): 163.

7. Rischin, *Promised City,* 93, 85; Deborah Dash Moore, *At Home in America: Second Generation New York Jews* (New York: Columbia Univ. Press, 1981), 3.

8. Lillian Wald, *The House on Henry Street* (New York: Holt, 1915), 21.

9. Mary Antin, *The Promised Land* (Boston: Houghton Mifflin, 1912), 277.

10. Moore, *At Home in America,* 90.

11. See also Elizabeth G. Stern, *My Mother and I* (New York: Macmillan, 1917), and Anzia Yezierska, "The Fat of the Land," in *Hungry Hearts* (Boston: Houghton Mifflin, 1920), and Laura Z. Hobson, *Laura Z: A Life* (New York: Arbor House, 1983), 12.

12. "Penalizing Parenthood," *Independent* 74 (March 20, 1913): 605.

13. Marshall Sklare, *Conservative Judaism: An American Religious Movement* (Glencoe, IL: The Free Press, 1955), 86.

14. Emily Solis-Cohen, Jr., *Woman in Jewish Law and Life: An Inquiry and a Guide to the Literary Sources of Information Concerning the Nature of Jewish Law and the Status Accorded to Women* (New York: Jewish Welfare Board Publications, 1932), 1.

15. Solis-Cohen, *Woman in Jewish Law,* 2.

16. Sklare, *Conservative Judaism,* 86–88.

17. Mel Scult, *Judaism Faces the Twentieth Century: A Biography of Mordecai Kaplan* (Detroit: Wayne State Univ. Press, 1993), 301–2.

18. Rabbi Samuel Gerstenfeld, "The Segregation of the Sexes," *The Jewish Forum* 7 (1924): 188.

19. Rabbi David Goldberg, "Women's Part in Religious Decline," *Jewish Forum* 4 (1921): 871–75.

20. Gilbert Klaperman, *The Story of Yeshiva University: The First Jewish University in America* (New York: Macmillan, 1969), 179–80.

21. National Council of Jewish Women, *The First Fifty Years* (New York: National Council of Jewish Women, 1943), 32–38.
22. Susan Weidman Schneider, *Jewish and Female* (New York: Simon and Schuster, 1984), 504.
23. E. M. Broner, *The Telling* (San Francisco: HarperSanFrancisco, 1993).
24. Letty Cottin Pogrebin, *Deborah, Golda, and Me: Being Female and Jewish in America* (New York: Doubleday, 1991), 205–34.
25. Sylvia Barack Fishman, *A Breath of Life: Feminism in the American Jewish Community* (New York: Free Press, 1993), 207.
26. Schneider, *Jewish and Female*, 47.
27. Maggie Wenig and Naomi Janowitz, *Siddur Nashim* (Providence, RI, 1976).
28. *Lilith* 14 (Fall/Winter 1985/86): 3.
29. Rivka Haut, "Women's Prayer Groups and the Orthodox Synagogue," in Susan Grossman and Rivka Haut, *Daughters of the King: Women and the Synagogue* (Philadelphia: Jewish Publication Society, 1992), 147.
30. Lynn Davidman, *Tradition in a Rootless World: Women Turn to Orthodox Judaism* (Berkeley: Univ. of California Press, 1991); Blu Greenberg, *On Judaism and Feminism: A View from Tradition* (Philadelphia: Jewish Publication Society of America, 1981); Tamar Frankiel, *The Voice of Sarah: Feminine Spirituality and Traditional Judaism* (San Francisco: HarperSanFrancisco, 1990).
31. Excerpted from *Letters of Rebecca Gratz,* ed. Rabbi David Philipson, D.D. (Philadelphia: Jewish Publication Society of America, 1929); for biographical information on Rebecca Gratz, see Rollin G. Osterweis, *Rebecca Gratz* (New York: G. P. Putnam's Sons, 1955).
32. Anzia Yezierska, *Bread Givers* (New York: Doubleday, 1925), 8–10; for biographical information on Anzia Yezierska, see Alice Kessler Harris's introduction to *Bread Givers.*
33. Excerpts from *A Sheaf of Leaves* (Chicago: private printing, 1911), 69, 72, 87; further biographical material is available in the article on Hannah Greenebaum Solomon by Sylvia Johnson in *Notable American Women,* ed. Edward T. James and Janet W. James (Cambridge, MA: Belknap Press, 1974), 3:324–25.

34. Correspondence to Haym Peretz, September 16, 1916, in Marvin Lowenthal, *Henrietta Szold: Life and Letters* (New York: Viking Press, 1942), 92–93. "The *Kaddish,* a sanctification of God, is recited by children in mourning for their parents at synagogue services during one year. By tradition, only male children recite the prayer. If there are no male survivors, a stranger may act as a substitute."

35. Address to the Hadassah Convention, October 20, 1936; *Hadassah Newsletter* 2, no. 11 (1922).

36. Excerpted from Cynthia Ozick, "Notes Toward Finding the Right Question: Fifteen Brief Meditations," *Lilith* no. 6 (1979): 19–29.

37. Interview by Raye T. Katz (a pseudonym of Aviva Cantor) in *Lilith* no. 14 (Fall/Winter 1985/86): 19–24.

38. Judith Plaskow, "Beyond Egalitarianism," *Tikkun* 5, no. 6 (November/December 1990): 79–81.

39. Shaina Sara Handelman, "Modesty and the Jewish Woman," in *The Modern Jewish Woman: A Unique Perspective,* ed. Raizel Schnall Friedfertig and Freyda Schapiro (Brooklyn: Lubavitch Educational Foundation for Jewish Marriage Enrichment, 1981), 19–31; reprinted with permission from *The Uforatzto Journal* (Summer 1979/*Kayitz* 5739).

40. Elyse Goldstein, "Take Back the Waters: A Feminist Re-appropriation of Mikvah," *Lilith* no. 15 (Summer 1986): 15–16.

41. Susan Grossman, "Finding Comfort After a Miscarriage," in *Daughters of the King,* ed. Susan Grossman and Rivka Haut (Philadelphia: Jewish Publication Society of America, 1992), 285–90.

42. This meditation was developed in consultation with Rabbi Joel Roth, head of the Law and Standards Committee of the Rabbinical Assembly, the Conservative movement's halachic decision-making body. At the time, the committee had just accepted a *teshuvah* (rabbinic opinion) on rituals appropriate for marking a miscarriage.

Chapter 4. Black Women:
From Slavery to Womanist Liberation

1. Rhys Isaac, *The Transformation of Virginia: 1740–1790* (Chapel Hill: Univ. of North Carolina Press, 1982), 70; Albert J. Raboteau, *Slave Religion: The "Invisible Institution" in the Antebellum South* (New York: Oxford Univ. Press, 1978), 291–311; C. Eric Lincoln, *Race,*

Religion and the Continuing American Dilemma (New York: Hill and Wang, 1984), 63.

2. Erskine Clarke, *Wrestlin' Jacob: A Portrait of Religion in the Old South* (Atlanta: John Knox Press, 1979), 7–8; Gayraud Wilmore, *Black Religion and Black Radicalism: An Interpretation of the Religious History of Afro-American People,* 2d ed. (Maryknoll, NY: Orbis Books, 1983), 15–17. Wilmore notes that the religion of West Africa entailed a highly involved ontological and ethical system. There was no rigid demarcation between the natural and supernatural. Animals appealed to Africans as symbolic representations of the environment in which humans exist. These may be related to the spirits of ancestors, but above all to a Supreme Being. This Supreme Being or God is above all gods and was known to the slaves as creator, judge, and redeemer.

3. Raboteau, *Slave Religion,* 66; Isaac, *Transformation of Virginia,* 70.

4. Melville J. Herskovits, *The Myth of the Negro Past* (Boston: Beacon Press, 1958), 214.

5. Isaac, *Transformation of Virginia,* 70.

6. Donald G. Mathews, *Religion in the Old South* (Chicago: Univ. of Chicago Press, 1977), 208.

7. Isaac, *Transformation of Virginia,* 306.

8. Darlene Clark Hine, "Lifting the Veil, Shattering the Silence: Black Women's History in Slavery and Freedom," in *The State of Afro-American History: Past, Present, and Future,* ed. Darlene Clark Hine (Baton Rouge: Louisiana State Univ. Press, 1986), 228.

9. Mathews, *Religion in the Old South,* 208. Mathews notes that in the process of conversion to Christianity, the wrath of Denmark Vesey and Nat Turner, the dialectic of white mission and Black piety gave impetus to a faith of liberation through an apocalyptic event.

10. Raboteau, *Slave Religion,* 243; Zora Neale Hurston, *The Sanctified Church* (Berkeley: Turtle Island Press, 1981), 79–80; Isaac, *Transformation of Virginia,* 300.

11. Isaac, *Transformation of Virginia,* 172.

12. Mechal Sobel, *Trabelin' On: The Slave Journey to an Afro-Baptist Faith* (Princeton: Princeton Univ. Press, 1988), 90.

13. Mathews, *Religion in the Old South,* 215.

14. Mathews, *Religion in the Old South,* 224–25.

15. Mathews, *Religion in the Old South,* 304.

16. Henry Highland Garnet, *Walker's Appeal, With a Brief Sketch of His Life* (New York: J. H. Tobitt, 1848). Walker's *Appeal to the Coloured Citizens of the World,* written in 1829, was steeped in religious imagery and prophecy. He predicted bloody retributive justice on white slaveholders as a necessary outcome unless emancipation was immediately declared. Earl Ofari, *Let Your Motto Be Resistance* (Boston: Beacon Press, 1972), 144–53. Henry Highland Garnet's "Address to the Slaves of the United States of America," written in 1843, built on Walker's *Appeal.* Garnet's address is stunning in its dissection of slavery as an evil in the sight of God and the submission to slavery as sinful. For him, it was better to die than live in submission.

17. Evelyn Brooks, "The Women's Movement in the Black Baptist Church, 1880–1920" (Ph.D. diss., University of Rochester, 1984), 146. Although Brooks concentrates on women of the Black Baptist church, her observations ring true for Black women across denominational lines during this period of African American religious history and experience. See also Evelyn Brooks Higginbotham, *Righteous Discontent: The Women's Movement in the Black Baptist Church, 1880–1920* (Cambridge: Harvard Univ. Press, 1993).

18. Brooks, "Women's Movement," 145. Black Christian society did allow exceptions to the rule of women's influence as positive. The characters of Delilah and Jezebel were not models for female behavior.

19. Brooks, "Women's Movement," 146.

20. Brooks, "Women's Movement," 140.

21. Willie Mae Coleman, "Keeping the Faith and Disturbing the Peace: Black Women: From Anti-Slavery to Women's Suffrage" (Ph.D. diss., University of California, Irvine, 1982), 88. Coleman notes that Black women took the *Virginia Baptist* to task for a series of articles that claimed that women who aspired to preach or desired suffrage were in violation of God's law. These Black sisters reminded churchmen that women outnumbered men in most churches and were crucial for the financial health of the church, and they note "when there is a question as to legislation or expenditure, then the men arise in their majesty and delegate to women the task of remembering that St. Paul said 'let the women keep silence.'"

22. Bert James Loewenberg and Ruth Bogin, ed., *Black Women in Nineteenth-Century American Life: Their Words, Their Thoughts, Their Feelings* (University Park: Pennsylvania State Univ. Press, 1976), 135; and William L. Andrews, ed., *Sisters of the Spirit: Three Black Women's Autobiographies of the Nineteenth Century* (Bloomington: Indiana Univ. Press, 1986), 29.

23. Brooks, "Women's Movement," 165.

24. Brooks, "Women's Movement," 133.

25. Brooks, "Women's Movement," 139.

26. Brooks, "Women's Movement," 149–53.

27. Brooks, "Women's Movement," 146.

28. Brooks, "Women's Movement," 147.

29. Coleman, "Keeping the Faith," 83.

30. Brooks, "Women's Movement," 168.

31. Brooks, "Women's Movement," 148. It is not clear from Oldham's rhetoric that she was advocating for the ordained ministry. It is most likely she was speaking for ministry in the broadest terms possible.

32. Brooks, "Women's Movement," 153.

33. Brooks, "Women's Movement," 153.

34. Coleman, "Keeping the Faith," 78.

35. Wilson Jeremiah Moses, *The Golden Age of Black Nationalism, 1850–1925* (New York: Oxford Univ. Press, 1978), 103.

36. Moses, *Golden Age,* 107.

37. W. E. B. DuBois, *Dark Waters: Voices from Within the Veil* (New York: Schocken Books, 1920), 84, n. 19.

38. Alice Walker, *In Search of Our Mothers' Gardens: Womanist Prose* (New York: Harcourt Brace Jovanovich, 1983), xi–xii.

39. Charles F. Heartman, ed., *Phillis Wheatley: Poems and Letters* (Miami: Mnemosyne Publishing, 1969), 23; Rosemary Radford Ruether and Rosemary Skinner Keller, eds., *Women and Religion in America,* vol. 2, *The Colonial and Revolutionary Periods* (San Francisco: Harper & Row, 1983), 252–53; and John Shield, ed., *The Collected Works of Phillis Wheatley,* The Schomburg Library of Nineteenth-Century Black Women Writers (New York: Oxford Univ. Press, 1988), 164–65.

40. Amanda Berry Smith, *An Autobiography: The Story of the Lord's Dealings with Mrs. Amanda Smith The Colored Evangelist, Containing an Account*

of Her Life Work of Faith, and Her Travels in America, England, Ireland, Scotland, India, and Africa, as an Independent Missionary, introduction by Bishop Thoburn of India (Chicago: Meyer & Brother, 1893).

41. Olive Gilbert, *Narrative of Sojourner Truth: A Bondswoman of Olden Time, Emancipated by the New York Legislature in the Early Part of the Present Century: With a History of Her Labors and Correspondence, Drawn from Her "Book of Life"* (Boston, 1875), 61–62, 65–68.

42. Ida B. Wells, *Crusade for Justice: The Autobiography of Ida B. Wells,* ed. Alfreda Duster (Chicago: Univ. of Chicago Press, 1970), 401–3.

43. Anna Julia Cooper, "Womanhood: A Vital Element in the Regeneration and Progress of a Race," in *A Voice From the South* (Aldine, OH: Aldine Publishing House, 1852), 14–19, 31, 40–41, 44–45.

44. Editor's note: five have been graduated since '86, two in '91, two in '92.

45. Rackham Holt, *Mary McLeod Bethune: A Biography* (Garden City, NY: Doubleday, 1964), 287–89.

46. Sara J. Duncan, "In Vindication of Vital Questions," in John T. Jenifer, *Centennial Retrospective History of the African Methodist Episcopal Church* (Chicago: Sunday School Union, African Methodist Episcopal Church, 1916), 141.

47. Sister Anna Smith, National Recording Secretary, "Minutes: 24th Annual Convocation," *The Whole Truth* 18, no. 1 (January 1942): 1. See also Lucille Cornelius, *The Pioneer History of the Church of God in Christ* (Memphis: Church of God in Christ Publishing House), 22–23.

48. See Jualyne E. Dodson and Cheryl Townsend Gilkes, "'Something Within': Social Change and Collective Endurance in the Sacred World of Black Christian Women," in *Women and Religion in America,* vol. 3, *1900–1968,* ed. Rosemary Radford Ruether and Rosemary Skinner Keller (New York: Harper & Row, Publishers, 1986), 111–12.

49. Typescript, National Conference of Black Sisters, 1968.

50. Nannie Helen Burroughs, *The Slabtown District Convention: A Comedy in One Act* (Washington, DC: Nannie H. Burroughs Publications/Nannie Helen Burroughs School, 1979). This is the twenty-second edition of a play that Miss Burroughs wrote early in her career.

51. Hurston wrote four novels. The first, *Jonah's Gourd Vine,* was written in 1934. *Their Eyes Were Watching God* (1937) studies the tension between communal values and the individual values of the chief protagonist, Janie Starks. The third novel, *Moses, Man of the Mountain* (1939), places the Moses story in the Black community. *Seraph on the Suwanee* (1948) is a study of the ironies and ambiguities of self-improvement and self-extension. She wrote many short stories, eight plays, an autobiography, *Dust Tracks on the Road* (1942), and collections of folklore that include *Tell My Horse* (1938) and *The Sanctified Church* (1981).

52. Zora Neale Hurston, *Jonah's Gourd Vine* (New York: Harper-Perennial, 1934), 173–82.

53. Toni Morrison, *Beloved* (New York: Alfred A. Knopf, 1987), 87–89.

54. Katie Geneva Cannon, "Moral Wisdom in the Black Women's Literary Tradition," in *Weaving the Visions: New Patterns in Feminist Spirituality,* ed. Judith Plaskow and Carol P. Christ (San Francisco: Harper & Row, 1989), 281–83, 285–87.

55. Original note to the document: Pierre L. Van Der Berghe, *Race and Racism: A Comparative Perspective* (New York: Wiley, 1967), 77.

56. Delores S. Williams, "The Color of Feminism: Or Speaking the Black Woman's Tongue," *Journal of Religious Thought* 44 (Spring/Summer 1986): 47–52, 54–55.

57. Original note to the document: Adrienne Rich, *Of Woman Born: Motherhood as Experience and Institution* (New York: W. W. Norton, 1976), 40.

58. Original note to the document: For a discussion of patriarchy in several contexts see Kate Millett, *Sexual Politics* (Garden City, NY: Doubleday, 1970); see also bell hooks's discussion in *Ain't I a Woman?* (Boston: South End Press, 1981). Elizabeth Dodson-Gray, *Patriarchy as a Conceptual Trap* (Wellesley, MA: Roundtable Press, 1982).

59. Original note to the document: Rich, *Of Woman Born,* author's interpolations.

60. Original note to the document: While many feminists are to be admired for refusing to take the white woman's traditional place upon the pedestal, few have turned down the privileges bestowed upon them by fathers, brothers and sons.

61. Original note to the document: Afro-American slave narratives contain many accounts about slave owners who fathered children by slave women and then sold these children as slaves.

62. Original note to the document: Black women should, as they name their experience, consider the following: "White males experience the world from the top side of history. White females experience the world from the underside of history. Black men experience the world from the underside of the underside of history. Black women experience the world from rock-bottom." Such a position for Black women logically suggests a different naming of reality and certainly a different view of history.

63. Original note to the document: For some years now I have heard many Black women say that they could not conceive of their own liberation apart from the liberation of the black family because Black children, female and male, are as oppressed by white-controlled American institutions as they (Black women) are.

64. Original note to the document: Democracy has no relation to demonarchy which posits beings intermediate between humans and the divine.

65. Jacquelyn Grant, "Womanist Theology: Black Women's Experiences as a Source for Doing Theology, with Special Reference to Christology," *Journal of the Interdenominational Theological Center* 13 (Spring 1986): 202–7.

66. Original note to the document: Cecil Wayne Cone, *Identity Crisis in Black Theology* (Nashville: African Methodist Episcopal Church Press, 1975), passim, esp. chap. 3.

67. Original note to the document: Bert James Lowenberg and Ruth Bogin, eds., *Black Women in Nineteenth-Century American Life: Their Words, Their Thoughts, Their Feelings* (University Park: Pennsylvania State Univ. Press, 1976), 267.

68. Original note to the document: Lowenberg and Bogin, eds., *Black Women in Nineteenth-Century Thought,* 265.

69. Original note to the document: Olive Gilbert, *Sojourner Truth: Narrative and Book of Life* (1850 and 1875; reprint, Chicago: Johnson Publishing, 1970), 83.

70. Original note to the document: Harold A. Carter, *The Prayer Tradition of Black People* (Valley Forge: Judson Press, 1976), 50. Carter, in

referring to traditional Black prayer in general, states that "Jesus was revealed as one who was all one needs!"

71. Original note to the document: Carter, *Prayer Tradition,* 50.

72. Cheryl Townsend Gilkes, "'Mother to the Motherless, Father to the Fatherless': Power, Gender, and Community in an Afrocentric Biblical Tradition," *Semeia* 47, ed. Katie Geneva Cannon (Atlanta: Scholars Press, 1989), 61–66.

73. Original note to the document: Thomas D. Hanks, *God So Loved the Third World: The Bible, the Reformation, and Liberation Theologies* (Maryknoll, NY: Orbis Books, 1981), ix.

74. Original note to the document: Hanks, *Third World,* 4.

75. Original note to the document: Elsa Tamez, *Bible of the Oppressed* (Maryknoll, NY: Orbis Books, 1982), 41.

76. Original note to the document: Tamez, *Bible of the Oppressed,* 41–45.

77. Original note to the document: John W. Blassingame, *The Slave Community: Plantation Slavery in the Antebellum South,* 2d ed. (New York: Oxford Univ. Press, 1979).

78. Original note to the document: Tamez, *Bible of the Oppressed,* 46–53.

79. Original note to the document: Orlando Patterson, *Slavery and Social Death: A Comparative Study* (Cambridge: Harvard Univ. Press, 1982).

80. Original note to the document: Tamez, *Bible of the Oppressed,* 53.

Chapter 5. Evangelical Women

1. For more information about Finney and women see Nancy A. Hardesty, *"Your Daughters Shall Prophesy": Revivalism and Feminism in the Age of Finney* (Brooklyn: Carlson Publishing, 1991), and *Women Called to Witness: Evangelical Feminism in the Nineteenth Century* (Nashville: Abingdon Press, 1984).

2. Donald W. Dayton, *Theological Roots of Pentecostalism* (Grand Rapids: Zondervan, 1987).

3. R. A. Tucker, "Crawford, Florence (1872–1936)," *Dictionary of Christianity in America,* ed. Daniel G. Reid et al. (Downers Grove, IL: InterVarsity Press, 1990), 325.

4. Susie Cunningham Stanley, *Feminist Pillar of Fire: The Life of Alma White* (Cleveland: Pilgrim Press, 1993).

5. See Edith L. Blumhofer, *Aimee Semple McPherson: Everybody's Sister* (Grand Rapids: Eerdmans, 1993).

6. The Scofield Reference Bible, the King James Version with notes and other "helps" provided by lawyer and pastor C. I. Scofield (1843–1921), became the undisputed Fundamentalist Bible.

7. Betty DeBerg, *Ungodly Women: Gender and the First Wave of American Fundamentalism* (Minneapolis: Fortress Press, 1990).

8. Janette Hassey, *No Time for Silence: Evangelical Women in Public Ministry Around the Turn of the Century* (Grand Rapids: Zondervan, 1986); Virginia Lieson Brereton, *Training God's Army: The American Bible School, 1880–1940* (Bloomington: Indiana Univ. Press, 1990); and Margaret Bendroth, *Fundamentalism and Gender, 1875 to the Present* (New Haven: Yale Univ. Press, 1993).

9. The group is now known as Evangelicals for Social Action, with offices at 10 Lancaster Ave., Philadelphia, PA 19151.

10. Ronald J. Sider, ed., *The Chicago Declaration* (Carol Stream, IL: Creation House, 1974), 2. The original fifty-three signers included Ruth L. Bentley, Sharon Gallagher, Nancy Hardesty, Wyn Wright Potter, Eunice Schatz, and Donna Simons.

11. The Evangelical and Ecumenical Women's Caucus meets biennially. Its mailing address is 6015 Mauritania Ave., Oakland, CA 94605. It publishes *Update.*

12. Christians for Biblical Equality publishes *Priscilla Papers.* Their address is 380 Lafayette Road South, Suite 122, Saint Paul, MN 55107-1216.

13. The Council on Biblical Manhood and Womanhood can be reached at P.O. Box 1173, Wheaton, IL 60189. Two leaders of the movement, Wayne A. Grudem and John Piper, have edited *Recovering Biblical Manhood and Womanhood* (Westchester, IL: Crossway Books, 1990).

14. *Daughters of Sarah,* the "Magazine for Christian Feminists," is published quarterly. Its address is 2121 Sheridan Road, Evanston, IL 60201.

15. S. Olin Garrison, ed., *Forty Witnesses: Covering the Whole Range of Christian Experience* (1888; reprint, Freeport, PA: Fountain Press, 1955), 138–39. Most are testimonies to the experience of holiness.

16. Elizabeth Cady Stanton, *Eighty Years and More: Reminiscences 1815–1897* (1898; reprint, New York: Schocken Books, 1971), 41–42. There is a problem with this account in that other biographers suggest that Stanton was at the Troy Female Seminary from 1830 to 1832. Finney held a revival at Beaman's church in the fall of 1826 but does not mention any meetings in Troy from 1830 to 1832 in his *Memoirs*.

17. Sarah M. Grimke, *Letters on the Equality of the Sexes and the Condition of Woman Addressed to Mary S. Parker, President of the Boston Female Anti-Slavery Society* (1838; reprint, New York: Burt Franklin, 1970), 4, 16–21.

18. Antoinette L. Brown, "Exegesis of 1 Corinthians, XIV., 34, 35; and 1 Timothy, II., 11, 12," *Oberlin Quarterly Review* (Oberlin, OH: James M. Fitch, 1849), 358, 360, 361, 363, 364–65, 367–68, 369–73.

19. Frances Willard, "President's Annual Address," *Minutes* (Chicago: Woman's Christian Temperance Union, 1888), 41–42, 45–46.

20. Phoebe Palmer, *Faith and Its Effects: Fragments from My Portfolio* (1845; New York: Joseph Longking, Printer, 1850), 85–86. She first used the altar terminology in *The Way of Holiness* (1843).

21. Garrison, ed., *Forty Witnesses*, 140–43.

22. Carrie Judd Montgomery, *The Prayer of Faith* (Oakland, CA: Office of Triumphs of Faith, 1880), 12–16.

23. Mrs. M. B. Woodworth-Etter, *Acts of the Holy Ghost, or The Life, Work, and Experience, of Mrs. M. B. Woodworth-Etter, Evangelist* (Dallas: John F. Worley Printing, [1912]), 108.

24. Sarah E. Parham, *The Life of Charles F. Parham: Founder of the Apostolic Faith Movement* (Joplin, MO: Hunter Printing, 1930; reprint, New York: Garland Publishing, 1985), 65–67. Agnes N. Osman LaBerge gives a slightly different account in her autobiography, *What God Hath Wrought* (Chicago: Herald Publishing, n.d.; reprint, New York: Garland Publishing, 1985), 28–30.

25. Hannah Whitall Smith, *The Christian's Secret of a Happy Life* (Old Tappan, NJ: Fleming H. Revell Company, 1942), 35–38.

26. John R. Rice, *Bobbed Hair, Bossy Wives, and Women Preachers* (Murfreesboro, TN, 1941), 18, 82.

27. John R. Rice, "Men and Their Sins," sermon delivered to men only at the First Methodist Church, Lewistown, Pennsylvania,

December 7, 1947. Printed in *Sword of the Lord* 61 (August 1, 1975): 11–12.

28. Kathryn Kuhlman, *I Believe in Miracles* (New York: Pyramid Books, 1962), 211, 213–14.

29. This is found in their brochure, a full-page ad run in *Christianity Today* (January 13, 1989), 41.

Chapter 6. Protestant Women and Social Reform

1. See, for example, Perry Miller, *The Life of the Mind in America from the Revolution to the Civil War* (New York: Harcourt, Brace & World, 1965), and Timothy Smith, *Revivalism and Social Reform* (Nashville: Abingdon Press, 1957; reprint, Gloucester: Peter Smith, 1976).

2. Barbara Welter, *Dimity Convictions* (Athens: Ohio Univ. Press, 1976).

3. Ann Douglas, *The Feminization of America Culture* (New York: Alfred A. Knopf, 1977).

4. Carolyn DeSwarte Gifford, "Women in Social Reform Movements," in *Women and Religion in America,* vol. 1, *The Nineteenth Century,* ed. Rosemary Skinner Keller and Rosemary Radford Ruether (San Francisco: Harper & Row, 1981), 296.

5. Harriet Beecher Stowe et al., *Our Famous Women: Comprising the Lives and Deeds of American Women* (Hartford, CT: A. D. Worthington, 1884), 59, quoted in Gifford, "Women in Social Reform Movements," 296.

6. See, for example, the work of the Mudflower Collective in *God's Fierce Whimsy* (New York: Pilgrim Press, 1985).

7. Elizabeth Cady Stanton, Susan B. Anthony, and Matilda Joslyn Gage, *History of Woman Suffrage* (New York: Fowler & Wells, 1881), 368–75.

8. J. T. Gracey, "Woman's Home Missionary Society," *Methodist Review* (September 1887), 652–53.

9. Ann Taves, ed., *Religion and Domestic Violence in Early New England: The Memoirs of Abigail Abbot Bailey* (Bloomington: Indiana Univ. Press, 1989), 75–77.

10. Mary Lyon, *The Power of Christian Benevolence Illustrated in the Life and Letters of Mary Lyon* (New York: American Tract Society, 1858), 182–83.

11. Angelina Grimke, *An Appeal to the Women of the Nominally Free States* (Boston: Isaac Knapp, 1838), 13–16, 60–61.

12. The Constitution and Circular of the New York Female Moral Reform Society; with the Addresses Delivered at Its Organization (New York: J. N. Bolles, 1834), 16–18.

13. Elizabeth Cady Stanton, *The Woman's Bible* (New York: European Publishing, 1891), 7–9, 11–12.

14. *Report of the International Council of Women* (Washington, DC: Rufus H. Darby, 1888), 26–29.

15. Frances E. Willard, *How to Win: A Book for Girls* (New York: Funk & Wagnalls, 1886), 48–57.

16. Gerda Lerner, ed., *Black Women in White America* (New York: Random House, 1972), 461–67.

17. Vida Dutton Scudder, *On Journey* (New York: E. P. Dutton, 1937), 336–39.

18. Georgia Harkness, *Grace Abounding: A Devotional Autobiography* (Nashville: Abingdon Press, 1963), 130–32.

19. "Point—Counterpoint," pamphlet (Washington, DC: Religious Coalition for Abortion Rights, 1985), 2, 27.

20. Christian Lesbians Out Together (CLOUT), press release, February 25, 1991.

Chapter 7. Women and Ordination

1. Samuel Hopkins, ed., *Memoirs of the Life of Mrs. Sarah Osborn* (Worcester, MA: Leonard Worcester, 1799).

2. Barbara Brown Zikmund, "Abigail Roberts: 'Female Laborer' in Christian Churches," *Historical Intelligencer* 2 (1982): 3–10.

3. See *Lucretia Mott: Her Complete Speeches and Sermons* (New York: Edwin Mellen Press, 1980), and Robert J. Leach, *Women Ministers: A Quaker Contribution,* Pendle Hill Pamphlet 227 (Wallingford, PA: Pendle Hill Publications, 1979).

4. See Elizabeth Cazden, *Antoinette Brown Blackwell: A Biography* (Old Westbury, NY: Feminist Press, 1983).

5. See Olympia Brown, *Suffrage and Religious Principle: Speeches and Writings of Olympia Brown,* ed. Dana Green (Metuchen, NJ: Scarecrow Press, 1983).

6. "Pastoral Letter," *General Assembly Minutes* (1832), 378, quoted in Lois A. Boyd and R. Douglas Brackenridge, *Presbyterian Women in America: Two Centuries of a Quest for Status* (Westport, CT: Greenwood Press, 1983), 94.

7. Ben M. Barrus, Milton L. Baughn, and Thomas H. Campbell, *A People Called Cumberland Presbyterians: A History of the Cumberland Church* (Memphis: Cumberland Presbyterian Press, 1972), 279–80. See also Louisa M. Woosley, *Shall Women Preach? or The Question Answered* (Caneyville, KY, 1891).

8. Boyd and Brackenridge, *Presbyterian Women in America,* 126–38.

9. Hazel Foster, "Ecclesiastical Status of Women," *The Woman's Pulpit* 40 (July–December 1964): 8.

10. Anna Howard Shaw, *The Story of a Pioneer* (New York and London: Harper and Brothers, 1915), 122–25.

11. Florence Resor Jardine, "The Methodist Uniting Conference and the Ministry of Women," *The Woman's Pulpit* 17 (May–June 1939): 1–4, and "Lady Ministers Win Full Status in Church," *Christian Advocate* 131 (May 24, 1956): 15.

12. James E. Will, "Ordination of Women: The Issue in the Church of the United Brethren in Christ," in *Women in New Worlds: Historical Perspectives on the Wesleyan Tradition,* ed. Rosemary Skinner Keller, Louisa L. Queen, and Hilah F. Thomas (Nashville: Abingdon Press, 1982), 2:290–97, and J. Bruce Behney and Paul H. Eller, *The History of the Evangelical United Brethren Church* (Nashville: Abingdon Press, 1979).

13. Phoebe Palmer, *The Promise of the Father* (Boston: Henry V. Degen, 1859), vi.

14. See the appendix in Juanita Evans Leonard, ed., *Called to Minister, Empowered to Serve: Women in Ministry in the Church of God Reformation Movement* (Anderson, IN: Warner Press, 1989); Rebecca Laird, *Ordained Women in the Church of the Nazarene: The First Generation* (Kansas City, MO: Nazarene Publishing House, 1993); and Benjamin T. Roberts, *Ordaining Women* (Rochester, NY: Earnest Christian Publishing House, 1891), 55.

15. See Elaine J. Lawless, *Handmaidens of the Lord: Pentecostal Women Preachers and Traditional Religion* (Philadelphia: Univ. of Pennsylvania Press, 1988). A summary of the book is found in Elaine J. Lawless, "Not So Different a Story After All: Pentecostal Women in the

Pulpit," in *Women's Leadership in Marginal Religions: Explorations Outside the Mainstream,* ed. Catherine Wessinger (Urbana and Chicago: Univ. of Illinois Press, 1993), 41–52.

16. Constant H. Jacquet, Jr., *Women Ministers in 1977* (New York: National Council of Churches, 1978), 7.

17. Raymond Tiemeyer, *The Ordination of Women: A Report Distributed by Authorization of the Church Body Presidents as a Contribution to Further Study, Based on Material Produced through the Division of Theological Studies of the Lutheran Council in the U.S.A.* (Minneapolis: Augsburg Press, 1970).

18. The following description is based upon a "Chronology of Events Concerning Women in Holy Orders," *The Witness* (Summer 1984), 4. See also Emily C. Hewitt and Suzanne R. Hiatt, *Women Priests: Yes or No?* (New York: Seabury, 1973), and Mary S. Donovan, *Women Priests in the Episcopal Church: The Experience of the First Decade* (Cincinnati: Forward Movement Press, 1988).

19. See Ted Harrison, *Much Beloved Daughter: The Story of Florence Li* (Wilton, CT: Morehouse-Barlow, 1985).

20. See Catherine M. Prelinger, "Ordained Women in the Episcopal Church: Their Impact on the Work and Structure of the Clergy," in *Episcopal Women: Gender, Spirituality and Commitment in an American Mainline Denomination,* ed. Catherine M. Prelinger (New York: Oxford Univ. Press, 1992), 285–309.

21. "Harris Chosen Anglican Woman Bishop," *The Woman's Pulpit* 67 (January–March 1989): 1, and "First Woman Consecrated Bishop of the Episcopal Church," *New York Times,* February 12, 1989, 1 and 14.

22. *Christian Century,* June 30–July 7, 1993.

23. Karen Kennelly, ed., *American Catholic Women: A Historical Exploration* (New York: Macmillan, 1989), 183–86.

24. The entire text of the statement is found in Carroll Stuhlmueller, ed., *Women and Priesthood: Future Directions* (Collegeville, MN: Liturgical Press, 1978), 212–25. See also Leonard Swidler and Arlene Swidler, eds., *Women Priests: A Catholic Commentary on the Vatican Declaration* (New York: Paulist Press, 1977).

25. Deborah Belonick, "The Spirit of the Female Priesthood," in *Women and the Priesthood,* ed. Thomas Hopko (Crestwood, NY: St. Vladimir's Seminary Press, 1983), 135–68.

26. See Constance Parvey, ed., *Ordination of Women in Ecumenical Perspective: Workbook for the Church's Future,* Faith and Order Paper 105 (Geneva: World Council of Churches, 1980).

27. See C. Eric Lincoln and Lawrence H. Mamiya, *The Black Church in the African-American Experience* (Durham: Duke Univ. Press, 1989), 274–89.

28. Elizabeth, *Elizabeth: A Colored Minister of the Gospel Born in Slavery* (Philadelphia: Tract Association of Friends, 1889), excerpt reprinted in *Black Women in Nineteenth-Century America,* ed. Bert J. Loewenberg and Ruth Bogin (University Park and London: Pennsylvania State Univ. Press, 1978), 127.

29. Jarena Lee, *Religious Experience and Journal of Mrs. Jarena Lee* (Philadelphia, 1836).

30. Amanda Berry Smith, *The Story of the Lord's Dealings with Mrs. Amanda Smith, The Colored Evangelist, Containing an Account of her Life Work of Faith, Her Travels in America, England, Scotland, India, and Africa as an Independent Missionary* (Chicago: Meyer and Brother, 1893). Excerpts are reprinted in *Black Women,* ed. Loewenberg and Bogin.

31. Jualynne Dodson, "Nineteenth-Century A.M.E. Preaching Women," in *Women in New Worlds,* ed. Hilah F. Thomas and Rosemary Skinner Keller (Nashville: Abingdon Press, 1981), 276–89.

32. Dodson, "Preaching Women"; see also Bishop Othal Hawthorne Lakey, *The History of the C.M.E. Church* (Memphis: C.M.E. Publishing House, 1985), 406, 408.

33. *Church of God in Christ Official Manual* (Memphis: Church of God in Christ Publishing House, 1973), 144–46.

34. A number of steps were taken in the Reform movement leading up to Priesand's ordination. The Reform tradition, which began in Germany, always tried to include women more fully in Jewish religious life. Women were counted in the *minyan* or quorum needed for worship; the daily prayer in which a Jewish man thanks God for not having been created a woman was abolished; women were admitted to formal religious instruction; and women and men were seated in the congregation together. Janet R. Marder, "Are Women Changing the Rabbinate? The Reform Perspective," in *Religious Institutions and Women's Leadership: New Roles Inside the Mainstream,* ed. Catherine Wessinger (Columbus: Univ. of South Carolina

Press, forthcoming). See also Ann Braude's discussion of Reform Judaism in chap. 3 of this volume.

35. Rebecca Alpert and Gail Milgram, "Women in the Reconstructionist Rabbinate," in *Religious Institutions,* ed. Wessinger.

36. Sydell Ruth Schulman, "Faithful Daughters and Ultimate Rebels: The First Class of Conservative Jewish Women Rabbis," in *Religious Institutions,* ed. Wessinger.

37. Schulman, "Faithful Daughters."

38. The documentation of the debate is found in Simon Greenberg, ed., *The Ordination of Women as Rabbis: Studies and Responsa* (New York: Jewish Theological Seminary of America, 1988); see especially 127–87.

39. Jack Wertheimer, *A People Divided: Judaism in Contemporary America* (New York: Basic Books, 1993), 148. See excerpts from an interview with Eilberg in chap. 3 of this volume, document 7.

40. Blu Greenberg, "Is Now the Time for Orthodox Women Rabbis?" *Moment: The Magazine of Jewish Culture and Opinion* 18 (December 1993): 50–53, 74.

41. Luther Lee, *Woman's Right to Preach the Gospel: A Sermon Preached at the Ordination of the Rev. Miss Antoinette L. Brown at South Butler, Wayne County, N.Y., September 15, 1853* (Syracuse, NY, 1853).

42. C. Duren, "Woman's Place in Religious Meetings," *Congregational Review* (January 1868), 22–29.

43. Lyman Richard Hartley, "Women as Ministers: The Pros and Cons," *New York Times Magazine,* April 10, 1947, 19, 59.

44. Madeline Southard, *The Woman's Pulpit* 1 (1924): 3; Madeline Southard, *The Woman's Pulpit* 4 (1928): 6; Florence Resor Jardine, "The Case for Women in the Methodist Ministry," *The Woman's Pulpit* 28 (April–June 1950): 2–3.

45. Phoebe Palmer, *Promise of the Father: or, A Neglected Specialty of the Last Days* (New York: W. C. Palmer, 1872), 28–30.

46. Margaret R. Seebach, "Shall Women Preach?" *Lutheran Quarterly* 33 (October 1903): 580–81.

47. Charles E. Raven, *Women and the Ministry,* with an American introduction by Elizabeth Wilson (Garden City, NY: Doubleday, Doran, 1929), 33–36.

48. "Progress Report," as reprinted in Hewitt and Hiatt, *Women Priests,* 111–16.

49. *Revised Interim Report of a Study on the Life and Work of Women in the Church* (Geneva: World Council of Churches, 1948), 39–49, and *Concerning the Ordination of Women* (Geneva: World Council of Churches, 1964), 5–6.

50. Jarena Lee, *Religious Experiences and Journal of Mrs. Jarena Lee, Giving Account of Her Call to Preach the Gospel: Revised and corrected from the Original Manuscript Written by Herself* (Philadelphia: published for the author, 1849), 14–17.

51. The complete documentation surrounding the debate on Conservative women rabbis at the Jewish Theological Seminary of America was published in book form as Simon Greenberg, ed., *The Ordination of Women as Rabbis: Studies and Responsa* (New York: Jewish Theological Seminary of America, 1988). See Joel Roth, "On the Ordination of Women as Rabbis," in that volume, 127–87. Excerpts printed here are 167–68 and 173–74.

52. Blu Greenberg, "Is Now the Time for Orthodox Women Rabbis?" *Moment: The Magazine of Jewish Culture and Opinion* 18 (December 1993): 52–53, 74.

Chapter 8. Gender in Utopian and Communal Societies

1. See Rosemary R. Ruether and Catherine Prelinger, "Women in Sectarian and Utopian Groups," in *Women and Religion in America,* vol. 2, *The Colonial and Revolutionary Periods,* ed. Rosemary Radford Ruether and Rosemary Skinner Keller (San Francisco: Harper & Row, 1983), 262–63, 288–94.

2. Ruether and Prelinger, "Utopian Groups," 263–66, 294–305.

3. Brian J. C. Berry, *America's Utopian Experiments: Communal Havens from Long-Wave Crisis* (Hanover, NH: Univ. Press of New England, 1992), 43–54, 116–28.

4. Ruether and Prelinger, "Utopian Groups," 260–62, 266–71.

5. Celia Morris Eckhardt, *Fanny Wright: Rebel in America* (Cambridge: Harvard Univ. Press, 1984).

6. Berry, *America's Utopian Experiments,* 98–105.

7. Berry, *America's Utopian Experiments,* 82–92, 107–15. Etienne Cabet claimed that socialism was the true Christianity in his book *True Christianity* (1846).

8. Berry, *America's Utopian Experiments,* 64–82, 93–98.

9. Berry, *America's Utopian Experiments,* 64–82, 93–98.

10. Rosemary R. Ruether, "Women in Utopian Movements," in *Women and Religion in America,* vol. 1, *The Nineteenth Century,* ed. Rosemary Radford Ruether and Rosemary Skinner Keller (San Francisco: Harper & Row, 1981), 52–53, 95–100; also Wendy Chmielewski et al., *Women in Spiritual and Communitarian Societies in the United States* (Syracuse: Syracuse Univ. Press, 1993), 52–67.

11. See Paul Kagan, *New World Utopias* (New York: Penguin, 1975), 19–35.

12. Kagan, *New World Utopias,* 48–83.

13. Berry, *America's Utopian Experiments,* 152–213.

14. Berry, *America's Utopian Experiments,* 129–37.

15. Chmielewski et al., *Women in Spiritual and Communitarian Societies,* 221–35.

16. Berry, *America's Utopian Experiments,* 214–27.

17. David van Zandt, *Living in the Children of God* (Princeton: Princeton Univ. Press, 1971); Steve Rose, *Jesus and Jim Jones* (New York: Pilgrim Press, 1979); Clifford Linedecker, *Massacre at Waco* (New York: St. Martin's Press, 1993).

18. Jim Wallis, *Agenda for Biblical People* (New York: Harper & Row, 1976).

19. Chmielewski et al., *Women in Spiritual and Communitarian Societies,* 201–20, 256–66; also Jon Wagner, ed., *Sex Roles in Contemporary American Communes* (Bloomington: Indiana Univ. Press, 1982), 172–210; Sue, Nelly, Carol, and Billie, *Country Lesbians* (Grants Pass, OR: Womanshare Books, 1976).

20. Jacob Boehme, *Mysterium Magnum* (London: John Watkins, 1924); Emmanuel Swedenborg, *Arcana Coelestia,* 8 vols. (New York: American Swedenborg Publishing Company, 1870–1874).

21. See Ruether, "Utopian Movements," 61–63.

22. Mary Baker Eddy, *Science and Health with Key to the Scriptures* (Boston: Christian Science Publishing Company, 1890), 16–17. See also Ann Douglas, *The Feminization of American Culture* (New York: Avon, 1977), 146–54.

23. Matilda Joslyn Gage, *Women, Church and State* (1893; reprint, New York: Arno Press, 1972), 21–23.

24. Charlotte Perkins Gilman, *His Religion and Hers* (New York: Century Press, 1923).

25. Carol Christ, *The Laughter of Aphrodite* (San Francisco: Harper & Row, 1987).

26. For example, Twin Oaks, in Louisa, Virginia, since 1984 has sponsored an annual Women's Gathering in August.

27. See Ruether and Prelinger, "Utopian Groups," 303–4.

28. See Roger Wunderlich, *Low Living and High Thinking at Modern Times* (Syracuse: Syracuse Univ. Press, 1992).

29. Adin Ballou, *History of the Hopedale Community* (Lowell, MA: Thompson and Hill, 1897).

30. See Raymond Lee Muncy, *Sex and Marriage in Utopian Communities in Nineteenth Century America* (Baltimore: Penguin Books, 1973), 212–13.

31. Sue et al., *Country Lesbians.*

32. Chmielewski et al., *Women in Spiritual and Communitarian Societies,* 119–32; also Lawrence Foster, *Women, Family and Utopia: Communal Experiments of the Shakers, the Oneida Community and the Mormons* (Syracuse: Syracuse Univ. Press, 1991), 17–42.

33. Ruether, "Utopian Movements," 81–87; see also Ruether, "Radical Victorians: The Quest for an Alternative Culture," in *Women and Religion in America,* vol. 3, *1900–1968,* ed. Ruether and Keller (San Francisco: Harper & Row, 1986), 12, 40–42.

34. Carolyn Kolmerten, *Women in Utopia: The Ideology of Gender in the American Owenite Communities* (Bloomington: Indiana Univ. Press, 1990), 111–41.

35. Ruether and Keller, eds., *Women and Religion in America,* 1:77–79.

36. Dorothy Day, *The Long Loneliness* (New York: Harper and Brothers, 1952), 240–43.

37. Chmielewski et al., *Women in Spiritual and Communitarian Societies,* 89–103.

38. Chmielewski et al., *Women in Spiritual and Communitarian Societies,* 182–200.

39. Anna Wheeler, with William Thompson, wrote the tract "The Appeal of One-half of the Human Race, Women, against the Pretensions of the Other half, Men, to Retain them in Political and Thence in Civil and Domestic Slavery" (1825); see Barbara Taylor,

Eve and the New Jerusalem: Socialism and Feminism in the Nineteenth Century (New York: Pantheon, 1983).

40. Carolyn Kolmerten, *Women in Utopia,* 68–101; also her article in Chmielewski et al., *Women in Spiritual and Communitarian Societies,* 38–51.

41. *Testimony of Christ's Second Appearing* (n.p.: United Society, 1856), 506, 514–18.

42. Hilda Adam King, *The Harmonists: A Folk Cultural Approach* (Metuchen, NJ: Scarecrow Press, 1973), 113–20.

43. Jeans McMahon Humez, ed., *Gifts of Power: The Writings of Rebecca Jackson: Black Visionary; Shaker Elderess* (Amherst: Univ. of Massachusetts Press, 1981), 154, 168, 174, 203.

44. "Goddess of Life," from *Pilgrim Warrior Songbook* (Greenfield, MA: n.d.), 2–3; available from 15 Abbott Street, Greenfield, MA 01301.

45. Julius F. Sachse, *The German Sectarians of Pennsylvania, 1742–1800: A Critical and Legendary History of the Ephrata Cloister and the Dunkers* (Philadelphia: n.p., 1900), 2:176–96.

46. John Humphrey Noyes, *Male Continence* (Oneida, NY: Office of the Oneida Circular, 1872), 11–12, 14–16.

47. Joseph Smith, *Doctrines and Covenants,* sec. 132 (1883; reprint, Greenwood Press, 1971).

48. Wilkinson Papers, Cornell University Archives, film 357.

49. Wilkinson Papers, Cornell University Archives, film 357; also Herbert Wisbey, *Pioneer Prophetess: Jemima Wilkinson, The Publick Universal Friend* (Ithaca: Cornell Univ. Press, 1964), 18, 30.

50. Frances Wright, *New Harmony Gazette,* January 30, 1828, 124; February 6, 1828, 132.

51. Charles Nordhoff, *Communist Societies of the United States* (New York: Harper and Brothers, 1875), 34–35, 37, 47–48.

52. George Garrison, "The Sanctificationists of Belton," *The Charities Review* 3 (November 1893): 29–46.

53. Ina May Gaskin, *Spiritual Midwifery* (Summertown, TN: Book Publishing Company, 1977); excerpt appeared in *Woman of Power* (Summer 1989), 29.

54. Ingrid Komar, *Living the Dream: A Documentary Study of Twin Oaks Community* (Louisa, VA: Twin Oaks Community, 1983), 181–87.

55. Batya Weinbaum, "Twin Oaks: A Feminist Looks at Indigenous Socialism in the United States," in *Women in Search of Utopia,* ed. Ruby Rohrlich and Elaine Baruch (New York: Schocken, 1989), 161–67.

Chapter 9. Seeing Red: American Indian Women Speaking of Their Religious and Political Perspectives

1. Inés Talamantez, "The Longest Walk," *Shantik: Journal of International Writing and Art* 4:2 (summer–fall), 1979.
2. Diane Bell, *Daughters of the Dreaming* (Minneapolis: Univ. of Minnesota Press, 1993).
3. "San Juan Pueblo," *Handbook of North American Indians,* Vol. 9 (Washington, DC: Smithsonian Institution, 1979).
4. Paula Gunn Allen, *Grandmothers of the Light: A Medicine Woman's Sourcebook* (Boston: Beacon Press, 1991).
5. Vickie Downey, "Tewa–Tesuque Pueblo," in *Wisdom's Daughters: Conversations with Women Elders of Native America,* ed. Steven Wall (New York: HarperCollins, 1993), 2–21.
6. Personal communication with Shirley Montoya.
7. Personal communication with Shirley Montoya.
8. Flora Jones is a Wintu religious leader and healer in northern California.
9. *Jesuit Relations and Allied Documents: Travels and Explorations of the Jesuit Missionaries in New France, 1610–1791* (Cleveland: Burrows Brothers, 1896–1901).
10. See Beatrice Medicine and Patricia Albers, eds., *The Hidden Half: Studies of Plains Indian Women* (New York: Univ. Press, 1983).
11. Ella Cara Deloria, *Waterlily* (Omaha: Univ. of Nebraska Press, 1988).
12. MALCS, *Mujeres Activas en Letras y Cambio Social* (Women Active in Letters and Social Change), is the major network for Latina women academics, writers, and social activists.
13. Rigoberta Menchu, *I, Rigoberta Menchu: An Indian Woman in Guatemala,* ed. Elisabeth Burgos-Debray, trans. Ann Wright (London: Verso Press, 1984).

14. See forthcoming book by Ines Talamantez, *'Isánáklésh Gotal: Introducing Apache Girls to the World of Spiritual and Cultural Values.*

15. Ines Hernandez-Avila, address given at the 1993 Annual Meeting of the American Academy of Religion, Washington, DC.

16. Original note to the document: Ines Hernandez-Avila, "Tejana Intonations/Nez Perce Heartbeat: Notes on Identity and Culture," *A/B: Autobiographical Studies* 7, no. 2 (Fall 1993): 298.

17. Original note to the document: In his forthcoming book, *Po'i Pentum Tammen Kimmappeh/The Road on Which We Came: A History of the Western Shoshone,* Steven Crum writes of his people: "Because of their hunting and gathering way of life, the extended families moved about or commuted within geographic 'orbits' inside their tribal territory. . . . And although the New moved about throughout the year, they still possessed a definite sense of place. . . . They did not wander aimlessly with no sense of belonging, but remained within niches inside the larger tribal territory."

18. Original note to the document: Maria Antonieta Rascon, "La Mujer en la Lucha Social," *Imagen y Realidad de la Mujer,* ed. Elena Urrutia (Mexico City: SeptDiana, 1977), 150.

19. Original note to the document: Vine Deloria, Jr., "Afterword," in Alvin M. Josephy, *America in 1492: The World of the Indian People before the Arrival of Columbus* (New York: Alfred Knopf, 1992), 429–30.

20. Original note to the document: Simon Brascoupe says, in "Indigenous Perspectives on International Development," *Indigenous Economics: Toward a Natural Order, Akwekon Journal* 9, no. 2 (Summer 1992): 429–30: "For the West to adopt Indigenous knowledge, they do not have to become 'indigenized,' but they do need to reflect on their own culture and benefit from lessons learned. The field of Indigenous knowledge extends to ecology, hunting and gathering, medicine and fishing."

21. This document is taken from Pilalau Khus's lecture to a religious studies class on myth and symbols at the University of California at Santa Barbara, April 7, 1994. The lecture was transcribed by D. Bell.

22. See forthcoming study in Inés Talamantez, *'Isánáklésh Gotal.*

23. For the beginnings of Mexican spiritualism, see Isabel Lagarriga Attias, *Magia y Religión entre los Espiritualistas Trinitarios Marianos*

(Mexico City: Departamento de Etnologia y Antropologia Social, Instituto Nacional de Antropologia e Historia, 1974).

24. These stages are described in Arnold van Gennep, *Rites of Passage* (1909; reprint, Chicago: Univ. of Chicago Press, 1960), 3–4.

Chapter 10. Women in American Religions: Growing Pluralism, New Dialogue

1. There has been no official census of American religious preference since the 1930s. These figures are estimates by the office of the World's Parliament of Religions in Chicago.
2. John Henry Barrows, ed., *The World's Parliament of Religions at the Columbian Exposition of 1893* (Chicago: The Parliament Publishing Company, 1893), 829–31, 968–78, 989–96; see also Robert S. Ellwood, ed., *Eastern Spirituality in America* (New York: Paulist Press, 1987), 5–43.
3. Ellwood, ed., *Eastern Spirituality,* 5–43.
4. J. Gordon Melton and Michael A. Köszegi, *Islam in North America: A Source Book* (New York: Garland Publishers, 1992).
5. This information was drawn from the program of the World's Parliament of Religions, August 28–September 4, 1993.
6. See Rosemary R. Ruether, "Women in Contemporary World Christianity," in *Today's Woman in World Religions,* ed. Arvind Sharma (Albany: State Univ. of New York Press, 1993), 267–301.
7. The most extreme effort to label Catholic feminists as witches engaged in a diabolic conspiracy to subvert the church is Donna Steichen, *Ungodly Rage: The Hidden Face of Catholic Feminism* (San Francisco: Ignatius Press, 1991).
8. Shelley Finson, ed., *Women and Religion: A Bibliographic Guide to Christian Feminist Liberation Theology* (Toronto: Univ. of Toronto Press, 1991).
9. Elisabeth Schüssler Fiorenza's major books on feminist hermeneutics are *In Memory of Her: A Feminist Theological Reconstruction of Christian Origins* (New York: Crossroad, 1983); *Bread Not Stone: The Challenge of Feminist Biblical Interpretation* (Boston: Beacon Press, 1984); *But She Said: Feminist Practice of Biblical Interpretation* (Boston: Beacon Press, 1992).

10. Some of Phyllis Bird's publications are: "The Place of Women in Israelite Cultus," *Ancient Israelite Religion,* ed. Paul Hanson et al. (Minneapolis: Fortress Press, 1987), 397–419; "Sexual Differentiation and Divine Image in the Genesis Creation Text," in *Image of God and Gender Models,* ed. Kari Borresen (Oslo: Solum Forlag, 1991), 11–34; and "Women's Religion in Ancient Israel," in *Women's Earliest Records,* ed. Barbara Lesko (Providence: Brown Univ. Press, 1989), 283–98. Some publications of Phyllis Trible are: *God and the Rhetoric of Sexuality* (Philadelphia: Fortress Press, 1978); and *Texts of Terror* (Philadelphia: Fortress Press, 1984). Publications of J. Cheryl Exum are: "You Shall Let Every Daughter Live: A Study of Exodus 1:8–2:10," *Semeia* no. 28 (1982): 63–82; and *Fragmented Women: Feminist (Sub)versions of Biblical Narratives* (Philadelphia: Trinity Press, 1993). Publications of Mieke Bal are: *Lethal Love: Feminist Readings of Biblical Love Stories* (Bloomington: Indiana Univ. Press, 1987); and *Murder and Difference: Gender, Genre and Scholarship in Sisera's Death* (Bloomington: Indiana Univ. Press, 1988). Publications of Katherine Sakenfeld are: "The Bible and Women: Bane or Blessing," *Theology Today* 32, no. 3 (October 1975): 222–33; and *Faithfulness in Action: Loyalty in Biblical Perspective* (Philadelphia: Fortress Press, 1985).

11. Drorah Setel, "Prophets and Pornography: Female Sexual Images in Hosea," in *Feminist Interpretation of the Bible,* ed. Letty Russell (Philadelphia: Westminster Press, 1985), 86–95; Tikva Frymer-Kensky, *In the Wake of the Goddesses: Women, Culture and the Biblical Transformation of Pagan Myth* (New York: Macmillan, 1992); Carol Meyers, *Discovering Eve: Ancient Israelite Women in Context* (New York: Oxford Univ. Press, 1988); Esther Fuchs, "For I Have the Way of Women: Gender, Deception and Ideology in Biblical Narrative," *Semeia* no. 42 (1988): 68–83; Marcia Falk, *The Song of Songs: A New Translation* (San Francisco: HarperSanFrancisco, 1990); Ross S. Kraemer, *Her Share of the Blessings: Women's Religion Among Pagans, Jews and Christians in the Greco-Roman World* (New York: Oxford Univ. Press, 1992); Savina Teubal, *Sarah the Priestess: The First Matriarch of Genesis* (Athens, OH: Swallow Press, 1984).

12. Deirdre Good, *Reconstructing the Tradition of Sophia in Gnostic Literature* (Atlanta: Scholars Press, 1987); Elizabeth Tetlow, *Women and*

Ministry in the New Testament (New York: Paulist Press, 1980; Winsome Munro, "Women Disciples: Light from Secret Mark," *Journal of Feminist Studies in Religion* 8 (Spring 1992): 47–64; Jane Schaberg, *The Illegitimacy of Jesus: A Feminist Theological Interpretation of the Infancy Narratives* (San Francisco: Harper & Row, 1987); Elaine Pagels, *The Gnostic Gospels* (New York: Random House, 1979); Pagels, *Adam, Eve and the Serpent in Genesis 1–3* (Claremont, CA: Institute for Antiquity and Christianity, 1988); Pheme Perkins, "Sophia and the Mother-Father: The Gnostic Goddess," in *The Book of the Goddess Past and Present,* ed. Carl Olsen (New York: Crossroad, 1985), 97–109; Sharon Ringe, ed., with Carol A. Newsom, *The Women's Bible Commentary* (Louisville, KY: Westminster/John Knox Press, 1992); Sandra Schneider, *Women and the Word: The Gender of God in the New Testament and the Spirituality of Women* (New York: Paulist Press, 1986); Luise Schottroff, *Itinerant Prophetesses: A Feminist Analysis of the Sayings of Source Q* (Claremont, CA: Institute for Antiquity and Christianity, 1991), and Schottroff, *Let the Oppressed Go Free: Feminist Perspectives on the New Testament* (Louisville, KY: Westminster/John Knox Press, 1993); Mary Ann Tolbert, *The Bible and Feminist Hermeneutics* (Chico, CA: Scholars Press, 1983); Mary Rose D'Angelo, "Abba and Father: Imperial Religion and the Jesus Tradition," *Journal of Biblical Literature* 3, no. 4 (Winter 1992): 611–30; Antoinette Wire, *The Corinthian Women Prophetesses: A Reconstruction Through Paul's Rhetoric* (Minneapolis: Fortress Press, 1990); Bernadette Brooten, *Women Leaders in the Ancient Synagogue: Inscriptional Evidence and Background Issues* (Chico, CA: Scholars Press, 1982); Karen Torjesen, *When Women Were Priests: Women's Leadership in the Early Church* (San Francisco: HarperSanFrancisco, 1993).

13. Letty Russell, *Human Liberation in a Feminist Perspective* (Philadelphia: Westminster Press, 1974); Russell, *Church in the Round: Feminist Interpretation of the Church* (Louisville, KY: Westminster/John Knox Press, 1993); Carter Heyward, *Touching Our Strength: The Erotic as Power and the Love of God* (San Francisco: Harper & Row, 1989); Anne E. Carr, *Transforming Grace: Christian Tradition and Women's Experience* (San Francisco: Harper & Row, 1988); Rebecca Chopp, *The Power to Speak: Feminism, Language, and God* (New York: Crossroad, 1989); Sallie McFague, *Models of God:*

Theology for an Ecological, Nuclear Age (Philadelphia: Fortress Press, 1987); McFague, *The Body of God: An Ecological Theology* (Minneapolis: Fortress Press, 1993); Rita Nakashima Brock, *Journeys by Heart: A Christology of Erotic Power* (New York: Crossroad, 1988); Rosemary R. Ruether, *Sexism and God-Talk: Toward a Feminist Theology* (Boston: Beacon Press, 1983); Elizabeth Johnson, *She Who Is: The Mystery of God in a Feminist Theological Perspective* (New York: Crossroad, 1992); Sharon Welch, *Communities of Resistance and Solidarity: A Feminist Theology of Liberation* (Maryknoll, NY: Orbis Books, 1985).

14. Renita J. Weems, *Just a Sister Away: A Womanist Vision of Women's Relationships in the Bible* (San Diego: Luna Media, 1988); Jacquelyn Grant, *White Women's Christ and Black Women's Jesus: Feminist Christology and Womanist Response* (Atlanta: Scholars Press, 1989); Katie G. Cannon, *Black Womanist Ethics* (Atlanta: Scholars Press, 1988); Emilie Townes, *Womanist Justice, Womanist Hope* (Atlanta: Scholars Press, 1993); Townes, *A Troubling in My Soul: Womanist Perspectives on Evil and Suffering* (Maryknoll, NY: Orbis Books, 1993); Delores S. Williams, *Sisters in the Wilderness: The Challenge of Womanist God-Talk* (Maryknoll, NY: Orbis Books, 1993); Toinette Eugene, "Moral Values and Black Womanist Ethics," *Journal of Religious Thought* 44, no. 2 (1988): 23–34.

15. Ada María Isasi-Díaz and Yolanda Tarango, *Hispanic Women, Prophetic Voice in the Church,* 2d ed. (Minneapolis: Fortress Press, 1992); Isasi-Díaz, *En la Lucha: A Hispanic Women's Liberation Theology* (Minneapolis: Fortress Press, 1993).

16. Sun Ai Park, ed., *In God's Image,* journal published since 1980; editorial office: Asian Women's Resource Center for Culture and Theology, 134–5 Nokbun-Dong, Eunpyong-Ku, Seoul, Korea.

17. Chung Hyun Khung, *The Struggle to Be the Sun Again: Introducing Asian Women's Theology* (Maryknoll, NY: Orbis Books, 1991).

18. Mary Hunt, *Fierce Tenderness: A Feminist Theology of Friendship* (New York: Crossroad, 1991); Carter Heyward, *Speaking of Christ: A Lesbian Feminist Voice* (New York: Pilgrim Press, 1989).

19. Susannah Heschel, ed., *On Being a Jewish Feminist: A Reader* (New York: Schocken, 1983).

20. Judith Plaskow, *Standing Again at Sinai: Judaism from a Feminist Perspective* (San Francisco: Harper & Row, 1990).

21. Leila Ahmed, *Women and Gender in Islam: Historical Roots of a Modern Debate* (New Haven: Yale Univ. Press, 1992); Juliette Minces, *The House of Disobedience: Women in Arab Society* (London: Zed Books, 1982); Nawal el Saadawi, *The Hidden Face of Eve: Women in the Arab World* (London: Zed Books, 1980); Bouthaina Shaaban, *Both Right and Left Handed: Arab Women Talk about Their Lives* (Bloomington: Indiana Univ. Press, 1991); Nahid Toubia, ed., *Women of the Arab World: The Coming Challenge* (London: Zed Books, 1988).

22. See Beverly Thomas McCloud, "African American Muslim Women," in *The Muslims in America*, ed. Yvonne Y. Haddad (New York: Oxford Univ. Press, 1991), 177–87.

23. Andrea Dworkin, *Right Wing Women* (New York: Coward, McCann, 1983).

24. Riffat Hassan, *Women's and Men's Liberation: Testimonies of the Spirit* (New York: Greenwood Press, 1991).

25. Chatsumarn Kabilsingh, *Thai Women in Buddhism* (Berkeley: Parallax Press, 1991); also Ayya Khema, *Be an Island unto Yourself* (Dodanduwa, Sri Lanka: Parappuduwa Nuns Island, 1986).

26. Sandy Boucher, ed., *Turning the Wheel: American Women Creating the New Buddhism,* 2d ed. (Boston: Beacon Press, 1993). See also Anne Klein, "Finding a Self: Buddhist and Feminist Perspectives," in *Shaping New Vision: Gender and Values in American Culture,* ed. Clarissa W. Atkinson, Constance H. Buchanan, and Margaret R. Miles (Ann Arbor: UMI Research Press, 1987), 195.

27. See, for example, Mary Daly's recent book, *Outercourse: The Bedazzling Voyage* (San Francisco: HarperSanFrancisco, 1992).

28. Carol Christ, *The Laughter of Aphrodite: Reflections on a Journey to the Goddess* (San Francisco: Harper & Row, 1987).

29. Starhawk, *The Spiral Dance: A Rebirth of the Ancient Religion of the Great Goddess* (Boston: Beacon Press, 1979, 1989); Starhawk, *Dreaming the Dark: Magic, Sex, and Politics* (Boston: Beacon Press, 1982).

30. Z Budapest, *The Holy Book of Women's Mysteries I* and *II* (Los Angeles: Susan B. Anthony Coven no. 1, 1979, 1980).

31. For an overview of the history of neopagan feminist spirituality, see Cynthia Eller, *Living in the Lap of the Goddess: The Feminist Spirituality Movement in America* (New York: Crossroad, 1993).

32. Paula Gunn Allen, *The Sacred Hoop: Recovering the Feminine in American Indian Tradition* (Boston: Beacon Press, 1986).

33. See Andy Smith, "For All Those Who Were Indian in a Former Life," in *Ecofeminism and the Sacred,* ed. Carol J. Adams (New York: Continuum, 1993), 168–71.

34. From Elisabeth Schüssler Fiorenza, "The Will to Choose or Reject: Continuing our Critical Work," in *Feminist Interpretation of the Bible,* ed. Letty Russell (Philadelphia: Westminster Press, 1985), 125–36.

35. Original note to the document: Adrienne Rich, "Disloyal to Civilization: Feminism, Fascism, Gynophobia" (1978), in *On Lies, Secrets, and Silence: Selected Prose 1966–1978* (New York: W. W. Norton, 1979), 307.

36. Original note to the document: From the ending chorus in Ntozake Shange, *For Colored Girls Who Have Considered Suicide/When the Rainbow Is Enuf: A Choreopoem* (New York: Macmillan, 1977).

37. Toinette Eugene, "Womanist Theology," from the *New Handbook of Christian Theology,* ed. Donald Musser and Joseph Price (Nashville: Abingdon Press, 1992), 510–12.

38. Adapted from Tarango and Isasi-Díaz, *Hispanic Women,* 1–7, 72–3, 109–10.

39. Original note to the document: Jose Miguez Bonino, *Doing Theology in a Revolutionary Situation* (Philadelphia: Fortress Press, 1975), 72.

40. From Judith Plaskow, "The Right Question Is Theological," in *On Being a Jewish Feminist: A Reader,* ed. Susannah Heschel (New York: Schocken, 1983), 223–33.

41. Original note to the document: Judith Hole and Ellen Levine, *Rebirth of Feminism* (New York: Quadrangle Books, 1971), ix–x.

42. Original note to the document: Simone de Beauvoir describes woman as the Other in *The Second Sex* (New York: Bantam Books, 1961), xvi–xxix and *passim.* Rachel Adler, in "The Jew Who Wasn't There: *Halakhah* and the Jewish Woman," *Response* 18 (Summer 1973): 77–82, makes use of this basic concept but without understanding its implications for halakhic change.

43. From Riffat Hassan, "Woman-Man Equality in the Islamic Tradition," *Harvard Divinity School Bulletin* 17, no. 2 (January–May 1987), 2–4.

44. From Rita Gross, *Buddhism After Patriarchy: A Feminist History, Analysis and Reconstruction of Buddhism* (Albany: State Univ. of New York Press, 1993), 127–28, 130–35. Some other writings of Gross are: Gross, ed., *Beyond Androcentrism: New Essays on Women and Religion* (Missoula, MT: Scholars Press, 1977); Rita Gross and Nancy Falk, eds., *Unspoken Worlds: Women's Religious Lives* (Belmont, CA: Wadsworth, 1989); and "Feminism from the Perspective of Buddhist Practice," *Buddhist-Christian Studies* 1 (1980): 73–82.

45. Original note to the document: Rita Gross, "Feminism from the Perspective of Buddhist Practice," *Buddhist-Christian Studies* 1 (1980): 73–82.

46. From Starhawk, *The Spiral Dance: A Rebirth of the Ancient Religion of the Great Goddess,* 2d ed. (San Francisco: Harper & Row, 1989), 16–29.

47. Original note to the document: Carol Christ, "Why Women Need the Goddess," in *Womanspirit Rising: A Feminist Reader in Religion,* ed. Carol P. Christ and Judith Plaskow (San Francisco: Harper & Row, 1979), 278.

CONTRIBUTORS

Anne Braude is associate professor of religious studies at Macalester College in St. Paul, Minnesota. She has written broadly on gender and ethnicity in American religious history. Her book, *Radical Spirits: Spiritualism and Women's Rights in Nineteenth Century America,* appeared in 1989.

Joanne Brown is professor of Church History and Ecumenics at St. Andrews College, Saskatchewan, Canada. She edited the book *Christianity, Patriarchy and Abuse* (1989) with Carole Bohn and contributed the lead article "For God So Loved the World."

Nancy Hardesty is currently visiting professor of religion at Clemson University, Clemson, South Carolina. She is author of *All We're Meant to Be: Biblical Feminism for Today* (1974) and *Your Daughters Shall Prophecy: Revivalism and Feminism in the Age of Finney* (1991).

Rosemary Skinner Keller is professor of religion and American cultural studies and dean of the faculty at Garrett-Evangelical Theological Seminary in Evanston, Illinois. She is co-editor of the three-volume documentary history *Women and Religion in America* (1981, 1983, and 1986) and has written numerous books and articles on women and religion.

Rosemary Radford Ruether is the Georgia Harkness professor of applied theology at Garrett-Evangelical Theological Seminary. She has written and edited numerous books and articles on women, theology, and social justice. She was co-editor with Rosemary Skinner Keller of *Women and Religion in America.*

Inés Talamantez is assistant professor of Native American religious studies at the University of California at Santa Barbara and managing editor of *New Scholar: An Americanist Review.* She is a frequent lecturer at conferences and universities. Her major research interests are Native American female initiation ceremonies and Native American attitudes toward the environment.

Emilie M. Townes, an ordained American Baptist, is associate professor of Christian social ethics at Saint Paul School of Theology. She is the author of *Womanist Justice, Womanist Hope* and *In a Blaze of Glory: Womanist Spirituality as Social Witness,* and editor of *A Troubling in my Soul: Womanist Perspectives on Evil and Suffering.*

Barbara Brown Zikmund has been president of Hartford Seminary, Hartford, Connecticut, since 1990. From 1981 to 1990 she was dean of the faculty and professor of Church history at Pacific School of Religion in Berkeley, California. She holds a B.D. and Ph.D. from Duke University and is ordained in the United Church of Christ.

INDEX

PERMISSIONS ACKNOWLEDGMENTS

Grateful acknowledgment is made to the following archives, authors, photographers, and publishers for permission to reprint texts or photos.

"Sister Blandina's Adventures in the Southwest," from *At the End of the Santa Fe Trail*, pp. 59–62, 75, Bruce Publishing Company: reprinted by permission of the Archives of the Sister of Charity, Mount St. Joseph, OH.

Journals and Letters of Mother Theodore Guerin, pp. 193–94: reprinted by permission of the Archivist of the Sister of Providence, St. Mary of the Woods, IN.

"Bishop England's Institute of the Sisters of Mercy," pp. 456–58: reprinted by permission of the Archivist of the Sisters of Charity of Our Lady of Mercy, Charleston, SC.

The Autobiography of Mother Jones, pp. 89–93: reprinted by permission of Charles H. Kerr Publishing Company, Chicago, IL.

Selected Writings of Dorothy Day, edited by Robert Ellsberg, Alfred Knopf Publishing Company: permission to reprint from Robert Ellsberg, Maryknoll, New York.

Excerpt from *Simple Gifts: The Lives of Pat and Patty Crowley*, pp. 98–99: reprinted by permission of Sheed and Ward, Kansas City, MO, and from Patty Crowley, Chicago, IL.

Excerpt from Sister M. Madeleva Wolff, *My First Seventy Years*, pp. 110–13, Macmillan Publishing Company: reprinted by permission of the Sisters of Holy Cross, St. Mary's Notre Dame, IN.

Excerpt from "Las Hermanas": permission to reprint from Yolanda Tarango.

Excerpt from *Mary McLeod Bethune: A Biography*, pp. 287–89: reprinted by permission of Doubleday, New York.

Excerpt from Toni Morrison, *Beloved*, pp. 87–89: reprinted by permission of International Creative Management, INC, New York.

Excerpt from Katie Geneva Cannon, "Moral Wisdom in the Black Woman's Literary Tradition": reprinted by permission of Katie Geneva Cannon.

Excerpt from Delores S. Williams, "The Color of Feminism": reprinted by permission of Delores S. Williams.

Excerpt from Jacquelyn Grant, "Womanist Theology": reprinted by permission of Jacquelyn Grant.

Excerpt from Cheryl T. Gilkes, "Mother to the Motherless: Father to the Fatherless": reprinted by permission of Cheryl T. Gilkes.

Photo of Womanist Scholars at the AAR: permission to print from the photographer, Susan L. Ebersold.

Excerpt from *Letters of Rebecca Gratz*, pp. 144–46 and 274–77, and from Susan Grossman and Rivka Haut, *Daughters of the King: Women and the Synagogue*, pp. 284–90: reprinted by permission of the Jewish Publication Society.

Selections from *Bread Givers* by Anzia Yezierska, copyright © 1925 by Doubleday, copyright © renewed 1952 by Anzia Yezierska, transferred to Louise Levitas Henriksen 1970. Reprinted by permission of Persea Books, New York.

Excerpt from *Henrietta Szold: Life and Letters* by Marvin Lowenthal. Copyright © 1942 The Viking Press, renewed © 1970 by Harold C. Emer and Harry L. Shapiro, Executors of the Estate. Used by permission of Viking Penguin, a division of Penguin Books USA, Inc.

Excerpt from Alice Seligsberg, Address to the 1936 Hadassah Convention and "The Woman's Way": reprinted by permission of the Hadassah Archivist, New York, NY.

Excerpts from Cynthia Ozick, "Notes Toward Finding the Right Question," copyright © 1979 by Cynthia Ozick. All rights reserved. By permission of the author and her agents, Raines and Raines.

Excerpts from an interview with Rabbi Amy Eilberg by Raye T. Katz, "Exploring the Link between Womanhood and the Rabbinate"; and Elyse Goldstein, "Take Back the Waters: A Feminist Appropriation of Ritual": reprinted by permission of *Lilith: The Independent Jewish Women's*

Magazine, New York, NY, and from the authors, Elyse Goldstein and Raye T. Katz (pseud. of Aviva Cantor, author of *Jewish Women/Jewish Men*, forthcoming from HarperSanFrancisco in Spring 1995).

Excerpt from Judith Plaskow, "Beyond Egalitarianism": reprinted by permission of *Tikkun Magazine, A Bimonthly Jewish Critique of Politics, Culture, and Society*, New York, NY.

Excerpt from Shaina Sara Handelman, "Modesty and the Jewish Woman" in *The Modern Jewish Woman:* reprinted by permission of the Lubavitch Educational Foundation for Jewish Marriage Enrichment, Brooklyn, NY.

Photo from *Tradition: Orthodox Jewish Life in America*, by Mal Warshaw. Copyright © 1976 by Mal Warshaw. Reprinted by permission of Pantheon Books, a division of Random House, Inc.

Photo of women's minyam: permission to print from the Brown University New Bureau Photo Library.

Excerpts from the Danvers Statement: reprinted by permission of the Council on Biblical Manhood and Womanhood, Wheaton, IL.

Excerpts from John Rice, *Bobbed Hair, Bossy Wives and Women Preachers*, and from "Men and their Sins": reprinted by permission of the Sword of the Lord Publishers, Murfreesboro, TN.

Excerpt from Georgia Harkness, *Grace Abounding*, pp. 128–32: reprinted by permission of Abingdon Press.

Excerpt of "Point-Counterpoint": reprinted by permission of the Religious Coalition for Abortion Rights.

Press release from CLOUT: reprinted by permission of CLOUT (Christian Lesbians Out Together).

Excerpts from "Women as Ministers: Pros and Cons," April 10, 1947: reprinted by permission of *The New York Times*.

Excerpts from *The Woman's Pulpit*, 1924, p. 3; 1928, p. 6; and 1950, pp. 2–3: reprinted by permission of *The Woman's Pulpit*.

Excerpts from *Women and the Ministry*, pp. 33–36: reprinted by permission of Doubleday, Doran and Company.

Excerpts from the *Revised Interim Report of a Study on the Life and Work of Women in the Church*, pp. 39–40: reprinted by permission of the World Council of Churches, Geneva, Switzerland.

Excerpt from *The Ordination of Woman as Rabbis:* permission to reprint from The Jewish Theological Seminary of America, New York.

Excerpt from article on Orthodox Women Rabbis, December, 1993: reprinted by permission of *Moment: The Magazine of Jewish Culture and Opinion.*

Photo of Bishop Barbara Harris: permission to print from Bishop Barbara Harris.

Photo of Rabbi Sally Priesand: permission to print from Rabbi Sally Priesand.

Excerpt from Rebecca Jackson, *Gifts of Power*, pp. 154, 168, 174, 203: reprinted by permission of the University of Massachusetts Press.

The song "Goddess of Life" from *The Pilgrim Warrior Songbook:* reprinted by permission of Sandra W. Boston.

Extracts from The Wilkinson Papers, #357: reprinted by permission of the Yates County Genealogical and Historical Society.

Excerpt from Ina May Gaskin, "Spiritual Midwifery on the Farm": reprinted by permission of Ina May Gaskin.

Excerpt from Batya Weinbaum, "Twin Oaks: A Feminist Looks at Indigenous Socialism in the United States," in Ruby Rohrlich and Elaine Baruch, *Women in Search of Utopia:* reprinted by permission of Schocken Books, published by Pantheon Books, a division of Random House, Inc.

Photo of Ina May Gaskin: reprinted by permission of Ina May Gaskin.

Photo of Frances Wright: reprinted by permission of New Harmony Society Archives.

Excerpt from Elizabeth Schüssler Fiorenza, "The Will to Choose or Reject: Continuing Our Critical Work": edited by and permission to print from Elizabeth Schüssler Fiorenza.

Toinette Eugene, "Womanist Theology" from Donald Musser and Joseph Price, *New Handbook of Christian Theology:* permission to reprint from Toinette Eugene and from Abingdon Press, Nashville, TN.

Excerpt adapted from Yolanda Taragon and Ada Maria Isasi-Diaz, *Hispanic Woman: Prophetic Voice in the Church:* edited by and permission to print from Ada Maria Isasi-Diaz and Yolanda Tarango.

Judith Plaskow, "The Right Question Is Theological": permission to reprint from Judith Plaskow.

Riffat Hassan, "Woman-Man Equality in the Islamic Tradition": permission to reprint from Riffat Hassan and from *The Harvard Divinity School Bulletin.*